Rehabilitation Counseling
Foundations–Consumers–Service Delivery

Randall M. Parker   *Carl E. Hansen*
University of Texas at Austin

Allyn and Bacon, Inc.
Boston   London   Sydney   Toronto

Library of Congress Cataloging in Publication Data

Main entry under title:

Rehabilitation counseling.

    Includes index.
    1. Rehabilitation—Addresses, essays, lectures.
2. Rehabilitation counseling—Addresses, essays,
lectures. I. Parker, Randall M., 1940–
II. Hansen, Carl E. [DNLM: 1. Counseling.
2. Handicapped. 3. Rehabilitation. HD7255.5 R3445]
HV1568.R434   362.4'0486   80–14979
ISBN 0–205–07094–9

Printed in the United States of America.

Contents

Preface   vii

Part I   Foundations of Rehabilitation Counseling   1

Chapter 1   History and Legislation of the Rehabilitation
Movement   7
William M. Jenkins

Chapter 2   Professional Status of Rehabilitation Counseling   37
David Brubaker

Chapter 3   Philosophy and Ethics in Rehabilitation
Counseling   59
Jerold D. Bozarth

Chapter 4   Rehabilitation Counseling Research   83
Brian Bolton

Part II   Rehabilitation Service Consumers—People
with Handicaps   103

Chapter 5   Extent of Disabling Conditions   109
Thomas L. Porter

Chapter 6   Impact of Disability on the Individual   143
Daniel W. Cook

Chapter 7   World of Work and Disabling Conditions   169
Jim L. Daniels

Part III   Rehabilitation Counseling Practice—Delivering Services to People with Handicaps   199

Chapter 8   Evaluation of Rehabilitation Potential   205
Jason W. Andrew

Chapter 9   Counseling for Personal Adjustment   227
Kenneth R. Thomas and Alfred J. Butler

Chapter 10   Placement and Career Development Counseling in Rehabilitation   261
David Vandergoot

Chapter 11   Managing the Delivery of Rehabilitation Services   295
Jennings G. Cox, Sean G. Connolly, and William J. Flynn

Appendix A   Selected Professional Organizations in Rehabilitation and Related Areas   325

Appendix B   Commission on Rehabilitation Counselor Certification (CRCC)   331

Appendix C   Council on Rehabilitation Education (CORE)   341

Appendix D   National Rehabilitation Counseling Association Ethical Standards for Rehabilitation Counselors   345

Index   358

Contributors

Jason W. Andrew, Ph.D.
Assistant Commissioner/Director
Nebraska Department of Education
Division of Rehabilitation Services
Box 94987
Lincoln, Nebraska 68509

Brian Bolton, Ph.D.
Coordinator
Arkansas Rehabilitation Research
& Training Center
University of Arkansas
West Ave. Annex
348 N. West Avenue
Fayetteville, Arkansas 72701

Jerold D. Bozarth, Ph.D.
Chairman
Department of Counseling and
Human Development Services
College of Education
The University of Georgia
Athens, Georgia 30602

David Brubaker, Ph.D.
Executive Director
National Rehabilitation Counseling
Association
1522 K Street, N.W.
Washington, D.C. 20005

Alfred J. Butler, Ph.D.
Chairman
Department of Behavioral Studies
Waisman Center
Waisman, Wisconsin 53706

Sean G. Connolly, Ph.D.
School of Allied Health Sciences

5323 Harry Hines Blvd.
Dallas, Texas 75235

Daniel W. Cook, Ph.D.
Senior Research Scientist
Arkansas Rehabilitation Research
& Training Center
University of Arkansas
346 N. West Avenue
Fayetteville, Arkansas 72701

Jennings G. Cox
School of Allied Health Sciences
5323 Harry Hines Blvd.
Dallas, Texas 75235

Jim L. Daniels, M.Ed.
Director
Job Readiness Clinic
University of Texas
Education Bldg. 306
Austin, Texas 78712

William J. Flynn, M.Ed.
Department of Rehabilitation
Science
School of Allied Health Sciences
5323 Harry Hines Blvd.
Dallas, Texas 75235

Carl E. Hansen, Ed.D.
Coordinator
Rehabilitation Counselor Education
Program
Department of Special Education
Education Bldg. 306
University of Texas
Austin, Texas 78712

William M. Jenkins, Ph.D.
*Coordinator of Rehabilitation
    Counselor Education
Department of Special Education
    and Rehabilitation
Memphis State University
Memphis, Tennessee 38152*

Randall M. Parker, Ph.D.
*Rehabilitation Counselor Education
    Program
Department of Special Education
Education Bldg. 306
University of Texas
Austin, Texas 78712*

Thomas L. Porter, Ph.D.
*Rehabilitation Counselor Education
Memphis State University
Memphis, Tennessee 38111*

Kenneth R. Thomas, Ed.D.
*Department of Studies in Behav-
    ioral Disabilities
University of Wisconsin—Madison
1500 Highland Avenue
Madison, Wisconsin 53706*

David Vandergoot, Ph.D.
*Director of Placement Research
Human Resources Center
Albertson, Long Island, New York
    11507*

Preface

This book is for students in Introduction to Vocational Rehabilitation Counseling courses. It is also intended to serve as a reference
volume for practicing rehabilitation counselors and as a resource for
students and practitioners in allied areas who wish to acquaint
themselves with this newly emerging profession.

As editors we found identifying, soliciting, and compiling the
material for the book an edifying and satisfying experience. The
discussion and planning stage involved identifying content areas we
believed were essential to a well-balanced presentation. Recognized
experts in these areas of rehabilitation counseling were then selected
to participate in this endeavor. As a result of their participation, the
resulting book, we sincerely believe, represents a contribution beyond the capabilities of any single author. To some extent consistency in style is sacrificed in an anthology, but this problem has
been minimized through careful editing.

The book is divided into three sections: Foundations of Rehabilitation Counseling; Rehabilitation Service Consumers—People
with Handicaps; and Rehabilitation Counseling Practice—Delivering Services to People with Handicaps. The sequence of the sections

and chapters within the sections follows a logical order, although instructors may want to modify this order in their courses. For example, some instructors may wish their students to begin with Chapter 2, Professional Status of Rehabilitation Counseling; followed by Chapter 3, Philosophy and Ethics in Rehabilitation Counseling; Chapter 1, History and Legislation of the Rehabilitation Movement; and finally Chapter 4, Rehabilitation Counseling Research. Others may wish to have students begin with Part II or Part III depending on their usual sequencing of topics within their courses.

Although each chapter is a significant and competent contribution, several are unique. Chapter 2 on professional status is an up-to-date conceptualization of the position rehabilitation counseling occupies in the process of becoming a profession. Chapter 3 on philosophy and ethics is the first thorough presentation of this topic for rehabilitation counselors. Chapter 7 on the world of work and disabling conditions presents a view of work from the perspective of a client who is participating in the rehabilitation process. Chapter 10 on placement and career development presents a model of career development as well as a review of extant theory and practice of vocational placement. Finally, Chapter 11 on managing service delivery is unique in content, depth, and scope.

We are proud of this book in spite of our recognition that the contributors are its true parents. This volume is, therefore, gratefully dedicated to them.

Randall Parker

Carl Hansen

Part I

*Foundations of
Rehabilitation Counseling*

The foundations of rehabilitation counseling may be conceptualized as resting on four structural cornerstones:

1. History and legislation;
2. Professionalization;
3. Philosophy and ethics;
4. Research.

Each of the four cornerstones have affected and will continue to influence the fabric of the rehabilitation movement in structure, direction, focus, impact, and outcome. Most people would initially identify legislation as the preeminent force in shaping programs for handicapped people. Legislation, however, is subject to frequent, sometimes violent changes. A cursory view of recent history shows the swings in program focus, funding, and function that can occur. During the Kennedy Administration programming for mentally retarded individuals was fostered; during the Johnson Administration economically disadvantaged people received attention; during the Nixon Administration rehabilitation programs were given no focus other than accountability and funding cutbacks, and more recently legislation has focused attention on both programming and funding for severely disabled individuals. These changes are not only violent, but also largely unpredictable. Long-term planning and development under such conditions is difficult to say the least. Although all four are interdependent, the remaining three cornerstones tend to lend more stability and continuity to the rehabilitation movement.

Rehabilitation counseling is an emerging profession dedicated to helping physically, mentally, and emotionally handicapped people attain their best possible physical, psychological, social, and vocational adjustment. There are about 19,000 rehabilitation counselors, one-third of whom are women. Seventy percent work in state rehabilitation agencies financed by both state and federal funds. The remaining 30 percent work in such settings as Veterans' Administration hospitals, rehabilitation centers, sheltered workshops, general hospitals, insurance companies, and mental health and mental retardation facilities (U.S. Department of Labor, 1978).

Recognized professions have certain characteristics in common. Professions are based on a systematic body of knowledge, possess professional authority and expertise, maintain public sanction and support, operate under ethical standards, and have a professional community or culture, often through the existence of professional organizations (Greenwood, 1957). When compared to recognized professions, such as law and medicine, rehabilitation counseling is regarded as an emerging profession; it has not developed in the aforementioned five criterion areas to the degree that established professions have. But rehabilitation counseling has made marked progress in the development of ethical standards and underlying counseling philosophies.

Philosophies and their implied views of the basic nature of human beings affect the operation of agencies as well as individual counselors. Are humans basically "good," "evil," or "blank slates" whose character is determined by their experiences? Many agencies and counselors tend toward the humanistic approach, believing that individuals are basically good, trustworthy, and if given the opportunity will grow in a positive, self-actualizing direction. Other facilities and counselors operate from a psychoanalytic framework, viewing humans as biological, hedonistic beings whose basic life drives are primitive and animalistic. Such views dictate that clients cannot always be expected to utilize services and choose directions that will maximize their potentials. A third predominant orientation is that of the behaviorists, who tend to view humans as learning machines, endowed with no preexisting nature. For them behavior is the result of stimuli in the environment; thus humans are not responsible for their behavior and are neither basically good nor evil. Agencies and counselors operating under the latter two philosophies will closely monitor client's behavior and use a variety of methods to elicit desired actions from clients. Behaviorists attempt to control client behavior through methods developed in experimental research.

Rehabilitation research, as well as current legislation, professional movements, and predominant philosophies, influence the direction of the contemporary practice of rehabilitation counseling. Medical, biomedical, human engineering, psychosocial, psychological intervention, and many other areas of research form the cutting edge of innovations in rehabilitation practice. Rehabilitation professionals including counselors must be capable of comprehending and evaluating the significance of research endeavors. Research in isolation is of little value; research communicated to practitioners leading to research utilization is a desirable, but difficult, goal. This difficulty has many roots, one being the quality of research itself. Berkowitz, Englander, Rubin, and Worrall (1975) reviewed available rehabilitation research, excluding demonstration, medical, and similar projects, funded primarily by Social and Rehabilitation Services, Public Health Service, and the Veterans' Administration from 1954 to 1973. From over 4,100 studies, 477 were selected dealing mainly with counseling, vocational training, placement services, and vocational evaluation. Although Berkowitz et al. deplored the quality of rehabilitation research, they gave moderate to high ratings to 56 percent of the studies on methodological adequacy and moderate to high ratings to 68 percent of the studies on their policy-utility (practical) value. Nonetheless, rehabilitation research needs improvement as does research utilization. One area requiring further attention is preservice and inservice training of rehabilitation counselors as research consumers. This endeavor alone will go a long way toward accomplishing the objective of efficient research utilization. The following four chapters deal with each of the four cornerstones in much greater detail.

In reading the following four chapters consider how past legislation has affected current professional trends, how philosophical beliefs have influenced current practice, and how research may be able to contribute to both the future development of rehabilitation counseling and the improvement of the delivery of services to people with handicaps.

REFERENCES

Berkowitz, M., Englander, V., Rubin, J., & Worrall, J. *An evaluation of policy-related rehabilitation research.* New York: Praeger, 1975.

Greenwood, E. Attributes of a profession. *Social Work,* 1957, *2*(3), 45–55.

U.S. Department of Labor. *Occupational outlook handbook.* Washington, D.C.: Government Printing Office, 1978.

Chapter 1

History and Legislation of the Rehabilitation Movement

William M. Jenkins

INTRODUCTION

Federal legislation of the past 60 years has reflected marked attitudinal changes in our society. Rehabilitation professionals generally recognize the relationship between societal values or pressures and legislative response, and they are sensitive to the impact of rehabilitation legislation on their profession and on people with handicaps. The study of the forces affecting adoption and implementation of past legislation leads to an awareness of the societal trends that play an important role in the development of proposed legislation, which in turn holds implications for the future direction of the profession.

The history of public attitudes toward disabled people can be grouped into three phases: a passive compassion, action for economic reasons, and action for social reasons. Each expansion in general social responsiveness to the problems of handicapped people has occurred in the years following a major national crisis. A study of the history of rehabilitation legislation provides in a microcosm the social attitudes of America, as well as the development of the philosophy of rehabilitation and the expansion of rehabilitation services through the years.

LEGISLATIVE BEGINNINGS OF
REHABILITATION

The history of the United States has been described by Rusalem
(1976) as a progression through a series of frontiers—geographic,
industrial, humanitarian, and scientific. Scurlock (1975) is in agreement with Rusalem's placement of the humanitarian movement in
the decades around the turn of the twentieth century. He characterized the federal Vocational Act of 1920 as "an expression of growing
public concern for the welfare of the individual citizen, and fore-
telling inevitable enactment of further far-reaching social legislation"
(p. 2).

Rehabilitation of handicapped people began with private phil-
anthropic and voluntary charitable organizations, as did most other
welfare services. These groups began programs of public education
about public responsibility (Meyers, 1968), which lead to laws in
several states (prior to passage of the first federal legislation for
civilian rehabilitation services) that authorized vocational rehabilitation programs.

Prior to World War I, the need for vocational education services had been a particular concern of Congress. Passage of the
Smith-Hughes Vocational Act of 1917 provided federal grants to
states to support vocational education, and was especially important
in that it set the precedent for federal funding of educational programs (Lassiter, 1972). The Act provided for vocational education
services to be operated by state and local communities in cooperation with the federal government, and created the Federal Board for
Vocational Education as the administrative agency for the program.

World War I added another dimension to vocational education,
and to the problem of rehabilitation for the disabled. The National
Defense Act of 1916 provided for opportunities for vocational training of soldiers while in active service, to help their return to civilian
life. The Smith-Sears Rehabilitation Act (PL 178) was passed by
Congress in 1918 in response to the needs of disabled veterans for
vocational training and placement. The Federal Board for Vocational Education was designated the administrative agency for the
program authorized under this act and was again named (in 1920)
as the obvious agency to implement the Smith-Fess Act of 1920
(PL 236). Placement of vocational rehabilitation services under
the administration of a board primarily concerned with vocational
education restricted implementation of rehabilitation programs for
many years.

Success of the veterans' rehabilitation program stimulated passage of the civilian vocational act (Smith-Fess Act of 1920, PL 236). The intent of the federal government was to encourage the states to provide for disabled citizens through provision of grants-in-aid to state agencies carrying out approved programs. Each state was to pass enabling legislation and establish a state board for administration of the program. Funds were to be allocated to the states according to population, with the states being required to match their allotment on a 50:50 basis (McGowan & Porter, 1967). Eight states had started programs of vocational rehabilitation, entirely state financed, before the Smith-Fess Act was passed, and within 18 months 34 states had become involved in the program. However, inadequate appropriations and a lack of support by many state administrative agencies made progress in the field irregular and slow for the next fifteen years (Kratz, 1960).

State boards of vocational education were named in the law as the implementing agencies in the states participating in this state-federal program. This, and placement of the Vocational Rehabilitation Act under the administration of the Federal Board for Vocational Education unfortunately reinforced the commonly held impression that its provisions were subsidiary to, or synonymous with, vocational education. The only difference noted at the time was that the vocational training services were being offered to a specific group of people, those with physical handicaps. The narrow concept of vocational rehabilitation during this period was probably due to the orientation toward education based on the personal experience and training of those responsible for administering the program. Emphasis was on retraining for employment in an occupation in which people could work despite their handicaps, that is, "training around" the disability rather than correcting or lessening the problem through medical or therapeutic treatment. Little more was offered than vocational training (Kratz, 1960).

Lassiter (1972) quotes from Section 2 of the Act of 1920:

> the term "person disabled" shall be construed to mean any person who, by reason of a physical defect or infirmity, whether congenital or acquired by accident, injury or disease, is or may be expected to be, totally or partially incapacitated for remunerative occupation; the term "rehabilitation" shall be construed to mean the rendering of a person disabled fit to engage in a remunerative occupation (p. 8).

The Federal Board interpreted this section to mean that services were restricted to only those persons with physical disabilities, and ruled that rehabilitation could be only vocational, excluding medical, physical, and social forms of rehabilitation (Obermann, 1968). Since medical correction or physical rehabilitation (purchasing prostheses, etc.) were not authorized under provisions of the act, the number of disabled who could be effectively served was limited. Those people who needed only counseling and job placement services were likewise excluded.

Preliminary proposals for the act had included all the elements of modern rehabilitation programs. Congress rejected this "unrealistic" comprehensiveness, but the adopted program, although small, did form a sound basis for further expansion (Switzer, 1969). Rusalem (1976) stated that this act opened the door for a new American attitude toward human problems: that the government "can and should function as a supportive intervenor in the lives of citizens who endure misfortunes" (p. 32).

Through the years since the inception of the state-federal vocational rehabilitation program, there had been several changes made in the organizational location of the program in both federal and state governments. These were tabulated by Lamborn (1970):

Organizational Location of Vocational Rehabilitation
Program in State Governments

1920–1943   State Board for Vocational Education (In two states the actual operation of the program was carried out by another department or commission under special arrangements with the State Board.)

1943–1954   State Board for Vocational Education, except where a rehabilitation commission was established prior to 1943 Act (one state); and State blind commission or other agency providing assistance or services to adult blind, if authorized to provide vocational rehabilitation to the blind.

1954–1965   State Board for Vocational Education, or an agency primarily concerned with vocational rehabilitation (independent agency); and State blind commission or other agency providing assistance or services to adult blind, if authorized to provide vocational rehabilitation to the blind.

1965–   State agency primarily concerned with vocational rehabilitation or vocational and other rehabilitation of disabled individuals, or State agency which includes at least two other major organizational units each of which administers

one or more of the major public education, public health, public welfare, or labor programs of
the state; and State blind commission or other
agency providing assistance or services to adult
blind if authorized to provide vocational rehabilitation to the blind.

(Lamborn, p. 13)

Organizational Locations of Vocational Rehabilitation Program in the Federal Government

1920–1933	Federal Board for Vocational Education
1933–1939	Office of Education
	Department of the Interior
1939–1943	Office of Education
	Federal Security Agency
1943–1953	Office of Vocational Rehabilitation
	Federal Security Agency
1953–1963	Office of Vocational Rehabilitation
	Department of Health, Education, and Welfare
1963–1967	Vocational Rehabilitation Administration
	Department of Health, Education, and Welfare
1967–1975	Rehabilitation Services Administration
	Social and Rehabilitation Service
	Department of Health, Education, and Welfare

(Lamborn, p. 12)

Reorganization of the Department of Health, Education, and Welfare in 1975 placed the Rehabilitation Services Administration (RSA)
in the Office of Human Development Services. Recent legislation has
once again changed the organizational location of RSA. On October
17, 1979, President Jimmy Carter signed PL 96–98 creating the
Cabinet-level Department of Education. Administrative responsibility for the State-Federal Rehabilitation Program was transferred
from HEW's Office of Human Development Services to the Office
of Special Education and Rehabilitation Services in the Department
of Education.

THE NATIONAL REHABILITATION ASSOCIATION (NRA)

Throughout the history of rehabilitation in the United States, the organization outside government that has been outstandingly responsible for legislative advancements has been the National Rehabilita-

tion Association (Whitten, 1975b). This Association, first proposed in 1923 and formally organized in 1925, was created to help promote the state-federal vocational rehabilitation program. It was founded by those working in rehabilitation together with a few associates in allied fields, who felt the need for a nongovernmental agency to work toward realizing the potential of vocational rehabilitation (Hanson, 1970). Aims of the NRA at the time of its formation were to see that the 1920 Act was made permanent and was adequately funded; additional aims included extending the scope of vocational rehabilitation program services and expanding the client population receiving services.

During the early years of its existence, the Association had little influence as an organization (Scurlock, 1975), although individual members played important roles in implementing passage of enabling legislation for continued funding of the vocational rehabilitation program. Accomplishments during the 1930s included influencing President Hoover to recommend extension of the Vocational Rehabilitation Act, even though federal expenditures were being reduced during the postdepression years. Whitten (1975b) also gives NRA credit for the inclusion of the vocational rehabilitation program in the first Social Security Act, which guaranteed the permanence of the program. Establishment of an NRA office in Washington in 1948 enabled the association to play a more active role in passage of rehabilitation legislation. Throughout the decades, most of the push for improvement in the rehabilitation program and for new legislation has come from within the vocational rehabilitation movement; NRA has sponsored all the basic federal rehabilitation legislation passed since 1943.

Hanson (1970) calls attention to the role of the NRA in providing a forum for discussion of rehabilitation issues, problems, and opportunities. Many rehabilitation professionals are currently concerned with the underutilization of this potential of the National Rehabilitation Association. Scurlock (1975) and Dowd and Emener (1978) call for the rehabilitation profession to be aware of the need for its input into planning and implementing rehabilitation legislation and services. Jenkins, Greer, and Odle (1978) point out that within the profession structures exist for making such contributions to policy making and implementation. In addition to the NRA with its interest group divisions and state chapters and chapter branches, other organizations in the profession include the National Council on Rehabilitation Education (NCRE), the Council of State Administrators of Vocational Rehabilitation (CSAVR), and the American Rehabilitation Counseling Association (ARCA), the division of the American Personnel and Guidance Association (APGA) that is concerned with the profession of rehabilitation counseling. (See Appendix A for further information concerning professional organizations related to rehabilitation.)

The National Council on Rehabilitation Education represents all rehabilitation educators and researchers who have as their major concern the preparation of rehabilitation personnel and maintenance of high professional standards. The Council of State Administrators of Vocational Rehabilitation is composed of the administrators of the public rehabilitation agencies in the states and territories. CSAVR was established in 1940, with the support of the Federal Administrator of the Vocational Rehabilitation Program, to provide state input into the state-federal program. It provides an opportunity for state vocational rehabilitation administrators to explore issues and act more effectively in matters of both state and national importance.

THE DEPRESSION YEARS:
THE DECADE OF THE 1930s

Growth of the program for vocational rehabilitation, from its beginning in 1920, was slow. The enthusiasm of workers in the field did not always extend to state administrations. Congressional appropriations tended to be relatively small, as were those of the states; many of the participating states provided only the minimum funds necessary to secure the federal grants. The federal government had no permanent commitment to the program; reaffirmation of the act and new appropriations had to be justified every few years. Permanent and expanded federal financial support for vocational rehabilitation was not assured until its inclusion in the Social Security Act of 1935.

Leaders in rehabilitation during this period seemed committed to the belief that *all* disabled people should have access to the vocational rehabilitation program, but such expansion of services was not proposed. Possibly there was public reluctance "to regard economic opportunity and self-esteem as rights of every individual, regardless of his misfortune" (Obermann, 1968, p. 265). Such recognition of human rights did not begin to develop until decades later. Although the social philosophy of the New Deal provided a favorable climate for the growth of the rehabilitation movement (Meyers, 1968), and the trend was toward broadening the scope of services offered, interpretation of the existing laws continued to be narrow.

During the 1930s, governmental priorities and programs were

constantly reappraised, new programs and agencies created, and old programs and agencies combined. The administrative agency for vocational rehabilitation was assigned to the Office of Education, within the newly created Division of Health, Education, and Welfare. Vocational rehabilitation in the states continued to be administered by the departments of education. Many supervisors of rehabilitation felt that an overemphasis on client training and an underemphasis on other services occurred because educators administered and evaluated the rehabilitation programs. The limiting provisions of federal laws and administrative directives continued to curtail expansion of the program during the 1930s.

LANDMARK LEGISLATION OF 1943: PUBLIC LAW 113

For more than twenty years, the vocational rehabilitation program had been meagerly financed, restricted in scope, and uneven in growth. Things were about to change. Entry of the United States into World War II created an immediate need for a more comprehensive vocational rehabilitation program and gave Congress the necessary motivation to enact Public Law 113. The primary purposes of this legislation were "first, to channel disabled manpower into war production and essential business as rapidly as possible and, second, to provide a comprehensive service to enable the disabled to prepare for and secure employment in peacetime pursuits" (Lassiter, 1972, p. 43).

In addition to greatly expanded funding, Public Law 113 made significant changes in the conceptualization of vocational rehabilitation. More comprehensive definitions of "disabled person" and "vocational rehabilitation services" made additional groups of handicapped people, especially those who were mentally ill and mentally retarded, eligible for a broader range of services. Many services previously administratively prohibited were then specifically authorized. A separate administration, the Office of Vocational Rehabilitation, was established in order to insure more effective program planning and development at both state and federal levels.

The 1943 legislation was important not only for its broadening the scope of rehabilitation services, but also for the changes in concepts within the profession and on the part of the general public. New approaches to rehabilitation practices were required because of manpower needs; employers and both the general public and rehabilitation professionals were looking at disabled people in a different light. Some vocational rehabilitation leaders remained conservative in their approach to rehabilitation, however, insisting that provision of personal adjustment services should not be included in vocational rehabilitation; they held that provision of any type of service that did not have as its purpose the reduction or removal of a disability causing a vocational handicap was not vocational rehabilitation (Kratz, 1960). While earlier counselor practice had been to serve only those clients who were clearly retrainable through the limited services permitted through narrow interpretation of legislation, Public Law 113 required that all clients either be served or referred to appropriate agencies (Thomas, 1970). However, the program of service to people with severe handicaps was limited because of the shortage of trained personnel, the lack of facilities, and the high cost of rehabilitating such people (Kratz, 1960).

THE HISTORY-MAKING YEAR: THE VOCATIONAL REHABILITATION ACT AMENDMENTS OF 1954 (PL 565)

The decade after 1943 has been recognized as a period of expansion and growth in vocational rehabilitation, especially in the area of medical/physical rehabilitation. Emphasis was placed on rehabilitation of severely physically disabled people, although services to the newly recognized groups of people who were mentally ill and mentally retarded remained at a minimum (Thomas, 1970). A gap still remained between needs and provision of services because of inadequate funds and facilities, and lack of trained personnel. Funding was clearly insufficient to meet the increasing demands from the public that rehabilitation take "a more responsible place in dealing with the broad problems of disability among the American people" (Switzer, 1964, p. 20).

The Eisenhower administration presented a favorable climate for expansion of rehabilitation services; conservatives, liberals, and moderates united in legislative approval. Support from the American public was also evident (Rusalem, 1976). Because of the passage of Public Law 565, President Eisenhower termed 1954 a "history-making year" for rehabilitation. At the time he signed the law, the President said that it "... re-emphasizes to all the world the great value which we in America place upon the dignity and worth of each individual human being" (Obermann, 1968, p. 316). The aim of the act was "to assist the states in rehabilitating physically (and mentally) handicapped individuals so that they may prepare for and engage in remunerative employment ... thereby increasing not only their social and economic well-being but also the productive capacity of the nation" (Lassiter, 1972, p. 45).

The provisions of this act greatly increased the financial base for funding rehabilitation services, provided special funding for extension and improvement of existing rehabilitation programs, and provided for research and training programs (Switzer, 1969). The law took into account the major problem of the shortage of professional personnel with specialized rehabilitation training, and grants were awarded to educational institutions preparing people for professional work in vocational rehabilitation. Another important section authorized funding for the expansion or establishment of rehabilitation facilities or workshops. Special project grants were made available for research and demonstration projects (Obermann, 1968).

Emphasis was placed on cooperative relationships with other agencies and organizations, both public and private. The Office of Vocational Rehabilitation served successfully as an initiating and coordinating agency, involving many different organizations, agencies, and disciplines in programs of research and development. State agencies, under the provisions of PL 565, were also able to initiate cooperative programs of service with other public agencies (Lamborn, 1970).

A new type of service, evaluation and work adjustment, serendipitously grew out of the Act of 1954. This service had as its focus helping "handicapped persons whose problem is primarily social or psychological rather than physical" (Thomas, 1970, p. 38). The development and expansion of evaluation and work adjustment services was based on the programs of research and demonstration, construction of rehabilitation centers, and professional training. Since 1954 the rehabilitation profession has become increasingly concerned with clients' motivation and work personality, as well as with their physical capacity for work.

The definitions of "disability" and "vocational rehabilitation services" were modified in PL 565. Eby (1964, p. 16) quotes from its provisions that the disabled person is "any individual who is under a physical or mental disability which constitutes a substantial handicap to employment, but is of such nature that vocational rehabilitation services may reasonably be expected to render him fit to engage in a remunerative occupation;" vocational services include "comprehensive diagnostic services; surgery, treatment and hospitalization; prosthetic devices; maintenance; tools, equipment, and initial stocks and supplies; transportation; acquisition of vending stands or other equipment; and establishment of public or other nonprofit rehabilitation facilities."

While the population of the country increased only 17 percent during the ten years from 1954 to 1964, the number of people rehabilitated almost doubled. In 1964, federal funding for vocational rehabilitation was five times the amount allocated in 1954 (Obermann, 1968). Extraordinary progress was made in providing services to mentally ill and mentally retarded people who were institutionalized. Emphasis was also given to placement of blind people in industry. During the late 1950s the role of the rehabilitation counselor became more that of a "coordinator" of service provision, with less opportunity for direct counseling and guidance service. Administrative pressures, as well as lack of funds and trained staff, often caused the exclusion of people who were severely physically handicapped or mentally handicapped from rehabilitation services. Priority was given those handicapped people "who could most easily have their disability removed or minimized and return to productive work" (Lassiter, 1972). The issue of whether to provide services for one severely handicapped person when ten to twenty less handicapped people could be helped to become productive citizens for the same money became both an administrative problem and a moral dilemma.

PEOPLE-ORIENTED LEGISLATION:
THE VOCATIONAL REHABILITATION
PROGRAM IN THE 1960s

The Kennedy Administration strengthened rehabilitation services through Social Security and welfare provisions. Upon introduction of the antipoverty program, vocational rehabilitation techniques were recognized as particularly applicable to the antipoverty effort, and Congressional committees responsible for these programs realized that a more comprehensive financial structure would be required for vocational rehabilitation to be effective in combatting social disabilities (Switzer, 1969).

Eby (1964) enumerated the problems facing the rehabilitation profession during the period by stating that rehabilitation, which should be the foremost resource in helping people with disabilities, was the last, because of inadequate financing. More effective ways to coordinate the rehabilitation services of voluntary and public agencies were needed in order to make better use of the available services. The rehabilitation profession needed to more effectively implement the democratic ideal of equality of opportunity. DiMichael (1971) listed important challenges for the era:

1. Solutions to the problems of the disadvantaged;
2. Reorganization of agencies for more effective coordination of services and for provision of a continuum of services to the client;
3. A greater focus on family dynamics in rehabilitating handicapped people, stressing the importance of including the family in the rehabilitation program.

Public Law 333, the Vocational Rehabilitation Amendments of 1965, provided a broadened legal and financial base, which insured continuation of the marked period of growth during the previous decade. This act doubled financial support from the federal government (McGowan & Porter, 1967), extended rehabilitation services to those with socially handicapping conditions, made evaluative services more available to state Division of Vocational Rehabilitation (DVR) applicants by waiving a previous item of eligibility ("a reasonable expectation that vocational services may render the individual fit to engage in a gainful occupation"), and provided for the operation of sheltered workshops (Lassiter, 1972, p. 48).

The portion of the 1965 Amendments that provided for extended evaluation to determine rehabilitation potential was of particular value to the rehabilitation profession in its efforts to provide for many of these handicapped individuals who formerly would have been quickly rejected because rehabilitation was not seen as feasible. Months of continuing evaluation of vocational, social, psychological, medical, and other factors, with provision of services as needs are identified, are often needed before a realistic determination of capacities and limitations of the client can be made (Smith, 1970).

Another piece of legislation that was of great importance to rehabilitation was that portion of PL 89-97 (Social Security Amendments) that changed the disability provisions and provided for payments of the costs of rehabilitation services from trust fund allocations. State vocational rehabilitation agencies were to be reimbursed from Social Security trust funds for rehabilitation services to those entitled to disability insurance benefits. This provision made it possible for rehabilitation services to be provided to many more disability insurance beneficiaries than would otherwise have been possible (McGowan & Porter, 1967).

During the first fifty years of the state-federal rehabilitation program, attention had been focused almost completely on the individual, but the Amendments of 1965 redefined rehabilitation services to "include follow-up services in maintaining an individual in employment, services to families of the handicapped individual when services can contribute to the rehabilitation of a group of individuals." This legislation, throughout its provisions, typified "the people-oriented character of the rehabilitation movement [and] ... clearly intended to bring the public and voluntary agencies into a closer working alliance so as to produce the very best of services for each disabled individual" (McGowan & Porter, 1967, p. 27).

The Rehabilitation Amendments of 1965 had marked implications for personnel training and service delivery. State vocational rehabilitation agencies were to be responsible for providing evaluation and work adjustment services to *all* "disadvantaged," many of whom would not be agency clients following the evaluation. The evaluative services would be a resource for other state, federal and voluntary agencies (Whitten, 1969). The acts were therefore a mandate to provide outreach, referral, and advocacy services. Agencies were to seek out clients, since many disadvantaged people never apply for services; to develop a more systematic referral service; and to evaluate clients more precisely. Systematic follow-up would be necessary to see that services needed from other agencies were actually received (Whitten, 1969).

The Act made many changes in the scope of state vocational rehabilitation agencies and their related activities, and in their relations with other programs at both state and federal levels (Lamborn, 1970). Funding for state VR agencies increased tenfold during the decade from 1958 to 1968. The number of handicapped people served in 1958 was approximately 250,000; in 1968, almost 700,000 were served. Rehabilitations increased from approximately 74,000 in 1958 to over 207,000 in 1968. Dramatic gains were made in providing services in categorical programs for people who were mentally retarded and mentally ill. In 1959, rehabilitated mentally retarded people comprised only 2.5 percent of the total number of rehabilitations; by 1967 the number had risen to 10.2 percent. Rehabilitation of mentally ill people in 1959 accounted for 4.5 percent of all rehabilitations; in 1967 this number had risen to 10 percent (Hunt, 1969).

The federal training grant program advanced significantly during the decade. In 1959, 1028 students in rehabilitation and allied areas received traineeships, while colleges received 197 teaching grants; in 1968 there were 5,918 traineeships and 477 teaching grants. Research and demonstration funds awarded increased from approximately $3,500,000 to over $21,000,000 during the decade. The research and demonstration project grant programs funded by the rehabilitation legislation of the period first focused mainly on physical disability; later research programs of major significance were carried out in the areas of retardation, mental illness, alcoholism, drug addiction, behavioral disorders, public offenders, and physically disabled people who were also socially and culturally disadvantaged. Utilization of research findings led to the development of new techniques of service, increased numbers of clients rehabilitated by state DVR, resulted in the absorption of demonstration projects into ongoing programs, and led to changes in federal and state legislation (Hunt, 1969).

The first major change in the organizational location of the vocational rehabilitation program in the Federal government came in 1967, with the reorganization of the Department of Health, Education, and Welfare. The Social Rehabilitation Service was established for the purpose of "providing a unified approach to the problems of needy Americans, with special emphasis on the family, and at the same time to assure continued special emphasis upon serving the aged, the handicapped, and children" (Hunt, 1969, p. 10). Reasons for the reorganization included dissatisfaction with the performance of public assistance programs and lack of coordination among the various human service units (DiMichael, 1971). This reorganization, favoring the rehabilitation concept and stressing a rehabilitation philosophy, was led by Mary E. Switzer (Commissioner of Vocational Rehabilitation from 1950–1967), and "provided greater visibility and national recognition for the total state/federal program" (Lassiter, 1972, p. 49). In the years following the creation of the Social & Rehabilitation Service, four major federal laws were passed: the 1967 and 1968 Vocational Rehabilitation Amendments, the 1967 Mental Retardation Amendments, and the Architectural Barriers Bill.

A note of caution was sounded by Whitten (1971, p. 2), warning that the Administration had "no real understanding of the accomplishments of rehabilitation and its potential in meeting human needs," and pointing out that the manpower and welfare legislation being sent to Congress at that time seemed to ignore the existence of the volunteer rehabilitation movement.

THE VOCATIONAL REHABILITATION
ACT OF 1973

Many problems were facing society in the early 1970s. In the area of human services, there were both a critical shortage of services and a misdistribution of those services available, with both redundancies and gaps in service provision and inefficiency in interprogram planning. DiMichael (1971, p. 15) viewed the coordination of services for handicapped people as a "national issue of grave concern." At the same time that vocational rehabilitation had been greatly expanded, other governmental agencies had also been expanded or created to provide some types of rehabilitation services. The federal government needed to simplify and coordinate its programs; practitioners hoped that this federal coordination might then cause the states to follow suit.

Administration spokespeople were advocating stricter fiscal justification of social programs and speaking of assessing these programs in regard to their economic outcomes. A constrictive managerial approach operated at both federal and state levels of vocational rehabilitation. Priority systems were again set up that emphasized serving those people with the potential to become wage earners with minimal cost to the program. Cost accounting seemed to take precedence over concern for people and their problems, with state rehabilitation agencies managing their programs on the basis of economic considerations rather than positive impact on disabled people (Rusalem, 1976).

During the late 1960s and early 1970s the Nixon administration threatened to substantially curtail the state-federal program. An HEW memo even advocated discontinuance of the program. Legislative leaders supporting rehabilitation challenged the administration to provide facts justifying such a proposal; none were forthcoming (Rusalem, 1976). Contraction and restriction of the vocational rehabilitation program continued during the Nixon years. Training programs for rehabilitation professionals were being phased out. Funding for rehabilitation research was reduced; programs and grant proposals had to be justified in terms of possible savings to the government rather than their benefit to disabled people. Much of the formerly centralized federal rehabilitation responsibility was distributed to a number of federal nonrehabilitation groups. Some rehabilitation-related agencies and rehabilitation-oriented programs for various groups were established independent of the existing rehabilitation agency structure. Fiscal support for voluntary rehabilitation agencies had to be provided through funding agencies other than the state-federal rehabilitation program. Rusalem (1976) stated that the rehabilitation agency administration passively accepted the new order of things, that its professional organizations were generally cautious, and that only a few of the rehabilitation leaders moved to counterattack the administration plans to undermine the program. Some disabled individuals recognized this passivity; some helped organize and lead grass-roots, client-directed movements against the weakening of the state-federal rehabilitation program.

In 1973 rehabilitation professionals found themselves in the middle of a confrontation between the legislative and administrative branches of government. Rehabilitation legislation became the test case for a power struggle between Congress and the President. The issue was not that of the proposed 1973 Rehabilitation Act Amendments, but "whether Congress or the President would control the development of legislation, and the appropriations to finance such legislation" (Whitten, 1973, p. 2). The machinery of the Executive Branch was brought to bear on Congress, and the Amendments were twice vetoed before their final passage in October of 1973.

There were several benefits accruing to rehabilitation as a result of this struggle for legislative power:

1. The profession more clearly understood how highly regarded its programs were, and how well they were supported, both by Congress and the public in general.

2. The profession received more publicity, all favorable, in the final two weeks of the struggle than in the previous ten years.

3. The rehabilitation movement was more unified than ever before.

Over 30 organizations concerned with the rehabilitation of the handicapped coordinated their efforts to override the veto. They were joined by many other groups and individuals with human service concerns (Whitten, 1973).

The principal objectives of the Rehabilitation Act of 1973 were:

a. To maintain and improve State/Federal programs of quality vocational rehabilitation services and to redirect the public rehabilitation program towards the expansion of services to the severely handicapped;

b. To provide the opportunity for active participation by the client in the development of the client's individualized written rehabilitation program;

c. To provide special attention to target groups whose rehabilitation problems are known to be difficult;

d. To promote the elimination of barriers in the environment which impede the handicapped in employment, housing, and transportation;

e. To utilize to the fullest possible extent community, State and Federal resources in the rehabilitation of the client and the extent to which those funds are marshalled to increase and improve:
   1. The supply of trained rehabilitation manpower;
   2. Rehabilitation knowledge and techniques;
   3. Rehabilitation facilities;

f. To promote and expand employment opportunities in the public and private sectors for handicapped individuals and to place individuals in gainful activities;

g. To provide education to the general public and handicapped population about the rehabilitation of the handicapped and to disseminate information pertaining to rehabilitation;

h. To develop a process of evaluation as to the effectiveness of present programming on different disability groups.

(Federal Register, p. 58959)

The Rehabilitation Acts and Amendments of 1973 and 1974 placed an increased emphasis on rehabilitation of severely handicapped people, requiring that each state agency establish an order of priority for services to people with handicaps, with severely disabled people receiving the highest priority. The severely disabled person was defined in the implementing regulations as "a handicapped individual who has a severe physical or mental disability which seriously limits his functional capacities (mobility, communication, self-care, or work skills) in terms of employability" (Whitten, 1974, p. 39). The Rehabilitation Act also included in its provisions the requirement that an individualized written plan for services be developed by the counselor and client together. This written plan was intended to provide for better continuity of the program, and most importantly, for clients' involvement in their own rehabilitation.

The rights of people with handicaps were addressed in Sections 502, 503, and 504 of the Acts of 1973 and 1974. Many people with handicaps have been unable to obtain employment, not because of lack of skills, but because architectural barriers and transportation difficulties have made it impossible for them to reach places of employment. Section 502 of the Act emphasized expanding the freedom of handicapped people through removal of such barriers, providing that public facilities should be fully accessible to all people with handicaps.

Another step forward was made with the affirmative action

provision of Section 503 of the 1973 Act that required that "employers who have a contract with an agency of the federal government shall, under certain conditions, take action to employ applicants who are handicapped" (Williams, 1976, p. 2). Sections providing for nondiscrimination against handicapped people were applicable only to those businesses participating in government programs, and did not include programs and activities of the federal government itself. The regulations published in 1974 contained no specific, effective enforcement procedures, so that compliance with this provision continues to depend upon effective education of employers about the competency of handicapped people in industry.

Section 504, a first step toward an expanded effort to establish civil rights for handicapped people, provided that no handicapped individual should be subjected to discrimination under any program or activity receiving federal financial assistance. Although the intent of Congress was to make this mandatory, no public enforcement mechanisms were created in the regulations. As Stapleton (1976) pointed out, even though laws provide the foundation for equal opportunity for the handicapped, unless they and their advocates demand enforcement, "existence of the laws is hollow" (p. 605). Legal mandates do not of themselves change the attitudes of society, or increase society's awareness of the needs of the individual.

RIGHT TO EDUCATION LEGISLATION

The Elementary and Secondary Education Act of 1965 was passed by Congress in order to improve educational opportunities for disadvantaged students. Amendments the following year added funds for special education and created the Bureau for the Education of the Handicapped (BEH). The Education for the Handicapped Act of 1970 made the Bureau a permanent part of the U.S. Office of Education. The Education Amendments of 1974 (PL 93-380) greatly increased federal funding for education of handicapped students, and also referred to the rights of handicapped students to public education (DeLoach & Greer, in press). Perhaps the most significant legislation in this area was passed by Congress in 1975, the Education for All Handicapped Children Act, PL 94-142, that mandates the right of all handicapped children to a free and appropriate public education. There is a close relationship between its provisions and those of the parts of Section 504 of the Rehabilitation Act of 1973 that are specific to elementary and secondary education. Both regulations mandate:

That a free appropriate public education be provided for handicapped persons,

That handicapped children be educated with non-handicapped children as much as possible,

That all handicapped children who are not receiving a free appropriate public education be identified and located,

That evaluation procedures be adopted for education classification and services, and

That procedural safeguards be established.

A number of states had passed laws that provided for appropriate educational services for handicapped people prior to passage of PL 94-142. Both state and federal legislation required mandatory services for handicapped people, resulting in greater compliance with the provisions. An added incentive for positive action toward making appropriate services available was the provision that Federal funds would be withheld whenever there was noncompliance with the law. As Cole and Dunn (1977) point out, noncompliance may place many school systems in double jeopardy, since the system not only may lose reimbursements under PL 94-142, but also may lose all HEW funding.

The need for more effective programs of vocational education for handicapped people, and for improving access to such programs, continued to be of major concern to both the rehabilitation and education professions. Vocational education for handicapped people was federally emphasized in PL 94-482, the Education Amendments of 1976. Comprehensive vocational education acts and career education legislation have been passed in many states since 1968. For example, the Vocational Education Act passed by the Tennessee 1973 General Assembly mandated that vocational facilities be provided to 50 percent of all students in grades 9 to 12, with counseling and prevocational courses made available to all students in grades 7 to 8 (Todd, 1978). Such an emphasis requires that teachers have a better understanding of the aims and purposes of vocational education, and that vocational teachers and curriculum specialists have training in modifying existing vocational curricula to suit handicapped individuals. Full and effective implementation of laws such as these and PL 94-142 should have a significant impact on the types and degree of services needed by handicapped people when they leave school and enter the labor market.

COMPREHENSIVE REHABILITATION
SERVICES AMENDMENTS OF 1978

Throughout the history of the state-federal rehabilitation program, federal monies for the program have been provided through appropriation resolutions and one to three year extensions of funding. Vocational rehabilitation administrators see this funding policy as a major problem in the implementation of comprehensive, long-range rehabilitation programs. Galvin (1978) as spokesman for the Council of State Administrators of Vocational Rehabilitation (CSAVR), called for passage of legislation for multiyear extension or permanent authorization of the Basic State-Federal Vocational Rehabilitation Program. Such permanent extension would increase the effectiveness and quality of rehabilitation services, according to Galvin, by allowing the state agencies to perform long-range planning and commit their resources to long-range projects and goals, to engage in cooperative long-range planning with private facilities and organizations, and to serve those individuals who are so severely handicapped that long-term commitments of time and resources are necessary for successful implementation of rehabilitation plans. Recommended for inclusion in such permanent authorization would be an "entitlement" feature, a funding mechanism that would give the states advance knowledge of the amount of Federal monies that would be received each year, thus aiding the state agencies in planning services and in requesting appropriations from state legislatures.

Provision in the Federal legislation of adequate funding to meet current objectives was seen as being of equal importance with long-term authorization. A recent CSAVR survey (Galvin, 1978) showed that states can match and effectively use a much greater Federal appropriation than was being recommended by the Administration. Galvin emphasized that

> the state rehabilitation agencies have the mission, personnel, experience, and support programs to develop and provide a program of comprehensive services needed to assist each eligible individual. What we . . . lack are the financial resources to make our comprehensive program available to all handicapped persons who could benefit from rehabilitation services. (p. 5)

The House Subcommittee on Select Education and the U.S. Senate Subcommittee on the Handicapped completed hearings in March and April of 1978 on legislation to amend and extend the Rehabilitation Act of 1973. Representatives of many professional groups and consumer organizations appeared before the Subcommittees to request statutory authority to serve severely handicapped people who have little or no vocational potential, as well as to plead for permanent authorization and adequate funding. Representatives of CSAVR strongly supported the proposed extension of the present rehabilitation program into the area of independent living rehabilitation (ILR), and recommended that the responsibility for administering the program be located in the state vocational rehabilitation agencies. An Independent Living Program (ILR) had been recommended in the legislation vetoed by President Nixon in 1972. The strong conviction in the profession that the ILR program was a concept "whose time has come" has since resulted in the development of such programs in several state agencies, using state funds. Such efforts have demonstrated the effectiveness of such programs and have shown the practicality of providing such services through existing state vocational rehabilitation agencies. In addition, the previously mentioned survey conducted by CSAVR revealed that state directors of vocational rehabilitation overwhelmingly favored the creation of an ILR program, with such services to be provided by the state vocational rehabilitation agency. Reasons for locating the ILR program within the existing state rehabilitation systems were given as follows:

1. Existing expertise and experience in working with and advocating for disabled people can be effectively utilized.
2. Possible duplication of services can be avoided.
3. Inter-agency coordination and cooperation for the benefit of the disabled client can be ensured.
4. The total needs of the severely handicapped person can be served.
5. State organizational "competition" can be avoided.
6. Public awareness of the needs of disabled people can be heightened, while confusion can be avoided.
7. Program accountability can be clearly established.
8. Cost-effectiveness can be assured.
9. A positive attitude of independence can be instilled in disabled persons who are served.

(Galvin, 1978, p. 11)

ILR was defined in the CSAVR Survey (Galvin, 1978) as a "program which would provide comprehensive rehabilitation services to improve the ability of severely handicapped people to live independently or function normally within their families or communities, without reference to a vocational goal" (p. 9). Since the program was envisioned to be an expansion of the existing program of rehabilitation services, it was argued that logically the state rehabilitation agency should administer the program. Duplication and overlapping of rehabilitation services could thus be minimized. An additional argument for such administration was that the program could be put into operation with less delay through the existing system of rehabilitation support services.

The Rehabilitation, Comprehensive Services and Developmental Disabilities Amendments of 1978 became law on November 6, 1978. Title VII of the law, Comprehensive Services for Independent Living, was designed to assist State Vocational Rehabilitation Agencies in providing independent living services for individuals with disabilities so severe that they presently have no potential for employment, but may benefit from rehabilitation services which will assist them to live independently. State Vocational Agencies were authorized to deliver vocational rehabilitation services and other comprehensive services to eligible clients, those who are unable to hold employment and/or who are unable to function independently in the family or community. An additional authorization under the act was that for grants to establish and operate centers for independent living. Handicapped individuals themselves were to be involved in administration and staffing of the centers, which were to provide a wide range of supportive services.

An additional new title, Employment Opportunities for Handicapped Individuals Act, was included in H.R. 12467 for the purpose of establishment of community service employment programs for handicapped individuals, thus providing opportunities for employment that would otherwise be unavailable. Other notable sections of the law provided for establishment of a National Institute of Handicapped Research, for establishment and support of Rehabilitation Research and Training Centers, and for establishment of a National Council on the Handicapped, with policy-making and advisory functions. Section 504 of the Rehabilitation Act of 1973 was broadened to mandate nondiscrimination under programs and activities of any federal agency, and the Architectural and Transportation Barriers Compliance Board was extended and strengthened. Rehabilitation services were also mandated for handicapped American Indians on federal or state reservations, and special projects were provided for migratory workers, blind people, deaf people, and for special recreation programs.

AN ENCOURAGING TODAY—
WHAT OF TOMORROW?

In an address to CSAVR in September of 1977, and again to the First General Assembly of the National Rehabilitation Association Conference in September 1978, the Commissioner for the Rehabilitation Services Administration, R. R. Humphreys, summed up recent accomplishments in the implementation of services to the handicapped:

> Section 504 regulations at last have been promulgated, and technical assistance plans to help implement those regulations are now under development.
>
> A new awareness on the part of industry and labor of the needs and demands of handicapped citizens has been generated by the affirmative action requirements of Section 503.
>
> The Secretary of Housing and Urban Development has established a new Office for Independent Living.
>
> The Architectural and Transportation Barriers Compliance Board is beginning to assert its authority through compliance orders.
>
> The White House Conference on Handicapped Individuals has concluded, and its recommendations, along with the plan for implementing them, soon will be forthcoming.
>
> The Education for All Handicapped Children Act is a reality. Major changes are underway in the nation's public school systems to accommodate handicapped youngsters.
>
> The nation now has an Administration that is committed to the elimination of discrimination against disabled people, and to the expansion of affirmative action.
>
> New and strong voices among disabled people are being raised, and are being heard. New handicapped groups are being formed. Coalitions and joint efforts to improve services and assert rights are becoming increasingly active.
>
> (Humphreys, 1977, p. 3)

Progress continues toward ensuring compliance with the provisions of Section 504 of the Rehabilitation Act of 1973. Recently issued proposed rules for implementing Section 504 have been published by the Department of Transportation (DOT) and the Department of Housing and Urban Development (HUD). The Department of Transportation administers federal financial assistance to local transit systems, highways, railroads, and airports. Although the newly issued rules (*Federal Register,* June 8, 1978) stress voluntary compliance, provision is made for withholding funds for noncompliance (Dept. of Transportation, 1978). The proposed regulations of HUD, published in the April 19, 1978, *Federal Register,* prohibit discrimination against handicapped people in federally funded housing programs and projects. Another important step toward the goal of a barrier-free society is seen in the Amendments to the Rehabilitation Act that give the Architectural and Transportation Barriers Board (created in 1973) greater authority to assure accessibility for handicapped people.

The final report of the White House Conference on Handicapped Individuals was presented to the President in March, 1978. This conference was authorized by the Rehabilitation Amendments of 1974 (PL 93-516). Over 100,000 concerned people took part in the 1976 state conferences and the 1977 National White House Conference. The most unusual and important feature of the conferences was that the recommendations that were made in the final report were formulated by some disabled people themselves. More than 50 percent of the voting delegates had disabilities; parents or guardians of handicapped people made up an additional 25 percent. The final report of the White House Conference contained 810 specific recommendations for insuring equal employment opportunities and social rights for the 36 million disabled citizens of this country. These recommendations called for:

> Immediate action to formulate national policy to insure that people with disabilities are able to participate fully in society and enjoy its benefits;
>
> Recognition of and response to unique needs of individuals with disabilities in education, welfare reform, tax policy, health insurance, transportation, housing, and other areas of distinct need; and
>
> Immediate action to provide consumer involvement in planning and decision making, including parents, guardians, disabled, aged and minority persons.
>
> ("Rehabilitation News," 1978, p. 7)

Input from the White House Conference, the President's Committee on Employment of the Handicapped, the Committee on Developmental Disabilities, and other nationally prominent groups and committees is of utmost importance to the Rehabilitation Services Administration in administration of the mandates of Congress to respond to the needs of all handicapped people.

Bowe (1978) states "America handicaps disabled people." This same point of view was expressed earlier by Mathias (1976), who felt that much of the "handicap," whether physical or psychological, of disabled people are imposed on them by society. He listed the basic human rights to which all American citizens are entitled, whether disabled or whole:

1. Every citizen with a disability should have the right to receive medical care for the protection of his or her well-being, and such additional special medical assistance as is required because of his or her disability.

2. Every citizen with a disability should have the right to receive an education to the fullest extent to which he or she is capable, paid for and provided through regular channels of American education. They should have available special educational help as needed by virtue of their disability.

3. Every citizen with a disability ought to be able to receive training for vocational and avocational pursuits as are dictated by his or her interests and talents.

4. Every citizen with a disability should have the right to work at any job for which he or she has the qualifications and interests, including sheltered and other subsidized forms of employment, if such is appropriate to their needs.

5. Every citizen with a disability should have access to barrier-free public facilities, including polling places, public buildings, general mass-transit systems, supplemental mass-transit systems, social and recreational facilities, shopping facilities and entertainment opportunities.

(Mathias, 1976, pp. 18–19)

The Rehabilitation Act of 1973 and the amendments that have followed, including the 1978 Amendments, mandate the provision of these rights, but many factors are impeding and will continue to impede their full implementation. Obvious factors, as pointed out by DeLoach and Greer (in press), are (1) the time required to implement a law after its passage, (2) the great number of people requiring services, (3) the attitudes of both professionals and the public toward implementation and toward their personal and corporate responsibilities in this regard, and (4) the large discrepancy between the amount of money needed for full implementation and the amount of money available. Money, facilities, and trained personnel remain, now as in 1920, obvious impediments to more effective service delivery. The constricted definition of vocational rehabilitation in the early years has broadened with passage of each piece of enabling legislation. This broader concept includes such areas as independent living, self-development, personal growth and social rehabilitation for those people without potential employability, in addition to the traditional services to those with vocational potential. Not all vocational specialists are in agreement with the inclusion of the less tangible objectives such as personal and social rehabilitation. Others disagree as to service delivery methods and the organizational structures through which such services should be provided. The federal-state rehabilitation program has, throughout its history, been recognized as one of the most successful of the many programs of the federal government. Increasing advocacy for special groups, increased public support from new sectors of society, and increased activity by special interest groups combine to exert great influence on the legislation and administration of rehabilitation programs. Jenkins, Greer & Odle (1978) remind the rehabilitation profession of its obligation to contribute to policy making as well as policy implementation, using existing organizations such as the National Rehabilitation Association as a framework within which to develop a more systematic leadership role. Jenkins et al. make the admonishing statement that "in a field dedicated to the discovery and actualization of the potential of less fortunate individuals, we have failed to look at ourselves and our programs in regard to our potential for controlling the thrusts and emphases of our efforts" (p. 30).

REFERENCES

Bowe, F. *Handicapping America: Barriers to disabled people*. New York: Harper & Row, 1978.

Clarification of final regulations to Public Law 94-142. *Amicus*, 1978, 3(1), 9.

Cole, R. W., & Dunn, R. A new lease on life for education of the handicapped: Ohio copes with 94-142. *Phi Delta Kappan,* 1977, 59(1), 3-6, 10, 22.

Cull, J. G., & Hardy, R. E. (Eds.). *Vocational rehabilitation: Profession and process.* Springfield, Ill.: Charles C Thomas, 1972.

DeLoach, C., & Greer, B. *Metamorphosis.* New York: McGraw-Hill, in press.

Department of Transportation issues proposed rules for Section 504 enforcement. *Amicus,* 1978, 3(4), 6.

DiMichael, S. G. Dimensions in coordinating rehabilitation services. *Journal of Rehabilitation,* 1971, 37(1), 14–16.

Dowd, E. T., & Emener, W. G. Lifeboat counseling: The issue of survival decisions. *Journal of Rehabilitation,* 1978, 44(3), 34–36.

Eby, C. L. Prologue. *Journal of Rehabilitation,* 1964, 30(5), 16.

Federal Register, December 19, 1975, 40(245), p. 58959.

Galvin, D. E. *Statement of the council of state administrators of vocational rehabilitation before the House subcommittee on select education,* Washington, D.C., April, 1978.

Hanson, H. H. Vocational rehabilitation and NRA. *Journal of Rehabilitation,* 1970, 36(5), 2.

House passes rehabilitation act amendments. *Amicus,* 1978, 3(4), 8.

H. R. 12467, Comprehensive rehabilitation amendments of 1978. *Congressional Record,* May 16, 1978, H3954–H3965.

HUD issues proposed rules to implement Section 504. *Amicus,* 1978, 3(4), 9.

Humphreys, R. R. The future of rehabilitation and the state-federal partnership. Paper presented at the meeting of the Council of State Administrators of Vocational Rehabilitation, San Diego, September, 1977.

————. Address given at the National Conference of the National Rehabilitation Association, Salt Lake City, September, 1978.

Hunt, J. A decade of progress. *Journal of Rehabilitation,* 1969, 35(1), 9–12.

Jenkins, W. M., Greer, B. G., & Odle, S. Conventional wisdom and rehabilitation: Is it really wise? *Journal of Rehabilitation,* 1978, 44(3), 28–30.

Kratz, J. A. Vocational rehabilitation, past, present and future in the United States. In C. H. Patterson (Ed.), *Readings in rehabilitation counseling.* Champaign, Ill.: Stipes, 1960.

Lamborn, E. The state-federal partnership. *Journal of Rehabilitation.* 1970, 36(5), 10–15.

Lassiter, R. A. History of the rehabilitation movement in America. In J. G. Cull & R. E. Hardy (Eds.), *Vocational rehabilitation:*

Profession and process. Springfield, Ill.: Charles C Thomas, 1972.

Malikin, D., & Rusalem, H. (Eds.). *Vocational rehabilitation of the disabled: An overview.* New York: New York University Press, 1969.

Mathias, C. Rehabilitation—The challenge—Past and future, *Journal of Rehabilitation,* 1976, *42*(1), 18–20.

McGowan, J. R., & Porter, T. L. *An introduction to the vocational rehabilitation process.* Washington, D.C.: U.S. Dept. of HEW, Rehabilitation Services Administration, 1967.

Meyers, J. K. The prophetic mission of rehabilitation: Curse or blessing. Statement. *Journal of Rehabilitation,* 1968, *34*(1), 27–29, 32–33.

Obermann, C. E. *A history of vocational rehabilitation in America* (5th ed.). Minneapolis: T. S. Denison, 1968.

Rehabilitation news. *Journal of Rehabilitation,* 1978, *44*(3), 6–7.

Rusalem, H. A personal recent history of vocational rehabilitation in America. In H. Rusalem & D. Malikin (Eds.), *Contemporary vocational rehabilitation.* New York: New York University Press, 1976.

Rusalem, H., & Malikin, D. (Eds.), *Contemporary vocational rehabilitation.* New York: New York University Press, 1976.

Scurlock, V. C. Never a sunset. *Journal of Rehabilitation,* 1975, *41*(4), 2.

Smith, E. N. Eligibility—An evolving concept. *Journal of Rehabilitation,* 1970, *36*(5), 23–25.

Stapleton, M. Rights to equality for disabled persons under federal and state law. *Rehabilitation Counseling Bulletin,* 1976, *19*(4), 597–606.

Switzer, M. E. The public program today. *Journal of Rehabilitation,* 1964, *30*(5), 20–24.

———. Legislative contributions. In D. Malikin & H. Rusalem (Eds.), *Vocational rehabilitation of the disabled: An overview.* New York: New York University Press, 1969.

Thomas, R. E. The expanding scope of services. *Journal of Rehabilitation,* 1970, *36*(5), 37–40.

Todd, J. D. Inservice preparation of teachers to implement the comprehensive vocational education act. *The Educational Catalyst,* 1978, *8*(2), 85–89.

Whitten, E. B. Disadvantaged individuals and rehabilitation. *Journal of Rehabilitation,* 1969, *35*(1), 2.

———. Handicapped people and the administration. *Journal of Rehabilitation,* 1971, *37*(1), 2.

————. Rehabilitation in 1973: A reassessment. *Journal of Rehabilitation*, 1973, *39*(3), 2, 43.

————. The rehabilitation act of 1973. *Journal of Rehabilitation*, 1974, *40*(2), 39–40.

————. Association development: Two themes traced. *Journal of Rehabilitation*, 1975a, *41*(4), 28–29, 51.

————. Twenty-five years of congressional activity. *Journal of Rehabilitation*, 1975b, *41*(4), 30–31.

Williams, C. L. Affirmative action: Do we have it? *Journal of Rehabilitation*, 1976, *42*(3), 2.

Chapter 2

Professional Status of Rehabilitation Counseling

David Brubaker

INTRODUCTION

The professional status of rehabilitation counseling is currently nebulous. Unlike the more "established professions," its emergence has been tied to federal legislative mandates and its development has been closely related to the expansion of the state-federal system of vocational rehabilitation. Additionally, rehabilitation counseling has had comparatively little time to complete the professionalization process. These and other problematic factors have led to a host of internal and external problems, and basic questions concerning rehabilitation counseling's professional status and direction remain unresolved.

For example, questions concerning role definition, title, and qualifications for initial employment and advancement have remained because of wide-ranging job roles. The ever-changing jurisdiction of the rehabilitation counselor adds difficulties in professional identity development. In certain settings, rehabilitation workers may function as a vocational counselor, psychotherapist, placement specialist, case coordinator, psychometrist, or administrator, or various combinations thereof. The rehabilitation counselor's educational attainment varies from high school graduate to doctorate; in addition, major fields of study are diverse. Furthermore, wide variations in job titles exist ranging from vocational rehabilitation counselor, vocational counselor, counselor, psychologist, rehabilitation specialist, to coordinator. Because of diversity in job title, duties, training, and experience, attempts to professionalize this group are inherently more difficult than in other more homogeneous occupations.

Complicating matters further are periodic substantive changes in the field's focus and direction, often emanating from federal legislation. There is considerable debate among leaders in rehabilitation counseling regarding the influence of government on the professionalization process. According to some, government has usurped the power of the occupation to define, control, and regulate itself, rendering it a relatively impotent, subservient, and highly unstable occupation. Conversely, others argue that rehabilitation counseling's ability to work cooperatively with federal and state government, while still maintaining a high degree of professional integrity, is evidence of the field's resiliency and enthusiasm. Thus, questions regarding government regulation and advantages and disadvantages of occupational institutionalization remain. The question of whether this field is doomed to marginal professional status because of these factors, must be adequately assessed.

The problem of determining entry level qualifications for rehabilitation counselors is illustrative of the basic professional quandry of the field. As distinguished from many other groups with professional aspirations, this field has, at present, no single nationally accepted vehicle for determining which people are competent to engage in rehabilitation counseling. Numerous and somewhat contradictory standards and regulations have been established by the Commission on Accreditation of Rehabilitation Facilities, the National Policy and Performance Council, the Council on the Rehabilitation Education, the Commission on Rehabilitation Counselor Certification and other public and private agencies. State rehabilitation departments have established guidelines for employment of rehabilitation counselors that entail minimums for experience, education, and other qualifications; as might be expected, they vary considerably among states. In conjunction with the National and American Rehabilitation Counseling Associations and other groups, the Commission on Rehabilitation Counselor Certification (see Appendix B) developed a certification procedure that includes experiential requirements and a written examination. Upon satisfactory completion of these requirements, an individual is designated as a Certified Rehabilitation Counselor (CRC).

All of these methods for determining competence have gained

acceptance in certain sectors of the rehabilitation field, but it appears that none have been universally used; however, the CRC designation has begun to gain preliminary acceptance by employers as well as counselors. For example, some employers rely heavily upon academic degrees or certification; others utilize subjective evaluations of applicants' qualifications. Some agencies require the master's degree, and others hire on the basis of personality, industrial experience, and other factors. Among state rehabilitation agencies there is a notable lack of consistency in employment standards (Crisler, 1977). Thus, rehabilitation counseling is one of the few professional occupations that a person may enter without relevant education or work experience.

Much has been written concerning the frustration of rehabilitation counselors who perform ambiguous and largely bureaucratic roles with questionable professional status. Some have submitted that this is a major cause of the relatively high attrition rate of rehabilitation counselors, many of whom leave the field to prepare for more prestigious and more professionalized occupations. Leaders of the rehabilitation counseling movement, although they concede the existence of many of these questions, are apt to refer to rehabilitation counseling as "the profession of . . .", or as a "new" or "emerging" profession. In contrast, physicians and other members of the so-called established professions sometimes consider rehabilitation counseling a paraprofessional occupation.

In light of the uncertain professional status of rehabilitation counseling, this chapter will seek to define and describe the notion of *profession* and apply the elements of the process of professionalization to the occupation of rehabilitation counseling. Finally, the more important professional issues confronting the field will be discussed.

THE NOTION OF PROFESSION

A bewildering assortment of definitions of *profession* have been tendered by students of occupational sociology. While these differences are generally a matter of emphasis, it is noteworthy that some authors avoid use of the term entirely. Although it is difficult to reach a near consensus on the definition of *profession* it seems certain that a sizable majority of authors view it as an ideal type of occupation that does not exist in the real world.

Perhaps the most common emphasis in defining a profession is on the knowledge base and the inherent responsibility of a particular occupation. For example, Whitehead (1948) defined a profession as "an avocation whose activities are subject to theoretical analysis and are modified by theoretical conclusions derived from that analysis" (pp. 73–74). According to Hall (1969), the stress on intellectual techniques is paramount; professions are organized around bodies of knowledge. While there is considerable debate over the relative importance of service and scientific discipline, Hall states that each can be primary characteristics of a profession. Interestingly, he separates the term *knowledge* from the term *research*, and suggests that the scientific quest for new knowledge is not a necessary prerequisite for professional status. As evidence he states that both law and the ministry are occupations that are generally accepted as professions, yet neither base their knowledge on scientific inquiry.

Moore (1970) states that a profession is an occupation "whose incumbents create and explicitly utilize systematically accumulated general knowledge in solving the problems posed by the clientele" (pp. 53–54). "The true professional," according to Jackson (1970), "is work-oriented to the highest degree possible. Work encompasses all aspects of his life" (p. 6). Gilb (1966) stresses that to be a professional "means to present a reliable, uniform face to the public; collectively, to have the public's confidence and respect" (p. 41). The essence of the professional ideal and the claim to professional status to some is that professionals profess to know better than their clients what ails them and their affairs.

While definitions of *profession* are both plentiful and diverse, relatively minor differences are found among occupational sociologists as to the distinguishing characteristics of professions, and a general consensus prevails that occupations exist along a continuum with highly professionalized occupations at one end and minimally professionalized occupations nearer the other end. Most authorities, notably Greenwood (1957), agree that professions are characterized by the possession of key elements: a systematic body of theoretical knowledge; professional authority; community sanction based upon relevance to basic social values; ethical codes and standards; and a professional culture. Considerable controversy remains as to the components and characteristics of these elements, as well as the relative importance of each, but substantial agreement exists about the elements themselves.

Systematic Body of Knowledge

One hallmark of a profession is the possession of advanced skills, knowledge, and understanding by its membership. Thus, the performance of professional service implicitly requires that members master a variety of specialized skills requiring lengthy periods of training. As Greenwood (1957) suggests, however, many occupations that do not otherwise qualify as professions often require a higher order of skills (e.g., diamond cutter, tool and die maker, and cabinet maker appear to require higher levels of intricate skill than do school teaching, social work, and nursing). The difference, he suggests, is the skills that typify a profession emanate from a basic "body of theory." This system of abstract theory and knowledge that helps to draw intellectual parameters for the specific domain of professional practice, also enables the occupation to "rationalize its operation in concrete terms" (p. 47). Thus, the acquisition of professional skill presupposes mastery of the basic body of professional knowledge. As opposed to lower-status occupations, the systematic study of theory is a fundamental attribute of professional preparation. Obviously, papers are not written on the theory of washing dishes. Because theoretical knowledge is basic to professional preparation, such training can be deemed both theoretical and practical in nature; but without basic theoretical preparation, students of a particular occupation cannot be considered prepared for a profession.

Generally, this intellectual foundation cannot be garnered in an on-the-job setting; formal schooling is essential. Thus, logical justification for the rise of the professional school can be made. Since theoretical knowledge is frequently more difficult to master than manual skills, it is easier to learn how to repair an automobile than to learn the theory of the internal combustion engine. As professionalization continues in an occupation, therefore, formalized education gradually replaces on-the-job or apprenticeship training because the increasing reliance on the theory dictates it. This evolutionary process culminates in university training and helps to both improve the competence of the profession and assure its status.

The generation of theoretical concepts and a research basis to the profession's body of knowledge requires adherence to the scientific method of inquiry. This adherence, in turn, reinforces the rationality of the occupation. This orientation functions to encourage critical thinking as opposed to "blind obedience" and implies a constant search for new methods and techniques to improve professional practice. Thus, the closer an occupation comes to the professional end of the continuum, the more rational and intellectually oriented it becomes. Conversely, those occupations at the other end of the continuum are generally more concretely oriented and non-intellectual in orientation.

Through the professionalization process there emerges the "researcher-theoretician" whose role is that of scientific investigator and theoretical systematizer. Frequently, a split within professional groups develops between the practitioners and theoreticians; this division can act as a boon or hindrance to an occupation, depending upon the ability of these professionals to function interdependently.

Professional Authority

The basis for an occupation's claim to professional status rests in the individual practitioner's overall superiority in expertise, which is predicated upon lengthy and rigorous study in both the theoretical and practical dimensions of the occupation. Comparatively, the layman is ignorant of this knowledge and must turn to the professional for assistance in areas germane to the professional's area of expertise. Such authority is at its highest when the number of members is small in relation to demand and when the clientele are not organized. When the clientele are organized, professional authority may be curtailed or eclipsed.

While occupations at all points along the professionalization continuum provide goods or services to the public, the key difference is the degree to which their authority is recognized by the public. For example, those occupations that are least professionalized have *customers* whom they hope to please ("the customer is always right!"), while highly professionalized occupations generally have *clients* or *patients*. While the customer determines the services he desires, the client must rely on the judgment of the professional as to the nature and type of service needed as well as the fee to be paid for the service.

Because clients lack the theoretical knowledge necessary to judge the professional's expertise, they are frequently unable to evaluate the competence of the person from whom they seek service. Again, the degree of professionalization of an occupation can be partially determined by the degree to which the people outside the occupation are able to competently arrive at judgments independent of the professional from whom they seek a service. In a minimally professionalized occupation (e.g., shoeshiner), customers feel free to criticize the service they receive in terms of price, quality, and timeliness, while the clients of the professional generally surrender this tendency to professional authority.

The maintenance of professional authority and autonomy is one reason that highly professionalized occupations have opposed advertising of professional services by members; for to encourage or even permit competitive advertising would imply the occupation's acceptance of the notion that the public is competent to judge professional needs, services, fees, and related matters. In essence, the physician (or member of another highly professionalized occupation) enjoys a monopoly with respect to decision making that falls within the general purview of the occupation. An additional element of this monopoly is the financial monopoly that the professional enjoys over his or her clients. Since clients are presumably unable to determine or treat their own needs, they must obtain professional services and pay prices that are often higher than the free market price. In addition, clients would often be in violation of the law were they to seek the services of a nonrecognized practitioner.

The professional's authority is restricted, however, to the areas in which he or she has been certified (by formal certification, possession of degrees, and so on). Parsons (1939) termed this phenomona functional specificity and indicated that because of the difficulty of infringing on the territory of another occupation, and the possibility of a corresponding decline in authority, professionals tend to function within well-defined parameters.

Community Sanction and Relevance
to Basic Social Values

Every occupation that seeks community sanction must strive to convince the public of its superiority within its proclaimed area of technical competence, its basic service orientation, and its relationship to the central values of society. The community's acceptance of this superiority will then lead to the approval of certain powers and privileges to the occupation, which may be bestowed either formally or informally.

Any occupation seeking professional stature must first establish and control training programs for entry-level personnel. This control is generally achieved through an accreditation process, which is in turn frequently controlled by a professional association. By regulation and control of the accreditation process, the occupation can thus regulate new entrants into the field and can also maintain control over curriculum, caliber of instruction, length of training, admissions procedures, and so on. This type of control is directly related to the degree of professionalization within the field and is not often found in occupations on the nonprofessionalized end of the continuum.

In order for this regulatory process to succeed, the aspiring profession must convince the public that no one should be entitled to professional status who has not attended an accredited training program prior to entrance and that the profession must be relatively autonomous. Again, anyone can call himself or herself a dishwasher, janitor, or philosopher, but a person claiming to be a lawyer or physician who lacks the requisite credentials is subject to legal prosecution. In addition, the profession will generally further attempt to monopolize its role in the community by seeking publicly approved, mandatory, state licensing. This is generally *claimed* to help the public by protecting them against fraud and incompetence, and almost always requires the newcomer to pass an examination in addition to having the required training. As a result, the professional monopoly is enhanced through the power of the state to punish violators of licensing legislation.

According to most students of professionalization, an important characteristic of a profession is the relation of the occupation's work to the central values of society. The extent to which this work assists in the attainment of these values is seen as one measure of a profession. For example, the relationship of law and medicine to the basic values of justice and health are an important basis for their status as professions. While societal values may be difficult to determine, aspiring professions tend to seek justification in abstract values upon which there is widespread consensus. Another criterion is the ability of the occupation to solve important problems within the society that only the occupation's members are trained to undertake.

The concept of autonomy or self-regulation is universally regarded as an important attribute of professional groups, which is expressed as the desire to control the activities of members, guard professional boundaries, and control access to the profession. In addition to this collective autonomy, each professionalizing occupation stresses the functional autonomy of the individual practitioner, which mitigates against supervision from outside of the profession and develops a tendency of refraining from open criticism of other members of the profession.

Autonomy and community sanction bring with them certain advantages. Immunity from community judgment on technical matters, confidentiality of communication, and professional protectionism grant the occupation a monopoly by community consent.

Ethical Codes

In order to protect the public from exploitation, professionalizing occupations have developed regulative codes of ethical behavior for members. Since grossly excessive fee schedules, rampant incompetence, or other widespread abuses could lead to a revocation by the public of the professional monopoly, these codes serve to protect both the members of the profession and the public.

Ethical codes are generally a combination of written documents (e.g., the Hippocratic Oath) and informal attitudes and behaviors that are expected of members of the profession. Included here would be a commitment to the general public welfare, a pledge of optimal performance, and fair fees. According to Parsons (1939), professional codes differ markedly from other occupational codes in that they are generally more binding, more public-service oriented, and more altruistic in tone than nonprofessional codes. While these codes may vary considerably by occupation, client-professional and colleague relations are almost always considered. Parsons indicates further that these codes usually pledge not only maximum performance, but also emotional neutrality, detachment, cooperation, equality of relationship, and mutual interdependence and consultation among colleagues. See Chapter 3 and Appendix D for further information concerning ethics.

Professional Culture

An important element of professionalization is the degree to which the occupation exhibits the characteristics of a community. In particular, this concept refers to a sense of esprit de corps, a distinctive culture, shared values, and shared norms. This culture tends to regulate the work behavior of its members, and even control nonwork activities such as political and recreational pursuits.

The presence of a professional community can be discerned if members are bound by a sense of identity and most of them view it as a terminal occupation. In addition, if the community has power over its members, if there is a consensus of role definitions, and if it carefully selects and indoctrinates new members, a professional community can be said to exist. Most authors have suggested that symbolism (distinctive insignia, logo, dress, ceremony) and the concept that professional people view their work as the all-encompassing facet of their lives are salient characteristics of professions.

A major role of the professional culture is the enculturation of new members—the fledgling professional. The new member must learn the social values and behavioral expectations of the new occupation. Hall (1969) indicates that the utilization of the professional organization as a major referent is important to the inculcation of these values in new members and students.

The failure to become satisfactorily enculturated can lead individuals to be deemed as a deviant by the professional culture, and can hinder their influence and success within the occupation. While the professional group encourages innovation in theory, it tends to discourage deviation from its social values and norms, not unlike the society at large.

The Key Elements: A Summary

The elements of a profession and the concept of a professionalization continuum are ideal notions. In reality, no occupation possesses each of these characteristics to a maximal degree, but these constructs aid in helping the observer compare occupations in terms of their relative degree of professionalization. These notions are sometimes not followed even by the "established professions," those that are recognized by the general public.

The Sequence of Professionalization

A consensus exists among occupational sociologists about the concept of sequential stages in the professionalization process. Generally, this process consists of the completion by an occupation of the criteria or elements of a profession. This process follows a predictable pattern in a chronological sequence, but movement can occur either toward professionalization or deprofessionalization. The sequential stages through which each occupation passes in this process are perhaps best delineated by Wilensky (1964) who includes: the creation of a full-time occupation; establishment of training schools; development of professional associations; formulation of a code of ethics; further definition of the area of occupational competence; and political agitation to protect the job territory of the occupation. It would appear that Wilensky's description of this process can be interpreted as a cumulative process in which the occupation increases, by stages, the socioeconomic and political power and mobility of its membership. Wilensky argues that while a popular generalization exists that occupations are becoming professionalized, this label is too loosely applied. He further argues that the basic elements of a profession are less important than is the sequence of events that take place during the professionalization process.

IS REHABILITATION COUNSELING A PROFESSION?

In viewing rehabilitation counseling in light of the criteria delineated previously, this occupation's current professional status is that of professional marginality; that is, while evolving toward the professional end of the continuum, it is notably lacking in a number of key elements, and has not completed the stages in the professionalization process. Not unlike other so-called marginal professions (such as pharmacy, engineering, and social work), rehabilitation counseling is a relatively new occupation that is often hampered by the bureaucratic nature of much of its employment. For a comprehensive treatment of professional marginality, see Etzioni (1969). The *body of knowledge* used in practicing rehabilitation counseling is not systematically organized and is not, in itself, unique. The knowledge base rests upon knowledge systems developed by other older disciplines (e.g., psychology, medicine). Considerable debate still persists as to the roles, functions, and definition of rehabilitation counseling, and about the theoretical framework from which it operates; indeed, the field is only now beginning to weave its components into a fabric of theory and spell out its functional specificity. Additional study is necessary to arrive at definitions that will show the unique nature of the field, but which are broad enough to encompass the myriad complex functions and roles that counselors may assume. In essence, the parameters of the field are only now beginning to be formulated.

The proliferation of so-called human service occupations has also made this definition difficult, for example, the emergence of the profession of mental health counseling. Among psychologists, social workers, rehabilitation counselors, and others, occupational roles have become blurred, and often a variety of occupations have claimed the same "turf."

Rehabilitation counseling has made considerable progress in delineating its area of expertise and has solidified its training programs at the master's degree level. The Council on Rehabilitation Education (CORE), the organization that accredits rehabilitation education programs, has developed a research-based accreditation process that has gained widespread acceptance in the field (see Appendix C). Formed in 1971, CORE has gained the support of the various constituencies within the field. The course content of these master's degree programs increasingly reflect the evolution of an accepted theory. The Commission on Rehabilitation Counselor Certification (CRCC), the certifying body of the field, moreover, has delineated core areas of practice that seem to reflect a consensus of support within the field:

1. Rehabilitation philosophy, history, structure, laws;
2. Medical aspects of disability;

3. Psychological aspects of handicapping conditions;
4. Occupational information and the world of work;
5. Counseling theory and techniques;
6. Community organization and resources;
7. Placement processes and job development;
8. Psychology of personal and vocational adjustment;
9. Evaluation and assessment;
10. Utilization of research findings and professional publications;
11. Delivery of rehabilitation services (CRCC, 1978).

Recent findings in the analysis of rehabilitation counselor job duties indicate that rehabilitation counselors spend most of their time performing noncounseling functions (Fraser & Clowers, 1978; Muthard & Salomone, 1969; Wright & Fraser, 1975), and many indicate that "counseling" itself is highly suspect in terms of effectiveness (Olshansky, 1976). Given the multitude of counseling-oriented occupations and the professional requirement for uniqueness, counseling may indeed be a weak basis for a claim of professional status. During the professionalization process, many occupations find it necessary to change the title of the occupation (e.g., inhalation therapist to respiratory therapist) in order to more adequately reflect the job functions of the occupation. Rehabilitation counseling may need to consider making such a change.

Professional authority within rehabilitation counseling is hampered by the bureaucratic settings in which many counselors function, and is also limited by government regulation. Often overwhelmed by feelings of powerlessness, not unlike members of other occupations in such settings, rehabilitation counselors often become alienated. This factor is seen to undermine not only the development of professional authority, but also the development of a professional culture as well.

Conflict has occurred about setting standards for entry into the field. Although several national organizations have developed such standards, the major measure taken thus far has been the certification of rehabilitation counselors by the Commission on Rehabilitation Counselor Certification. While a weaker measure than state licensing, the certification of counselors is, within the framework of professionalization, a major step toward professional status. Certification has its critics, for example, Miller (1971) who sees the procedure as a professional game and asks, "How do you certify a wide diversity of persons to do something that escapes definition and seems to keep changing as well as requiring different skills in different locales?" (p. 84).

Certification, a voluntary effort, has met with considerable success. Many employers have begun to use certification as an employment requirement, and certification has begun to be cited in federal regulations (e.g., final regulations for Intermediate Care Facilities for the Mentally Retarded, *Federal Register*, June 3, 1977).

Many rehabilitation counselors are employed in state rehabilitation agencies that set their own employment standards. The standards employed by these agencies vary considerably. Some require master's degrees in rehabilitation counseling or a closely related area, while others frequently hire inexperienced and untrained people as rehabilitation counselors. According to U.S. Congressman Frederick Richmond:

> Many employers continue to hire persons with no rehabilitation counseling experience to fill beginning positions. In far too many cases, non-professional criteria are used to make hiring decisions. Employers sometimes base the hiring decision on political or personal reasons rather than on professional standards. The end result of this process is the inadequate delivery of services to the handicapped. This situation is not acceptable. A sufficient number of qualified counselors exists to ensure that disabled individuals receive the best possible care (*Congressional Record*, April 18, 1978).

To remedy this situation, Richmond introduced a bill in 1978 in the U.S. House of Representatives (HR 12130) to amend the Rehabilitation Act of 1973 to require that rehabilitation counselors hired under provisions of the Act meet minimum professional standards of preparation. Sponsored by the National Rehabilitation Counseling Association (NRCA), HR 12130 incorporates the standards developed by CRCC. Passage of this or similar legislation would be a major step forward in increasing the field's professional authority. Other legislative initiatives have been taken as well. NRCA-sponsored licensing bills have been introduced in New York and Massachusetts, and American Personnel and Guidance Association-sponsored omnibus counseling bills have been introduced in Arkansas, Idaho, Ohio, and Virginia. At this time only the Virginia and Arkansas bills have become law, although other bills are also likely to gain passage. It seems clear that professionalization will continue in terms of Wilensky's last stage—the legislative protection of the occupation. However, rehabilitation counseling may not have the necessary political power to gain independent legislation and may have to satisfy itself with inclusion as a subspecialty of generic counseling as has been done in Virginia.

One serious impediment to the greater development of professional authority is the division of the field. When compared with social work, engineering, teaching and other "emerging" professions, rehabilitation counseling is very small in numbers. Thus, the existence of competing professional associations tends to dilute the ability of the field to achieve its goal of more rapid professionalization. The National and American Rehabilitation Counseling Associations have split their membership in such a way as to divert fiscal resources to duplicated services and thereby have rendered the field relatively impotent in generating the political and financial resources necessary to compete with the larger, better established occupations.

Rehabilitation counseling currently lacks sufficient input into the state and federal bureaucracy to enable the field to achieve full professional status. The occupation should attempt to gain a greater degree of influence over the rehabilitation-government bureaucracy. Constructive input from counselors regarding duties, evaluation of performance, advancement, ethical standards, and so on, is necessary. To thwart the possibility of the field's blending into the bureaucracy and becoming just another white collar service occupation, ways should be formulated to professionalize within this setting. In order to do this, leaders of state and federal rehabilitation agencies ideally should be chosen from counselor ranks, and procedures for mandating rehabilitation counselor input into the bureaucratic decision-making process should be instituted.

One major advance would be to require that state directors of vocational rehabilitation programs meet certification standards. This could be done through an amendment to the Rehabilitation Act. Another approach toward the same goal would be to have the NRCA *Code of Ethics* incorporated into state employment guidelines and job descriptions. This step would tend to give counselors additional autonomy and aid them in becoming recognized by the bureaucracy as professionals as opposed to mere white collar workers.

Rehabilitation counseling's relevance to basic social values is reflected largely in legislative support nationally and at the state and local levels. This support has, generally, manifested itself in approval of expenditures for expanding the state-federal system of vocational rehabilitation, and in laws protecting handicapped individuals. Thus far direct support for rehabilitation counseling has not been widely expressed. The occupation, while having garnered broad public support on philosophical issues of general concern, has relatively little public visibility and status. While highly professionalized occupations such as dentistry and law are immediately recognized by the average citizen, little is known about rehabilitation counseling. The field should endeavor to enlighten the public about its service orientation and mission, and develop a positive public image regarding its professional status. Successfully done, this would lead to increased community sanction of its activities.

Ethical codes have been developed in rehabilitation counseling, but not unlike other human service occupations, have remained essentially unenforceable. While highly developed in content, the NRCA *Code of Ethics* is not widely employed by the practicing counselor and has not been adopted by the entire field, being in competition with other codes, notably APGA's *Ethical Standards*. While the trends suggest the eventual acceptance of the NRCA code (e.g., by CRCC and others), at this time there is no single code with which all rehabilitation counselors identify.

Although exhibiting many of the characteristics of a professional culture, the field has not as yet defined this aspect of professionalization. The proliferation of organizations in the field compete for members. NRCA and the American Rehabilitation Counseling Association (ARCA) are the prime referents of rehabilitation counselors, although some members identify with the American Psychological Association, National Rehabilitation Administration Association, and a host of other small groups. In order to professionalize the field further, steps should be taken to coordinate the activities of these organizations. Measures have been taken, recently, by NRCA and ARCA to work more closely in areas of mutual concern.

The development of a professional culture could be enhanced by a number of other changes. Many counselors hold master's degrees from CORE-approved graduate programs; others hold only undergraduate degrees, frequently in fields unrelated to rehabilitation counseling. Given the growth of these graduate programs, legislative initiatives, and recognition, this situation should gradually change. In time, professional training will become an employment prerequisite; those without proper credentials will be precluded from entering the field, and the culture will be strengthened.

The relative newness of the field is also a hindrance to professionalization. Medicine, the "queen of the professions," has had many years to develop the symbols, ideals, and other trappings of a profession. Rehabilitation counseling has only recently begun its journey toward professional status.

Still another difficulty in developing a professional culture is the lack of a long-term commitment to the field by many new entrants. While growing occupational mobility is a societal trend, it is still unusual for professionals to leave their calling. A high degree of occupational commitment appears lacking in many counselors as reflected in studies that suggest a high rate of job turnover (Sussman & Haug, 1970; Anderson, 1963; Dunning, 1972). It appears that many new entrants use rehabilitation counseling as a catapult for upward socioeconomic mobility, and as a transitional rather than terminal type of employment. Too, many counselors are quick to reach the top of the state pay scales, forcing them into administrative positions in order to advance in status and salary. While many within the occupation have espoused the career ladder concept, which would provide higher pay and more responsibilities for career counselors, this appears unlikely to occur on a widespread basis in the near future.

FUTURE TRENDS

A number of issues will increasingly have a significant impact upon the development of rehabilitation counseling, especially in the larger arena of the regulation of those claiming to be a part of the rapidly expanding ranks of allied health practitioners.

Proliferation of Occupations

Currently more than 100 occupations can qualify as allied health manpower; each being involved with patient care and community or environmental health. In some occupations, various levels of personnel are specifically recognized (e.g., respiratory therapists and respiratory therapy technicians), and in many cases each level has formed its own professional association and certifying agency. Given the rapidly rising cost of health care and the demand for cost containment and accountability, there has been and continues to be considerable demand for giving closer scrutiny to those newer occupations that are now claiming professional status. Indeed, many people feel that the older, more established occupations could often fulfill the functions of these newer occupations through delegation of authority to paraprofessionals, and through the expansion of existing roles and functions.

As a result of this concern, the United States Department of Health, Education, and Welfare was required by the Health Training Improvement Act of 1970 to make suggestions for containing the rapid and seemingly uncontrolled expansion of new professions. The Department's 1971 *Report on Licensure and Related Health Personnel Credentialing* called for a moratorium on the development of new certification bodies and state licensing acts. Since the release of this report, debate has continued. Nevertheless, the implications are ominous; in an allied health-bueaucratic-governmental climate that is growing less sympathetic to the demands of the new occupations, only the best organized, most articulate new entrants can hope to survive as viable health occupations.

Credentialing

In 1977, the U.S. Public Health Service issued a report entitled *Credentialing Health Manpower* that made a variety of recommendations for improving the health manpower delivery system in general and the licensing and certification of health professionals specifically. Concerned with a rapidly expanding, inconsistent, and often haphazard credentialing system, it called for the development of a National Voluntary System for Allied Health Certification. Not surprisingly, the implication was that if the private sector could not develop uniform national credentialing standards, the federal government would.

As a result, the National Commission for Health Certifying Agencies (NCHCA), a voluntary, private body, was formed. The Commission established national standards to certify bodies that attest to the competency of individuals participating in the health care delivery system; to grant recognition to certifying bodies that voluntarily meet the standards; and to monitor the adherence to the standards by the certifying bodies which it has recognized (NCHCA, 1977). The Commission recognizes two membership classifications including national organizations as well as certifying bodies meeting the Commission's standards. At this time, rehabilitation counseling is represented by NRCA in the former category, but is not represented in the latter. The recognition by NCHCA of CRCC would be helpful to rehabilitation counseling's claims to professional status.

The topic of competency measurement was also considered in the 1977 Public Health Service Report, with the recognition that more attention to the development of valid methods for measuring competency (and equivalency) must be forthcoming. Many critics have charged that existing methods for determining competence are faulty and that the possession of academic degrees and the passage of examinations does little to insure competence. Rehabilitation counseling has yet to develop such a scale like many other occupations, but many come under increasing pressure to do so.

Continued Competence

The era of the license-for-life is rapidly coming to an end. *Credentialing Health Manpower* (U.S. Public Health Service, 1977), Cohen (1977), the National Health Council (1978), and others have pointed to the need for measuring the continued competence of each occupation's members, with the individual occupations charged to develop such a method. Relicensing and recertification will probably become a reality in most professional areas; for example, in many states public school teachers must take a certain number of courses to maintain their teaching certificates.

In rehabilitation counseling, the Commission on Rehabilitation Counselor Certification has instituted a "Plan of Certification Maintenance" (1977) that requires certified rehabilitation counselors to accumulate a minimum of 30 clock hours of continuing education each year in order to maintain their CRC status. Although this meager beginning does not insure the continued competence of the individual counselor, it is a valuable first step toward the development of a viable mechanism for encouraging continued competence.

"Private" Rehabilitation Counseling

While rehabilitation counselors have worked for many years in private settings such as sheltered workshops, rehabilitation centers, and so on, a new group of "privately" employed counselors has begun to emerge. Recent changes in the Workman's Compensation laws in some states have led to private practice opportunities for rehabilitation counselors. The increasing feasibility of rehabilitation through private insurance carriers and corporations (e.g., Sears and Roebuck) has also led to employment opportunities. Given the decline in the expansion of the state-federal system of vocational rehabilitation, in the future a growing percentage of rehabilitation counselors may be employed in the private profit-making sector of the economy.

CONCLUSION: PROFESSIONAL MARGINALITY

Rehabilitation counseling presents an excellent example of a marginal or emerging profession and illustrates the process of professionalization. Rehabilitation counseling's status in terms of its knowledge base and community sanction is unclear to both the occupation and the public. Ranking in the middle range of the professionalization scale on both of these measures is common among professionalizing occupations of a marginal nature (e.g., social work, engineering).

As is typical of marginal professions, rehabilitation counseling's members vary radically with respect to the amount of knowledge they possess and on variables such as educational attainment they vary widely. Some members of this occupation are clearly nonprofessional; most exhibit only certain characteristics of professionals. The elite of the occupation (e.g., directors of graduate programs, higher level administrators), have taken the lead in developing professionalism within the rank-and-file and in seeking public recognition for rehabilitation counseling as a profession. This relatively small element of the membership clearly ranks high on the professionalization scale.

As is typical of emerging professions, the leaders within rehabilitation counseling, while acknowledging the field's shortcomings, compare them with the inadequacies found in the established professions in years past. This observation gives the clear implication that the field can, and will, progress to full professional status. In order to express the community orientation of the occupation, marginal occupations are apt to develop and publish a code of ethics early in the professionalization process. As is the case here, however, the knowledge base lacks sufficient development to permit the specificity needed to permit the practitioner to apply it in concrete cases. Hence, the code is filled with generalities, and no effective enforcement of its provisions exists.

In an effort to spur the developing profession, the professional elite of marginal professions often attempt to strengthen the occupation's professional associations, mainly for the socialization and education of members, for public relations purposes, and for the defense of occupational interests. Unfortunately, rehabilitation counseling is still a divided field with competing associations. The total membership base has remained at approximately 20,000 professionals, but the total membership in these organizations has remained at less than 10,000, while the number of such associations has increased (e.g., most recently the American Mental Health Counselors Association and the National Association of Rehabilitation Professionals). With the proliferation and duplication of such national associations, the overall effectiveness of these groups necessarily diminishes. As an incentive for the least professional members to become more so, marginal occupations develop titles ("fellow") and legal restrictions upon practice. Rehabilitation counseling has begun this process.

The leaders of marginal occupations seek to develop and strengthen the professional school programs that train new entrants. The relative flexibility of American universities has permitted such programs, and marginal professional schools are oftentimes upgraded by the universities. This process has been beneficial to rehabilitation counseling. Emerging professions are attentive to the value of public relations efforts in generating public support for the field. Unfortunately, rehabilitation counseling has made little or no progress in this area; it lacks broad public recognition.

Finally, marginal professions that succeed in their efforts to professionalize are quick to be seen as invaders by other better established occupations. Rehabilitation counseling has come into conflict with generic counseling, social work, psychology and other fields during this process, and the conflict continues as to role definitions, employment domain, salary, and a host of related issues.

Thus, while rehabilitation counseling has not achieved recognition as a profession, this emerging profession has begun to make major strides in the process of professionalization. Surely, this fact presents both the rehabilitation student and the practicing rehabilitation counselor with the challenge to continue this process.

REFERENCES

Anderson, L. (Ed.) Counselor Attitudes, counselor performance, and turnover as they relate to counselor section. Conference Report of the Fifth Annual Vocational Rehabilitation Administration Region VI Research Conference. Minneapolis: Industrial Relations Center, University of Minnesota, 1963.

Brubaker, D. *The professionalization of occupations: A case study of rehabilitation counseling.* Unpublished Doctoral Dissertation, Southern Illinois University at Carbondale, 1977(a).

———. Professionalization and rehabilitation counseling. *Journal of Applied Rehabilitation Counseling,* 1977b, 8(4), 208–218.

Cohen, H. New directions in regulating health manpower. In J. Hamburg (Ed.), *Review of allied health education: 2.* Lexington, Kentucky: The University Press of Kentucky, 1977.

Commission on Rehabilitation Counselor Certification. *Plan of Certification Maintenance.* Chicago: Commission on Rehabilitation Counselor Certification, 1977.

Commission on Rehabilitation Counselor Certification. *Some com-*

monly asked questions about rehabilitation counselor certification. Chicago: Commission on Rehabilitation Counselor Certification, 1978.

Crisler, J. Results of the career ladder survey in state rehabilitation agencies. *Journal of Applied Rehabilitation Counseling,* 1977, 8(4), 218–227.

Dunning, C. *Counselor employment turnover in the North Dakota and Wyoming state rehabilitation agencies.* Unpublished Doctoral Dissertation, University of Northern Colorado, 1972.

Etzioni, A. *The semi-professions and their organization.* New York: Free Press, 1969.

Fraser, R., & Clowers, M. Rehabilitation counselor functions: Perceptions of time spent and complexity. *Journal of Applied Rehabilitation Counseling,* 1978, 9(2), 31–35.

Gilb, C. *Hidden hierarchies: The professions and government.* New York: Harper and Row, 1966.

Greenwood, E. Attributes of a profession. *Social Work,* 1957, 2(3), 45–55.

Hall, R. *Occupations and the social structure.* Englewood Cliffs, New Jersey: Prentice-Hall, 1969.

Jackson, J. (Ed.). *Professions and professionalization.* London: Cambridge University Press, 1970.

Miller, L. A reaction to the certification of rehabilitation counselors. *Rehabilitation Counseling Bulletin,* 1971, 15(2), 84–85.

Moore, W. *The professions: Role and rules.* New York: Russell Sage Foundation, 1970.

Muthard, J. & Salomone, P. The roles and functions of the rehabilitation counselor. *Rehabilitation Counseling Bulletin,* 1969, 13, 1–SP.

National Commission for Health Certifying Agencies. *Bylaws.* Washington, D.C.: National Commission for Health Certifying Agencies, 1977.

National Health Council. *Credentialing of health manpower and the public interest.* New York: National Health Council, 1978.

Olshansky, S. Counseling, State VR Agencies, and related matters. *Rehabilitation Literature,* 1976, 37(9), 263–268.

Parsons, T. The professions and the social structure. *Social Forces,* 1939, 17, 457–467.

Sussman, M., & Haug, M. *From student to practitioner: Professionalization in rehabilitation counseling.* Working Paper #7, Cleveland: Dept. of Sociology, Case-Western Reserve University, 1970.

U.S. Department of Health, Education, and Welfare. *Developments in health manpower licensure.* Washington, D.C.: U.S. Department of Health, Education, and Welfare, 1973.

U.S. Public Health Service. *Credentialing health manpower.* Washington, D.C.: U.S. Public Health Service, 1977.

U.S. Public Health Service. *Report on licensure and related health personnel credentialing.* Washington, D.C.: U.S. Public Health Service, 1971.

Vollmer, H., & Mills, D. *Professionalization.* Englewood Cliffs, N.J.: Prentice-Hall, 1966.

Whitehead, A. *Adventures in ideas.* London: Pelican Books, 1948.

Wilensky, H. The professionalization of everyone? *American Journal of Sociology,* 1964, 70(2), 137–158.

————. The dynamics of professionalism: The case of hospital administration. *Hospital Administration,* 1972, 7(2), 14–17.

Wright, G., & Fraser, P. Task Analysis for the Evaluation, Preparation, Classification, and Utilization of Rehabilitation Counseling—Tract Personnel. *Wisconsin Studies in Vocational Rehabilitation.* Monograph XXII, of the University of Wisconsin, Regional Rehabilitation Research Institute, 1975.

Chapter 3

Philosophy and Ethics in Rehabilitation Counseling

Jerold D. Bozarth

The questions addressed in this chapter are: What have been some of the philosophical influences on rehabilitation counseling in ancient history? What have been some of the philosophical influences on rehabilitation counseling in recent history? What are the influences of the philosophical questions? What is the basic nature of human beings? What propositions do the philosophical influences suggest might aid in the development of a coherent philosophy? What are the current and future directions of the philosophy of rehabilitation counseling?

The author expresses appreciation to Drs. J. Crisler, T. Field, R. Parker, S. Rubin, and J. Sink for information and suggestions for this chapter.

The importance of exploring the philosophy and ethics of rehabilitation counseling is especially apropos during this time of intensified struggle to clarify the professional image of rehabilitation
counseling. This struggle is highlighted by movements toward national counselor certification, state licensing for counselors, and national accreditation of rehabilitation counselor education programs
(see Chapter 2). The lack of explicit statements dealing with the
philosophical foundations of rehabilitation counseling may be detrimental to the future of rehabilitation counseling as a profession.
The rapid growth of rehabilitation counseling has been inimical to
the development of either a unified theory or a coherent statement
of underlying philosophy. Without an understanding of philosophical
foundations, the profession is apt to continue to be reactive and political in its attempts to become recognized. The influences of multiple disciplines (e.g., medicine, counseling psychology, vocational
psychology), and diverse philosophies (psychoanalytic, behavioristic, existential-humanistic) magnify the need for rehabilitation personnel to undertake this task. Formulating a statement of philosophy
and developing ethical standards are basic ingredients in the development of a viable profession.

PHILOSOPHY OF REHABILITATION COUNSELING

The difficulty of identifying the underlying philosophical tenets of
a profession in any concrete and specific way lies in the level of ab-
straction of the term *philosophy*. One dictionary definition is:

> Philosophy is the discipline which seeks wisdom and searches
> for truth through logical analysis rather than factual or em-
> pirical observations (Webster, 1974).

Philosophy is further defined as "the sum of the ideas and convictions of an individual or group." The ideas and convictions associated with a profession emerge from history, situational events,
and multiple bodies of knowledge.

Philosophical inquiry about rehabilitation counseling is basically
no different from any area of philosophical inquiry. Philosophy deals
with three major questions: What is real (Ontology)? What is
true (Epistemology)? What is good (Axiology)? But the basic
philosophical question for individuals is: What is the meaning of

life? Responses to this latter question from either an individual or group perspective will, in part, be predicated upon responses to another philosophical question: What is the basic nature of human beings? This question, along with those previously mentioned, are considered in this chapter in order to analyze and ferret out some of the philosophical bases of rehabilitation counseling.

Philosophical Influences on Rehabilitation Counseling in Ancient History

The historical perspective of rehabilitation counseling has been presented by Obermann (1965) and Garrett (1969) among others, and is also covered in the first chapter of this book. Shontz (1975) and Rubin and Roessler (1978) have summarized the philosophical influences on rehabilitation counseling, several of which are noted here.

Thought was revolutionized in the fifteenth century B.C. by Democritus who asserted that objects were constructed of atoms that were particles in motion. The soul was considered a special kind of atom that dispersed into the air at death. The classical doctrine of the four elements—earth, air, fire, and water—was developed in the fifteenth century B.C. by Empedocles. Both Plato's explication of dualism and Aristotle's description of life functions influenced the development of philosophical presuppositions of rehabilitation counseling presented later in this chapter.

Others who set the stage for the presuppositions were Hippocrates, Galen, and Paracelsus. Hippocrates determined that mental life was attributable to the brain rather than to the heart. Galen was the first person known to collect and record relevant medical knowledge. Paracelsus recognized that the physician does not heal, but aids the healing process.

Both the scientific study and humane treatment of mentally ill people progressed rapidly in the early years of the Roman Empire. However, demonology resurged by 200 A.D., and the Middle Ages were marked by neglect and/or abuse toward disabled individuals. The Renaissance renewed rehabilitation concepts as evidenced by increased attention to people who were poor or deaf. It was nearly the nineteenth century before naturalistic science began to predominate.

Several attitudes in early history that initiated the development of a philosophy of rehabilitation were:

1. Handicapped individuals were viewed as individuals who could be assisted rather than rejected.
2. Suggestions for resolutions of the problems of handi-

capped people were primarily from an authoritarian context. Legal and religious potentates were often the individuals who claimed to have the solutions to the problems of handicapped people. These authorities most often dictated plans for the handicapped people to follow.

3. A general trend existed for handicapped people to be considered part of the populus rather than as either "gifted" omnipotent beings, or individuals to be discarded because of their afflictions.

However, it was not until the nineteenth century that the general philosophical influences of the past began to form more definitive directions for disabled people.

Philosophical Presuppositions of Rehabilitation Counseling in Recent History

The nineteenth century brought with it considerable advances in rehabilitation. Increased efforts were undertaken by individuals and groups for certain disabilities. Gallaudet fostered education for deaf people; Valentin Hauy established a school for blind people in Paris; a residential school for the mentally retarded individuals was opened in Massachusetts; Dorothea Dix promoted services for mentally ill people; and physically disabled individuals were accorded more attention and treatment.

The twentieth century heralded industrialization, increased legislation, and increased financial support for program development. The identification of the philosophical presuppositions of rehabilitation counseling is considered in this section by first describing several stages of development. These stages have not always been clearly separate from each other. They are presented with accompanying major thrusts of behavior and intervention strategies. The stages are identified as:

1. Medical stage;
2. Vocational stage;
3. Psychological evaluative stage;
4. Psychological developmental stage;
5. Psycho-socio-political stage.

The influence of several major theoretical frameworks—medicine, psychoanalysis, behaviorism, and existentialism-humanism—are considered influential philosophical factors.

1. *The medical stage* (1900–1945) refers to systematic modern medical rehabilitation of disabled individuals. It was at this stage that the major attempt was to restore disabled patients to physical functioning. The intervention strategies were those of medical service, provision of prostheses, and suggestions that patients enter work settings that would accommodate their limitations. The basic assumptions were that the physician's diagnosis and treatment were correct and that the physician knew the patients' problems more clearly than the patients. Remediation of the physical limitations and appropriate placement in a receptive physical setting were the areas of emphasis early in this stage. Little consideration was given to patients' views or attitudes. The diagnostic and prescriptive model was predominant.

2. *The vocational stage* (1935–1955) refers to the stage of emphasis upon the return of disabled individuals to productive work. The emphasis was upon collecting, synthesizing, and presenting pertinent information to the clients followed by actively assisting the clients in pursuing an acceptable course of action. This stage marked the beginning of the vocational guidance movement in the United States. More than any other psychological philosophy, the psychoanalytic philosophy was most influential in the guidance movement. The basic tenets of psychoanalytic philosophy as related to major philosophical presuppositions of guidance are summarized by Beck (1963):

> A deterministic world view is taken. The world was thought to exist and move in accordance with cause-and-effect 'laws' of nature. . . .
>
> A deterministic view is taken, also, of the life of man. Man's being is thought to be composed of two definite parts, the mental and the physical. . . . The therapist could therefore see more objectively the relationships involved in the client's problem.
>
> "Objective viewing" by the therapist was deemed the chief means of untangling relationships which might be too threatening or too symbolic for the client to cope with effectively.
>
> Early life patterns and experiences may appear again in different guise, hidden from the consciousness of the organism.
>
> Responsibility was held to be a pseudo-concept since the whole pattern of a person's life was thought to be almost totally determined by factors (forces, drives, instincts, early experiences) beyond his power to alter. . . .
>
> After catharsis and a logical working through of the

meanings involved in the client's experiences, the therapist
was to point out what the client might do, or lead him to see
what he might do, to alleviate his suffering. . . . (pp. 57–58)

This stage placed primary emphasis upon finding the client the
right job and encouraged them to "get working." There was more
attention to job placement than to client development. Stereotypes
of specific disabilities were often promoted by the focus on efficiency. For example, a commonplace idea was that appropriate training for the paraplegic was horology.

3. *The psychological evaluative stage* (1955–1970) offered
more attention to the attitudes of and situational impingements on
the client. There was still a predominant influence from psychoanalytic philosophy; and there was more emphasis upon counselees
making their own decisions. The philosophy of instrumentalism,
espousing commitment to democracy and to free choice of occupations, influenced this stage. The goals of the Deweyan Instrumental-
ists were consistent with the commitments of the guidance movement and of rehabilitation counseling. A major emphasis was still,
however, upon the counselor's assessment and ascription of the
"right man for the right job."

4. *The psychological developmental stage* (1955–1979) began
to stress the potential of the client, the necessity of participation of
the client in self-choices, and particularly the counselor-client relationship. The humanism of Carl Rogers had significant impact in
rehabilitation counseling as it did for other areas of counseling and
psychotherapy.

This stage was accompanied by a gradual emphasis upon
change of the counselor's function. It was a time of the emergence
of counseling psychology that emphasized treatment that was developmental rather than remedial, educational rather than medici-
nal, and emphasized normal human development rather than pathology (Super, 1977, p. 14).

Although the importance of the counselor-client relationship
was emphasized, the other influences on rehabilitation counseling
remained. Rehabilitation counseling continued to focus upon vocational goal setting, assessment of client potential, and provision of
services (medical, vocational, and educational) for clients. The influence of the diagnostic-prescriptive model continued to be part of
the rehabilitation counseling model.

Nonetheless the postulates of Rogers (1957) had major impact
on the field of counseling including rehabilitation counseling. The
importance of the relationship, the client's perception of the world,

and the necessity of the counselor to be a real person provided the base for a major philosophical thrust.

5. The *psycho-socio-political stage* (1970–present) is the term used to refer to the current stage of rehabilitation counseling. This stage is characterized by increased federal influence and by an intensified formal struggle for professional identity.

Although the humanistic influence continued, several additional philosophical influences appeared to gain momentum during this stage. These thrusts include strong political efforts to influence legislation to mandate the role of rehabilitation counselors, develop certification for rehabilitation counselor education programs, and become better recognized as a politically influential profession. This stage appears to consist of a stronger move toward competency-based instruction, packaged training programs, and increased attention to evaluative-diagnostic-assessment procedures. Much of this move is sponsored by legislative and financial support from the federal government. In addition, education programs tend to be heavily laden with behavioristic approaches and increased emphasis on systematic development models (Carkhuff, 1972; Akridge, Means, Milligan, & Farley, 1976; Means & Roessler, 1976; Rubin, Means, Rice, Bozarth, & Milligan, 1975; Lasky, Dell Orto, & Marinelli, 1977). This stage seems representative of the proclivity in rehabilitation counseling toward pragmatism, action, and technology. The trend appears to be one of moving toward a more behavioristic philosophy for humanistic purposes. There is a focus, however, upon the expertise, skills, and services that the rehabilitation worker can offer the client. These philosophical influences will be noted in the next section.

The struggle for a unique professional identity appears as paramount in rehabilitation counseling as in many other counseling professions. The practically exclusive focus on professional development appears to have resulted in less opportunity and fewer attempts to develop the profession from philosophical presuppositions.

Views Concerning the Nature of Human Beings

Four major philosophical influences on rehabilitation counseling pertaining to the question, What is the nature of humans?, are:

1. The physiological-medical model that is diagnostic and prescriptive;
2. The psychoanalytic model that is an interpretive model;

3. The behavioristic model that is an action-oriented and goal-oriented model;

4. The existential-humanistic approach that emphasizes the human-to-human encounter and authenticity of the counselor.

The *physiological-medical model* emphasizes the diagnosis and evaluation of the individual's disability and finding ways to heal or remedy that disability. An organism, a malfunctioning organ, or the loss of organ function requires therapeutic intervention by the physician. Intervention may take place with the application of medicines or surgical procedures. The underlying response to the philosophical question regarding the nature of humans is that people have physiological characteristics that can be treated medically when a disability occurs.

The basic assumption of the *psychoanalytic approach* is that human behavior is determined by the ebb and flow of psychic energy and by irrational and unconscious forces. Psychopathology results from the inadequate resolution of one or more psychosocial stages. Psychotherapy focuses on the uncovering of unconscious materials. The role of the counselor is to teach the client the meaning of present behavior as related to previous experiences.

The *behavioristic approach* assumes that all behavior is learned and that humans are shaped by sociocultural conditioning. It is a deterministic view of behavior since behavior is a product of conditioning. This approach focuses on overt behavior, establishment of precise treatment goals, development of a treatment plan, and objective evaluation of outcomes. The counselor-client relationship is not emphasized. The role of the therapist is one of being active, directive, and expert in behavior modification techniques, such as systematic desensitization, implosive therapy, and operant conditioning.

The *existential-humanistic approach* emphasizes responsibility, choice, freedom, and self-determination. Humans are assisted toward development of personal potential and toward discovering their own uniqueness. The influence of the client-centered approach falls within this domain (Corey, 1977). Three pivotal questions raised by each of these four approaches concerning the nature of humans are:

1. Can we trust individuals to move in positive and healthy directions if provided with a nonthreatening atmosphere?

2. Do people have the potential to resolve their own problems?

3. Can people become self-responsible when given the opportunity?

These questions are implicit in the philosophical development of a professional. More specific propositions related to the philosophy in rehabilitation counseling are discussed in the next section.

A Philosophical Framework for Rehabilitation Counseling

The philosophical influences in history are diverse and, at times, contradictory. These influences and their ramifications are identified in the series of philosophical propositions that follow. Further elaboration of both philosophical influences of history and of other impinging factors are discussed with each proposition. The following propositions, then, are those viewed as being the most important for the development of a philosophical framework for the profession of rehabilitation counseling.

Proposition 1: **All individuals possess human dignity and worth regardless of their disabilities or limitations.** The evolution of the treatment of benign neglect and/or absolute abuse from ancient times and the Middle Ages to development of rehabilitation programs for disabled people in the nineteenth century illustrates the increasing acceptance of this concept. The increase of humanitarian values has been reflected even more so in the past few decades by such programs as Roosevelt's New Deal, Eisenhower's Dynamic Conservatism, Kennedy's New Frontier, and Johnson's Great Society (Rubin & Roessler, 1978).

More recently, Mathias (1976) stresses that each disabled individual should have the right to any employment "for which he or she has the qualifications and interests, including sheltered and often subsidized forms of employment, if such is appropriate to their needs" (p. 19).

Garrett (1969) refers to several philosophical concepts related to this proposition in his historical review: "The philosophical concept which in essence sums up our entire approach is that rehabilitation is a practical expression of the American ideal of the human dignity and worth of the individual" (p. 30).

Proposition 2: **Disabled individuals can become self-sufficient and can contribute to society.** One of the current arguments in favor of rehabilitation has been that of savings to taxpayers. Rehabilitation services result in economic benefits exceeding economic costs at a ratio of approximately eight to one (Conley, 1969). Reedy (1972) indicates that expenditures for rehabilitation services comparable to public assistance payments often allow disabled welfare recipients to become self-supporting.

In reviewing ideals basic to rehabilitation, Garrett (1969) states,

> The first concept is that the principle of equality of opportunity for all citizens imposes an obligation on the American people to provide special services for persons who are disabled, in order that they may be physically and vocationally prepared for employment and participation in privileges and responsibilities of American citizenship. (p. 29)

Proposition 3: **Productive activity, employment and/or maximum vocational independence is an important psychological benefit to individuals.** Working individuals are more apt to feel positive about themselves, more inclined to have self-respect, and feel better about themselves as contributors to society. For example, efforts by the Illinois State Mental Health System and the Jewish Vocational Workshop of Chicago (Gellman, Gendel, Glaser, Friedman, & Neff, 1957) have demonstrated remarkably diminished psychopathology in patients who were out of the hospital and working in sheltered workshop settings.

Bolton (1976) and others (Bozarth & Rubin, 1977) have identified psychological adjustment as an important dimension for rehabilitation client improvement. Holding a job provides the worker with a social and physical environment, with feelings of satisfaction, and with financial support.

Proposition 4: **Individuals' participation and determination of their own plans and destinies are essential elements in rehabilitation.** Studies in industry offer additional philosophical components relevant to rehabilitation counseling. Industrial management studies (Likert, 1961; Likert, 1976) have, among other things, found that when people can participate in their own plans success is more likely to follow. Rehabilitation counseling models have emphasized client participation (Bozarth & Rubin, 1972), and the Individualized Written Rehabilitation Plan (IWRP) as a rehabilitation counselor's requirement is reflective of this emphasis.

Proposition 5: **Diagnostic techniques, therapeutic interventions, environmental alteration, and activation of services for cli-**

ents can be combined to produce effective results. The philosophical attitude of using concurrent multiple approaches existed since the inception of rehabilitation counseling (McGowan & Porter, 1967). Approaches such as Lazarus's multimodal therapy (Lazarus, 1976) and community psychology and psychiatry have incorporated similar comprehensive "helping" philosophical attitudes.

Behavior modification techniques have demonstrated that reinforcement of success is a principle that aids people to improve their life situations (Franks, & Wilson, 1975). The development of total environments, such as, rehabilitation centers, sheltered workshops, and structured work environments provide total social support systems for disabled people. In addition, legislative and federal mandates have provided impetus to social action for handicapped people.

In summary, the development of the philosophy of rehabilitation counseling was influenced by many sources including history, philosophies of other professions, and other multiple sources. The philosophical concepts delineated in this chapter appear to be basic to the underlying philosophy of rehabilitation counseling. Another component of philosophy, that of ethics, will be reviewed in this examination of the philosophical components and their influence on the practice of rehabilitation counseling.

The next section is directly relevant to the assumptions about the nature of human beings. Ethical principles of conduct are predicated upon these assumptions. Since ethics is measured by behavior, the fundamental beliefs of whether, for example, humans are basically good or evil, are critically intertwined with the determination of appropriate professional conduct.

ETHICS IN REHABILITATION COUNSELING

The philosophical concepts of a profession are fundamental to the development of ethical standards. Ethics is the study of how people treat each other and concerns questions about right and wrong (Black, 1965). Ethics has been defined as a philosophical discipline concerned with people's conduct that utilizes such terms as "ought," "should," and "wrong" (Ogunyilieka, 1977–1978). Webster (1974) defines ethics as: "the discipline dealing with what is good and bad and with moral duty and obligation." But in this instance it specifically refers to "the principles of conduct governing an individual or group. . . ."

At one level, the principles of conduct of the behaviorist, humanist, and psychoanalytic counselor will differ. The behaviorist will function as a counselor who can manipulate the client's environment for the benefit of the client. The psychoanalyst will behave as though the client will act in destructive ways until the counselor has provided the opportunity for appropriate insights. The humanist will act in a way that places maximum responsibility on the client.

It is, perhaps, that the set of moral principles and values of each individual is the base for truly "ethical" behavior. Individuals who are responsible and who act with integrity and trust with co-workers, supervisors, and clients are the foundation for ethical practice in a profession. Obermann (1973) summarizes this idea by reviewing the rationale of questions associated with the code of ethics for rehabilitation counselors. He states:

> It was suggested that it would be reasonable to assume that persons of good will, sophistication and discipline as individuals trained to a professional level could be expected to be, would know what is "right" and would proceed in an ethical manner in their various professional practices and relationships. Responsible, democratically oriented persons should be accorded the trust and prerogative to set their own individual standards of behavior. If there is merely general acceptance of the Golden Rule, misunderstandings and misinterpretations in specific situations could be resolved without involvement beyond one's immediate peers, supervisors, employers, or clients (p. 214).

Obermann suggests that this is an attractive argument, but that professional associations have not accepted such arguments and have "... required that consensual rules be provided for guidance on what is 'right' and 'proper' in certain ambiguous situations" (p. 214). Professions depend on stated rules for conduct. One of the major requirements of a "profession" is that a code of ethics is applied by the members of the profession.

It is interesting that the implication is that the development of an ethical code is more to meet the requirements of developing a profession than for dealing with what is "good" and "bad." Several questions may be used to evaluate ethical codes: Does the ethical code provide consensual rules for guidance of what is "right" and "proper" in ambiguous situations? Do ethical codes reflect the basic assumption that humans can be trusted? Are ethical codes for the protection of clients or the propagation of professionals?

The major purposes of an ethical code are noted as the following:

1. Provides a position on standards of practice to assist each member of the profession in deciding what he should do when situations of conflict arise in his work;

2. Helps clarify the counselor's responsibility to the client and protects the client from the counselor's violation of, or his failure to fulfill, these responsibilities;

3. Gives the profession some assurance that the practices of members will not be detrimental to its general functions and purposes;

4. Gives society some guarantee that the services of the counselor will demonstrate a sensible regard for the social codes and moral expectations of the community in which he works;

5. Offers the counselor himself some grounds for safe guarding his own privacy and integrity. (Shertzer & Stone, 1974, pp. 391–392)

The question of whether or not ethical codes accomplish such purposes has not been extensively studied. Actually, ethical codes are predicated upon legalistic logic, that is, the guidelines must be interpreted by governing bodies and by cases of precedent for any given code violation or specific question.

Differences among the ethical standards of the American Psychological Association (APA), the American Personnel and Guidance Association (APGA), and National Rehabilitation Counseling Association (NRCA) appear to be minimal. The content of the APGA and NRCA ethical standards code are reflected in the following headings:

APGA	NRCA
General	Counselor–Client's Family
Counselor-Counselee Relationship	Counselor–Client's Employer
Measurement and Evaluation	Counselor–Counselor
Research and Publication	Counselor–Other Professions
Consulting and Private Practice	Counselor–Agency Supervisor
Personnel Administration	Counselor–Community
	Counselor–Other Programs Agencies and Institutions
	Counselor–Maintenance of Technical Competency
	Counselor Research

The American Psychological Association (APA, 1977) Code of Ethics is based on nine principles dealing with: (1) responsibility; (2) competence; (3) moral and legal standards; (4) public statements; (5) confidentiality; (6) welfare of the consumer; (7) professional relationships; (8) utilization of assessment techniques; and (9) pursuit of research activities.

The general theme of ethical standards for these groups is that "members are dedicated to the enhancement of the worth, dignity, potential and uniqueness of each individual and thus to the service of society" (APGA, 1976). The specification of ethical standards enables members to clarify the nature of their responsibilities; standards serve to stimulate greater concern and self-examination by members for their own professional functioning. The major responsibility of the counselor is to the client; however, the fact that the client is affected by other relationships necessitates ethical responsibility to others as well (e.g., to family members of the client, to the counselor's employer, to other agencies, to society, and to the profession).

The ethical codes of these three organizations are convergent. The divergences among these three ethical codes are primarily with the interpretations of such areas as counselor-therapist competence and training. For example, one APA standard involves the concept that psychologists remain receptive to their own psychological functioning. For example, if cognizant of personal problems interferring with work performance, the psychologist should seek competent psychological assistance. The APA Standards appear to be more specific than either APGA or NRCA standards and ascribe more emphasis to private practice procedures, research, and teaching than do either APGA or NRCA standards.

A brief review of the major areas of ethical standards for rehabilitation counselors (NRCA Ethics Sub-Committee, 1972) offers a more concrete idea of the standards (see Appendix D for the complete Code of Ethics). The major thrusts in the ethical standards code for rehabilitation counselors are as follows:

1. Counselor–client: The code that indicates that the primary obligation of the rehabilitation counselor is to the client. "In all his relationships he will protect the client's welfare and will diligently seek to assist the client toward his goals" (p. 218). The specifics of the code include such areas as confidentiality, illegal behavior of a client, safeguarding of client records, observation of professional standards in the personal

relationship of the client, and responsible action on the client's behalf in emergency situations.

2. Counselor–client's family: The counselor is reminded to recognize the important role of the client's family in the client's rehabilitation. "He will strive to enlist the understanding and involvement of the family as a positive resource in promoting the client's rehabilitation plan and in enhancing his continued effective functioning" (p. 221).

3. Counselor–client's employer or prospective employer: The code notes that it is the rehabilitation counselor's obligation to protect the client-employer relationship by apprising the employer of the client's capabilities and limitations. The counselor "will not participate in placing a client in a position that will result in damaging the interests and welfare of either or both the employer or the client" (p. 222).

4. Counselor–counselor: "The rehabilitation counselor will relate to his colleagues in the profession so as to facilitate their on-going technical effectiveness as professional persons" (p. 222). The code encourages counselors to urge their colleagues to observe ethical rules and professional standards, to not knowingly withhold information from colleagues that would increase colleague effectiveness, to not disseminate information about colleagues that would be erosive to their professional position, to refrain from expressing opinions or behavior that might be discrediting to colleagues or to the profession, and to give active support to colleagues who experience pressures because of observing ethical and professional principles.

5. Counselor–other professionals: "The rehabilitation counselor will conduct himself in his interdisciplinary relationships in such a way as to facilitate the contribution of all the specialists involved for maximum benefit of the client and to bring credit to his own profession" (p. 224).

6. Counselor–his employer, agency, supervisor: "The rehabilitation counselor will be loyal to the agency that employs him and to the administrators and supervisors who supervise him. He will refrain from speaking, writing, or acting in such a way as to bring discredit on his agency" (p. 225). The counselor is encouraged to attempt to amend regulatory and administrative conditions of employment that require

him or her to act in an unethical or unprofessional manner and to attempt to resolve differences through discussion and other communications with appropriate persons in the agency.

7. Counselor–community: The code indicates that the professional status of the rehabilitation counselor imposes higher standards of conduct than for nonprofessional individuals. The rehabilitation counselor "will use his specialized knowledge, his special abilities, and his leadership position to promote understanding and general welfare of handicapped persons in the community, and to promote acceptance of the viable concepts of rehabilitation and of rehabilitation counseling" (p. 226).

8. Counselor–other programs, agencies, and institutions: The code encourages the counselor to "... follow procedures and insist on the arrangements that will foster maximum mutual facilitation and effectiveness of services for the benefit of the client" (p. 227).

9. Counselor–maintenance of technical competency: The code states that the counselor is "... obligated to keep his technical competency at such a level that his clients receive the benefit of the highest quality of services the profession is capable of offering" (p. 228).

10. Counselor–research: "The rehabilitation counselor is obligated to assist in the effort to expand the knowledge needed to serve handicapped persons with increasing effectiveness" (p. 228).

Further divergences between the NRCA ethics code and the APGA and APA ethic codes appear to be the following:

1. The NRCA code focuses on the duties and functions and responsibilities of the rehabilitation counselor. Both APGA and APA codes focus on members of the organizations and their responsibilities to clients regardless of the particular job role.

2. The NRCA code of ethics focuses upon a relationship of the counselor to others, while the codes of ethics of APGA and APA attend more to areas of competency, such as test interpretation, research precautions, and consultation.

3. There is more explicit reference to the counselees' freedom of choice in the APGA and APA codes than in the NRCA code of ethics. However, the role of the coun-

selor in developing individualized client plans is specifically noted in the NRCA code of ethics.

4. The NRCA code of ethics is directed primarily toward employees, whereas the ethical codes of the other two organizations are directed more toward private practitioners.

5. The APA ethical code especially emphasizes the ethical responsibility of professionals to society and their collective influence on social issues related to discrimination against women, minority groups, and elderly people.

Other convergences of the three codes of ethics are generally that:

1. All of the codes can serve to stimulate greater concern by members for their own professional functioning and for the conduct of fellow professionals.

2. The three codes of ethics are clear that the primary responsibility of the organization member is to the client, and that responsibilities in other areas have to do with the relationship of those areas to the client.

3. The three codes of ethics offer a developed set of guidelines for members.

The guidelines of the ethical codes are not always easily interpretable nor do interpreters always agree with one another. Final interpretations are usually determined by an ethics committee comprised of members of the profession. Several examples of interpretations of ethical violations are noted below. The cases have been altered to assure anonymity of those involved.

First, a rehabilitation counselor in a state mental hospital discovered that his female client who had moved from in-patient to out-patient status said she was unable to have satisfactory sexual relations with her husband. The counselor, who was familiar with some of the recent work on sex therapy, arranged for the client and her husband to go through a form of systematic desensitization while the counselor observed them. This sequence of systematic desensitization entailed the counselor's observing them in (1) self-masturbation, (2) mutual masturbation, and (3) coitus. A coworker reported the counselor to their employer.

Multiple questions arise concerning this possible violation of ethics, including: What was the motive of the counselor? Was the intention of the counselor to help the client or was the action based on the counselor's needs? Was the counselor qualified for this type of therapy? Was this a therapeutic endeavor that was part of the rehabilitation counselor's job? In this case, the counselor resigned his job prior to referral to an ethics committee.

Second, a rehabilitation counselor in a state agency used allocated case funds both to pay for newspaper ads and to pay people to find jobs for his clients. An administrator in the agency complained that such allocation of funds was unethical, if not illegal. The counselor documented that his job placements had increased 200 percent; that his job placements were over 200 percent more than the average job placements of counselors in the state; and that his clients tended to remain on the job at least twice as long as the average duration of employment by other clients in the agency. Although the case was not referred to the ethics committee, the counselor resigned. It can, perhaps, be seen from this case that the questions of right and wrong are often difficult to resolve.

CURRENT STATUS OF PHILOSOPHY AND ETHICS

The development of ethics in rehabilitation counseling appears to parallel ethical developments in other fields. The commonalities among the APA, APGA, and NRCA Codes are more remarkable than their differences.

The NRCA Code, in particular, suggests that the profession of rehabilitation counseling is markedly humanistic. Disabled clients are to be valued, respected, and considered responsible members of society. However, most of the treatment and service strategies in rehabilitation counseling are behavioristic in function. There is an increased focus on evaluation and prescription for determination of client plans and objectives. Given the emphasis in both past and recent history on the importance of authoritative determinations, this is not surprising. In some ways the profession is a unique admixture of humanism and behaviorism. Clients are uniformly designated as the major participants in their rehabilitation plan and the extent of participation is even mandated by law with the requirements for a written rehabilitation plan. It is perhaps noteworthy that the need was felt to *mandate* client participation in the rehabilitation counseling process. Rehabilitation counseling appears to be a control-oriented profession that has high humanistic objectives.

The federal government has strongly influenced the philosophy of rehabilitation counseling. In some ways, the federal expectations of this field have given the profession little time to reflect on its philosophy. The result is that the rehabilitation counselor is a multi-based, multifaceted, multiskilled, and multidirected individual. Ugland (1978) notes several demands placed on the rehabilitation counselor by federal regulations and law. The requirements include that the counselor be:

1. Qualified to use all of the traditional skills and tools necessary for effective counseling in career exploration and choice;
2. Knowledgeable about the house care and health care delivery system;
3. Skilled in coordination and sequencing of diverse service;
4. Goal-oriented rather than process-oriented;
5. Expert in the processes of purchase of goods and services and resource managements;
6. Knowledgeable about and skilled in all the techniques used in securing and retaining employment with particular sophistication in dealing with employer prejudiced toward handicapped persons and the facilitating affirmative employment practices;
7. Capable of performing effectively in the role of expert witness (p. 3).

Certainly, Ugland's comments reflect the multiple base of influence on rehabilitation counseling. These features, in turn, suggest a functional model for the rehabilitation counselor. It appears to be essential that the profession take time to consider its philosophical foundations and identify its unique and functional model. Consideration of those features noted by Ugland and the philosophical propositions noted earlier suggest several prominent categories for the performance of the rehabilitation counselor. These include:

1. The rehabilitation counselor focuses upon the strengths of the individual client as a way to intervene in limitations posed by specific handicaps. The general refrain of a client's plea of "I need help" is more specific: "I need help to overcome my handicap."
2. The rehabilitation counselor focuses primarily on the area of work. Although work may be associated with independent client functioning or nonremunerative employment, there is the role of reasonable expectation

for the individual to reach and maintain some performance level.

3. The rehabilitation counselor is often required to be an expert prognosticator. That is, the counselor must predict the probable success of a handicapped individual in a particular training program, job, or other activity.

4. The rehabilitation counselor is action oriented. The counselor, as an integral part of the role definition, is involved in assisting the client with utilizing community resources, finding a job, and being an active client advocate.

5. The rehabilitation counselor is expected to be a combined resource of therapeutic interactionist, vocational counselor, vocational prognosticator, community organizer, and client advocate (Bozarth & Gianforte, 1978).

A functional model would certainly incorporate these dimensions especially the roles of therapeutic responder, vocational diagnostician, and community facilitator. A functional model should be developed using these three dimensions as the core to the model. The term *therapeutic responder* designates the utilization of psychological skills garnered from the knowledge base of psychological principles. The term *vocational diagnostician* implies the utilization of evaluative skills to predict the likelihood of client success in jobs, training programs, etc. The term *community facilitator* implies the utilization of community resources in highly skillful ways. This includes utilizing the knowledge of organizational development, group facilitation, and consultation skills. A model that would identify rehabilitation counseling in this way would better assimilate the philosophical assumptions of existential humanism and behaviorism, in addition to offering counselors a clear identity base.

Future Trends

The philosophical base of rehabilitation counseling possesses both strengths and weaknesses. The broad, developmental philosophical base is interdisciplinary in nature, drawing on the strengths of other professions and several major philosophical frameworks. The major weakness is the difficulty of developing a cohesive and consistent professional definition due to a broad knowledge base, diverse philosophical influence, and growing demands of society.

Field and Emener (1978, p. 63) note several factors that contribute to the growing professional identity of rehabilitation counseling.

> First, there is a significant and obvious need for our society and other societies to respond to the needs of the disadvantaged, the disabled, and the handicapped. . . . Secondly, there is the persistent and ever growing response to this need. . . . And, thirdly, the more we work and study and research, the more we will be able to effectively refine the substance of our work.

The profession of rehabilitation counseling can become stronger from this multiple baseline foundation. The unique model of rehabilitation counseling is that of offering a multifaceted service model for client facilitation toward an eventual goal of vocational, social, and psychological rehabilitation.

The future trends of rehabilitation counseling are apt to be influenced by many factors. The extent to which these factors will direct the knowledge base and the philosophy of rehabilitation counseling will be determined by the extent to which the specifics of this philosophy are crystalized and identified. The philosophical base is clear and unique. The base developed to date seems to include a marriage between behaviorism and humanism, which are contradictory in their view of the nature of humans as well as in other important areas. Further synthesis of these two philosophies will be a formidable task. A careful development and clarification of the philosophical base as a model will channel the continuing evolution of the philosophy and ethics of rehabilitation counseling in the future.

REFERENCES

Akridge, R. L., Means, R., Milligan, T., & Farley, R. C. *Interpersonal skills training: Basic helping skills for rehabilitation workers.* Fayetteville, Ark.: University of Arkansas, 1976.

American Personnel & Guidance Association. *Ethical standards casebook.* Washington, D.C.: APGA, 1976.

American Psychological Association. Revised ethical standards of psychologists. *APA Monitor,* 7(3) (March), 1977.

Beck, C. E. *Philosophical foundations of guidance.* Englewood Cliffs, N.J.: Prentice-Hall, 1963.

Black, A. D. *The first book of ethics*. New York: Franklin Watts, 1965.

Bolton, B. Case performance characteristics associated with three counseling styles. *Rehabilitation Counseling Bulletin*, 1976, *19*(3), 464–468.

Bozarth, J. D., & Gianforte, G. Rehabilitation counseling: Some quandaries and reactions. In W. Emener (Chair.), *Issues and identity crises in rehabilitation counseling as a profession*. Symposium presented at the meeting of the National Rehabilitation Association, Salt Lake City, 1978.

Bozarth, J., & Rubin, S. *Facilitative management in rehabilitation counseling: A case book*. Springfield, Ill.: Stipes, 1972.

————. Empirical observations of rehabilitation counselor performance and outcome: Some implications. *Rehabilitation Counseling Bulletin*, 1977, *19*(1), 294–298.

Carkhuff, R. R. New directions in training for the helping professions: Toward a technology for human and community resource development. *The Counseling Psychologist*, 1972, *3*, 12–30.

Conley, R. Benefit-cost analysis of the vocational rehabilitation program. *Journal of Human Resources*, 1969, *4*(2), 226–252.

Corey, G. *Theory and practice of counseling and psychotherapy*. Monterey, Calif.: Brooks-Cole, 1977.

Field, T., & Emener, W. G. Editorial: Rehabilitation counseling as a profession. *Journal of Applied Rehabilitation Counseling*, 1978, *9*(3), 63.

Franks, C. M., & Wilson, G. T. *Annual review of behavior therapy: Theory and Practice*. Vol 3. New York: Brunner/Mazel, 1975.

Garrett, J. F. Historical background. In D. Malikin & H. Rusalem (Eds.), *The vocational rehabilitation of the disabled*. New York: New York University Press, 1969, pp. 29–38.

Gellman, W. G., Gendel, H., Glaser, N. M., Friedman, S. B., & Neff, W. S. *Adjusting people to work*. Chicago: Jewish Vocational Service, 1957.

Lasky, R., Dell Orto, A., & Marinelli, R. *Structural experimental therapy applied to rehabilitation* (SET-R). Paper presented at the annual meeting of the American Personnel and Guidance Association, Dallas, 1977.

Lazarus, A. *Multimodal behavior therapy*. New York, Springer, 1976.

Likert, R. *New patterns of management*. New York: McGraw-Hill, 1961.

Likert, R., J. G. *New ways of managing conflict*. New York: McGraw-Hill, 1976.

Mathias, C. Rehabilitation—The challenge: Past and future. *Journal of Rehabilitation,* 1976, *42*(1), 18–20.

McGowan, J. T., & Porter, T. L. *An introduction to the vocational rehabilitation process.* Washington, D.C.: U.S. Government Printing Office, 1967.

Means, B., & Roessler, R. *Personal achievement skills leader's manual and participant's workbook.* Fayetteville, Ark.: Arkansas Rehabilitation Research and Training Center/Arkansas Rehabilitation Services/University of Arkansas, 1976.

NRCA Ethics Sub-committee. Ethical standards for rehabilitation counselors. *The Journal of Applied Rehabilitation Counseling,* 1972, *3*(4), 218–228.

Obermann, C. E. *A history of vocational rehabilitation in America.* Minneapolis: Dennison, 1965.

———. A code of ethics for rehabilitation counselors. *The Journal of Applied Rehabilitation Counseling,* 1973, *3*(4), 214–215.

Ogunyilieka, B. G. "Term paper." In R. A. Lassiter, and W. R. Ruel (Eds.), *Ethics in rehabilitation: Thoughts about values and professional behavior in rehabilitation.* (Monograph No. 3) Virginia: Regional Rehabilitation Continuing Educational Program and Virginia Commonwealth University, 1977–78.

Reedy, C. Developing trends in rehabilitation. In J. C. Cull & R. E. Hardy (Eds.), *Vocational rehabilitation: Profession and process.* Springfield: Charles C Thomas, 1972, p. 80.

Rogers, C. R. The necessary and sufficient conditions of therapeutic personality change. *Journal of Consulting Psychology,* 1957, *21,* 95–103.

Rubin, S. E., Means, B. L., Rice, B. D., Bozarth, J. D., & Milligan, G. T. *Facilitative case management: Instructors manual.* Fayetteville, Ark.: University of Arkansas, Arkansas Rehabilitation Research and Training Center, 1975.

Rubin, S. E., & Roessler, R. T. *Foundations of the vocational rehabilitation process.* Baltimore: University Park Press, 1978.

Shertzer, B., & Stone, S. *Fundamentals of counseling.* Boston: Houghton-Mifflin, 1974.

Shontz, F. *The psychological aspects of physical illness and disability.* New York: Macmillan, 1975.

Super, D. E. The identity crises of counseling psychologists. *The Counseling Psychologist,* 1977, *7*(2), 13–15.

Ugland, D. Letter. *Spotlight: Minnesota Rehabilitation Association,* June, 1978.

Webster's New Collegiate Dictionary: A Merriam Webster. Springfield, Mass.: G. & C. Merriam Company, 1974, p. 392.

Chapter 4

Rehabilitation Counseling Research

Brian Bolton

INTRODUCTION

The ultimate goal of research projects in rehabilitation is the improvement of services to disabled clients. Because rehabilitation counselors are the primary agents in the service delivery system, it is important that they are aware of the findings of contemporary rehabilitation research. By incorporating research-based knowledge into their counseling practices, rehabilitation professionals assure that handicapped people receive optimal services. Thus, the objective of this chapter is to introduce students and practitioners to the essential characteristics of scientific method and research design so that they can become intelligent consumers of rehabilitation research.

IS REHABILITATION RESEARCH NECESSARY?

The beginning student may well ask the question, "Why do research when we already know what works on the basis of practical experi-

---

This chapter is based on selected materials from Chapters 1, 4, and 10 in B. Bolton, *Rehabilitation Counseling Research*. Baltimore, Maryland: University Park Press, 1979, with permission of the author and publisher. Readers interested in an in-depth review of research methodology in rehabilitation counseling are referred to this volume.

ence?" or slightly rephrased, "Research only tells us what we already know." While much research in the social and behavioral sciences does confirm common sense expectations, some does not. Practical experience in counseling and rehabilitation provides considerable evidence, *subjectively* interpreted by the practitioner, regarding more effective and less effective service procedures. Most research projects in rehabilitation are simply systematic investigations of practical experience. The primary goal of the research enterprise is the attainment of useful knowledge by *objective,* replicable methods. The following section summarizes an investigation that produced results contrary to the investigators' expectations. The obvious point being made is that research does not always tell practitioners what they already know.

A STUDY OF PSYCHIATRIC REHABILITATION

Barbee, Berry, and Micek (1969) reported the results of a study undertaken to investigate the relationship between participation in a work therapy program and measures of treatment duration and rehospitalization for psychiatric patients. The subjects were patients at the Fort Logan (Colorado) Mental Health Center who were randomly assigned to participant (experimental) and nonparticipant (control) groups at the time of their admission. The experimental treatment, work therapy, has been heralded as a highly useful technique for preparing long-term patients for return to independent functioning outside the psychiatric institution. By communicating more realistic expectations of a job, work therapy reduces the patients' fear of leaving the security of the institution and eases their transition into the community.

Follow-up interviews with the 100 experimental (work therapy) and 149 control (no work therapy) subjects were conducted 3, 12, and 24 months after each patient's first substantial indication of improvement. The two groups were compared on four (dependent) variables using statistical significance tests: (1) length of intensive treatment, (2) length of total hospital stay, (3) rate of readmission to any psychiatric facility, and (4) readmission rate to the Fort Logan Medical Health Center.

Which group of subjects (work therapy or control) spent less time hospitalized? Which group had the lower readmission rates? In other words, using the four dependent variables as criteria, was the work therapy program at Fort Logan successful?

Contrary to the investigators' expectations (referred to as hypotheses), the results indicated that the experimental subjects had significantly longer stays in both intensive treatment and total hospitalization than did the control subjects. Although there was no difference between the groups with respect to readmission to all psychiatric facilities, the work therapy patients had significantly more readmissions to Fort Logan.

What might have accounted for these unanticipated results? The authors suggest that the work therapy program, as it was operated at Fort Logan, may have fostered institutional dependency rather than lessening it. They recommended that work therapy programs be established in the community in order to avoid contributing to hospital dependency. In fact, a longitudinal investigation of the effects of a community-based work therapy program on the rehabilitation of chronic patients at Chicago State Hospital supported this recommendation (Soloff, 1967). Soloff's study will be reviewed later.

THE SCIENTIFIC METHOD

The study by Barbee et al. (1969) is clearly an important contribution to the advancement of knowledge about rehabilitation services. The results of their investigation suggest that the vocational workshop may have to be modified to achieve optimal effectiveness with hospitalized psychiatric patients. However, the results of this study may be unique to the setting (Fort Logan) as well as to the particular disabled population. Great caution must be exercised in generalizing from the research findings of any given study. No single study ever provides conclusive evidence about anything; knowledge is advanced by the orderly accumulation and synthesis of research results. Rehabilitation practice can only achieve a scientific foundation through the systematic evaluation of current procedures and the flexible adaptation of experimental innovations. Basic to the attainment of an empirical foundation for any applied discipline is adoption of a set of rules or procedures referred to as the scientific method.

The scientific method is no more than a refinement of common sense. The primary characteristics of this fundamental approach to answering questions and solving problems are outlined in this section. Two global assumptions underlie the methods of science (Underwood, 1957, pp. 3–6).

1. Determinism: It is assumed that there is *lawfulness* in the events of nature as opposed to random, spontaneous activity. Every natural event is assumed to have a cause. The task of scientific endeavors is to discover the *orderliness* about observed phenomena.

2. Finite causation: It is assumed that every natural event has a discoverable and limited number of conditions which influence it. The task of scientific investigation is to identify the *specific causes* of observed events.

A scientific study begins with the phrasing of a research question. The question may evolve out of a practical problem or be the logical product of theoretical speculation. An example of the former might be "Does work therapy improve the probability of successful rehabilitation of psychiatric patients?" while the latter would be illustrated by "Is work satisfaction a function of the correspondence between an individual's abilities and the ability requirements of the work environment?" (This is an abbreviated restatement of Proposition II of the Minnesota Theory of Work Adjustment; see Dawis, 1976). In order for the research question to be amenable to scientific procedures, it must be translated into testable terms. The scientific method requires empirical data that can be evaluated objectively as a basis for addressing the research question. Someone other than the original investigator should be able to repeat the steps of any research study and arrive at the same conclusions. In other words, scientific research studies are subject to scientific verification in accordance with the principle of replicability.

There is no such thing as proof in the realm of empirical research. Theorems are proved in mathematical studies in the sense that they are the logical end-products of a series of *deductions* from previous statements, that is, axioms, postulates, and other theorems. Scientific investigations utilize empirical data, that is, observable phenomena that are translated by objective procedures into numerical form. Questions are answered tentatively as more evidence is collected; the criterion for assessing the state of knowledge in any given area of research activity is the total weight of the evidence. The logical process is *inductive:* the scientific method rests on arguments from a few cases to a defined universe of phenomena.

Measurement and Statistics

Two important topics merit attention at this point because they are cornerstones of the scientific method as it is applied to behavioral research. First, the translation of the research question into testable terms, or equivalently, the reduction of specified observable phenomena to empirical data, involves the process of measurement. Acceptable measuring instruments must be reliable and valid at a minimal level. Reliable instruments yield similar results when repeated; for example, a yardstick can provide a fairly reliable assessment of the surface dimensions of a dining room table in that the figures obtained on three consecutive days would probably not vary too much. An instrument is valid if it measures what it purports to measure. The yardstick constitutes a valid measuring instrument if the goal is an assessment of the *size* of the table; it may not be a valid measure of the *value* of the table.

The second important operation in the application of the scientific method of behavioral data occurs after the measuring process is complete. Statistical procedures provide an objective device for translating the empirical data into probability statements that constitute evidence regarding the research question. For example, the result of a statistical significance test might be a statement such as, "The probability of finding a difference as large as that obtained, if treatment A and treatment B are really equally effective, is less than one in a hundred. Therefore, it is concluded that treatment A is more effective than treatment B with chronic, male psychiatric patients." It should be emphasized that the statistical significance test cannot prove treatment A to be more effective than treatment B. It can only associate a probability value with the empirical data collected by the investigator.

RESEARCH STRATEGIES

Some basic principles of research design were introduced in the summary of the study of psychiatric rehabilitation, for example, random assignment, control group, and hypotheses. In this section three common research strategies or designs are discussed and illustrated using examples from the rehabilitation research literature. Emphasis is given to the essential characteristics of an adequate research design. The investigation summarized first illustrates a common design, referred to as the *one-group pretest-posttest* design, which, unfortunately, is methodologically weak. A discussion of the specific weaknesses follows.

Survival Camping: A Rehabilitation Treatment

Collingwood (1972) reported the development, implementation, and evaluation of "Camp Challenge," a three-week camping program designed as a demonstration and service project for male problem youth in Arkansas. The program was developed on the premise that the survival camping process provides a context in which effective interpersonal behaviors can be learned, and self-discipline and self-respect can be enhanced. Practitioners viewed the program as an initial therapeutic client service to prepare the youth for the vocational rehabilitation process in terms of more appropriate behavior and attitudes.

The total camp program (*experimental treatment*) lasted approximately three weeks. There were four basic stages to the program: (1) basic training, (2) backpacking expedition, (3) counseling, and (4) follow through. The participants spent the first eight days at a resident camp learning to work together as a team, becoming proficient in the basic camping and survival skills, and getting into physical shape. Following basic training, the group, which consisted of five leaders and 21 delinquency-prone male adolescents, went on a nine-day backpacking expedition through the Ozark mountains. Toward the end of the nine days, pairs of boys went on 24-hour survival details, where they had to secure their own shelter, food, and fire. After returning to the resident camp the participants spent two days in group counseling, individual consultation with the leaders, recreation, and equipment cleanup. After leaving the program, the boys reported to their rehabilitation counselors. A concrete rehabilitation plan was then developed with the aid of camp staff reports and personal consultations.

Twenty-one boys between the ages of 15 and 18 began the program with 19 successfully completing it. Of the boys who completed the program, three were from one of the training schools in Arkansas, ten were from the Arkansas Rehabilitation Service First Offender Program, and six were from a large rehabilitation facility.

The impact of the camping program on the participants was assessed through a variety of measures. The hypothesis that guided the design of the program and the selection of the research instruments was that successful completion of the program would result in an increase in physical fitness that would facilitate an increase in positive body attitude, which in turn would increase their general self-concepts and feelings of internal control in their lives. The specific measures were: four basic fitness tests, the Body Attitude Scale, the Index of Adjustment and Values (self-concept), an Internal-External Control Scale, the Jesness Personality Inventory, the Behavioral Rating Inventory and the Behavioral Problem Checklist (completed by parents and counselors), and three questionnaires designed to evaluate the program.

The results of the statistical analyses clearly supported the research hypothesis. Furthermore, the behavioral ratings by parents and counselors were consistent with the objective and self-reported measures: they noted an increase of positive behaviors and a decrease in the frequency of negative behaviors. In responding to the Program Assessment Questionnaire, the rehabilitation counselors indicated that the program had a definite positive effect upon the boys, especially in terms of increasing their rehabilitation potential. A follow-up contact four months after the program terminated revealed that almost all of the participants in the program were engaged in positive activities (vocational training, school, employment) that was in direct contrast to their status prior to the program.

The author concluded that "In summary, all the data and measurements obtained point out that the camp program made a substantial impact upon the participants and facilitated relevant behavioral and attitudinal changes" (Collingwood, 1972, p. 31). Is this a reasonable conclusion? Does the research design allow practitioners to accept the proposition that a survival camping experience can facilitate (cause) positive changes in attitudes and behavior in delinquency-prone youth? To answer this question, it is necessary to consider in detail some possible sources of weakness or invalidity in the design.

INADEQUACY OF THE ONE-GROUP PRETEST-POSTTEST DESIGN *

An important distinction exists between the *internal* validity and the *external* validity of research designs. Internal validity is concerned with the question of whether or not it was the experimental treatment that *caused* the measured effect. External validity refers to the extent to which the obtained results can be *generalized* to other settings, treatments, and populations. Both types of validity are required if any research investigation is to add to the reliable extension of knowledge. Internal validity is the first requirement, however, because to generalize an unspecifiable effect would be meaningless. In practice, the two classes of validity often appear to be competing in that it may be difficult to have both; the tighter a research study becomes (it utilizes more laboratory controls), the less realistic it

* This section relies to a great extent on the survey by Campbell, D. T., & Stanley, J. C. *Experimental and quasi-experimental designs for research.* Chicago: Rand-McNally, 1966.

is, and thus, the less representative (generalizable) are the results; on the other hand, the more the investigation approaches a field study (and becomes realistic and therefore generalizable) the more difficult it is to insure the controls necessary to achieve internal validity.

The study by Collingwood must be viewed critically and the results labelled tentative at best. The lack of a *control* (untreated) group of subjects who received the same pretest and posttest measures precludes the unequivocal conclusion that survival camping effected the positive changes that were recorded for the experimental group. In the absence of a control group it is impossible to know which changes, if any, could be attributed to the experimental treatment, and which were due to other factors.

The one-group pretest-posttest design is relatively weak because several sources of improvement, in addition to the experimental treatment, may be plausible. Additional sources of error may be:

1. *History:* specific events occurring between the pretest and posttest measurements in addition to the experimental variable, for example, the announcement that the principal investigator was appointed to the President's Council on Physical Fitness could have served to positively influence subjects (a hypothetical example).

2. *Maturation:* processes within the subjects operating as a function of the passage of time *per se,* for example, adolescent boys grow in spurts with amazing developmental changes often occurring during the summer months. Furthermore, in remedial situations, a process of spontaneous remission analogous to wound healing may be mistaken for the specific effect of the treatment.

3. *Testing:* the effects of taking a test upon the scores at a second testing (referred to as *reactive effects*). The process of measuring may even change what is being measured (due to cues, practice, etc.). For example, the pretest physical fitness evaluation may have merely provided the subjects with an opportunity to learn and practice the evaluation tests.

4. *Instrumentation:* changes in the observers or knowledge of the experiment on the part of raters may produce changes in the obtained measurements. For example, the parents and rehabilitation counselors who

completed the behavioral ratings of the participants may have been influenced by their knowledge of the program.

5. *Statistical regression:* apparent improvement from pretest to posttest that occurs because the subjects were selected for their extreme scores on related measures. Regression effects are not suspect when the group is selected for independent reasons; thus, statistical regression does not seem to be a legitimate criticism of the survival camping study.

These five sources of error may jeopardize the internal validity of the one-group pretest-posttest design; the external validity of the design may be limited by:

6. *Reactive effect of pretesting:* the pretest might increase or decrease the subject's sensitivity or responsiveness to the experimental variable and thus make the results obtained for a pretested population unrepresentative of the effects of the experimental treatment for the unpretested population. Therefore, the appropriate conclusion may be that the pretest-treatment combination produced the measured effect, that is, the pretest becomes an integral part of the treatment. (But the generalizability of the study must still be qualified by the question regarding internal validity.)

Collingwood's study of the effects of survival camping on delinquency-prone youth would have been greatly strengthened by the use of a control group. The ideal study would have begun with a sample of 40 potential participants and *randomly assigned* them to two groups of 20 subjects each. One group would have been arbitrarily (randomly) selected to receive the survival camping program. All subjects would take the pretest/posttest series of measures and their parents and counselors would complete the behavioral ratings *without* knowing who participated in the experimental program and who were control subjects. The five threats to internal validity listed would be neutralized by such a design, which is called the *pretest-posttest control group design.*

However, contrary to popular opinion, pretesting is *not* essential to an adequate experimental design. The *random assignment* of subjects to groups insures that the groups are similar (within the limits of statistical sampling) on all possible subject characteristics. Matching is *not* an appropriate procedure for the purpose of equating groups; however, it may be a useful adjunct technique for reducing statistical error variance, as illustrated in the next study. The strongest experimental design, then, is the *posttest-only control group design*. An outstanding example of this design is summarized next.

A Work Therapy Research Center

Soloff (1967) described a study of the influence of an extramural rehabilitation workshop program on the potential for rehabilitation of hospitalized chronically ill mental patients conducted between 1960 and 1965 by the Chicago Jewish Vocational Service. To test the *hypothesis* that the workshop service, which was located three miles from the state hospital, improved the prospects of patients for rehabilitation, the effects of two alternative rehabilitation services were studied: (1) the standard hospital services routinely offered to all in-patients at the Chicago State Hospital, and (2) a daily recreational therapy program located outside of the hospital at the Chicago Mental Health Center.

Subjects entered the Project from selected wards of the state hospital. They were matched in groups of three, according to age, sex, ward of residence, length of hospitalization, and marital status, and *randomly assigned* to one of the three service programs. The 149 subjects took part over the five-year period: 55 in the workshop sample, 57 in the state hospital sample, and 37 in the recreational therapy sample, since the latter program operated for three years only.

The workshop program was a simulated work situation in which, for a period of nine months, clients worked six hours a day, after an initial stage of shorter hours. At first, clients traveled to and from the workshop on a bus provided by the hospital; within three months, most had left the bus to travel by public transportation. Besides the workshop, services included individual counseling, job placement, follow-up counseling, and, where necessary, family counseling.

The program was evaluated by comparing results for the three groups on seven major criteria. These were (1) the proportion of subjects who were "successful," that is, met one or more of the following conditions: discharged from the hospital, worked in competitive employment, or took part in an ongoing, prevocational or activity program in the community; (2) the proportion of subjects discharged from the state hospital within one year of the completion of their programs; (3) the proportion of subjects so discharged who were in the community six months or more without rehospitalization; (4) the proportion of discharged subjects continuously in the community for at least one year following discharge; (5) the average number of weeks in the community for those subjects who were discharged; (6) the proportion of subjects who obtained competitive employment; and (7) the proportion of working subjects who retained employment for at least six months.

An analysis of the comparative results for the three programs according to the seven criteria supported the hypothesis that the workshop program, as provided off the grounds of the hospital, added a significant dimension to the prospects for success of chronically ill, state hospital patients. The proportion of workshop subjects exceeded that of both of the other programs on six of the seven criteria. The recreational therapy program had more positive results than the state hospital program on the same six criteria.

When subjected to tests of statistical significance, the differences in results among the three programs on the seven criteria fell into three groups. First, on the overall success criterion, workshop program results were significantly superior to those of the state hospital program (57 percent vs. 30 percent, $p < .01$). Results for the recreational therapy program (43 percent) fell between those of the other two and were not significantly different from either. Second, on the criteria of discharge from the state hospital, securing employment, and maintaining employment, workshop program results were superior to those of the state hospital program at a somewhat significant level ($p < .10$). Results for the recreational therapy program again fell in the middle and were not significantly different from either of the other two. Third, on the other four criteria, none of the program differences were statistically significant.

These results suggest a pattern. The workshop program results were most superior to the results of the regular state hospital program on those criteria where the staff exerted the most direct influence on subjects. Once subjects were in the community or employed, their contacts with staff diminished or stopped, and the influence of the staff in helping maintain gains was minimized. An analysis of staff ratings of community adjustment for those clients who had been discharged supports the results of the above pattern in that no statistically significant differences were found by program.

Three of the major conclusions derived from the study were:

1. It is possible to improve the chances for rehabilitation of chronically ill, state mental hospital patients through the use of a rehabilitation workshop program located

off the grounds of the hospital. It may be possible to do so using a recreational therapy program, but this not so clear.

2. The superiority of workshop program results is most evident at this point just after program completion when the staff's direct influence is the greatest. Once clients are in the community, and this is, of course, relevant only for those clients who get there, differences in adjustment between program groups tend to disappear.

3. While the results of the workshop program in securing competitive employment are clearly superior, the percentage of people getting jobs (25 percent of the total workshop sample) was small. The percentage maintaining employment over six months was still smaller. The success of the program is much more striking in promoting discharge than in promoting employment.

Ex Post Facto Investigations

The *ex post facto* (or retrospective) design is fairly common in field studies. It is not a true experimental design because the independent variable (treatment) is *not manpulated* by the investigator. Rather, subjects are *selected* because they have or have not been exposed to the experimental variable. In other words, subjects are assigned to treatment groups by procedures beyond the control of the researcher. The ex post facto design is appropriate when random assignment of subjects to groups is difficult or impossible.

A well-known example from medical sociology concerns the alleged relationship between smoking and lung cancer. In the simplest analysis, the observed statistical correlation cannot be interpreted as "smoking causes lung cancer" because smokers select themselves (they are not randomly assigned) into the experimental group; smokers and nonsmokers differ in many other ways and any of these other differences (singly or in combination) might predispose smokers to lung cancer. The important point is that observed differences cannot be attributed (causally) to the subject difference that was the basis for classification into the comparison groups. Many ex post facto studies include an attempt to match the natural groups on relevant variables in order to rule out alternative causes, e.g., smokers and nonsmokers may be matched on age and marital status.

The results of ex post facto studies can never be statements of cause and effect similar to the results of true experiments. But the ex post facto investigation does serve as a useful hypothesis-generating procedure; its tentative conclusions are *suggestive* of causal relationships that can be evaluated in carefully controlled experimental studies. The strength of the ex post facto design is that it describes the situation as it exists without experimental tampering. Thus, external validity, from a descriptive point of view, is excellent. The retrospective design is illustrated with the following large-scale investigation of the rehabilitation counseling process in state agencies.

Rehabilitation Counselor Behavior and Client Outcomes

The Counselor Client Interaction Project (Bozarth, Rubin, Krauft, Richardson, & Bolton, 1974) was a five-year, nationwide field study that addressed the following broad research question: "What kinds of counselors are effective with what kinds of clients in producing specific types of rehabilitation outcomes?" This question assumes that all counselors are not equally effective with all clients and therefore, that an *interaction* exists between rehabilitation counselor styles and different types of clients. Another way of stating the interaction is to say that client variables *moderate* the relationship between counselor styles and the outcome measures [see Bolton & Rubin (1974) for a detailed presentation of the interaction model].

Eleven state agencies and two agencies for the blind, each with ten counselors who served ten clients, comprised the study sample. Due to the many problems that occur in conducting field studies, the final sample for the longitudinal data analyses (initial intake through follow-up six months after closure) contained less than 250 clients. However, each of the clients completed a battery of psychological tests (Tennessee Self-Concept Scale, Sixteen Personality Factor Questionnaire, and Mini-Mult) at intake, four months after intake, and twelve months after intake. In addition to routinely collected demographic data, the Rehabilitation Gain Scale was completed at the three points noted above. Six months after closure the Minnesota Survey of Employment Experiences was mailed to the client. The project was clearly designed to focus on changes in client functioning in the areas of vocational adjustment and self-reported personality adjustment.

The *independent* variables of primary concern were the counselor's affective qualities and verbal behavior that were quantified via ratings from tape recordings of the actual counseling interviews. Each counselor in the study who mailed in one or more tapes for at least two clients received rating scores on the three interpersonal skill dimensions of empathy, respect, and genuineness, and twelve behavioral subroles, for example, information seeking—specific; information giving—administrative; communication of values, opinions, and advice; and listening/client talk. Demographic data and information reported by the counselor were also collected.

Some of the major conclusions derived from the extensive data analyses were:

1. Rehabilitation counselors are not a homogeneous group performing in a unitary manner. Three interaction styles were identified: information providers, therapeutic counselors, and information exchangers.

2. Rehabilitation counselors spend the majority of their job roles engaged in information-seeking, information-giving, and advice-giving behaviors.

3. Higher levels of interpersonal skills tended to be related to higher vocational gain at closure, higher monthly earnings at follow-up, positive psychological change ten months or more following intake, and greater job satisfaction at follow-up.

4. Lower levels of empathy and respect were associated with less vocational gain and a lower proportion of clients whose case files were closed as rehabilitated for the psychologically disabled.

5. Vocational adjustment and client-reported psychological adjustment emerged as independent dimensions of client change during the rehabilitation process.

The final step in the interpretation of the results of the Counselor Client Interaction Project was the translation of the data-based conclusions into *implications* for rehabilitation counseling practice. The following general implications were drawn:

1. Allow the rehabilitation counselor's work role to be more flexible; consider the revision of work emphases and rewards.

2. Include more interpersonal skill training for rehabilitation counselors—it pays off.

3. Begin to move toward the differential assignment of rehabilitation clients to counselors.

4. Consider psychological adjustment as a possible rehabilitation goal in itself.

From the design perspective, the important point to be noted about this investigation is that it is an ex post facto investigation.

The independent variables (counselor interpersonal skills and sub-role behaviors) were only measured; they were *not* manipulated. Counselors assigned themselves to the high, medium, and low sub-role conditions, and interpersonal skill levels by virtue of their counseling behavior. The counselors in the three groups probably differed on many other relevant behavioral dimensions. Therefore, the conclusions stated indicate that various kinds of counselor behaviors are *associated* with certain kinds of changes in client adjustment, but should *not* be interpreted as *causal* factors in the absence of additional, confirming evidence. An experimental design that could test the tentative conclusions from the Counselor Client Interaction Project would require that counselors be randomly assigned to sub-role usage conditions or interpersonal skill levels and then instructed or trained to function in a manner consistent with their group assignment. The criterion variables could be measured and, if differences were obtained, appropriate causal inferences could be made. Despite its weaknesses, the retrospective investigation is an important research strategy, but the results and conclusions that emerge are generally not a sufficient basis for the revision of rehabilitation counseling practice.

While this discussion of research designs is generalizable to all types of rehabilitation research, the presentation of the studies selected for illustrative purposes are necessarily brief. Interested readers would benefit from a careful reading of the section on rehabilitation counseling research in *Rehabilitation Counseling: Theory and Practice* (Bolton & Jaques, 1978). For information on measurement methodology and the use of psychological tests in rehabilitation, see the *Handbook of Measurement and Evaluation in Rehabilitation* (Bolton, 1976). Finally, any of the several dozen textbooks on elementary statistics and research methods would serve as a good starting point for students who wish to pursue these topics.

RESEARCH UTILIZATION

As stated at the beginning of this chapter, rehabilitation research is conducted for the purpose of discovering useful knowledge that can be applied in rehabilitation programs to improve services to disabled people. In fact, there is scant evidence that the tremendous amount of money and energy expended on research projects has had any significant impact on the efficacy of rehabilitation practice. This realization provided the impetus for intensive study of the research utilization process during the last decade. The basic problem is simply that of getting the results of research projects incorporated into rehabilitation counseling practice.

Barriers to Research Utilization

Three major barriers to the utilization of research results can be identified. These obstacles serve as a starting point for solving research utilization problems.

1. Research projects are often designed without any input or participation from the practitioners who will ultimately constitute the vehicle for the application of the research findings. When practitioners are not active participants in the design of studies, questions of major significance may be overlooked or inappropriately framed and, thus, the eventual results may be inapplicable. The study by Glaser and Taylor (1973) strongly suggests that the *involvement* of practitioners and administrators in planning and conducting research is the major factor in determining the eventual success of a research project.

2. Research findings are generally not reported in a form that encourages the utilization of results. Most reports (journal articles, monographs, books) are written for researchers and other academically oriented people, *not* for practitioners. Clearly, the mode of dissemination must be appropriate for the needs and professional interests of the target audience. (This is not to suggest that research reports should be watered down for practitioners; studies must be reported carefully in order to minimize the possibility that results will be misinterpreted or overgeneralized.) The Rehabilitation Services Administration (RSA) has developed a comprehensive program for the dissemination and utilization of research results that is designed to accelerate the translation of research into practice.

3. Resistance to change is a natural characteristic of individuals and organizations that often impedes the utilization of research findings. Halpert (1966) points out that the practitioner, who derives his satisfaction from meeting people's needs, is motivated against changing from practices that apparently have been successful. Thus, the results of research must be presented to potential consumers in convincing and nonthreatening ways.

The RSA Research Utilization Program

An important distinction exists between the dissemination of research results and their utilization. Dissemination refers to the distribution process while utilization is concerned with the actual usage of the results by practitioners. Dissemination is a *necessary* prerequisite for utilization, but widespread availability of research reports does not *guarantee* that they will be read or used by the target audience. Thus, a comprehensive utilization program must include techniques for helping individuals and organizations to adopt new ideas and alter service procedures. The RSA Research Utilization Program encompasses a variety of dissemination and utilization components (Garrett, 1970):

1. All RSA-supported research and demonstration grants must conclude with a final project report that states the *Significant Findings and Implications for Rehabilitation Practice* on the inside cover.

2. Research BRIEFs (Bring Research Into Effective Focus) are distributed separately to disseminate project findings to a wider audience. Each BRIEF contains a summary of the research project, an overview of the major findings, and a discussion of the implications for practice. The BRIEF's uncomplicated format and minimal length (front and back of a looseleaf notebook page) are intended to be attractive to the busy counselor or administrator.

3. Research utilization (RU) specialists have been assigned to RSA Regional Offices to implement the "county agent" concept that the Agriculture Department has successfully employed for many years. The RU specialists function as initiators of change in the rehabilitation service delivery system in state agencies. Several states have also established RU specialist positions.

4. Research utilization laboratories have been established at the Chicago Jewish Vocational Service and The Institute for the Crippled and Disabled in New York City to study and enhance the utilization process.

5. Rehabilitation research and training centers in four areas (medical, vocational, mental retardation, and deafness) conduct applied research and translate results into training programs that are conducted for rehabilitation practitioners in a variety of settings.

6. Regional research institutes conduct programmatic research on designated topics of broad interest (counselor functioning, job placement,·attitudinal barriers)
and disseminate their findings nationally.

Several of these research utilization efforts have been evaluated
using standard research procedures. The results indicate that the
use of research by practitioners can be increased by programs that
help practitioners to incorporate research-based knowledge into their
counseling styles. A special issue of the *Rehabilitation Counseling
Bulletin* entitled "Research Utilization in Rehabilitation" (Bolton,
1975) summarizes the state-of-the-art in this important area of rehabilitation research.

SUMMARY

While much research in the behavioral sciences serves only to confirm common sense expectations, some does not. An investigation
that did not support practical experience and clinical intuition found
that work therapy provided on the hospital grounds did not improve
the rehabilitation success rates of psychiatric inpatients.

The primary goal of the research enterprise is the attainment
of useful knowledge following a set of procedures known as the scientific method. The scientific method requires empirical data that
can be evaluated objectively as a basis for addressing research questions. Two important aspects of the application of the scientific
method to behavioral phenomena are the process of measurement
and the use of tests of statistical significance.

A common research strategy, which is methodologically weak,
is the one-group pretest-posttest design. The lack of a control group
of subjects precludes the conclusion that the experimental treatment
caused any of the measured changes. Other possible sources of invalidity fall within the categories of history, maturation, testing,
instrumentation, and statistical regression. The random assignment
of subjects to experimental and control groups ensures that the
groups are similar on all possible subject characteristics. A recommended experimental design is the posttest-only control group design.

The ex post facto design is fairly common in field studies. It is
not a true experimental design because the independent variable is
not manipulated by the investigator. Subjects are selected because
they have or have not been exposed to the experimental variable.

The results of such retrospective studies can never be statements of cause and effect, but their tentative correlational conclusions are suggestive of causal relationships that can be evaluated in true experimental studies.

Rehabilitation research is conducted for the purpose of improving services to disabled people. Three barriers to the utilization of research are (1) failure to include practitioners in the planning of projects, (2) technical research reports that are not written for practitioners, and (3) the natural tendency of individuals and organizations to resist change. The RSA Research Utilization Program includes six components: (1) dustjacket summaries on research reports, (2) BRIEFs of research projects, (3) regional research utilization specialists, (4) two research utilization laboratories, (5) research and training centers, and (6) regional research institutes.

REFERENCES

Barbee, M. S., Berry, K. L., & Micek, L. A. Relationship of work therapy to psychiatric length of stay and readmission. *Journal of Consulting and Clinical Psychology*, 1969, 33, 735–738.

Bolton, B. (Ed.). Research utilization in rehabilitation. *Rehabilitation Counseling Bulletin*, Special Issue, December, 1975.

———. *Handbook of measurement and evaluation in rehabilitation.* Baltimore: University Park Press, 1976.

———, & Jaques, M. E. (Eds.). *Rehabilitation counseling: Theory and practice.* Baltimore: University Park Press, 1978.

Bolton, B., & Rubin, S. A research model for rehabilitation counselor performance. *Rehabilitation Counseling Bulletin*, 1974, *18*, 141–148.

Bozarth, J. D., Rubin, S. E., Krauft, C. C., Richardson, B. K., & Bolton, B. *Client counselor interaction, patterns of service, and client outcome: Overview of project, conclusions, and implications.* Arkansas Studies in Vocational Rehabilitation: 19. Fayetteville: Arkansas Rehabilitation Research and Training Center, 1974.

Collingwood, T. R. *Survival camping: A therapeutic mode for rehabilitation problem youth.* Fayetteville: Arkansas Rehabilitation Research and Training Center, 1972.

Dawis, R. V. The Minnesota Theory of Work Adjustment. In B. Bolton (Ed.), *Handbook of measurement and evaluation in reha-bilitation*. Baltimore: University Park Press, 1976.

Garrett, J. Using research findings to enhance services to people. In D. Patrick (Ed.), *Expanding services to the disabled and dis-advantaged: Implications for research utilization in delivery of services and manpower planning*. Birmingham: University of Alabama Research and Training Center, 1970.

Glaser, E. M., & Taylor, S. H. Factors influencing the success of applied research. *American Psychologist*, 1973, *28*, 140–146.

Halpert, H. P. Communications as a basic tool in promoting utilization of research findings. *Community Mental Health Journal*, 1966, *2*, 231–236.

Soloff, A. *A work therapy research center*. Chicago: Jewish Vocational Service, 1967.

Underwood, B. J. *Psychological research*. New York: Appleton, 1957.

Part II

*Rehabilitation Service
Consumers—People
with Handicaps*

Throughout recorded history handicapped people have been a source of concern for nonhandicapped people. This concern has resulted in marked variations in treatment throughout history, ranging from persecution to protection and even reverence. Although the variations of treatment of people who are handicapped are not as marked today, prejudice, avoidance, and isolation, as well as humanistic caring coexist in the United States (Obermann, 1965).

Still consumers of rehabilitation services contend that their cause has too long been denied, ignored, or simply not heard by the public at large. Perhaps their numbers are simply too small to be heard, but statistics belie this speculation.

In 1972 the Social Security Administration (SSA) estimated that 15.6 million people aged 20 to 64 in the noninstitutionalized population were disabled. Of these 7.7 million were unable to work at all or unable to work regularly; 3.5 million were able to work regularly but not in the same job as before the onset of disability; and 4.4 million were able to work full time, regularly, and at the same job, but with limitations in the nature or amount of work they could do. About four-fifths had at least one physical activity limitation, and the most frequent disabilities were musculoskeletal and cardiovascular conditions. The median age at onset of disability was 41 years and the median duration was 5 years. Compared to non-disabled people, the disabled individuals were older, poorer, less educated; more likely to be black, live in the South, have a rural residence; and were more likely to be divorced, separated, or widowed.

It is easy to be confused when reading statistics regarding the extent of disabling conditions. Most estimates are based on surveys of a particular sample of the population. For example, the SSA study cited selected only noninstitutionalized persons aged 20 to 64 years. Other estimates may be quite different because they were done at a different time and were based on a different sample. For example, the Urban Institute (1975) estimated that as of July 1, 1975, there were 23.3 million noninstitutionalized disabled people aged 18 to 64. Finally, all such surveys are subject to sampling error and may lack the degree of precision the naive person might expect.

Nonetheless, people who have a disability appear to comprise a substantial percent (roughly 10 to 15 percent) of the population of the United States. This data prompts alternative hypotheses. Perhaps the impact of disability is so severe that people with a disability expend virtually all of their energy meeting basic physiological and safety needs (Maslow, 1954) and are unable to pursue more lofty goals. Clinical data lends support to this hypothesis. Numerous studies have been conducted concerning the psychological impact of disability and the process of adjustment to disability (e.g., see Bray, 1978; Kerr, 1961; Meyer, 1971; Shontz, 1975; and Wright, 1960). Although there are significant variations in the descriptions of the course of the adjustment process, most authors include aspects of the following phases: shock, protest and denial, depression, acceptance, and adaptation. The psychological trauma of disability may be so severe that an individual may never reach the acceptance or adaptation phase. Even though an individual may progress to the later stages of adjustment, subsequent stress may lead to regression in adjustment. One potential source of stress is the family. Families go through a process of adjustment to the family member's disability, similar to the process the individual goes through. At any given time, however, the family may be at a different point in the process than the disabled individual, leading to a variety of problems in communication and relationship. Bray (1978) presents one view of the parallel adjustment process spinal cord injured individuals and their families appeared to go through. He found that the initial stages of adjustment took as long as two years for the average spinal cord injured person and his or her family. From a broader perspective, adjustment to disability is a continuing, never-ending process not only for disabled persons and their families, but also for the community at large.

The economic impact of disability on the community is considerable. Berkowitz (1974) estimated that the "cost" of disability was $35.5 billion in 1970, $51.6 billion in 1973, and will be $222.8 billion by 1990. The cost, which appears to be increasing geometrically, adds impetus for state and federal governments to increase efforts at rehabilitation. This impetus is heightened when the cost effectiveness of the state-federal rehabilitation programs is considered. Studies (Urban Institute, 1975) reveal that for vocational rehabilitation, one of the few social programs for which benefit/cost analyses have been made, there was a return of $18.11 in 1970 and $20.37 in 1972 by clients for every dollar spent for rehabilitation services. This was determined by figuring the ratio of paid earnings to program costs, which is the most straightforward model of benefit/cost analysis. Note in Chapter 5 that in spite of the cost effectiveness of state rehabilitation programs and the growing extent of disability, both the funding and outcomes of state vocational rehabilitation agencies have recently been declining!

Prejudicial public attitudes may be an additional factor in the inability or reluctance of society to fully meet the needs of people with handicaps. Although publicly voiced attitudes may be somewhat positive in tone (Wright, 1960), more recent research suggests that *interaction strain* occurs when a handicapped and nonhandicapped people interact and that the nonhandicapped people may not be aware of their own marked behavioral reactions toward disabled people (Kleck, 1966; Kleck, 1969; Kleck, Ono, & Hastorf, 1966). An important effort of rehabilitation counseling is to educate the public and modify people's attitudes about disabled people away from pity and toward realistic acceptance.

Another hypothesis that might explain the apparent lack of public action to meet the needs of people with handicaps is that handicapped people and their advocates do not have sufficient economic or political strength to attract public attention to their needs. As stated earlier this group as a whole is financially poorer than nonhandicapped people, and avenues to attain wealth are often shut off to them. People with handicaps, for example, face numerous barriers in attaining employment. Even though Section 504 of the 1973 Rehabilitation Act and the 1978 amendments (see Chapter 1) mandate nondiscrimination based on handicapping conditions in employment, numerous barriers to employment still exist. Architectural, attitudinal, and bureaucratic barriers are still rampant in our society.

A final alternative would be to discount the original premise that implies that the needs of consumers have had little positive impact on the public. A number of effective consumer-oriented organizations for people with handicaps do exist, for example, the American Foundation of the Blind, the Epilepsy Foundation of America, the National Association for Retarded Citizens, the National Association of the Deaf, the National Federation of the Blind, and the National Paraplegia Foundation (see Bowe, 1978). These and many other groups now have a unified voice particularly in influencing federal legislation through the American Coalition of Citizens with Disabilities, which is a nationwide umbrella of 65 organizations of and for the disabled. However, in spite of the growing influence of such groups and the increasing general knowledge of the difficulties society imposes on people with handicaps, the public and most assuredly rehabilitation practitioners must maintain a continuing awareness of and sensitivity to the rights, needs, and desires of people with handicaps. The following three chapters will further develop the topics of the extent of disability, the impact of disability on the individual, and the world of work and disabling conditions.

REFERENCES

Berkowitz, M. Cost burden of disability and effects of federal program expenditures, Final report. New Brunswick, N.J.: Disability and Health Economics Research, Bureau of Economics Research, Rutgers University, 1974.

Bowe, F. *Handicapping America: Barriers to disabled people*. New York: Harper & Row, 1978.

Bray, G. Rehabilitation of spinal cord injured: A family approach. *Journal of Applied Rehabilitation Counseling*, 1978, 9, 70–78.

Kerr, N. Understanding the process of adjustment to disability. *Journal of Rehabilitation*, 1961, 27, 16–18.

Kleck, R. Emotional arousal in interactions with stigmatized persons. *Psychological Reports*, 1966, 19, 1226.

———. Physical stigma and task-oriented interactions. *Human Relations*, 1969, 22, 53–60.

———, Ono, H., & Hastorf, A. The effect of physical deviance upon face-to-face interaction. *Human Relations*, 1966, 19, 425–436.

Maslow, A. *Motivation and personality*. New York: Harper, 1954.

Meyer, G. The psychodynamics of acute blindness. *Ophthalmology Digest*, October, 1971, 31–37.

Obermann, C. *A history of vocational rehabilitation in America*. Minneapolis, Minn.: Dennison, 1965.

Shontz, F. *The psychological aspects of physical illness and disability*. New York: Macmillan, 1975.

Social Security Administration. First findings of the 1972 survey of the disabled: General characteristics, Report No. 1, Kathryn H. Allen. Washington, D.C., Social Security Administration, 1972.

Urban Institute. Report of the comprehensive service needs study. Washington, D.C.: Urban Institute, 1975.

Wright, B. *Physical disability—A psychological approach*. New York: Harper, 1960.

Chapter 5

Extent of Disabling Conditions

Thomas L. Porter

INTRODUCTION

There is a familiar story about a Dutch boy who held back a flood by stopping a leak in a dike. It is doubtful that this lad was concerned about the exact amount of water behind that dike. Most rehabilitation workers are faced with a similar situation—an unending flow of cases. As one client leaves the process, several more are waiting. Additional personnel and resources seem to increase instead of reduce the number of potential clients. However, knowledge regarding the magnitude of the problem is relevant. It helps in understanding the demands for increased productivity and is necessary information for those people involved in long-range planning and in obtaining funds.

A recent publication by the President's Committee on Employment of the Handicapped (no date) entitled *Facts About Handicapped People* offers the following warning: "A wise man once said that too much information can stand in the way of knowledge. This can especially be true when one tries to extract pertinent information about handicapped people from the various sources of statistical data."

An abundant amount of information and estimations exist regarding the extent of disability among residents of the United States. Much of it is contradictory and difficult to interpret. The more specific the data, the more misleading it becomes in terms of the total picture, i.e., handicapped people tend to have more than one impairment. But not all impairments constitute disabilities or handicaps. Definitions will be discussed in the next section of this chapter.

The following thirteen "key facts" from *Facts About Handicapped People* provide an overview of the population that may be in need of specialized rehabilitation services.

1. One in eleven people is handicapped.
   - Over 11 million noninstitutionalized Americans aged 16 to 64 reported that they had permanent work disabilities in 1970.
   - This is 9 percent of all people aged 16 to 64.
   - By sex: 10 percent of all men; 8.5 percent of all women.
2. Many Americans have long-term disabilities.
   - Over 6 million Americans aged 18 to 64 had been disabled for five years or longer in 1970, which is more than half of those with permanent disabilities.
   - Over 4 million people had been disabled 10 years or longer, which is more than one-third of those with permanent disabilities.
3. Disability increases with age.

Percent Disabled 6 Months or More

Age	Total Disabled	Male	Female
16–24	4.5	5.9	3.1
25–34	5.0	5.7	4.4
35–44	7.6	8.1	7.2
45–54	12.7	13.4	12.0
55–64	21.0	22.1	20.0
Total	9.3	10.1	8.5

4. The disabled population is considerably older than the general population.
   - Fifteen percent of the total U.S.A. population was 55 to 64 years old in 1970. More than double that percentage—35 percent—of the handicapped population was between 55 and 64 years old.
   - Thirty-eight percent of the total population was between 35 and 54 years old; 42 percent of the handicapped population was between 35 and 54.
   - For the younger ages—16 to 34—it's an entirely different story! Forty-seven percent of all the population; only 23 percent of the handicapped population.

5. Handicapped people have less schooling than non-handicapped people.
   - Thirty-seven percent of disabled Americans 18 to 64 did not go beyond elementary school compared with 18 percent of the general population.
   - Eighty-five percent of disabled people did not go beyond high school compared with 75 percent of the general population.
   - Only 5 percent of disabled people had some college education compared with 11 percent of the general population.

6. Disabilities limiting work capabilities are more prevalent among minorities than among whites.
   - Nine percent of whites 18 to 64 reported permanent work disabilities in 1970 (11 percent for men; 8 percent for women).
   - Thirteen percent of blacks 18 to 64 reported such disabilities (13 percent for both men and women).
   - Ten percent of people of Spanish origin reported such disabilities (10 percent for men, and 9 percent for women).

7. More disabled people are heads of households than in the general population.
   - Forty-three percent of the disabled population 18 to 64 were heads of households compared with 39 percent of the general population.
   - Thirteen percent of all households in the disabled population were headed by women compared with 10 percent headed by women in the general population.

8. A higher proportion of disabled people have never worked than persons in the general population.

   - Four percent of handicapped men 18 to 64 had never worked compared with 2 percent of the total male population.
   - Sixteen percent of disabled women had never worked compared with 11 percent of all women.

9. Far fewer handicapped people than the general population are employed.

   - Forty-two percent of handicapped adults were employed in 1970 compared with 59 percent of the general population. Handicapped people not employed include both (a) those ready and willing to work who are seeking work and (b) those who are not officially in the labor force (defined as not working and not looking for work) for a variety of reasons. Some of these reasons have more to do with the physical and attitudinal barriers of society than with the disabilities of those individuals.
   - By sex: 58 percent of handicapped men were employed compared with 76 percent of all men; 24 percent of handicapped women were employed compared with 42 percent of all women.

10. Disability strikes primarily in adult years.

   - Eighty-two percent of disabled people aged 18 to 64 acquired their disabilities after age 17. By this time they had already received their basic education and had acquired normal work aspirations. Of these. . .
   - Thirty-two percent became disabled during early career years (18 to 34).
   - Forty-one percent became disabled between 35 and 54.
   - Nine percent became disabled after age 54.

11. Handicapped people aged 14–64 have lower earnings than nonhandicapped people.

   - The average handicapped person's income was about $1,000 below the average for the total population (Median income 1969: disabled people, aged 16 to 64, $1,800; total population, aged 16 to 64, $2,700). (These averages appear low since they include many people who are not working or working part-time.)

- Among men the difference is even more striking (Median income 1969: handicapped men, $4,200; total, $6,200).
- Forty-five percent of men in the general population but only 31 percent of handicapped men made over $7,000 in 1969.

12. Disabled people with jobs held proportionately fewer professional, technical, and managerial jobs than did the general population.

    - Twenty-one percent of employed disabled men held professional, technical, and managerial positions compared with 26 percent of the total male population.
    - Fifteen percent of all disabled women employed held professional, managerial, and technical positions compared with 20 percent of all employed women.
    - Disabled men were more likely than nondisabled men to have clerical, sales, service, or laborers' jobs.
    - Twenty-two percent of disabled women were laborers or service workers compared with 17 percent of all employed women.

13. Disability takes a variety of forms.

    - Twenty-six percent of the disabled had cardiovascular disorders, including heart trouble and high blood pressure.
    - Twenty-five percent had muscular or skeletal conditions, including arthritis, rheumatism, and back trouble.
    - Ten percent had mental disorders, including mental retardation and mental illness.
    - Nine percent had respiratory and related disorders, including asthma.
    - Nine percent had disorders of the nervous system, including epilepsy, multiple sclerosis, and paralysis.
    - Five percent had digestive disorders.
    - Three percent had diabetes.
    - Three percent had visual impairments.
    - Ten percent had other and unspecified conditions. (It is estimated that deafness is the nation's most prevalent disability. However, no breakdown for deafness was included in this profile.)

DEFINITIONS

A review of the rehabilitation related literature and definitions used by public programs for disabled people reveals a melange of uses of the terms "impairment," "disability," and "handicap." It seems that the terms can mean whatever the user wants them to mean.

The Urban Institute (1975, p. 25) makes the following distinctions:

> Our preference is to call the residual limitation resulting from congenital defect, disease, or injury an *impairment*. A person with an impairment, then, may or may not have a *disability*, an inability to perform some key life functions. When the inability is such that the environment imposes impediments to the individual's goals for travel or work, for example, the individual has a *handicap*.

Hamilton (1950, p. 17) differentiates between disability and handicap. His definitions are:

Disability—a condition or impairment, physical or mental, having an objective aspect that can usually be described by a physician.

Handicap—the cumulative result of the obstacles which disability interposes between the individual and his maximum functional level. The handicap is the measure of the loss of the individual's capacity, wherever evident.

These definitions emphasize disability as a medical diagnosable fact, while a handicap is determined by the extent of functional limitation.

The problem of definition is further complicated by the emphasis placed on the rehabilitation of the "severely handicapped person" by the Rehabilitation Act of 1973.

In this Act, the severely handicapped person is defined as:

One who has a severe physical or mental disability that seriously limits his or her functional capacities (mobility, communication, self-care, self-direction, work therapy or work skills) in terms of employability;

One whose vocational rehabilitation can be expected to require multiple vocational rehabilitation services over an extended period of time; and

> One who has one or more physical or mental disabilities
> resulting from amputation, arthritis, blindness, cancer,
> cerebral palsy, cystic fibrosis, deafness, heart disease,
> hemiplegia, hemophilia, respiratory or pulmonary dys-
> function, mental retardation, mental illness, multiple
> sclerosis, muscular dystrophy, musculoskeletal disor-
> ders, neurological disorders including stroke and epi-
> lepsy, paraplegia, quadriplegia, and other spinal cord
> conditions, sickle cell anemia and end-stage renal dis-
> ease, or another disability or combination of disabil-
> ities determined on the basis of an evaluation or reha-
> bilitation potential to cause comparable substantial
> functional limitation.

The report by the Urban Institute (1975) contains a review
(pp. 721–738) of operational definitions of individuals who are severely handicapped. This report would be a good starting point for
the interested reader.

The rehabilitation worker is faced with the dilemma of combining objective medical evidence with subjective client factors. Impairments may or may not lead to important functional limitations.
For example, consider the case of a college student who entered the
military and lost an arm. He returned to college and completed law
school under the G.I. Bill and now practices law, earning $40,000
per year. If the veteran had been a service station attendant prior
to his impairment his problems after discharge could have been very
different. Or, consider the waitress that suffers a cosmetic disfigure-
ment. Her ability to perform the physical aspects of her job have
not been altered, however her employer and customers may react
to her differently. Or, think about the very different implications of
a below-the-knee amputation across a variety of occupations, for
example, an accountant versus a carpenter.

The occurrence of a medical impairment may cause a more
substantial personal problem to surface. Consider the male day laborer, married with seven dependents, who develops a hernia and
can not engage in strenuous activity. For many individuals a hernia
would be only an inconvenience that could be repaired using personal funds or insurance benefits, without suffering very much in
terms of lost earnings. But the day laborer cannot do the only work
he knows, has accumulated very little money, and has no medical
insurance. The following questions come to mind: What is this man's
disability? Is it the hernia, or his inability to pay for the necessary
medical services? Should rehabilitation services be limited to repair
of the hernia, or should rehabilitation efforts be directed to the root

of the problem, that is, the man's lack of resources to care for his own needs? For this man, his hernia is a handicap because of his lack of resources and not because of the objective medical problem. These definitions and questions must be kept in mind when considering the data presented in this chapter.

STATISTICS

It is difficult to specify the number of citizens that could profit from vocational rehabilitation services. Haber (1969) presented the data contained in Table 5-1.

Table 5–1 Noninstitutionalized Disabled Population: Ages 18 to 64

Major Disabling Conditions	Number
Arthritis or rheumatism	2,201,000
Heart trouble	2,018,000
Back or spine impairments	1,952,000
Mental illness–nervous trouble	902,000
Loss or impairment of limbs	874,000
Asthma	677,000
Diabetes	487,000
Urogenital disorders	451,000
Visual impairments	433,000
Neoplasms	301,000
Stroke	257,000
Chronic bronchitis	220,000
Mental retardation	212,000
Thyroid	205,000
Deafness	187,000
Paralysis	184,000
Epilepsy	171,000
Tuberculosis	168,000
Emphysema	149,000
Multiple sclerosis	102,000
Total	17,753,000

Of course, not all these individuals need the type of services provided by vocational rehabilitation agencies.

Worrall and Schoon (1975) estimated that 5,401,700 noninstitutionalized disabled Americans could profit from vocational rehabilitation (VR) services. In 1971 the National Center for Health Statistics reported that five million of the 18 million disabled adults between the ages of 18 and 64 years could benefit from VR assistance. The Rehabilitation Services Administration (USDHEW, 1972b) estimated that there were 4.6 million persons aged 16 to 64 who needed vocational rehabilitation. In contrast, the previously cited figures published by the President's Committee on Employment of the Handicapped (no date) indicate 11 million working age Americans report they had permanent work impairments. It could be that a sizeable proportion of this 11 million, however, are suitably employed in spite of their impairment.

In summary, it appears that the size of the population in need of vocational rehabilitation services is between five and six million. If disabled individuals over age 65 and others regardless of their vocational potential are included, then the population in need of services would be much larger.

The extent of the problem is overwhelming. In fiscal year 1977, only 291,204 individuals were reported to have been rehabilitated by the state-federal agencies. Yet each year over 450,000 disabled people enter the group who need vocational rehabilitation (Vocational Rehabilitation Administration, 1965). This annual number of new potential clients is quite possibly much larger now with the reductions in infant mortality, extended life expectancy, and improved medical services. It would appear that every year rehabilitation efforts get further behind. However, in fiscal year 1977 there were a reported 1,881,671 clients on the rolls of the VR agencies. So it is encouraging to note that at least one-third of the population estimated to be in need of services are being served.

CHRONIC CONDITIONS

The major chronic conditions that cause activity limitations are heart conditions and diabetes, which together affect about 7 percent of the population of all ages combined. Also noteworthy is the heavy concentration of chronic conditions among people with low income, particularly conditions that limit personal mobility. Two additional trends are evident in this area: the increasing rate of mental health care episodes (particularly outpatient care episodes) and the rising percentage of people who are 65 or older in nursing homes, which now ranges from about 1 percent among males 65 to 74 years old to a peak of 29 percent among females 85 years old and over (Bureau of the Census, 1977).

The U.S. National Center for Health Statistics reports that in 1974 there were 29,292,000 Americans with activity limitation caused by chronic conditions. Of these 9,511,000 were age 65 and over: 10,327,000 were between 45 and 65 years of age: and 9,454,000 were under age 45. This report indicates that approximately two-thirds of those with activity limitation caused by chronic conditions are 45 years of age or older. More females (approximately one million) are included in the total figure, however this difference is in the population over age 65. For the Center's 1973 Health Interview Survey, they sampled 41,000 households (120,000 individuals). The reported estimates regarding the portion of the employed population that suffer limitation of activity due to chronic conditions are relevant to providers of rehabilitation services.

ESTIMATES OF THE SEVERELY DISABLED POPULATION

The Urban Institute (1975, pp. 772–773) provided the following summary of their efforts to estimate the number of severely disabled people in the United States. They found that:

1. Most sources of data do not contain information on handicapping conditions at all; a few focus on disabilities. The primary information useful for population estimates reports only the inability to work attributed to some health condition or disability. There is no current, ongoing system for data collection on the characteristics or number of handicapped people for vocational rehabilitation purposes.

2. A comparison of the major sources of data on the disabled population results in different estimates even when controlling for year of survey, definition of disability, and severity. Their estimates are based on what they considered the most methodologically sound parts of different approaches. They estimated that in 1975 there were approximately the following numbers of most severely handicapped persons in the United States, when severe disability is considered analogous to severe handicap:

Noninstitutional severely disabled	
population	8,280,000
Under age 18	180,000
18–64	4,200,000
65 and over	3,900,000
Institutional population	1,787,000
Total U.S. population with most severe	
handicaps	10,067,000

These estimates are compatible with those presented earlier. This total of ten million includes citizens under age 18 and over 65, and the institutional population. The previous estimates did not.

3. In general, the severely disabled noninstitutional population are older, more female, slightly more nonwhite, less well educated, and slightly more southern, and they have more than one impairment compared to the less severely disabled people.

4. The largest states have the largest absolute number of severely disabled. The most frequent disability types are musculoskeletal and cardiovascular impairments, followed by mental and nervous system disorders.

HEALTH CARE EXPENDITURES

The tremendous increase in per capita health care expenditures from about $8 per month in 1955 to about $40 per month in 1975 has been associated with an increasing share of this cost being borne by health insurance systems and public funds. In 1955, about 60 percent of health care expenditures were met by direct private payments. By 1975, that proportion was down to 33 percent. Moreover, price increases (inflation) account for just over half of the increase in aggregate health care expenditures during the 1965 to 1975 period, while increased utilization and quality improvements account for over one-third of the total increase (Bureau of the Census, 1976).

DISABLING CONDITIONS

This section contains information related to the prevalence and/or incidence of selected disabling conditions. The *Disability and Rehabilitation Handbook* (1978) edited by R. M. Goldenson, J. R. Dunham, and C. S. Dunham was a helpful resource in the compilation of these data. This extremely comprehensive handbook contains a wealth of information of interest and importance to professionals in rehabilitation settings.

A warning: The reader must keep in mind while reviewing these data, that the reports of disabling conditions can be misleading since, more often than not, one individual will have more than one disorder, that is, an individual with arthritis, hypertension, and a visual disorder may very well be counted once for each condition.

The specific disabilities selected for inclusion in this section were based primarily on the characteristics of the 294,400 people rehabilitated in fiscal year 1978 (U.S. Department of Health, Education, and Welfare, 1979). The categories, with approximate percentages, reported were: mental illness (27%), orthopedic (18%), mental retardation (13%), visual (12%), hearing (8%), circulatory (4%), amputations (3%), and other disabilities (15%).

Mental Illness

Mental illness was indicated as the principal cause of disability for 14 percent of the people rehabilitated in 1966 (McGowan & Porter, 1967, p. 14) as compared to 27 percent in 1978. Prior to the mid-1950s, very few individuals were declared eligible for rehabilitation services because of mental illness.

A discussion of the characteristics of the full range of psychiatric disorders is not appropriate for this chapter, however, the criteria for the states to use (*Rehabilitation Services Manual,* Section .3005.03, 1974) in reporting the severely disabled mentally ill people follows:

> *Psychotic disorders:* If now requiring institutional care in a mental hospital or psychiatric ward of a general hospital; or has history of being institutionalized for treatment for three months or more, or on multiple occasions; or meets the description for moderate or severe.
>
> > *Moderate:* Definite disturbances of thinking, with definite but mild disturbances in behavior. Includes hospital discharges who require daily medication to avoid rehospitalization. With provision of rehabilitation services, capable of maintaining themselves in the community and of engaging in low-stress competitive employment, but at least initially requiring continuing supervision, guidance, motivation, and support. Misunderstanding of instructions, activity,

self-isolation, or overreaction in gesture, speech or emotion may be displayed during the Vocational Rehabilitation process, and may cause concern to people in the work milieu.

Severe: (a) Severe disturbances of thinking and behavior that entail potential harm to self or others; (b) in the extreme, severe disturbances of all components of daily living, requiring constant supervision and care. Unable to communicate readily; have difficulty differentiating between their fantasies and reality; behavior is disruptive and often menacing to others; shouting, vulgarity, carelessness of dress and excretory functions, or possible suicidal attempts necessitate continuing observation, professional intervention and medication, especially during early stages of the rehabilitation process; and (c) persons with the provision of rehabilitation services, may be capable of maintaining themselves in the community and engaging in limited or sporadic productive activity, but only under continuing supervision in sheltered or protective environment, including halfway houses.

Psychoneurotic disorders: If now requiring institutional care in a mental hospital or psychiatric ward of a general hospital; or has a history of being institutionalized for treatment for three months or more, or on multiple occasions; or meets the description for moderate or severe.

Moderate: Stress reactions which modify patterns of daily living. Can maintain themselves in the community and perform adequately in low-stress competitive employment with the provision of rehabilitation services. May require medication and continuing supervision, motivation, and support at least during early postplacement. Their fears, indecision, loss of interest, or occasional odd behavior will be evident during the rehabilitation process, and may moderately interfere with job performance and other workers' activities in employment when stressful situations arise.

Severe: Stress reactions to daily living that result in continuing regression and tissue-organ pathology. Capable of productive work but only under sheltered, noncompetitive conditions in a highly structured or protective environment, at least initially. May require continuing medication. Bizarre and disruptive behavior, loss of interest in activities of daily living, problems with memory and concentration will be evident in the counseling process and, with their interference with other workers, necessitate continuing supervision, guidance, motivation, and support by professional staff in the work situation. Conversion reactions, poor eating, and cleanliness habits may create considerable health problems.

Precise information about the number of mentally ill individuals in the United States is difficult to obtain. Estimates vary widely. The Urban Institute (1975, p. 372) requested information from two associations regarding this question. Their responses were:

The National Association for Mental Health: How many people are we talking about? We don't know. The services are disconnected, and control dispersed; there is no uniform reporting system. Furthermore, their impact on society is far in excess of their numbers. Witness the recent state-wide scandals in New York and California. Many receive attention only from the police, courts, and correctional systems.

The 1957 Commission on Chronic Illness reported 109 in every 1,000 people have a mental disorder and 49 percent of the people entering state mental hospitals have been there at least once before. The more often patients have been admitted to a mental hospital, the more likely they are to return in the future.

The National Center for Health Statistics reports that 10 percent of the people with chronic conditions are unable to carry out major activities due to mental problems. The National Institute of Mental Health Biometry Branch is currently conducting a study on chronically mentally ill people.

International Committee Against Mental Illness: There is no really hard data as to the number of persons—in terms of either incidence or prevalence—encompassed within the major categories of mental disorders. Such data as exists are usually extrapolations of limited and usually unrepresentative epidemiological studies in specific communities, for example, the Midtown Manhattan Study, or are based on standard institutional reports from a number of Federal and State agencies giving statistics on admissions, readmissions, discharges, etc. from such facilities as Veterans' Administration hospitals, state and county mental hospitals, private psychiatric facilities, community mental health centers, psychiatric departments of general hospitals, outpatient clinics, and similar service units.

The difficulty in assessing the chronicity or degree of

severity of many psychiatric syndromes is due in part to the dynamic fluidity of the psychophysiological processes involved. Judgments as to service needs and anticipated functional capacity of the physically disabled—the blind, deaf, paraplegics, etc.—although taking into account the derivative psychological concomitants of such disabilities—are generally less complex than parallel judgments required to be made for the psychiatrically disabled.

For 1973, the Bureau of the Census (1977) reports that there were 24 Americans per 1,000 population that received either inpatient or outpatient care at a mental health facility. This is compared to 11 per 1,000 population in 1955.

Dunham (1978) reports that at the present time an estimated 21,500,000 people in the United States suffer from mental or emotional illness severe enough to require psychiatric or psychological treatment. This is 10 percent of the total population. The total includes an estimated 500,000 mentally ill children.

Similarly, Felton, Perkins, and Lewin (1966) estimate that "... at any given time, 1 out of every 10 persons manifests symptoms which warrant a diagnosis of psychiatric disorder, and 1 out of every 7 persons, sometime during his life, seeks professional help in resolving the problems which precipitate these disorders" (p. 155). Apparently there is a wide discrepancy between the number of people who need mental health service and the number that seek or receive such services.

Orthopedic Disabilities

A complete listing of all the bone, joint, and muscle disabilities would be extensive. Hylbert (1976, p. 71) reports that there are ten million Americans who suffer some *significant* limitation of activity due to disabilities of the musculoskeletal system. This estimate may be conservative.

Felton et al. (1966, p. 31) indicate that orthopedic disabilities may result from *congenital deformities* affecting the spine or one or more extremities, from *infection* (osteomyelitis); from *metabolic disorders* (gout); from *endocrine disorders* (bone deformities); from *neoplastic disease* of the bone (osteosarcoma); from *circulatory or vascular diseases* (Buerger's disease); from *degenerative disease* (arthritis); from *trauma* (including fractures and soft tissue injury); from *neurologic lesions* in the brain (cerebral palsy), the spinal cord (poliomyelitis), or the peripheral nerves (localized post-traumatic paralysis); or from *psychological disorders* that may induce hysterical immobility.

Specific information about people with severe spinal cord injuries and arthritis is presented below since these conditions are of particular importance to rehabilitation workers.

Howell (1978b) estimates that there are 150,000 paraplegics and quadriplegics in the United States; with 5,000 to 10,000 incidences per year. Three-fourths of these are male, and the age period when most incidences occur is between 15 and 30.

The Arthritis Foundation (1976) estimates that there are 3,500,000 Americans disabled by arthritis and that 22 million citizens require medical care for this condition. Osteoarthritis is the most common form; however, it is estimated that 5 million individuals suffer from rheumatoid arthritis and one million from gouty arthritis. Even though older people are more likely to be affected, a recent public service announcement reported that 250,000 children are seriously impaired by arthritic conditions.

Mental Retardation

Mentally retarded individuals function at low intellectual level. Typically they have a short attention span, difficulty in learning, and frequently evidence emotional problems. Felton et al. (1966) indicate that generally, degrees of mental retardation are established in terms of intelligence quotients as follows:

IQ below 25—severely retarded

IQ 25–50—moderately retarded

IQ 50–75—mildly retarded (approximately 85 percent of
    the total)

However, the American Association on Mental Deficiencies (Grossman, 1973) insists that low intellectual function be accompanied by problems in *adaptive behavior* in order for an individual to be labeled retarded. Heber (1965) estimates that over half of the people with IQs between 60 and 70 have adaptive behavior problems. He further suggests that the proportion increases to 95 percent at an IQ of 55.

Approximately 6 million people (3 percent of the population) in the United States are mentally retarded. Of these, approximately 400,000 are over age 65 and 2.6 million are under 20 years of age. The remaining 3 million are of working age (20 to 64). Half of these are working in the economy and an additional 650,000 are gainfully occupied (most as unpaid family workers). Approximately 240,000 mentally retarded individuals are institutionalized in 24-hour care settings, including those in penal institutions (Turem & Conley, 1972). These statistics indicate that over 500,000 retarded adults in the community are not gainfully occupied either at work, keeping house, or as students. Experts in the field tend to believe that most of the nonemployed adults who are retarded have potential for development that would reduce their dependence on others.

Blindness and Visual Impairments

Any discussion of the blind population requires agreement on a definition of blindness. Often statistics are reported and statements made as if a universally accepted definition of blindness existed. This consensus, however, does not exist (Goldberg, 1975).

One of the most widely accepted definitions of blindness is that of legal, economic, or administrative blindness as contained in the 1935 Social Security Act. This definition states that an individual can be considered to be legally blind whose vision in the better eye is no greater than 20/200 with best correction, or whose field of vision is limited to 20 degrees or less (Aranda, 1974; Goldstein & Josephson, 1975; Liska, 1973).

Another definition of blindness that is coming into use is the functional definition. This states that an individual shall be considered blind if he or she is unable to read newspaper print with glasses (Clark, 1968; Goldstein & Josephson, 1975). This definition seems to be more functional as it is more geared to measuring visual functioning and efficiency than mere distance acuity, and is less concerned with identification of hard core cases of blindness. The use of this less restrictive functional definition of blindness, especially with respect to the elderly and rehabilitation populations has been proposed (Clark, 1968; National Society for the Prevention of Blindness (NSPB) 1966; Geriatric Focus, 1967; Goldstein & Josephson, 1975).

The definition used to identify blindness has an effect on the estimates of blind people. There is a wide discrepancy between the estimates of the number of people who are legally blind and those who are functionally blind. For example, the National Society for the Prevention of Blindness (1966) reported there were approximately 430,000 legally blind and 1,000,000 functionally blind individuals in the United States. Goldstein and Josephson (1975) reported estimates ranging from 300,000 legally blind to 1,277,000 functionally blind people. Estimates of the number of elderly blind people also show this disparity, as Inkster (1976) reported there were from 200,000 to 900,000 elderly visually impaired people in the United States. Smith (1971) estimates that in the United States one-half million elderly people are blind but says that many "hidden blind persons" have yet to be identified as blind by the various governmental agencies.

The proportion of elderly blind people among the total blind population has been estimated to be approximately one-half when the age used for classifying people as elderly is 65 years (Burnside, 1974; Inkster, 1976). When the age of 55 is specified for inclusion into the elderly group, the proportion rises to nearly two-thirds of the total blind population (Scott, 1969).

Rates of blindness are reported to be higher for males below 65 years of age, but then higher for females in the age group over 65 years (Clark, 1968; Geriatric Focus, 1967; Goldstein & Josephson, 1975).

The rate of blindness among the nonwhite population has been reported to be approximately twice that of white population (Clark, 1968). But this rate varies across different age groups. Goldstein and Josephson (1975) reported that in the age group from 65 to 74 years, the rate for the nonwhite population was nearly three times that for the white population. In the 75 to 84 age group the rate for nonwhites was nearly twice that of whites.

There is a marked increase in the rates of blindness with age. The rate in the 65 to 74 age group is almost double that of the 45 to 64 age group. The rate triples for the 75 to 84 age group and then doubles again for those people 85 and older (Goldstein & Josephson, 1975). It has also been reported that 96 percent of all newly reported cases of blindness involve people over 65 years of age.

Deafness and Hearing Impairments

A census was undertaken in 1970 to determine the size, distribution, and principal demographic, educational, and vocational characteristics of the deaf population (Schein & Delk, 1974). There is no legal definition of deafness as there is for blindness. The National Census of the Deaf Population (NCDP) selected a definition that is significant and meaningful in education, rehabilitation, sociology, and psychology. They define deafness as ". . . the inability to hear and understand speech." The report points out that definitions of deafness have tended to take the age at which the loss occurred into account. The reason probably involves the fact that the earlier hearing is lost the more severe are the consequences to speech and language development. People who become deaf after developing speech usually retain it, while prelingually deaf children have great difficulty acquiring speech. Language development also is more seriously disrupted by early childhood deafness than by deafness occurring in teenage.

The NCDP focused on a group at the extreme end of the hearing impairment continuum that it labeled prevocationally deaf. This group consists of people who could not hear and understand speech and who had lost (or never had) that ability prior to 19 years of age.

The number of prevocationally deaf people is over 410,000. They are the most seriously handicapped among the 1.8 million deaf people, but the deaf as such, regardless of age at onset, are the most seriously handicapped among the 13,400,000 people who have impaired hearing.

The prevalence rates for prevocational deaf people were higher in the 6 to 16 and 17 to 24 age groups than they were in the 25 to 44 age group, which will mean an upsurge in demand on both secondary and postsecondary educational programs and on vocational rehabilitation agencies in early 1980s.

Cardiovascular Disabilities

The American Heart Association (no date) reports that in 1974 cardiovascular disease was the leading cause of death in the United States (1,035,273, or 54 percent of the total number of deaths). Cancer accounted for 360,472 deaths, accidents 104,622, and for all other causes there were 434,021 deaths. In addition they state that heart disease costs the nation 26 billion dollars each year.

Felton et al. (1966) divide cardiovascular disorders into five categories:

> *Congestive Heart Failure:* Congestive heart failure is not a disease of the heart but a complication of either a cardiovascular disease or a disease of the pulmonary system. The disorder is a general circulatory failure which occurs when the heart is unable to put out sufficient blood to meet the requirements of the body. (p. 79)

> *Arteriosclerotic Heart Disease:* The most common cause of heart disease is hardening and narrowing the coronary arteries which supply the heart muscle itself, and the resultant

failure of the heart to receive the supply of oxygen it requires. (p. 79)

Rheumatic Heart Disease: Rheumatic heart disease (sometimes called valvular heart disease) is of particular concern to vocational rehabilitation counselors because it takes its major toll among persons between the ages of 25–45, who, without the impairment, might be assumed to be functioning at their occupational peak.

The disease develops as the result of rheumatic fever, usually incurred in childhood, as a complication of a streptococcal infection. (p. 80)

Hypertensive Heart Disease: Hypertension is characterized by increased peripheral resistance in the small vessels. An additional force is required to move the blood through the circulatory tree; hence, the increased blood pressure. The maintenance of this additional pressure over a prolonged period of time increases the workload of the heart, and hypertensive heart disease develops.

Persistent, untreated hypertension may injure any of the vital organs, including the heart. The causes of primary (or essential) hypertension are not known, although obesity is recognized as a predisposing factor as is a positive family history, and it appears that certain personality configurations are associated with the disease. In approximately 5 percent of the cases, hypertension is secondary to renal or endocrine disorders, or other vascular diseases. (p. 81)

Congenital Heart Disease: A cardiac defect which is present at birth usually makes its presence known almost immediately. The infant will suffer from dyspnea and may be cyanotic in appearance, if his blood is being shunted into the arterial system without first having been oxygenated.

Houd (1978, p. 318) states that a total of 31,290,000 people in the United States have some form of heart and blood vessel disease: 23,660,000 have hypertension; 4,050,000, coronary heart disease; 1,770,000, rheumatic heart disease; and 1,810,000 stroke. In addition, she points out that by 1980 there will be approximately 90 million people over age 45 in America—the age group in which cardiac disease is most prevalent.

Amputations

Hylbert (1976, pp. 104–105) reports that there are approximately 400,000 people in the United States who have had major amputations. He provides the following breakdown:

Birth to age 16: Approximately 25,000, with most being congenital and involving upper extremities.

Age 17 to 55: Approximately 175,000 with most resulting from injuries involving the lower extremities. About three-fourths of this group are male.

Age 56 and up: Approximately 200,000, with most resulting from diabetic or cardiovascular conditions and generally of the lower extremities.

Other Disabling Conditions

Fifteen percent of the people rehabilitated in 1978 did not fit into one of the above categories. A few other disabilities were selected for inclusion in this section that are relevant to rehabilitation workers.

Alcoholism. The Rutgers Center of Alcohol Studies (1976) estimated that in 1975 there were 5,750,000 alcoholics 20 years old and over in America. An alcoholic is defined as, a person who cannot choose whether or not to drink, and who, if he or she drinks, is unable to choose whether he or she shall stop." Other estimates of the incidence of alcoholism are higher, that is, The National Council on Alcoholism estimates 9 million alcoholics.

The Rutgers statistics indicate that of the 5,750,000 alcoholics, 4,800,000 are male and that 950,000 are female. The three states with the highest incidence of alcoholism (approximately 6,500 per 100,000 population) are Nevada, California, and Rhode Island. In contrast, Hawaii, Alabama, and Idaho are reported to have the lowest incidence (approximately 1,800 per 100,000 population).

Cancer. Cancer per se, is not an impairment. It causes impairments such as amputations, brain damage, and heart and liver failure. Therefore, there is significant overlap between the incidence of cancer and the incidence of other impairments.

According to the American Cancer Society (1977), one in four people, or 55 million Americans now living, will have cancer. They estimate that 10 million citizens are currently under medical care for cancer.

Epilepsy. The Epilepsy Foundation of America (no date) estimates that there are between one and four million U.S. citizens that have an epileptic disorder. They state that age, race, and sex are not related to the prevalence of epilepsy.

Kidney Disease. Metcalfe (1978) states that kidney transplantation and dialysis are accepted methods of treating end-stage renal disease; however, she reports that not all patients can benefit from these treatments. An estimated 50 million Americans (of which 10,000 to 11,000 individuals have end-stage renal disease) are identified each year who would benefit from dialysis or transplantation. Approximately 3,100 patients received kidney transplants and 5,000 to 6,000 new patients began maintenance dialysis in 1974.

Multiple Sclerosis. MS is a disease of the central nervous system; little is known about its etiology or treatment. The disease can affect virtually all body functions that are related to the central nervous system. Generally, the disease is not recognized before age 15 and the modal age of onset is around 30. More women than men are affected and the National Multiple Sclerosis Society (1974) estimates that about 50,000 Americans have MS.

Muscular Dystrophy. In this disease, the nervous system is intact and the primary disease is in the muscle. It is a hereditary disease that usually begins in the early years of life. There is a progressive deterioration of the skeletal and/or voluntary muscles, which generally is painless. Effective treatment modalities have not been discovered. The National Institute of Neurological and Communication Disorders and Stroke (no date) estimates that 200,000 Americans are afflicted with some form of muscular dystrophy.

Cerebral Palsy. This permanent impairment of motor function results from brain damage usually incurred before or during birth. In addition to motor dysfunction, there may be mental retardation, impairment of hearing, vision, or speech, and behavioral dislocations. The characteristic motor pattern includes spastic paralysis, athetosis, and tremor. Hylbert (1976, p. 129) reports that approximately 750,000 Americans suffer from cerebral palsy.

THE PROVIDERS OF REHABILITATION SERVICES

In 1973 the Rehabilitation Services Administration (Gellman, 1974) estimated that there would be over a 100 percent increase in the number of people rehabilitated by 1978 (from 300,000 to 612,000), and that there would be a 33 percent increase in the number of rehabilitation personnel. This increase has not occurred. At the end

Table 5–2 Vocational Rehabilitation Counselors:
Selected Years, 1950 through 1974

Year	Estimated Number of Counselors	Employed in State VR Programs	Employed in Hospitals, Schools, or Other Settings[1]
1973	17,700	12,500	5,200
1974	17,000	12,000	5,000
1971	14,800	10,400	4,400
1969	12,000	8,500	3,500
1967	9,700	7,200	2,500
1965	6,200	4,200	2,000
1960	3,000	2,000	1,000
1955	1,800	1,200	600
1950	1,500	1,000	500

[1] Includes those employed by voluntary health agencies and other organizations with rehabilitation interests.

Sources: U. S. Department of Health, Education, and Welfare, Rehabilitation Services Administration, Division of Statistics and Studies: Quarterly Manpower Report, Fiscal Year, 1970. December, 1970. Also, prior editions. U. S. Department of Health, Education, and Welfare, Rehabilitation Services Administration, Division of Manpower Development.

of Fiscal Year 1977 there were only 291,204 people rehabilitated and no marked increase in the numbers of personnel employed by rehabilitation agencies.

Rehabilitation clients need a wide range of services from health care, applied psychology, and educational professionals. Goldenson (1978) divides rehabilitation professions into (1) medical specialists, (2) nonmedical specialists, and (3) allied medical and paramedical professionals. He reports that 3.8 million individuals are working in these fields, including approximately 350,000 physicians.

In addition to the full range of medical specialists, the following is a partial listing of the professionals that are engaged in the delivery of rehabilitation services to people with disabilities. The special educator, social worker, rehabilitation psychologist, vocational evaluator, work adjustment coordinator, job placement spe-

Table 5–3 Schools Offering Graduate Training Programs in
Rehabilitation Counseling, and Number of Students and
Graduates: Selected Years 1959–60 through 1974–75

Academic Year	Schools	Students[1]	Graduates[1]
1974–75	78	1,800	900
1973–74	72	1,084	542
1972–73	72	2,070	1,035
1971–72	69	1,853	1,024
1970–71	69	1,927	1,062
1969–70	71	2,024	1,009
1968–69	71	1,972	1,018
1967–68	68	1,684	800
1965–66	39	1,140	559
1963–64	34	857	415
1961–62	32	646	231
1959–60	29	566	243

[1] Estimated.

Source: Unpublished data from the U. S. Department of Health, Education, and Welfare, Rehabilitation Services Administration. Division of Manpower Development, Data for United States and Puerto Rico.

cialist, speech pathologist and audiologist, administrator, art therapist, corrective therapist, clinical psychologist, music therapist, occupational therapist, rehabilitation engineer, orthotist and prosthetist, physical therapist, and recreation therapist are all concerned with rehabilitation clients.

The rehabilitation counselor orchestrates the efforts of these professionals in addition to developing and maintaining a counseling relationship with handicapped clients. The agency is personified in the counselor, and through the counselor, the client's initial perception of vocational rehabilitation is formulated. The counselor establishes a professional relationship with the client, continuing from the onset or recognition of the disability to the attainment of greatest competitive capacity. The counseling relationship is a dynamic, ongoing process in which the personalities of the counselor and the client interact in such a way as to maximize present vocational assets and foster realistic self-acceptance in the client. The counselor's counseling responsibilities may include work with various members of the client's family.

Table 5-2 contains information regarding the growth in numbers of rehabilitation counselors, and Table 5-3 provides data regarding the increase in graduate training programs for rehabilitation counselors. Since the work of the rehabilitation counselor is central to the provision of services, the number of these counselors employed is probably a good index of the utilization of other professionals in rehabilitation settings.

At this time, the employment of service providers is obviously more a function of the availability of public funds for rehabilitation services, than it is a function of the size of the population in need. Therefore, any projections regarding the need for rehabilitation professionals will have to be based on the state of the economy and the funding available.

OUTCOMES: 1976–77

With regard to the activities of the state-federal rehabilitation agencies' efforts in behalf of handicapped citizens, a summary of the Annual Report to the President and Congress for Fiscal Year 1976 is presented below.

Fiscal Year 1976 will best be remembered as a year when caseloads in state rehabilitation agencies contracted sharply and when so many historical caseload patterns were broken, if not shattered. Compared to Fiscal Year 1975, fewer cases entered state agency caseloads during Fiscal Year 1976, fewer advanced successfully to later stages of the rehabilitation process, fewer were rehabilitated, and fewer remained in agency caseloads on June 30, 1976, than on the same date a year earlier. The downturn in caseload activity was so pervasive that its effects can be seen in many different ways.

Decline in New Cases

One surprising trend breaker was the decline in the number of new referrals in Fiscal Year 1976 to 1.0 million, a decrease of about 15 percent from the prior year and the first annual decrease in 17 years. It is not clear why this drop in new referrals occurred. It is possible that the decrease reflects a movement away from referral sources less likely to refer severe cases, as well as a determination on the part of agencies to spend more of their available funds on cases already in the rehabilitation stream than on looking for new cases. This determination may have been occasioned by the fact that, on the average, greater sums of money are needed to successfully serve severe than nonsevere cases. Another factor accounting for lowered referral activity and, indeed, decreased caseload activity, in general, are limitations placed on many agencies in the hiring of new personnel brought about by tight budget requirements. In these agencies, outreach efforts have probably been affected. Reports have been received, too, that new administrative duties mandated by the Rehabilitation Act of 1973, which require considerable counselor time and attention, have had an adverse impact on the ability of state agencies to work productively with their caseloads.

In addition to fewer new referrals in Fiscal Year 1976, there were fewer people recorded as applying for services (down 14 percent from Fiscal Year 1975), fewer people entering extended evaluation (down 7 percent), and fewer people accepted for vocational rehabilitation (down 14 percent).

Acceptance Rate: An All-Time Low

An examination of the number of cases accepted for rehabilitation services indicates that the long established pattern of yearly increases was reversed; the decline was the first in 22 years. The number of these cases, about 460,000, was the lowest in six years. They represented only 42 percent of the nearly 1.1 million cases processed for eligibility for rehabilitation services in Fiscal Year 1976. The acceptance rate in Fiscal Year 1975 was 46 percent. The 42 percent acceptance rate in Fiscal Year 1976 was the lowest ever recorded since this measure was introduced in Fiscal Year 1943. Interestingly, the acceptance rate has declined in every year since Fiscal Year 1970 when nearly 54 percent of all cases processed for eligibility were accepted for services. This persistent decline, which has accelerated since the passage of the Rehabilitation Act of 1973, is consistent with the assumption that as severely disabled people become a larger proportion of all referrals, a relatively smaller number of these referrals can be accepted for services. It is also consistent with the assumption that cases of marginal eligibility status that had been accepted for services in the past are now being turned down.

Decline in Likelihood of Advancing
in VR Process

After the aforementioned declines in new referrals, new applicants, new extended evaluation cases, and new cases accepted for rehabilitation are duly noted, it must be pointed out that the likelihood of a client reaching a more advanced level of the rehabilitation process was less in Fiscal Year 1976 than in the previous year. For example, relatively fewer referrals processed in Fiscal Year 1976 reached the applicant stage than in Fiscal Year 1975. In addition, relatively fewer applicants were accepted for rehabilitation services; relatively fewer cases receiving extended evaluation were deemed eligible for rehabilitation; and relatively fewer cases closed from the active statuses could be rehabilitated. The last finding bears some elaboration because it, too, represents another break with the past.

Rehabilitation Rate: A 30-Year Low

Of all cases closed from the active statuses either rehabilitated or not rehabilitated in Fiscal Year 1976, only 63 percent were rehabilitated compared to 70 percent in Fiscal Year 1975. The rehabilitation rate in Fiscal Year 1976 was the lowest in 30 years in a program where a 75 percent rate had been typical for a long time. Although Fiscal Year 1976 was the sixth consecutive year in which a decrease in the rehabilitation rate was observed, most of the decline from the 77 percent rate in Fiscal Year 1970 had occurred since the Rehabilitation Act of 1973 was passed. It is difficult to explain the sharp drop in the rehabilitation rate, particularly in the last year. It is true that agency caseloads now contain more clients who are severely disabled, and that they are, as a group, more difficult to successfully rehabilitate than nonseverely disabled people. This explanation is not fully satisfactory, however, because the observed rehabilitation rate in Fiscal Year 1976 among nonseverely disabled people was only 65 percent compared to 60 percent among the severely disabled. Thus, the rehabilitation rate for even nonsevere cases is not in line with the historical pattern of 75 percent. Possibly the typical nonsevere case today is simply more difficult to rehabilitate than was the typical case, whether severe or not, two or more years ago. This situation might have arisen as a result of greater care being exercised by agencies in judging the eligibility of mildly disabled cases that, presumably, would have been easier to rehabilitate.

Another explanation for the lowered rehabilitation rate is that agencies have tightened their closure standards as a result of audits and a heightened awareness of the need to conduct a "quality" rehabilitation program. It is possible, therefore, that more attention is being given to such closure criteria as the completion of a program of services insofar as possible, the provision of substantial services, and placement into a suitable occupation for a minimum of 60 days.

Decline in Caseload Levels

Another measure of caseload contraction is found in the lowered number of cases in agency caseloads on June 30, 1976, compared to June 30, 1975. The overall decline was from about 1.3 million to 1.2 million, or 7 percent. Still another break with the past is seen in the number of cases on June 30, 1976, that were in the active statuses, that is, they had previously been accepted for rehabilitation services; but as of the last day of the fiscal year those services had not yet been completed. These active cases numbered about 756,000, a 3 percent decline from the level attained on June 30, 1975, and the first such end-of-year decrease in 22 years. In addition, cases in the referral status on June 30, 1976, were 20 percent less than on the same date a year earlier; applicants were down by 12 percent, and extended evaluation cases, by 4 percent.

Rehabilitations: Severe and Nonsevere Cases

All caseload activity is conducted with the ultimate aim of vocationally rehabilitating disabled individuals into jobs commensurate both with their abilities and limitations. In Fiscal Year 1976, state agencies recorded 303,300 successful rehabilitations, a decline of over 6 percent from the number rehabilitated in the prior year—the second consecutive yearly decrease after 20 years of uninterrupted growth. Of these 303,300 people, 122,900 or nearly 41 percent were severely disabled. In Fiscal Year 1975 only 36 percent of all rehabilitations were of severely disabled people compared to only 32 percent in Fiscal Year 1974. This nine-point increase in only two years is quite remarkable because the mix in client characteristics tends to change gradually over the years.

In addition to increasing their share of all rehabilitations, the number of severely disabled people has risen in absolute terms. The Fiscal Year 1976 total of about 122,900 rehabilitations was 6 percent more than in Fiscal Year 1975 which, in turn, was almost 2 percent more than the Fiscal Year 1974 total. These modest percentage gains stand in stark contrast to the losses in rehabilitations of nonseverely disabled people. For the latter group, the decline was 13 percent in Fiscal Year 1976 to 180,400 after a 16 percent drop in Fiscal Year 1975. A high of 247,100 rehabilitations was attained in Fiscal Year 1974.

The Outlook

Continued gains in the proportion of total rehabilitations for severely disabled people can be expected in the near future because 49 percent of all cases accepted for rehabilitation services in Fiscal Year 1976 were people who were severely disabled, which was more than enough to raise the proportion of rehabilitations among severely disabled people above the 41 percent experienced in Fiscal Year 1976.

The outlook for increases in the absolute numbers of severely disabled people is less certain. On the positive side is the rise in the number of cases of severely disabled people in the active statuses, that is, in receipt of rehabilitation services, of nearly 20,000 from 330,800 on July 1, 1975, to 350,600 on June 30, 1976. On the negative side is the actual decrease in rehabilitations of severely disabled people of about 5,700 in the last six months of Fiscal Year 1976 compared to the same period in the previous fiscal year. Most of this loss, some 4,900 cases, occurred in the fourth quarter alone. The factor that will likely determine a gain or loss in rehabilitations of severely disabled people in the near future is the degree to which new cases are brought into the active statuses, which, in turn, will largely hinge on other factors such as funding, outreach efforts, and availability of experienced staff.

For nonseverely disabled people, the near-term would seem to be "more of the same." Active cases among this group fell by nearly 43,000 from 448,200 on July 1, 1975, to 405,600 on June 30, 1976. With severe cases becoming a larger proportion of agency caseloads and with agencies directing more of their efforts toward them, continued declines in the rehabilitation of the nonseverely disabled people can be expected. Questions about the ability of state agencies to meet the genuine needs of eligible nonseverely disabled people have begun to arise.

In general, the increased responsibility imposed upon each rehabilitation counselor by the Rehabilitation Act of 1973 and the current limitation imposed by many states on increasing counselor staff will likely constrict caseload size.

With regard to the work to be done, it is obvious that there is a huge discrepancy between what is being accomplished and what remains to be done. Mary E. Switzer (1962) coined a fitting title for all rehabilitation efforts; that is, "The Work Is Never Done."

Gellman (1974) reported that the prevalence of physical disability is increasing as the population grows and as medical, biological, and technical advances lengthen the life span. The change in life expectancy from 63.3 years in 1943 to 71.9 years in 1974 has increased the number of people in our society prone to illness or injury (Bureau of the Census, 1977). The National Health Education Committee (1976) estimates that improved medical knowledge saved 8 million lives between 1944 and 1967 and that of the 7.5 million still alive, about 63 percent were not working. Indeed, "The Work Is Never Done."

REFERENCES

American Cancer Society. *What is reach to recovery?* New York: American Cancer Society, 1977.

American Heart Association. *Heart facts: 1977.* Dallas: American Heart Association, 1977.

Aranda, R. R. CILS: *A model for the social rehabilitation of older persons with severe visual impairment.* New York: New York Infirmary, Center for Independent Living, 1974.

Arthritis Foundation. *Primer on the rheumatic diseases* (7th ed.). Atlanta: Arthritis Foundation, 1976.

Bureau of the Census, U.S. Department of Commerce. *Social indicators 1976: Selected data on social conditions and trends in the United States.* Washington, D.C.: U.S. Government Printing Office, 1977.

Burnside, I. M. Nurses's perspective: Blindness in long-term care facilities. *The New Outlook for the Blind,* 1974, *68,* 145–150.

Clark, L. L. (Ed.). *Proceedings of the research conference on geriatric blindness and severe visual impairment.* New York: American Foundation for the Blind, 1968.

Cohen, A. Y. *Alternatives to drug abuse: Steps toward preventing.* Rockville, Maryland: National Clearinghouse for Drug Abuse, 1975.

Dunham, C. S. Mental illness. In R. M. Goldenson, J. R. Dunham, & C. S. Dunham (Eds.), *Disability and rehabilitation handbook.* New York: McGraw-Hill, 1978.

Epilepsy Foundation of America. *Facts about epilepsy.* Washington, D.C.: Epilepsy Foundation of America, no date.

Farmer, R. E. Drug-abuse problems. In R. M. Goldenson, J. R. Dunham, & C. S. Dunham (Eds.), *Disability and rehabilitation handbook.* New York: McGraw-Hill, 1978.

Felton, J. S., Perkins, D. C., & Lewin, M. *A survey of medicine and medical practice for the rehabilitation counselor.* Washington, D.C.: U.S. Government Printing Office, 1966.

Gellman, W. Projections in the field of physical disability. *Rehabilitation Literature,* 1974, *35,* 2–9.

Geriatric Focus. *Problems and service needs of the aged blind.* New York: Geriatric Focus, 1967.

Goldberg, I. D. Definitions of blindness. In L. L. Clark (Ed.), *Proceedings of the research conference on geriatric blindness and severe visual impairment.* New York: American Foundation for the Blind, 1975.

Goldenson, R. M. Rehabilitation professions. In R. M. Goldenson, J. R. Dunham, & C. S. Dunham (Eds.), *Disability and rehabilitation handbook.* New York: McGraw-Hill, 1978.

Goldenson, R. M., Dunham, J. R., & Dunham, C. S. *Disability and rehabilitation handbook.* New York: McGraw-Hill, 1978.

Goldstein, H., & Josephson, E. The social demography of vision impairment in the United States. *Public Health Reviews,* January 1975, 5–38.

Grossman, H. (Ed.). *Manual on terminology and classification in mental retardation* (1973 revision). Washington, D.C.: American Association on Mental Deficiency, 1973.

Haber, L. *Epidemiological factors in disability: I. Major disabling conditions. Social security survey of the disabled, 1966—Report No. 6.* Washington, D.C.: U.S. Department of Health, Education and Welfare, Social Security Administration, 1969.

Hamilton, K. *Counseling the handicapped in the rehabilitation process.* New York: Ronald Press, 1950.

Haring, N. G. "The severely handicapped." In Norris G. Haring, *Behavior of exceptional children* (2nd ed.). Columbus, Ohio: Charles E. Merrill, 1978, pp. 195–230.

Heber, R. F. *Special problems: The vocational rehabilitation of the mentally retarded.* Washington, D.C.: U.S. Department of Health, Education and Welfare, 1965.

Houd, H. Cardiac disorders. In R. M. Goldenson, J. R. Dunham, & C. S. Dunham (Eds.), *Disability and rehabilitation handbook.* New York: McGraw-Hill, 1978.

Howell, L. Disabling birth defects. In R. M. Goldenson, J. R. Dunham, & C. S. Dunham (Eds.), *Disability and rehabilitation handbook.* New York: McGraw-Hill, 1978a.

———. Spinal cord injury. In R. M. Goldenson, J. R. Dunham, & C. S. Dunham (Eds.), *Disability and rehabilitation handbook.* New York: McGraw-Hill, 1978b.

Hylbert, K. W. *Medical information for human service workers.* State College, Penn.: Counselor Education Press, 1976.

Inkster, D. E. *Selection, education and placement of senior peers in a program to serve older visually impaired adults.* New York: New York Infirmary, Center for Independent Living, 1976.

Liska, J. S. What does it mean to be "legally blind." *The New Outlook for the Blind,* 1973, 67, 19–20.

McGowan, J. F., & Porter, T. L. *An introduction to vocational rehabilitation process.* Washington, D.C.: U.S. Government Printing Office, 1967.

Metcalfe, V. M. Kidney disease. In R. M. Goldenson, J. R. Dunham, & C. S. Dunham (Eds.), *Disability and rehabilitation handbook.* New York: McGraw-Hill, 1978.

Mital, M. A., & Pierce, D. S. *Amputees and their prostheses.* New York: Little, Brown, 1971.

National Advisory Committee on Handicapped Children. *First Annual Report.* Washington, D.C.: U.S. Office of Education, 1968.

National Association for Retarded Citizens. *Mental retardation.* Mimeo, 1978.

National Council on Alcoholism. *Alcoholism.* New York: National Council on Alcoholism, no date.

National Health Education Committee. *The killers and cripplers: Facts on major diseases in the United States today.* New York: David McKay, 1976.

National Institute of Neurological and Communication Disorders and Stroke. *Muscular dystrophy: Hope through research.* Bethesda, Maryland: National Institute of Neurological and Communication Disorders and Stroke, no date.

National Multiple Sclerosis Society. *Multiple sclerosis research.* New York: National Multiple Sclerosis Society, 1974.

National Society for the Prevention of Blindness (NSPB). *Factbook.* New York: National Society for the Prevention of Blindness, 1966.

President's Committee on Employment of the Handicapped. *Facts about handicapped people.* Washington, D.C.: U.S. Government Printing Office, no date.

Rutgers Center of Alcohol Studies. *Statistics on consumption of alcohol and alcoholism.* New Brunswick, N.J.: Rutgers Center of Alcohol Studies, 1976.

Schein, J. D., & Delk, M. T. *The deaf population of the United States.* Silver Springs, Maryland: National Association of the Deaf, 1974.

Scott, R. A. *The making of blind men.* New York: Russell Sage Foundation, 1969.

Smith, P. S. Aging and blindness: A public symposium. *The New Outlook for the Blind,* 1971, *65,* 201–203.

Switzer, M. E. The work is never done. *Rehabilitation Record,* 1962, *3,* 12–15.

Travis, L. E. (Ed.). *Handbook of speech pathology.* New York: Appleton-Century-Crofts, 1957.

Turem, J., & Conley, R. *Roles of the retarded.* Washington, D. C.: The Joseph P. Kennedy, Jr., Foundation, 1972.

U.S. Department of Health, Education, and Welfare. *Annual report to the President and the Congress on Federal activities related to the administration of the Rehabilitation Act of 1973 as amended: Fiscal year 1976.* Washington, D.C.: Office of the Secretary, 1977.

————. *Annual report to the President and the Congress on Federal activities related to the administration of the Rehabilitation Act of 1973 as amended: Fiscal year 1978.* Washington, D.C.: Office of the Secretary, 1979.

U.S. Department of Health, Education, and Welfare, Social and Rehabilitation Services, Rehabilitation Services Administration. *Rehabilitation services manual.* Washington, D.C.: U.S. Government Printing Office, 1974.

U.S. Department of Health, Education, and Welfare, Social and Rehabilitation Service, Rehabilitation Services Administration. *RSA long range plan, FY 1974–1978.* (Draft) May 15, 1972a.

————. *Statistical notes, No. 30.* Washington, D.C.: U.S. Government Printing Office, June, 1972b.

U.S. Public Health Service, National Center for Health Statistics. *Current estimates from the health interview survey, United States—1970.* DHEW Pubn. No. (HSM) 72–1054. Washington, D.C.: U.S. Government Printing Office, May, 1972.

U.S. Department of Health, Education, and Welfare, National Center for Health Statistics. *Health interview survey: 1971.* Washington, D.C.: U.S. Government Printing Office, 1973.

U.S. Department of Health, Education, and Welfare, Rehabilitation Services Administration. *State vocational rehabilitation agency fact sheet booklet, FY 1977.* Washington, D.C.: U.S. Government Printing Office, 1978.

Urban Institute. *Report of the comprehensive needs survey.* Washington, D.C.: (HEW Contract #100-74-0309), Urban Institute, 1975.

Veterans' Administration. *Disabled war veterans.* Washington, D.C.: Veterans' Administration, 1977.

Vocational Rehabilitation Administration, U.S. Department of Health, Education, and Welfare. *Annual Report: Fiscal Year 1964.* Washington, D.C.: U.S. Government Printing Office, 1965.

Worrall, J. D., & Schoon, C. Methodologies for the estimation of the vocational rehabilitation target population: An exploratory analysis. In S. E. Rubin (Ed.), *Studies on the evaluation of state vocational rehabilitation agency programs: Final report.* Fayetteville: Arkansas Rehabilitation Research and Training Center, 1975.

Chapter 6

Impact of Disability
on the Individual

Daniel W. Cook

INTRODUCTION

Chronic illness and physical impairment often result in some residual disability, that is, functional limitations in performing basic daily activities. It is perhaps natural to assume that physical disability would affect a person's psychosocial adjustment. Indeed a person's reponse to the debilitating effects of physical impairment is a universal consideration in rehabilitation. Unfortunately, the psychosocial impact of disability remains a complex subject. For example, in reviewing over 250 studies on psychological adjustment and physical disability, Shontz (1971) concluded that specific types of disability are not associated with specific personality characteristics and that different types of physical disability do not cause specific kinds of maladjustment. But physical disability does affect individuals' behavior; physical disability can, and often does, have a profound impact on individuals' psychological adjustments to their disabilities.

The study of how and why disability affects any individual's behavior is currently being conducted on two fronts, the study of

Development of this chapter was supported, in part, by a Rehabilitation Services Administration, Rehabilitation Research and Training Center Grant (16-P-56812, RT-13).

individuals' responses to their disability, and the impact of society's response to people with disabilities. Since personality can be defined as those enduring behavior characteristics of an individual, classical personality theories should be able to explain how any one individual might adjust to a physical disability. And since a physical disability can act as a stimulus to others, the views of society toward disability are important. This chapter is divided into two parts, the first summarizes the personality theories of Sigmund Freud, Carl Rogers, and Kurt Lewin; covers the application of each theory in understanding the psychological impact of physical disability; and gives examples of research linking each theory to the study of physical disability. The second part discusses the attitudes of society toward disability, the attitudes of rehabilitation professionals toward disability, and methods of fostering attitude change.

FREUD'S PSYCHOANALYTIC THEORY

Psychoanalytic theory has three aspects: the procedures devised by Freud to study mental processes, the techniques for the type of psychiatric treatment practiced by Freud and his followers, and a psychology developed by Freud to describe and explain why people behave as they do. It is Freud's psychology that has had the most influence on explaining the impact of disability on the individual.

In essence Freud (1963) formulated a dynamic psychology, hydraulic in nature, which states that psychic energy is exchanged and transferred throughout a closed system. Energy comes from basic metabolic processes and is transformed into psychic energy via the instincts. Instincts were postulated as internal forces that are never truly satisfied. Hence the person is always subject to these forces or tensions.

Freud hypothesized three main structural concepts, the id, ego, and superego. The id is made up of the instincts, is the source of psychic energy, remains unconscious, and continually strives to reduce instinctual tensions through pleasurable satisfaction of instinctual needs. The id seeks to reduce tension in any way possible, even in ways that may be socially unacceptable or detrimental to the individual. Thus the id is engaged in constant conflict with the ego that seeks to channel the energies of the pleasure seeking id into meeting needs in a reality-oriented manner. The third structural concept, the superego, develops out of the ego as the child learns what society considers moral behavior. According to Freud a child's basic personality is fixed by age five.

Freud's theory of personality follows a conflict model (Maddi, 1972) in that there is a constant interplay of driving and restraining forces. The ego must maintain a balance between these forces. When the forces become excessively out of balance the ego is flooded with anxiety, and if the ego cannot deal with this anxiety by rational means, ego defenses come into play. These ego defenses are unconscious and serve to protect the individual by distorting reality, and thus reducing anxiety. If the defenses markedly distort reality the individual becomes maladjusted and the defenses are counterproductive.

Freud's Theory and Physical Disability

Perhaps Freud's greatest contribution to understanding the impact of disability on the individual was his conceptualization of the ego defenses. There are at least four defense mechanisms continually referred to in the literature on adjustment to physical disability; they are: repression, projection, reaction formation, and regression.

Through repression the ego is able to keep painful memories, conflicts, and perceptions from conscious awareness. Ideas that are particularly anxiety provoking are simply put out of a person's awareness. Repression allows for an evasion of anxiety, guilt, and interpsychic conflicts. Projection refers to the attribution of unconscious feelings, needs, or conflicts to another person. A particularly unacceptable feeling, such as hostility toward a physician, may be expressed as, "He hates me," rather than as, "I hate him." A disabled person who feels inadequate and is unable to tolerate that feeling might project the anxiety producing feeling to others as, "Nobody knows enough to really help me." Reaction formation is the expression of feelings opposite to those really felt at an unconscious level. A parent with an unacceptable aversion to a disabled child might overprotect and attempt to meet the child's every need. The newly disabled person may resent those people they are dependent on and express that resentment through excessive displays of love and affection. Both projection and reaction formation are compensation defenses. People who experience anxiety relieve that anxiety by overdeveloping other personality traits. Regression is an escape defense in which an individual reverts to fantasy as a form of coping with psychic stress. Basically a person using regression as a defense will revert to an earlier developmental period and may exhibit the childlike behavior and negativism associated with earlier developmental periods.

Freud's Theory and Adjustment to Disability

While Freud did recognize the influence the mind can have over the body (e.g., conversion hysteria) in formulating his theory, he did not specifically deal with the psychological impact of physical disability. One passage, however, illustrates the applicability of Freud's insights to physical disability.

> A capable working-man earning his living is crippled by an accident in the course of his employment; he can work no more, but he gets a small periodical dole in compensation and learns how to exploit his mutilation as a beggar. His new life, although so inferior, nevertheless is supported by the very thing which destroyed his old life; if you were to remove his disability you would deprive him for a time of his means of subsistence, for the question would arise whether he would still be capable of resuming his former work. When a secondary exploitation of the illness such as this is formed in a neurosis we can range it alongside the first and call it "secondary advantage through illness." (Freud, 1963, p. 334)

Like any functional psychological theory, Freud's theory is detailed enough to make specific predictions about how physical disability might affect an individual. Of course within the rehabilitation field, ego defenses have received the most attention as potential adjustment mechanisms in adapting to physical disability.

Freud's theory predicts that the person with a disability would most likely exhibit psychological problems if they became impaired before the age of five, while the personality was still developing. English (1971a) suggests that immaturity and "passive-aggressiveness" are the salient personality traits exhibited by people disabled early in life. Meng (1938) describes disability-related maladjustment as developing from hostile impulses that stem from the child's blaming the parents for the impairment. Since these hostile impulses are perceived as being unacceptable, they are likely to be repressed, and the impairment is unconsciously considered justifiable punishment for the unacceptable feelings. According to Meng (1938) the chief task of helpers is to diminish disability associated anxiety by bringing to consciousness the blame of parents—the basis of repressed hostility and guilt.

Research Evidence for Freud's Theory

Most of the research concerning Freud's theory has focused on interpretation of individual case studies. Indeed, one of the major criticisms of the theory is that it is not easily empirically tested. However, in an extensive review of the research literature, Maddi (1972) concludes that the idea of psychological defense is tenable, although not exactly as specified by Freud. Hirschenfang and Benton (1966) analyzed Rorschach responses of paraplegics and quadriplegics. They reported that paraplegics, "manifested certain characteristics indicating childlike immediate needs for gratification" (p. 41) that could be construed as providing support for Freud's regression hypothesis. In general, however, the bulk of the research is at best equivocal. Even such popular notions as "compensation," the concept derived from psychoanalytic theory that disabled people develop special compensatory abilities, for example, that blind people have superior hearing, has not been supported (McDaniel, 1976, p. 4). Freud's original ideas remain of great importance, although they have been largely adapted and modified by more recent theorists with respect to the psychological consequences of physical disability.

ROGERS'S SELF-CONCEPT THEORY

Carl Rogers, like Freud, developed his theory of personality largely through therapeutic relationships with clients. His theory (Rogers, 1951; 1961) is based on a phenomenological approach to personality development and change. That is, Rogers relies on subjectivity, defining reality as how people perceive their immediate experiences. Of course, Rogers assumes that the real world exists, however, he sees people's subjective perceptions of reality as all important.

The self-concept is the central structural construct of Rogers's theory. Various theorists have used the concept of self in different ways. Probably the most common definition of the self-concept is those feelings, evaluations, and perceptions toward oneself that define who one is. Rogers further defines the self-concept as "the organized, consistent conceptual Gestalt composed of perceptions of the characteristics of the *I* or *me* and the perceptions of the relationships of the *I* or *me* to various aspects of life, together with the values attached to these perceptions" (Rogers, 1959, p. 200).

Contrary to Freud, who asserted that biological forces motivate the person, Rogers suggested one motivational tendency, people's need for self-actualization, for people's self-concept to be congruent with their experiences. Although Rogers did put forth other needs, the need for positive regard, for example, these are all seen as subservient to the basic motive, the tendency of people to maintain and enhance themselves.

According to Rogers, behavior is caused; the psychological cause of behavior is the human way of perceiving. Human beings are considered rational, forward moving, and goal seeking rather than reactive. The ideal situation is to actualize people's potentiality, and to be open to new experiences.

Rogers's Theory and Physical Disability

Of all the personality theorists, Rogers has probably had the most impact on the field of rehabilitation counseling. His influence stems from the fact that his system of psychotherapy, out of which came his theory of personality, broke away from the disease model of maladjustment popular at the time. Also his approach was refined in academic settings and popularized during the period university-based rehabilitation counseling programs were being established.

Rogers's elaboration of the self-concept construct, and his conceptualization of the self versus ideal-self discrepancy have contributed to understanding the impact of disability on the individual. Perhaps most important is the emphasis Rogers attached to personal experiences. Unquestionably, individuals' self-concepts, values, feelings, and judgments of self-worth guide their behavior; it follows then that it is not disability *per se* that psychologically influences the person, but rather the subjective meaning and feelings attached to the disability. Thus Rogers's theory would explain why a relatively minor physical impairment might be construed as catastrophic by some people, and why some extremely severely impaired individuals are psychologically well adjusted. The ideal-self is comprised of those values and meanings that the person holds in high regard. The self versus ideal-self discrepancy becomes important when the way people view themselves differs from the way they wish to view themselves.

Rogers's Theory and Adjustment to Disability

Rogers defined a psychologically adjusted person as one who is "fully functioning." Such a person is open to new experiences, has a self-concept that is congruent with actual experience, and has a value system similar to the value systems of other well-adjusted people (Rogers, 1951).

Maladjustment can occur when there is incongruence between experiences and the way individuals view themselves. This incongruence can occur when individuals are exposed to conditions of worth, or negative as well as positive evaluations. Because individuals seek to maintain consistent self-concepts, either negative or positive evaluations, depending on the relationship of the evaluation to their self-concept, may be screened out and blocked from awareness through denial or distortion—two psychological defenses in Rogers's theory. Both denial and distortion falsify experiences in order to make them consistent with the self-concept. Defensive behavior has been described by Rogers (1959) as

> the organism's response to experiences which are perceived or anticipated as threatening, as incongruent with the individual's existing picture of himself in relationship to the world. These threatening experiences are temporarily rendered harmless by being distorted in awareness, or being denied to awareness. (p. 187)

For example, consider a relatively well-adjusted lumberjack who suffers a spinal cord injury. Assume that his self-image is one of independence and physical prowess, and, as a result of his injury, he is placed in an extremely dependent and socially devalued position, and is in fact unable to meet his own self-expectations. The disability represents a threat to his self-concept. In the extreme case this individual might deny his new physical reality through such statements as, "I haven't changed at all," or he might distort reality by alluding to the disability as temporary, "I'll be walking and cutting trees in six months." This incongruence between the subjective reality of the person and the objective reality of the disability can act to impede rehabilitation. A person may fail to "accept" the limiting aspects of the disability, even to the point of maintaining a self-picture that completely disregards the new state. If reality distortion becomes incorporated into the self-concept, the person will tend to become rigid and closed to the experiences needed for successful rehabilitation to occur.

Rogers (1961) stated that in order for the maladjusted person to change, helpers must offer certain conditions considered necessary and sufficient for change to occur. If the core counselor conditions of congruence, warmth, and empathic understanding are present and perceived by the client, a therapeutic relationship, safe and secure from threat, is established. In the counseling relationship that is free of threat, the client can look at incongruencies, experience them, and finally assimilate the previously distorted experiences into a reorganized self. Following successful therapy, individuals are more self-directed, responsible, and open to new experiences.

Research Evidence for Rogers's Theory

Hundreds of research studies have evaluated Rogers's method of facilitating client change and personal growth. Relatively fewer studies have examined the adequacy of his conceptualization of personality to describe the impact of disability. Most of the research has studied the effects of disability on self-concept. For example, Berry and Miskimins (1969) found that compared to normal people, psychiatric patients had poorer self-concepts, but that psychiatric patients with the best self-concepts had better vocational outcomes than patients with poorer self-concepts. Berry, Dunteman, and Webb (1968) reported that physically disabled clients who had favorable self-concepts and low self versus ideal-self discrepancies had the most rapid recovery from disability and return to work. Roessler and Bolton (1978) reviewed twelve studies dealing with the influences of the self-concept on disability and concluded that:

> (1) Disabled persons report lower self-esteem [the evaluative component of the self-concept] than nondisabled persons, and (2) some disability conditions have greater impact on the self-concept than others. . . . [But] the data supporting the second conclusion are much more tenuous than those that support the first, because few studies have directly compared the self-concepts of persons with different types of disabilities. (Roessler & Bolton, 1978, p. 26)

A study conducted by Lipp, Kolstoe, James, and Randall (1968) is particularly relevant to Rogers' concept of denial as a defense. Lipp et al. tested the idea that disabled people are threatened, psychologically, by their disability and do, in fact, deny disability. To test for the presence of denial, Lipp et al. had physically disabled and nondisabled subjects view slides of normal and physically disabled people, presented by a tachistoscope, a device that varies the amount of time a slide is shown. The investigators found that disabled subjects took significantly longer to recognize the slides of disabled people than the physically normal subjects did. Lipp et al. concluded "that disability is unacceptable to the disabled and that they defend against this threat by the mechanism of denial" (p. 74).

LEWIN AND SOMATOPSYCHOLOGY

Kurt Lewin's field theory (Lewin, 1935; 1936) is social psychological in nature and forms a bridge between personologists (Freud and Rogers) who have been primarily concerned with the developmental dynamics of the individual, and social psychologists who have been concerned with the influence of social factors on individual behavior. Lewin's theorizing stressed the importance of *contemporaneity*, the idea that behavior can best be understood in its immediate manifestations, and the importance of understanding the individual in relation to the larger environment. Lewin argued that in order to understand why people behave as they do, analysis must begin with the total situation.

By beginning analysis with the total situation, Lewin sought to go from the general to the specific. To Lewin the most general situation is the life space, the total psychological world consisting of everything that is observed, sensed, and inferred. The life space represents the psychological environment (E) out of which the person (P) is differentiated. Thus the life space consists of all those things that determine the behavior of an individual at any particular moment. In algebraic terms, behavior (B) is a function (f) of the life space (L), $B = f(L)$ and $B = f(P, E)$; this equation represents a person by situation interaction paradigm popular in psychology today.

Somatopsychology and Physical Disability

Lewin's theory has stimulated the most theoretical work in conceptualizing the psychological effects of physical disability, as exemplified in the writings of Barker, Wright, Meyerson, and Gonick (1953), and Dembo, Leviton, and Wright (1956). These writers have adapted and modified Lewin's theory incorporating such Lewinian ideas as the accessibility of, and barriers to, goals in the life space; here-and-now behavior; and personal-social expectations into a point of view called *somatopsychology*. Somatopsychology makes the assumption, largely verified (Shontz, 1971), that "there is no substantial indication that persons with an impaired physique differ *as a group* in their *general or overall adjustment*" and "there is no clear evidence of an association between types of physical disability and particular personality characteristics" (Wright, 1960, pp. 373–374). Somatopsychologists focus on the person by situation interaction, stressing that it is the personal meaning of the disability in conjunction with the stimulus value the disability holds for others in a person's life space that is important in understanding psychological adjustment to disability. Thus somatopsychology studies "those variations in physique that affect the psychological situation of a person by influencing the effectiveness of his body as a tool for action or by serving as a stimulus to himself or others" (Barker et al., 1953, p. 1).

Somatopsychology and Adjustment to Disability

Wright (1960) has written extensively on somatopsychology, delineating situations that confront disabled people and determining how
the disabled people cope with them. According to Wright (1960)
disabled people may assume an inferior status position as a result of:

1. Having *dual identifications* with the disability group
   they are part of as well as with the larger nondisabled
   population;
2. By engaging in *"as if"* behavior wherein they deny or
   cover up their disability acting "as if" they were not
   disabled;
3. Engaging in the *idolization of normal standards* by
   which disabled people strive to reach unattainable
   standards of "normal" performance;
4. The *eclipse of behavior possibilities* in that attention
   is focused on deficit behaviors rather than on asset
   behaviors.

Wright (1960) divided adjustment to disability into succumbing
versus coping behaviors. She emphasizes the perceptions of disabled
people toward their disabilities and on the perceptions of "nondisabled people" toward the disabled people. Using "as if" behavior,
idolizing normal standards, and eclipsing behavior possibilities are
all seen as succumbing to disability. To the somatopsychologist, coping, or adjustment to physical disability occurs when:

1. One *enlarges the scope of values,* and embraces other
   than disability related values;
2. *Subordinates physique,* limiting the importance placed
   on physical appearance and physical ability;
3. Contains the *spread* of disability by limiting disability
   to the impact of the actual impairment;
4. Places emphasis on *asset values,* while limiting comparative values (Wright, 1960).

The emphasis on asset versus comparative values has received
particular attention as a primary attribute in adjustment to physical
disability. Comparative values are evaluations made in reference to
some standard, for example, "normal" behavior; asset values are
evaluations based purely on the intrinsic qualities of the person be-

ing evaluated. Comparative values made by disabled people themselves, or by others toward people with disabilities are potentially
devaluing. Asset values are potentially psychologically rewarding
because they focus on the inherent positive qualities of a person in
a particular situation.

Research Evidence for Somatopsychology

Barker et al. (1953) present a detailed case analysis of two postpolio
girls. Both girls were the same age, in current excellent health, and
had the same IQ and education. One, Marcia, was much more physically affected by her disability than the other, Beverley. Even though
Beverley was less severely disabled and had many more social opportunities open to her, she was the more socially and psychologically maladjusted of the two.

Barker et al. interpreted Beverley's maladjustment as the result
of role marginality. They saw Beverley as striving for normality and
in conflict because she was caught between an underprivileged (disabled) and a privileged (normal) social position. Beverley had
problems in determining what behaviors were appropriate in ambiguous social situations. Beverley, to use Wright's (1960) terminology
had "dual identifications." Marcia had a rather clear understanding
of her position as a person with a disability and was able to adapt
her behavior to different situations. Marcia had accepted the limitations of her disability without devaluing herself. On the basis of this
case analysis, Barker et al. hypothesized that role marginality would
lead to conflict and social maladjustment.

Goldberg (1974) tested the somatopsychological proposition
that physical disability acts as a negative stimulus and leads to social
discrimination. He compared visibly disabled people (facial burns)
with a group of invisibly disabled (congenital heart disease) on ten
adjustment measures. On all measures the invisibly disabled people
were better "adjusted." The invisibly disabled people also had significantly better self-image. The major implication of the study is
that visible disability can lead to negative social evaluations, which
in turn may be incorporated into disability related self-evaluations.

ATTITUDES AND DISABILITY

Of utmost importance in understanding the impact of physical disability on the person is the study of attitudes; attitudes of the general public and rehabilitation professionals as they affect the adjust-

ment of disabled people. Basically attitudes are evaluations made toward an object, person, or idea. Attitudes consist of three components, feelings and cognitions, the internal expressions of an attitude, and an external expression manifested as behavior or movement toward or away from that being evaluated. The relationship between the internal and external components of an attitude is not well understood. It is generally believed that internal evaluations guide behavior, but that overt behavior depends, in part, upon the situation. Thus a person may be prejudiced, but override that prejudice depending upon the situation of the negatively evaluated object. A well-known psychological principle is that people do not always behave in predictable ways. Attitudes are, however, considered to serve as predispositions to behave in certain ways.

Attitudes Toward People with Disabilities

Because disabled people are often perceived by nondisabled people as "different" the prevailing theoretical view is that they tend to be classed as deviant from the majority and are forced into an "inferior" social position with those negative evaluations given other minority groups. Associating disability with minority group status has the potential of stigmatizing the person with a disability. Certain undesirable qualities are attributed to disabled people, merely because they are physically impaired. Gellman (1959) suggested that when society defines a person's role as deviant, that evaluation results in a self-definition of inferiority leading to adaptation of a marginal role in society.

Confounding the idea that disability is associated with negative evaluations has been the finding that in measuring attitudes toward people with physical disabilities, publicly expressed attitudes are generally positive (Comer & Piliavin, 1975). One probable reason that public attitudes toward disabled people tend to be positive is that in verbalizing public attitudes, people generally do not express negative feelings. This tendency is referred to as a social desirability bias and has been found in studies of attitudes toward disability (Feinberg, 1967). Popular attitude measurement instruments, e.g., the Attitude Toward Disabled Persons Scale (ATDP) (Yuker, Block, & Younng, 1966) are often unidimensional, that is, they measure a continuum of positive to negative affect. Since this dimension is readily apparent to most people taking these measures, they are able to, and in fact do, select the most socially desirable responses. This bias is a serious drawback of attitude measurement.

Siller (1976) and his associates have taken a multidimensional approach to measuring attitudes toward disability. He has isolated seven dimensions underlying attitudes toward disability that are "fairly comprehensive in describing the attitude domain for a wide range of conditions" (p. 72). They are:

1. Interaction strain—uneasiness in the presence of disabled persons and uncertainty as how to deal with them;

2. Rejection of intimacy—rejection of close, particularly familial, relationships with the disabled;

3. Generalized rejection—a pervasive negative and derogatory approach to disabled persons with consequent advocacy of segregation;

4. Authoritarian virtuousness—ostensibly a "prodisabled" orientation, this factor is really rooted in an authoritarian context which manifests itself in a call for special treatment that is less benevolent and more harmful than it seems;

5. Inferred emotional consequences—intense hostile references to the character and emotions of the disabled;

6. Distressed identification—personalized hypersensitivity to disabled persons who serve as activators of anxiety about one's own vulnerability to disability;

7. Imputed functional limitations—devaluation of the capacities of a disabled person in coping with his environment (Siller, 1976, p. 72).

Siller's (1976) research suggests that attitudes toward disability are complex, but that there are underlying, essentially negative components of attitudes toward disability.

Research has examined underlying correlates of attitudes toward disability, attitudes toward *disability per se* contrasted against attitudes toward a *person* with a disability, and the uniformity of attitudes toward different types of disability. Yuker (1965) summarizes a series of studies using the ATDP scale and concluded that, "In many respects prejudices toward the disabled are similar to prejudices toward other groups" (Yuker, 1965, p. 16). Cowen, Bobgrove, Rockway, and Stevenson (1967) found, in fact, that people who were prejudiced toward deaf people also tended to be prejudiced toward blacks and other minority groups. Chesler (1965) studied ethnocentrism, the belief that one's culture is superior to another, and attitudes toward disability. Using the Intergroup Relations Scale to measure ethnocentrism, and the ATDP scale to measure attitudes toward disability, Chesler found that negative attitudes toward disability were significantly related to ethnocentrism and concluded: "For some purposes the physically disabled can be conceptualized as a minority group subject to many of the same attitudinal and behavioral predispositions as are ethnic minorities" (p. 881). English (1971b) surveyed the literature on other correlates of attitudes toward disability and concluded that females have more favorable attitudes toward disability than do males, and that one's age, race, and nationality are not related to attitudes toward disabled people.

Central to understanding the impact of societal attitudes is the question, "Is there a common stereotype of a person with a disability?" Siller and Chipman (1965) correlated general attitudes toward physical disability with attitudes toward specific types of disabilities. The correlations were significant, leading Siller and Chipman (1965) to conclude that able-bodied people do hold stereotypical attitudes toward disability. While the correlations were statistically significant, they were so modest (.26 to .36) that they may have been statistical artifacts. Whiteman and Lukoff (1964, 1965) have studied attitudes toward blindness. They found that whereas blindness was the most negatively evaluated *type* of disability, blind *people* were generally favorably evaluated, that is, seen as socially competent. Based on the available research, McDaniel (1976) has concluded that "there does not appear to be a universal stereotype of the 'physically disabled person' . . . negative attitudes and evaluations [toward the disabled] may be more related to the *condition of the disability per se*" (p. 37).

Presumably those specific disabilities that are the most negatively evaluated are also the most aversive to the general public. In ranking attitudes toward specific disabilities, emotional disorders consistently receive the most negative evaluations (MacDonald & Hall, 1969). Among the physical disabilities, blindness tends to be the most negatively evaluated (Gowman, 1957; Whiteman & Lukoff, 1965). Harasymiw, Horne, and Lewis (1976) studied 4,459 able-bodied subjects' acceptance of 22 disability types. Their findings indicated a relatively stable ranking of disability according to social acceptance across their various subsamples (e.g., high school students, teachers, general population). Their major conclusion was, "that those disabilities that are least debilitating and facilitative of productivity (e.g., ulcer, asthma) are most accepted; however, those that may be termed as self-imposed (e.g., drug addict, ex-convict) . . . are the least accepted" (p. 101). Shurka and Katz (1976) also found that perceived responsibility for the disability is important in determining attitudes toward a person with a disability, as is the contextual cause of disability. In the Shurka and Katz (1976) study, people with a war related disability received the most favorable evaluations, presumably since they personally were not responsible for causing their disability.

Kutner (1971) cautions, however, that in assessing attitudes toward specific disabilities, the rankings are seldom consistent across different studies, and are confounded by the varying emotional responsiveness of people to "labeling." Vander Kolk's (1976) finding that stress, as measured by analysis of nondisabled subjects' affective responses to various disability labels, was highly variable across subjects and types of disabilities, supports Kutner's caveat.

Attitudes of Rehabilitation Professionals
Toward Disability

Extensive reviews of the attitude toward disability literature (English, 1971b; Kutner, 1971; McDaniel, 1976) note the paucity of research on the attitudes of rehabilitation professionals toward disabled people. Given that attitudes are assumed to affect behavior, the attitudes of professionals can exert a tremendous influence on the impact of disability on individuals and the professionals' interactions with them.

Ideally, rehabilitation professionals should be free from bias and prejudice. Unfortunately, that is not the case. Schofield and Kunce (1971) found that rehabilitation counselors did tend to stereotype disabled clients, were inconsistent in how they viewed clients with similar disabilities, and that their attitudes did influence counselor-client interactions. Pinkerton and McAleer (1976) hypothesized that of four chronic disabilities, renal failure, heart disease, cancer, and paraplegia, rehabilitation counselors would hold the least favorable attitudes toward cancer. They also hypothesized that counselor behavior, as measured by counselor projected case performance, would correlate with the counselor's attitudes toward disability. Using the ATDP as a measure of attitudes, the hypotheses were confirmed. Counselors were most negative toward cancer as a disability, and were likely to project less case service to clients with cancer than to clients with other equally severe disabilities. Pinkerton and McAleer (1976) interpret their finding as a reflection of the counselors' own fear of cancer.

Two other studies have documented that, like the general public, rehabilitation professionals may hold differential attitudes toward specific disabilities. Krauft, Rubin, Cook, and Bozarth (1976) rank-ordered rehabilitation counselors' ATDP scores toward eight disabilities, from most to least positive as: amputations, heart disease, epilepsy, orthopedic impairment, deafness, cerebral palsy, spinal cord injury, and mental retardation. Counselors who held less positive attitudes toward disabled people in general had significantly fewer of their clients with the three least favorable disabilities complete a rehabilitation program than did counselors with more favorable attitudes toward disabled people. Byrd, Byrd, and Emener (1977) studied employers', rehabilitation counselors', and rehabilitation counseling students' perceived "employability" of 20 different types of disability. Byrd et al. were concerned with the similarity of attitudes among the groups. Counselors and students were most similar in their rank orderings, employers and students the most dissimilar. However, inspection of the mean rankings per disability presented by Byrd et al. clearly revealed that practicing rehabilitation counselors were the most negative in their general perceptions of employability of disabled persons. On the five-point Likert scale used to rate each disability, counselors *averaged* a score of four or above, that is, said they would be unlikely, or very unlikely to hire a person with a particular disability for eight (e.g., blindness, cerebral palsy, paraplegia) of the twenty disabilities presented. Employers were as negative on only one disability—alcoholism. Students had no average ratings as negative as counselors for any disability.

One of the most consistent findings in the literature on attitudes toward disability is that women tend to possess more favorable attitudes than men do. Cook, Kunce, and Getsinger (1976) found that sexual differences in evaluating the disabled may be moderated by counselor effectiveness. Cook et al. asked resident hall counselors to evaluate the personality characteristics of pictures of men. One-half of the sample was given additional and biasing information suggesting that some of the men depicted were disabled. When the sample was split by supervisor's judgment of counselor effectiveness, there were no significant differences by sex for the more effective counselors given either biased or unbiased instructions. There were significant sex differences among the less effective counselors in that with biasing instructions, women upgraded their "personality" ratings, and men downgraded their ratings. If rating personality characteristics from pictures of people can be construed as an ambiguous task, then it is apparent that the more effective counselors tended to suspend judgment when given a biasing set, whereas the less effective counselors may have added structure to the task by relying on stereotypical and/or prejudiced attitudes; perhaps men downgraded the disabled by taking a hardnosed, "make-them-face-reality" approach and possibly women upgraded disability because of an over-nurturing attitude.

As with the general population, rehabilitation professionals are not immune from negative or potentially biasing attitudes toward disability. The findings that counselors do hold negative attitudes toward specific disabilities may stem from projected fears as implied by Pinkerton and McAleer (1976), from experience, as suggested by Byrd et al. (1977), or from ineffectiveness as suggested by Cook et al. (1976), and Krauft et al. (1976). Given the potential of attitudes to modify behavior, it becomes efficacious to design methods for changing negative attitudes toward disability.

Changing Attitudes Toward Disability

Within the social psychology literature there are many competing theories of how attitudes can be changed. Some theories assume that attitudes will change in order to be more congruent with behavior, others assume that behavior change will cause attitude change. Research has suggested that attitudes toward disability are related to situational determinants, vary according to type of disability, and are generally resistant to change. Research has also suggested that attitudes toward disability are complex in that seemingly neutral or even positive attitudes may consist of negative underlying components that are manifested in subtle ways, e.g., through job discrimination and aversiveness in interpersonal interactions.

It is paradoxical that in stigmatizing disabled people, able-bodied people attribute some positive traits to those who suffer misfortune. Occasionally the nondisabled even attribute special powers, awareness, or sensitivity to people who have experienced a disability. For example, a number of studies (Mitchell, 1976; Mitchell & Allen, 1975; Mitchell & Frederickson, 1975) have documented that physically disabled counselors are preferred by able-bodied clients. In these studies, subjects perceived the disabled counselors as possessing "an enhanced ability to understand and empathize." It is a pragmatic concern whether these positive, yet stereotypical attitudes, should be modified.

Some of the literature implies that interpersonal interactions with disabled people produce "interaction strain," or an uncertainty and discomfort in able-bodied people regarding how to respond to disabled people in interpersonal situations. Kleck, Ono, and Hastorf (1966) documented that nondisabled people experienced "interaction strain" reflected in their maintaining greater physical distance, and terminating the interaction more quickly with the disabled. Marinelli and Kelz (1973) found that people who interacted with a visibly disabled person experienced significant anxiety, and Davis (1961) has explored the various strategies the visibly disabled people adopt to reduce interaction strain.

The experimental approach used in the study of interpersonal interaction between nondisabled and disabled people is potentially powerful in isolating ways to modify attitudes. Traditional attempts to modify attitudes toward people with disabilities have focused on direct persuasion, providing information about physical disability, and in instigating direct contact with disabled people. The use of direct persuasion, for example, "Hire the handicapped . . . It's Good Business," has done little to open employment opportunities for disabled people. As Olshansky (1966) noted, if it were truly considered "good business" employers would need little exhortation to hire the handicapped. Merely providing information about physical disability can reduce misconceptions and ignorance, thus changing the cognitive component of an attitude. On the other hand, mere contact with disabled people may invoke the aforementioned interaction strain and modify attitudes in a negative direction, an unfortunate outcome observed by Cowen, Underberg, and Verrillo (1958).

It appears that it is not contact or information alone but contact between able-bodied and disabled people when both are of equal status, and the combination of information about disability and contact with disabled people that are the most powerful attitude change strategies (Anthony, 1972). For example, Evans (1976) was able to demonstrate in an experimental study that conduct alone did not affect the attitudes of able-bodied people. Contact in which the disabled person specifically provided information to put the nondisabled person at ease did significantly increase the positive attitudes of the nondisabled person. A major implication of this study was that in providing relevant information about physical disability the disabled people can minimize interaction strain. Another version of the information-contact strategy has been shown to modify attitude toward disability.

Sadlick and Penta (1975) reported that they were able to successfully modify the attitudes of nurses toward quadriplegia. In this study, nurses watched a 17-minute film of a successfully rehabilitated quadriplegic, who provided information regarding his injury, feelings about being disabled, and changes brought about by his injury. The attitude change stimulated by this technique was reportedly long lasting. Similarly Cook, Kunce, and Sleater (1974) compared discussion groups, didactic lectures, and the viewing of a series of videotapes depicting select behaviors and attitudes toward mentally ill people, as to their relative effectiveness in fostering attitudinal and behavioral change in a group of psychiatric aide trainees. Videotape training was superior in facilitating actual interpersonal behaviors of the aides. In these two studies it is important to note that desirable attitudinal and behavioral change were instigated vicariously through modeling.

These studies have demonstrated that attitudes of rehabilitation professionals and college students toward disabled people can be favorably modified. A much more difficult problem is the modification of attitudes of society in general. Experts in the field have considered several strategies. Wright (1975) argued for attending to a "handicap" not as something inherent in the person, but as a barrier in the environment restricting the disabled person from interaction with the able-bodied people. Interestingly, Langer, Fiske, Taylor, and Chanowitz (1976) conducted a series of experiments in which they tested the hypothesis that physically disabled people are avoided because of the conflict over a desire of the able-bodied people to stare at the physically disabled despite the norm against staring at people. Langer et al. found support for their hypothesis and also discovered that when disability as a "novel stimulus" is reduced, interaction avoidance was reduced. Wright's (1975) suggestions and Langer's et al. (1976) findings suggest that when environmental barriers are reduced and disabled people enter public places previously denied them, avoidance of interpersonal interactions will also be mitigated.

To summarize, the measurement of attitudes presents formidable methodological problems to the study of attitudes toward disability. However, the research to date suggests that people prejudiced toward minority groups are likely to be prejudiced toward people with disabilities; that there appears to be no general stereotype of "a person with a disability" among nondisabled people; that different types of disabilities are evaluated differentially, although the evaluations are highly variable; and that rehabilitation professionals can and sometimes do develop negative attitudes toward disabled people. Although attitudes may be related to situational determinants, they are assumed to act as predispositions to behavior, and once formed are likely to be resistant to change. The most effective method of modifying negative attitudes toward disability has been the pairing of information about disability with contact with people with a disability, especially when the information is provided by a disabled person.

CONCLUSION

With the possible exception of the somatopsychologists, no person-ologist or social psychologist has specified a theory of how physical disability affects the individual. Rather, research has followed an empirical-descriptive paradigm and practitioners have opted for an eclectic, pragmatic, and largely atheoretical approach to helping individuals with disabilities. There are, however, various minithe-ories that have adapted components of broader social-psychological theories to explain and predict the impact of disability on the individual. For example, Thomas (1966) applied role theory to understanding disability, Asher (1973) utilized Heider's balance theory of sentiments in changing attitudes toward the disabled, McDaniel (1976) adapted achievement motivation theory to predict performance levels of disabled people, and Cowen (1960) suggested psychological stress as a primary disability related adjustment variable. Currently developmental psychology has influenced theorists (e.g., Kerr, 1961; Shontz, 1975) to hypothesize that people experiencing physical impairment move through various stages of adjustment.

Developmental adjustment paradigms assume that upon becoming disabled an individual traverses various phases, such as shock, depression and mourning, denial, and acceptance. While psychological adjustment *per se* is undoubtedly a developmental process, identifying specific stages in adjustment to disability has proved to be a difficult task. This difficulty is partly because terms are often used interchangeably, for example, confusing the concept of "mourning" used by Wright (1960) as a reaction to disability with the concept of mourning used by Kubler-Ross (1969) as a reaction to dying. Also, the concept of psychological denial as an adjustment stage has been popularized by rehabilitationists. Specifically, denial of disability has appeared in the rehabilitation literature as a postulated primary facet of adjustment to disability. Whereas various studies purport to have documented "denial" as a fact, few have linked the "fact" to the explanatory structure of a theory. Thus, there is semantic confusion regarding the meaning of denial. Clearly, testing key hypotheses as developed by various theorists would add to the knowledge on how disability affects the individual. These difficulties pose a challenge to researchers for the development of more comprehensive theories, clearer constructs, and further empirical research.

REFERENCES

Anthony, W. A. Societal rehabilitation: Changing society's attitudes toward the physically and mentally disabled. *Rehabilitation Psychology*, 1972, *19*, 117–126.

Asher, N. W. Manipulating attraction toward the disabled: An application of the similarity-attraction model. *Rehabilitation Psychology*, 1973, *20*, 156–164.

Barker, R. G., Wright, B. A., Meyerson, L., & Gonick, M. R. *Adjustment to physical handicap: A survey of the social psychology of physique and disability* (2nd ed.). New York: Social Science Research Council, Bulletin 55, 1953.

Berry, J. R., Dunteman, G. H., & Webb, M. H. Personality and motivation in rehabilitation. *Journal of Counseling Psychology*, 1968, *15*, 237–244.

Berry, K. L., & Miskimins, R. W. Concept of self and posthospital vocational adjustment. *Journal of Consulting and Clinical Psychology*, 1969, *33*, 103–108.

Byrd, E. K., Byrd, P. D., & Emener, W. G. Student, counselor, and employer perceptions of employability of severely retarded. *Rehabilitation Literature*, 1977, *38*, 42–44.

Chesler, M. A. Ethnocentrism and attitudes toward the physically disabled. *Journal of Personality and Social Psychology*, 1965, *2*, 877–882.

Comer, R. C., & Piliavin, J. A. As others see us: Attitudes of physically handicapped and normals toward own and other groups. *Rehabilitation Literature*, 1975, *36*, 206–221, 225.

Cook, D. W., Kunce, J. T., & Getsinger, S. H. Perceptions of the disabled and counseling effectiveness. *Rehabilitation Counseling Bulletin*, 1976, *19*, 470–475.

Cook, D. W., Kunce, J. T., & Sleater, S. M. Vicarious behavior induction and training psychiatric aides. *Journal of Community Psychology*, July 1974, 294–297.

Cowen, E. L. Personality, motivation and clinical phenomena. In L. H. Lofquist (Ed.), *Psychological research and rehabilitation*. Washington, D.C.: American Psychological Association, 1960, pp. 112–171.

Cowen, E. L., Bobgrove, P. H., Rockway, A. M., & Stevenson, J. Development and evaluation of an attitude to deafness scale. *Journal of Personality and Social Psychology*, 1967, *6*, 183–191.

Cowen, E. L., Underberg, R., & Verrillo, R. T. The development and testing of an attitude to blindness scale. *Journal of Social Psychology*, 1958, *48*, 297–304.

Davis, F. Deviance disavowed: The management of strained interaction by the visibly handicapped. *Social Problems,* 1961, *9,* 121–132.

Dembo, T., Leviton, G. L., & Wright, B. A. Adjustment to misfortune: A problem of social-psychological rehabilitation. *Artificial Limbs,* 1956, *3,* 4–62.

English, R. W. The application of personality theory to explain psychological reactions to physical disability. *Rehabilitation Research and Practice Review,* 1971a, *3,* 35–47.

———. Correlates to stigma towards physically disabled persons. *Rehabilitation Research and Practice Review,* 1971b, *2,* 1–18.

Evans, J. H. Changing attitudes toward disabled persons: An experimental study. *Rehabilitation Counseling Bulletin,* 1976, *19,* 572–579.

Feinberg, L. B. Social desirability and attitudes toward the disabled. *Personnel and Guidance Journal,* 1967, *46,* 373–381.

Freud, S. *A general introduction to psychoanalysis.* New York: Liveright, 1963.

Gellman, W. Roots of prejudice against the handicapped. *Journal of Rehabilitation,* 1959, *25*(1), 4–6, 25.

Goldberg, R. T. Adjustment of children with invisible and visible handicaps: Congenital heart disease and facial burns. *Journal of Counseling Psychology,* 1974, *21,* 428–432.

Gowman, A. G. *The war blind in American social structure.* New York: American Foundation for the Blind, 1957.

Harasymiw, S. J., Horne, M. D., & Lewis, S. C. A longitudinal study of disability group acceptance. *Rehabilitation Literature,* 1976, *37,* 98–102.

Hirschenfang, S., & Benton, J. Rorschach responses of paraplegic and quadriplegic patients. *International Journal of Paraplegia,* 1966, *4,* 40–42.

Kerr, N. Understanding the process of adjustment to disability. *Journal of Rehabilitation,* 1961, *27*(6), 16–18.

Kleck, R., Ono, H., & Hastorf, A. H. The effects of physical deviance on face-to-face interaction. *Human Relations,* 1966, *19,* 425–436.

Krauft, C. C., Rubin, S. E., Cook, D. W., & Bozarth, J. D. Counselor attitude toward disabled persons and client program completion: A pilot study. *Journal of Applied Rehabilitation Counseling,* 1976, *7,* 50–54.

Kubler-Ross, E. *On death and dying.* New York: Macmillan, 1969.

Kutner, B. The social psychology of disability. In W. S. Neff (Ed.),

Rehabilitation Psychology. Washington, D.C.: American Psychological Association, 1971, pp. 143–167.

Langer, E. J., Fiske, S., Taylor, S. E., & Chanowitz, B. Stigma, staring and discomfort: A novel-stimulus hypothesis. *Journal of Experimental Social Psychology,* 1976, *12,* 451–463.

Lewin, K. *A dynamic theory of personality.* New York: McGraw-Hill, 1935.

———. *Principles of topological psychology.* New York: McGraw-Hill, 1936.

Lipp, L., Kolstoe, R., James, W., & Randall, H. Denial of disability and internal control of reinforcement: A study using a perceptual defense paradigm. *Journal of Consulting and Clinical Psychology,* 1968, *32,* 72–75.

MacDonald, A. P., & Hall, J. Perception of disability by the nondisabled. *Journal of Consulting and Clinical Psychology,* 1969, *33,* 654–660.

McDaniel, J. W. *Physical disability and human behavior* (2nd ed.). New York: Pergamon Press, 1976.

Maddi, S. R. *Personality theories: A comparative analysis.* Homewood, Ill.: Dorsey, 1972.

Marinelli, R. P., & Kelz, J. W. Anxiety and attitudes toward visibly disabled persons. *Rehabilitation Counseling Bulletin,* 1973, *16,* 198–205.

Meng, H. Zur sozialpsychologic der korperbeschandigten: Ein beitrag zum problem der praktischen psychohygiene. *Schweizer Archiv fur Neurologie and Psychiatrie,* 1938, *40,* 328–344. Cited in R. O. Barker, B. A. Wright, L. Meyerson, & M. R. Gonick, *Adjustment to physical handicap: A survey of the social psychology of physique and disability* (2nd ed.). New York: Social Science Research Council, Bulletin 55, 1953.

Mitchell, J. C. Disabled counselors: Perceptions of their effectiveness in a therapeutic relationship. *Archives of Physical Medicine and Rehabilitation,* 1976, *57,* 348–352.

Mitchell, J., & Allen, H. Perception of a physically disabled counselor in a counseling session. *Journal of Counseling Psychology,* 1975, *22,* 70–73.

Mitchell, D. C., & Frederickson, W. A. Preferences for physically disabled counselors in hypothetical counseling situations. *Journal of Counseling Psychology,* 1975, *22,* 477–482.

Olshansky, S. Hire the handicapped week: A critique. *Rehabilitation Literature,* 1966, *27,* 295–298.

Pinkerton, S. S., & McAleer, C. A. Influences of client diagnosis-cancer on counselor decisions. *Journal of Counseling Psychology*, 1976, *23*, 575–578.

Roessler, R., & Bolton, B. *Psychosocial adjustment to disability.* Baltimore, Maryland: University Park Press, 1978.

Rogers, C. R. *Client-centered therapy; its current practice, implications, and theory.* Boston, Mass.: Houghton Mifflin, 1951.

———. A theory of therapy, personality, and interpersonal relationships, as developed in the client-centered framework. In S. Koch (Ed.), *Psychology: A study of a science* (vol. 3). New York: McGraw-Hill, 1959, pp. 184–256.

———. *On becoming a person.* Boston, Mass.: Houghton Mifflin, 1961.

Sadlick, M., & Penta, F. B. Changing nurse attitudes toward quadriplegics through use of television. *Rehabilitation Literature*, 1975, *36*, 272–278.

Schofield, L. F., & Kunce, J. T. Client disability and counselor behavior. *Rehabilitation Counseling Bulletin*, 1971, *14*, 158–165.

Shontz, F. C. Physical disability and personality. In W. S. Neff (Ed.), *Rehabilitation Psychology.* Washington, D.C.: American Psychological Association, 1971, pp. 33–73.

———. *The psychological aspects of physical illness and disability.* New York: Macmillan, 1975.

Shurka, E., & Katz, S. Evaluations of persons with a disability: The influence of disability context and personal responsibility for the disability. *Rehabilitation Psychology*, 1976, *23*, 65–71.

Siller, J. Attitudes toward disability. In H. Rusalem & D. Malikin (Eds.), *Contemporary vocational rehabilitation.* New York: New York University Press, 1976, pp. 67–79.

Siller, J. E., & Chipman, A. Personality determinants of reaction to the physically handicapped II: Projective techniques. Studies in reaction to disability: VIII. New York: New York University Press, 1965.

Thomas, E. J. Problems of disability from the perspective of role theory. *Journal of Health and Human Behavior*, 1966, *7*, 2–14.

Vander Kolk, C. J. Physiological and self-reported reactions to the disabled and deviant. *Rehabilitation Psychology*, 1976, *23*, 77–83.

Whiteman, M., & Lukoff, I. F. A factorial study of sighted peoples' attitudes toward blindness. *Journal of Social Psychology*, 1964, *64*, 333–353.

———. Attitudes toward blindness and other physical handicaps. *Journal of Social Psychology*, 1965, *66*, 135–145.

Wright, B. A. *Physical disability: A psychological approach.* New York: Harper, 1960.

————. Social psychological leads to enhance rehabilitation effectiveness. *Rehabilitation Counseling Bulletin,* 1975, *18,* 214–222.

Yuker, H. E. Attitudes as determinants of behavior. *Journal of Rehabilitation,* 1965, *31,* 15–16.

Yuker, H., Block, J., & Younng, J. *The measurement of attitudes toward disabled persons.* Albertson, N.Y.: Human Resources Center, 1966.

Chapter 7

World of Work and Disabling Conditions

Jim L. Daniels

INTRODUCTION

Work and disability have both been addressed by many different disciplines, including such diverse fields as anthropology, philosophy, biology, and psychology. Each contributes its own perspective to the understanding of these essential aspects of life. Rehabilitation, which deals with effects of disability on the whole person, is at the crossroads of many disciplines. Vocational rehabilitation deals more specifically with the relationship between the world of work and people who have physical or mental handicaps. Basic competencies required in vocational rehabilitation include knowledge about disabling conditions, information concerning the world of work, and skills to modify the interaction between the effects of disability and work. This chapter is written from a vocational rehabilitation perspective and will integrate extant views of the world of work with information concerning people with disabilities.

WORLD OF WORK

The world of work can be analyzed from two different perspectives. The first is the external or rational view of the work structure and its organization. The second perspective is work as perceived by the worker.

Rational View

Competitive Work. When it comes to occupational terminology, some terms such as *job, career, occupation, work,* and *position* are often used interchangeably (Bolles, 1978). Although Bolles's point is well taken with regard to a specific job seeker, some general terms, are helpful to the people who want to understand the system of jobs and how they relate to each other. Occupations may be categorized by industry, job content, worker characteristics, or socioeconomic status (Shartle, 1964) as well as by status, and setting. The *Dictionary of Occupational Titles* (1977) identifies over 35,000 job titles in 23,000 occupations. Given a large number of variables, any scheme attempting to describe the total occupational structure is either forced into complexity or must sacrifice detail to describe the total. Most attempts to categorize the types of work arrive at some nine to thirteen categories. The number and type of categories derived depend on the criteria utilized for grouping the jobs. The *Dictionary of Occupational Titles* (D.O.T.) (Department of Labor, 1977) lists nine general fields called occupational categories. These categories were derived by grouping jobs according to an analysis of their similarity in function. Table 7-1 compares this system with two other systems. The second column represents the categories of the *Encyclopedia of Careers and Vocational Guidance* (Hopke, 1967) that lists nine general fields called occupations and careers. This particular system has a clearer focus on white collar than blue collar jobs. In this system some of the jobs are categorized according to the content of the work (e.g., sales, managerial), whereas others are defined by the level of skill involved (e.g., skilled, professional). The third column represents thirteen career groups defined in the *Career Data Book* (Flanagan, Tiedeman, Willis, & McLaughlin, 1973). Similar to column two, this system focuses on white collar as opposed to blue collar occupations. This grouping is based on the content area of the work rather than on an analysis of common functions. Thus, each system is limited by the criteria utilized to group occupations. Any particular system should be judged on the relevance of the groupings to the needs of the target population. If the counselor is working with people who are primarily interested in professional or technical positions, then the *Career Data Book* will be most helpful. If working with a target population that has a broad range of occupational characteristics, then the D.O.T. classification system may be the most useful.

The distribution of employment by industry is also an aid to understanding the occupational structure in the United States. Table

7-2 presents the relative distribution of employees by industry over the last half century (U.S. Department of Labor, 1976). Each decade has seen greater incremental increases in the total number of employees. Manufacturing, wholesale, and retail trade are consistently the largest employing industries over time, whereas mining, contract construction, finance, insurance, and real estate are consistently the smallest employing industries. Service and government employment has demonstrated the largest relative increase, with government employment increasing dramatically as a result of programs initiated during the depression of the 1930s. Throughout the twentieth century industries providing services have been steadily increasing in employment and have surpassed goods-producing industries in numbers of jobs. In 1945 each offered approximately 27 million jobs, but in 1975 goods-producing industries employed 27 million, while those in service-producing industries numbered 54 million (U.S. Department of Labor, 1976).

Blue collar or white collar distinctions are utilized frequently in discussing occupations and in reporting employment statistics. For the past thirty years the trend has been a relatively greater increase in white collar occupations than in blue collar (blue collar/white collar ratio, 1945—9:7, 1975—5:7). This trend seems significantly correlated with increasing job complexity and specialization and increasing educational requirements (U.S. Department of Labor, 1976).

Noncompetitive Employment. Not all work comes in the form of well-defined jobs. Many functions essential to the fabric of society, culture, and economy are performed daily without supervision and with no direct remuneration. Few could deny that minding the children, mowing the yard, washing dishes or clothes, cooking a meal, cleaning the house, repairing possessions, or a thousand other mundane tasks are forms of work. All these functions correlate with job positions in the competitive employment structure; the difference is that these tasks are performed within a family or community unit for rewards other than money, and that there is no competition between groups of people to perform these tasks. On an objective level, the houseparent trades management of the house for room and board, affection, and security; family farm workers perform work for similar rewards; and children in most families perform chores with the same payoff. You may ask your mechanic neighbor for assistance in tuning your car and later assist him in preparing his income tax with no money changing hands. These types of goods and service exchanges were much more prevalent in the earlier years

Table 7-1 A Comparison of Three Systems
of Occupational Categories

Source	Dictionary of Occupational Titles	Encyclopedia of Careers and Occupations	Career Data Book
Name	Occupational Categories	Careers and Occupations	Career Groups
	1. Professional, Technical, and Managerial	1. Managerial and Official 2. Professional 3. Semiprofessional and technical	1. Engineering, Physical Science, Math, and Architecture 2. Medical and Biological Sciences 3. Business Administration 4. General Teaching and Social Service 5. Humanities, Law, Social, and Behavioral Science 6. Fine Arts, Performing Arts 7. Technical Jobs
WHITE COLLAR	2. Clerical and Sales	4. Clerical 5. Sales	8. Proprietor Sales 9. Secretarial, clerical, office workers

172

3. Service

4. Agricultural, Fishery, Forestry, and Related

5. Processing

6. Machine Trades
7. Bench Work

8. Structural Work

9. Miscellaneous

BLUE COLLAR

6. Service

7. Farming

8. Semiskilled— unskilled
9. Skilled

10. Community and Public Service

11. General Labor

12. Mechanics, Industrial Trades

13. Construction Trades

173

Table 7-2 * Numbers** of Employees on Nonagricultural Payrolls and Rank Order by Numbers for Selected Years

Industry	1920 Rank	1920 Number	1930 Rank	1930 Number	1940 Rank	1940 Number	1950 Rank	1950 Number	1960 Rank	1960 Number	1970 Rank	1970 Number	1974*** Rank	1974*** Number
Mining	6	1.24	8	1.01	8	.92	8	.90	8	.71	8	.62	8	1.00
Contract Construction	8	8.48	7	1.37	7	1.29	6	2.33	6	2.88	7	3.38	7	3.00
Manufacturing	1	10.66	1	9.56	1	10.98	1	15.24	1	16.79	1	19.35	1	19.00
Transportation and Public Utilities	3	3.99	3	3.68	5	3.04	5	4.03	5	4.00	5	4.49	5	4.00
Wholesale and Retail Trade	2	4.47	2	5.79	2	6.75	2	9.38	2	11.39	2	14.91	2	17.00
Finance, Insurance, Real Estate	7	1.17	6	1.47	6	1.50	7	1.91	7	2.67	6	3.69	6	3.50
Services	5	2.26	4	3.37	4	3.68	4	5.38	4	7.42	4	11.612	3	14.00
Government	4	2.60	5	3.14	3	4.20	3	6.02	3	8.35	3	12.53	3	14.00
Total		27.35		29.42		32.38		45.22		54.23		70.645		78.50

* Source: U.S. Department of Labor, Bureau of Labor Statistics, Bulletin 1312-9, 1972.
** Numbers in millions.
*** Source: U.S. Department of Labor, Occupational Outlook Handbook (1976).

174

of this country. The influences of technology, specialization, and ur-banization have decreased the amount of these less formal exchanges of work. The houseparent is not normally placed in a competitive position with regard to parenting children or managing the house-hold; neither is a child with regard to chores. Most people perform noncompetitive work, and its importance should not be overlooked when discussing the world of work. If these tasks were no longer performed or suddenly became formalized jobs, the effects on the economy and society would be devastating. Unless people are com-pletely disabled, they will normally have some of these noncompeti-tive tasks to perform whether they work competitively or not.

Worker's Perspective

The previous section discussed work and job without being con-cerned about the person who performs the tasks or holds the job title. However, generally work and job are identified as human ac-tivities. This section will view work from the workers' perspective in the work setting and from the job seekers' perspective.

On a personal level work is one of the primary mechanisms through which adults earn emotional and financial stability, social status, and material rewards (Neff, 1968). On a larger level the world of work is woven into the fabric of every aspect of life. The question, "What do you want to be when you grow up?" plagues us until we "grow up," then everyone begins to ask, "What do you do?" In the United States there tends to be a generalized expectancy that people must work—the so-called work ethic. Where people work and what they do determines their standard of living, prestige, recreational patterns, social interaction, and self-image. Much of the individual lifetime is devoted to preparing for, serving, and retiring from the performance of some function (job). Once in a job each worker brings certain characteristics to the job based on his or her feelings about the job tasks and his or her expectation of the role work is to play in his or her life. What is work to one person may be play to another (i.e., the professional athlete compared to the week-end sportsperson). Some people enjoy the tasks they perform. This enjoyment may stem from their value toward people, self, accom-plishment, security, wealth, or a variety of other values. Others see the job only as a means (money) to the end—enjoyment of their leisure time.

Once in a job position certain attributes of the job are gener-alized to the worker. Job titles such as doctor, professor, or judge are most often associated with high degrees of status, monetary reward, intelligence, and ability. Conversely, job titles such as garbage collector, laborer, and janitor are normally associated with high degrees of physical stamina. The person holding the job is perceived as having the same attributes as the job.

Occupational choice can influence the individual's environment in many areas at any given point in time and have a pervasive influence over the lifetime of the individual (Ginzberg, Ginzberg, Axlerad & Herma, 1951; Super, 1957). Many factors become important from the viewpoint of the individual when considering a specific job. The individual must consider both factors about himself or herself and about the jobs available. Carlson, Dawis, England, and Lofquist's (1963) distinction between job satisfaction and job satisfactoriness (the former referring to the worker's feeling toward the job and the latter indicating the adequacy of the worker's job performance) actually describes the difference between these internal and external judgments made about job appropriateness.

The Work Environment. The worker encounters not a set of jobs but rather a group of individuals who perform specific jobs. The system of jobs within an organization represents a *formal structure* that describes the *stated* functions, responsibilities, and relationships among the elements necessary to the success of the enterprise. The *informal structure* comprised of the personalities of the employees and their interaction frequently parallels the formal structure. Getzel and Guba (1957) labeled these dimensions of organizational behavior nomothetic (formal) and idiopathic (informal). The informal work structure may be equal in importance to an individual's formally defined position.

Managerial philosophy and leadership style may also have a tremendous impact on a given individual's satisfaction with a particular job. What position management assumes with regard to McGregor's (1962) Theory X and Theory Y will influence the type of employment offered. Management that treats its workers as if people are basically lazy and must be punished if they are to work (Theory X) will provide radically different employment situations than management that ascribes to the notion that people basically want to work and need to be provided with appropriate circumstances in which to achieve (Theory Y).

Another important organizational variable is the leadership style exercised by the supervisor. Those whose supervisory style is laissez-faire will provide different work environments than a more autocratic supervisor. The intricacies of these aspects of within-work-setting variables are brought up to emphasize the uniqueness of each job and to point to the areas of organizational and administrative theory as fruitful resources for further exploration.

DISABILITY/HANDICAP AND WORK

An important distinction in vocational rehabilitation is made between what constitutes a disability and a handicap (Zawada, 1973). The term disability refers to an impairment or functional limitation in one or more body systems, while the term handicap refers to an inability to perform in a way dictated by situational circumstance. This distinction may be utilized to explain the observed fact that effects of any given disability vary among individuals. Consequently, even with the same impairment (disability), one person may work and another may not. Even from a surface view the relationship between disability and work is complex. Consider Figure 7-1 that represents the relationship between work, disability, and handicap. Notice that work is divided into competitive and noncompetitive areas and disability is divided into mild, moderate, and severe categories so that these can be considered in the interaction also. This discussion introduces the parameters of the interaction that will be explored in more depth in the remainder of this section. Examining

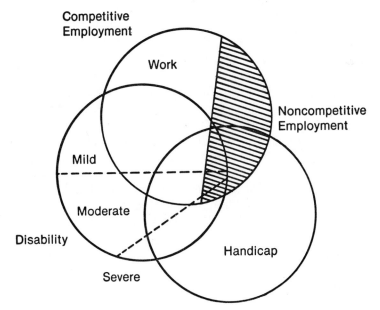

Figure 7–1 Relationship Between Work, Disability, and Handicap

the position of work in Figure 7-1 reveals that the effects of a disability or handicap are only partially related to work. Frequently the effects are felt in other areas, such as leisure, self-care, socialization, or other life functions. As illustrated, handicap causes relatively more interference with competitive employment than does disability:

1. Not all disabilities result in handicaps either within or outside of the work situation and, conversely, not all handicaps result from disability. Since 1954 (Brown vs. Board of Education) minority status and lack of education have been identified as handicapping conditions.

2. A sizable number of disabilities create no or only minimal handicaps to work (Levitan & Taggert, 1977).

3. A number of people who have both a disability and a handicap are in the work force; although the numbers decrease as the severity of disability increases. Levitan and Taggert (1977) report that one-seventh of the severely disabled are employed compared to 71 percent of the occupationally disabled people, and 74 percent of nondisabled people.

4. The more severe the disability, the more likely it is to be handicapping (Zawada, 1973).

5. Handicap more than disability is likely to keep an individual out of the competitive work force.

A handicap is present only when an individual characteristic (disability) has a negative effect on an individual's performance within a specific environment. The technician who is hard of hearing may experience little difficulty in repairing a malfunctioning turntable but could not perform adequately as a quality control expert in audio systems. The physically "normal" person who is only five feet tall would be substantially handicapped in the professional basketball ranks. Thus an employment handicap is present only when an individual lacks the ability to perform job tasks. Handicaps occur as a result of disability, disadvantage, overwhelming circumstance, age, experience, or any other physical or mental characteristic, but do not bear a one-to-one correspondence with any of these characteristics.

Disability and Work

A disability is only one characteristic of an individual, and its effect on the individual will be a function of a myriad of factors—some intrinsic to the individual, others ecological in nature. The total individual and not just the disability must be considered when discussing disability in relationship to work. The halo effect, the tendency of people to generalize from one characteristic to the whole person (Wright, 1960; Vuris, 1970), tends to obscure the spectrum of abilities possessed by an individual. The range of limitations within any given disability, from mild to severe, must also be considered. Even with identical limitations two people may respond differently, that is, a limitation imposed by a disability will vary among individuals.

Given these considerations, there are no specific statements that can be made about how a particular disability relates to specific jobs. Obviously the term disability itself implies a loss of function, but the effect of the loss of function on the person's ability to perform work can only be situationally determined. Factors such as age at time of disability, predisablement history, degree of disability, and course of adjustment to disability have equally important relationships to the world of work as do specific types of disability (Berkowitz, Johnson, & Murphy, 1976).

People with disabilities form an extraordinarily heterogeneous group in that they possess the same range and variety of variance in regard to any physical, mental, or behavioral trait as the nondisabled population (Wright, 1960). Generalizing from this statement it follows that people with disabilities will be found in most job positions, in most fields, and at all levels of the employment hierarchy (Rusk, 1963; Barsch, 1962). This statement is necessary to avoid misunderstandings about the effects of disability. True, a quadriplegic is not likely to become an olympic sprinter nor a person without sight a stunt car driver, but these are extreme situational impossibilities. These disabilities would not necessarily prevent individuals from being counselors, programmers, or computer operators. Work limitations of people with disabilities are based primarily on the functional limitations directly related to the disability and the person's reaction and adjustment to the disability. These factors operate within the social context of the individual, and the relationships are mutually interactional.

But the use of general disability labels impedes understanding a person's abilities. Basing an opinion of a person's ability on the label *amputee* would ignore many salient points. Different limitations are associated with the nature and extent of amputation. A double amputee will face problems different from those of a single amputee. There are also differences in limitation depending on where the amputation is made. The person who lost a little toe by amputation will suffer little, if any, impairment. These illustrations only scratch the surface of the variation within the disability label *amputee*. When the total physical, mental, and emotional status of a person is also taken into account then the variations become almost infinite. There is no valid way of determining an exact and immutable relationship among jobs and disabilities. Any such stereotyping represents an oversimplification and is grossly misleading. For example, even if experience were to reveal that mentally retarded people as a group were highly successful in food service work, it is difficult to determine the degree to which the success was a result of inherent characteristics of this group or whether other factors, e.g., low pay and job availability, were the basis for this finding. Counselor, teacher, parent, and employer expectations have also contributed to the formation of vocational stereotyping of disabled people. It would be easy to construct a table of vocational stereotypes for several disability groups. For example:

Mentally Retarded	Service occupations, Bus boy, Janitor
Epileptics	Clerical occupations, File clerk, Ticket clerk
Blind	Social service, Clerical occupations, Counselors, Receptionists
Orthopedic	Bench work, Assembly, Machinists
Deaf	Machine trades, Printing press operators

Unfortunately, vocational decisions are frequently based on such generalized expectations. Poorly matched or premature person-job arrangements can be damaging both to clients' self-perceptions and employer receptivity to hiring individuals with handicaps (Landy & Griffith, 1958).

Disability Factors Influencing Work. Certain general factors of disabilities have important relationships with the world of work (Baxt, 1959). The nature of the disability will dictate different considerations in the involvement of an individual with the world of work (is the disability stable, growing progressively worse, improving, or intermittent). In the case of a disability that is constant, like stable, congenital blindness, the vocational limitations inherent in the lack of sight will remain relatively constant. The same is true of an adventitious condition like traumatic paraplegia. Once the adjustment to the disability is made, the vocational limitations faced by the individual will be relatively stable. Diabetes, conversely, may involve frequent changes in status of the disability. If the diabetes is allowed to become acute before treatment begins then a rapid increase in functioning may occur as the insulin injections start to stabilize the effects of the condition. However, diabetes may also lead to a progressive worsening of an ability as in the case of diabetic retinopathy where vision often progressively deteriorates. Similar patterns of progressive improvement or regression are also prevalent in mental disabilities, drug abuse, cancer, and multiple sclerosis. Other disabilities typically have only intermittent vocational effects. Epilepsy, migraine headaches, phobias, and situational emotional disturbances are all disabilities where the effects occur for short periods and the person usually has no functional limitations during periods when the disability is not active.

The time since onset of disability is another factor that frequently influences the individual's participation in the world of work. Generally speaking, the longer the time period since disablement the greater the opportunity for effective treatments to have occurred and the more likely the person will have progressed through the various stages of adjustment. The sooner the individual receives services after disability the better the chance for successful rehabilitation (Waters, Geham, & Barrette, 1970). People who have congenital disabilities or were disabled during childhood will most often have experienced a wide range of rehabilitation interventions designed to lessen the effects of the disability prior to entering the work force. Thus the person disabled early in life is more likely to have had involvement with some service that has either removed the effects of the disability or enabled the person to cope more adequately with those effects (Haber, 1973). In all cases of disability, factors such as financial circumstance at time of disability, quality and number of services provided in the home locale, and family and personal feelings toward treatments will influence the rate of adjustment.

The age of the individual at the time of onset of disability will also provide valuable information about how a disability will affect an individual's work life (Waters et al., 1970). People who are disabled earlier in life will have had fewer life and work experiences on which to base vocational decisions. The nondisabled individual is introduced to work first through example of others, then through home chores, then part-time work before entering full-time work. Disabilities that occur during any one of these stages will interfere with the individual's vocational information gathering. For instance, the person with no sight is unable to observe the wide variety of jobs encountered in the normal course of living. Sighted youngsters normally observe workers when traveling with parents to the store, to restaurants, and to pay bills. Blind children do not get this incidental exposure unless companions describe their surroundings. The same lack of access occurs with the congenitally deaf, severely mobility impaired, and overprotected individuals. Since many developmental disabilities delay the overall learning of skills in many areas, these disabilities will also interfere with development of vocational awareness and work skills. Such circumstances are usually less relevant for people who were disabled after they have had some significant work experience. Many people who suffer adventitious disabilities will have been successful as workers. This means they will have developed general work skills including punctuality, cooperation, and social skills, as well as a specific work skill such as typing, welding, programming, or counseling. These skills often provide a basis for the development of new areas of work; frequently, existing skills may be transferred to more accommodative settings through human and environmental engineering. A casual perusal of the want ads in any newspaper will show the premium placed on experience. Those disabled people who possess successful work experience will have less difficulty gaining acceptance as workers.

Each disability and each person's reaction to a disability must be dealt with individually. The factors of type and severity of impairment also are important when considering how a disability relates to the world of work. In general, the more severe the disability and the more body systems involved in the disability, the more difficulties that will be encountered when trying to accommodate that individual within the world of work.

Handicapping Aspects of Disability. Rehabilitation workers are most often concerned with enabling a person with a disability to reenter the work force as an end goal. Much of the work is in fostering new skills in their clients. However, many of the barriers between the disabled individual and the world of work are beyond the individual's or rehabilitation agencies' control. Architecture, attitudes, and established orders and procedures often are the most handicapping aspects of disability. These problems, if alleviated, would place the person with a disability on equal footing with those without a disability: trying to maximize their skills, minimize their liabilities, and match this pattern to jobs where corresponding abilities are required. Each person would fail or succeed based on the extent of his or her efforts. In fact the process of selective placement is accomplished by 70 percent of the general population without professional intervention (Hollander, 1967).

Disability is a powerful factor in the world of work and the world of the individual. Millions of man-hours are lost to disability at work, not to mention the personal effects of disability.

Some handicaps are inherent in the disability, while others are imposed by society (Dembo, Diller, Gordon, Levitan, & Sherr, 1973). For example, loss of sight handicaps an individual's performance in visual tasks; however, many blind people are discriminated against in employment because of employer attitude that a sightless worker is bound to be incompetent or a hazard. Keep in mind that each individual will vary with regard to the handicapping effects inherent in a particular condition. A discussion of some of the more common handicaps imposed by society follows.

1. *Physical Barriers.* People affected with physical disorders may face concomitant physical handicaps. The physical world was not made to accommodate people with blindness, deafness, seizures, or cerebral palsy (Dembo et al., 1973). Obviously, severe physical disabilities require individuals to learn new ways of coping in most areas of their lives. Some individuals with disabilities may learn to cope with the effects to the maximum extent possible. The abilities they lack, once this maximum adjustment is made, constitute the true handicap of the condition as this factor will handicap across all situations where the lost ability is required. The auto accident victim with legs paralyzed at first is dependent on others for many life functions that later he or she will be able to do alone (transferring from bed to chair or chair to car, going to the bathroom, giving skin proper care, or driving a car).

The external world may handicap disabled individuals in many ways. The inconvenience to the person in a wheelchair of not being able to reach the public water fountain is minor compared to the many architectural barriers that stand between some disabled individuals and the world of work. Generally, architectural barriers are associated with physical disabilities, although the communication problems of mentally retarded, deaf, or learning disabled people are sometimes complicated by difficult-to-understand signs. Architectural barriers are those physical aspects of buildings or machinery that limit a disabled person's access, use, or mobility. People in wheelchairs are often restricted by narrow or hard-to-open doors; rampless curbs; stairs; nonadapted toilet facilities; elevator buttons, telephones, and water fountains placed too high; too steep ramps; and tight parking places. When the work station has these types of problems, then the wheelchair-bound person has been significantly handicapped by the physical plant. Employers often feel justified in not hiring disabled people who would face real or imagined problems such as these. If hired, those individuals must find ways to cope with these barriers or suffer their effects during their employment tenure. People who use crutches or a cane, have leg braces, leg prostheses, or walkers will be bothered by stairs and hard-to-open doors.

For visually impaired people, orientation to new places often presents the most difficult problem, but the stability of the physical arrangement is also important. Needed adaptations may include braille or large print labels for doors, elevators, and vending machines. Relief maps of a city or the interior of a building may also be helpful. Most severely visually impaired people also need a period of mobility orientation to new surroundings. Architectural problems relating to deafness are centered around communication difficulties. Loss of hearing interferes with perception of auditory warning signals and unassisted use of many communication devices, for example, the telephone.

In considering these and other architectural handicaps, the distinction made by Jeffrey (1973) between adapted, specialized, or accessible housing may be applied to the work station. Adapted work stations are those in which there would be no barriers regardless of the ambulatory ability of the personnel. Specialized work stations are those where certain disabilities would not be handicapping, and accessible work stations would be situations requiring only minimal adaptations.

2. *Attitudinal Barriers.* Abundant evidence indicates that another type of barrier exists between people who are disabled and the world of work. Attitudinal barriers that result in employment discrimination toward people labeled "disabled" or "handicapped" are often more handicapping than physical barriers. Frequently, employer attitudes are based on the same stereotypes as those of the general public. Generally attitude surveys of employers have asked the employer to respond to a disability label. Evidence indicates that these labels evoke certain stereotyped responses (Sinnick, 1968; Torre & Askenasy, 1963). Such stereotyped views of people who are handicapped are based largely on misinformation and generalizations about the "handicapped" in general or specific types of handicaps, as well as confusion of the handicap/disability distinction.

People included in the mentally ill group may display psychotic, neurotic, or emotionally disturbed behavior or have a history of such behavior, psychiatric treatment, or hospitalization. Employers view "mentally ill" individuals as dangerous, unpredictable, unreliable, and susceptible to breakdown. They fear more interpersonal problems with coworkers, more time spent on supervision, and lower levels of productivity (Pirdell, 1958; Torre & Askenasy, 1963). Employers view all of these characteristics as cutting into their profits.

Included in the physically disabled category are all disabling conditions that result from an impairment or loss of a physiological function. General employer perceptions are that a physical disability negatively affects safety on the job; that employing physically handicapped people results in higher insurance costs, more sick leave, and necessary physical plant modifications; and that coworkers and customers will react negatively to the presence of a person with a physical handicap (Felton, 1962; President's Committee on Employment of the Handicapped, 1970).

The mentally retarded label is included separately because it does not fit into the other categories and includes all those people who are correctly or incorrectly labeled retarded. Employers often view retarded people as incapable of learning, needing constant supervision, and causing interaction strain on customers and coworkers (Phelps, 1965).

These employer attitudes reflect the general attitude that a handicap is the essential and salient characteristic of a potential employee. Actually there is little objective data to support any of these perceptions. Evidence from diverse sources shows that when selectively placed, handicapped workers are equal to or better than nonhandicapped workers on job performance, motivation, attendance, persistence, and safety (Texas Rehabilitation Commission, 1974). These facts, however, are not nearly as likely to change attitudes as will a positive employment experience with a qualified handicapped worker (Strauch, 1970; Anthony, 1972). Nevertheless, attitudinal barriers frequently result in overt or covert discrimination if an applicant's disability is known, even though such discrimination is prohibited by law (Section 504 of the Rehabilitation Act of 1973).

3. *Procedural Barriers.* Attitudinal barriers are often operationalized into restrictive procedures or arbitrary standards that inhibit employment of otherwise qualified people. Many times individuals are refused employment because the job description indicates that a certain educational certificate is required (i.e., high school diploma, college degree). Such practices are discriminatory when the possession of a certificate has not been demonstrated to be directly related to minimal job performance.

Some occupations are barred to people with disabilities based on set company policy even though a specific individual may possess the requisite job skills (Sterling, 1967; Jackson, 1974; Pirdell,

1958). Such set policies then become the real handicap, not the person's disability. When companies require physical examinations, the examining physician's report may be powerful in determining whether the applicant is suited for work with that organization. The difficulty with this procedure is that the physician is less likely to possess in-depth knowledge about the job tasks than about the physical characteristics of an individual. Thus, they may be excluding from employment people who would be able to perform all essential job functions.

Another procedural barrier is found in the employment process of large companies, when applicants must receive unanimous approval from several people in order to be hired whereas only one "no" will prevent hiring (Barshop, 1959). Even though a first-line supervisor may be receptive to hiring someone with a disability, the personnel office may screen the individual out or vice versa.

Entry into many occupations is dependent on union membership. Unions try to select into the entry-level positions individuals who will be able to progress upward through the skill level of the trade, which also functions as a procedural barrier to the employment of disabled people (President's Committee on Mental Retardation and Employment of the Handicapped, 1969). Consider an individual who possesses the necessary skills and interests to be a bricklayer's assistant but has little potential beyond that. The union requirement that this individual be capable of becoming a journeyman or master bricklayer excludes him or her from the entry-level occupation. These examples are cited to illustrate the types of barriers created by procedures. Procedural barriers are often more intractable to change than either attitudinal or physical barriers because they require the alteration of a system as opposed to a situational modification or individual change.

INTERVENTIONS

The two previous sections have described the world of work and explored how disabling conditions influence an individual's relationship to work. Knowledge of these factors, however, is not sufficient for the rehabilitation worker. Active interventions are required both in assisting clients to develop their employability and in modifying the world of work so that it can accommodate a wider range of variation in human function. This section will discuss intervention strategies involved in assisting people to enter or reenter the world of work.

Understanding and Adapting the World of Work

In order to effectively implement selective placement, the rehabilitation worker (or job seeker) must know about the labor market and how to influence hiring practices. Labor market analysis is a process that helps understand and organize the complex of jobs in a given locale. The first step in this process is to get an overview of the total local labor market. A framework for viewing the system should be chosen, such as the *Dictionary of Occupational Titles*. The United States Department of Labor, the U. S. Office of Employment, and their state and local offices will have general information available, such as number of people working in various occupations covered by unemployment insurance, numbers of job vacancies by occupation on monthly and yearly summaries, most-sought occupations, and wage levels. Local Chambers of Commerce can also be helpful sources of information on local businesses as can the yellow pages of the telephone directory and local newspapers. Manufacturers' indexes and construction permits awarded will give a notion of expansions in the employment market. Once this general information is collected it should be organized into the framework previously selected. Priorities for further investigation can be set (i.e., visiting all the large employers, making contact with a wide variety of employers, or focusing on a specific industry or job). One satisfactory way to obtain more detailed information is through the plant survey that allows the rehabilitation worker to get to know the employer, understand the employment procedures, and know more specifically the range of jobs and their skill requirements. Job analysis is the process of identifying the relevant functions and requirements of any given job. Models of job analysis range from the most minute examination of function to a more broadly based examination. Since it is a virtual impossibility for any one individual to know the details of all jobs in a community, each rehabilitation worker must decide if it is more important that he or she know some specific jobs in depth or have a general understanding of a wide range of jobs. Table 7-3 presents an outline for a general job analysis. In-depth understanding of the employment market takes time and should be approached through an organized system of contacts based on priorities of size, potential sales, and need.

Even when the most complete job survey is accomplished and the rehabilitation worker has an in-depth understanding of his clients' strengths and weaknesses, there are circumstances in which selective placement necessitates the adaptation of the employment market. Some employment barriers to a certain disability may be

Table 7–3 Job Analysis

Section	General	Example—Janitor
Functional purpose	Brief paragraph describing overall objective of job.	Perform semiskilled routine work to clean and care for buildings and premises.
Major tasks	List of major tasks that taken together equals whole job.	1. Sweeping 2. Mopping 3. Stripping and waxing 4. Dusting 5. Cleaning windows 6. Collecting and taking out garbage 7. Cleaning plumbing equipment 8. Replenishing supplies 9. Reports repair needs to supervisor
Job setting	1. Description of physical environment 2. List of equipment and machines present and used 3. What kinds of people are present and to what extent must they be dealt with	1. Generally employed in building or institution 2. Mostly indoor work with minor outside tasks 3. Day and/or night work 4. May work around hazardous machinery (furnaces, heaters, and other machines in area to be cleaned) 5. Uses vacuum cleaner or buffer 6. May have to climb ladders, scaffolding, or stairs 7. May work in crowded buildings, often as part of work crew
Worker qualifications	1. Physical requirements 2. Psychological requirements 3. Requisite skills and/or training	1. Sufficient strength and stamina to perform all the required tasks 2. Good foot, hand, eye coordination 3. Good natural balance for climbing 4. Ability to understand and follow oral and written instructions

removed by job modification. This may come in the form of restructuring the job tasks or modification of the work environment. A job may be restructured to allow a number of workers to perform relatively less complex jobs, that is, a group of workers assemble typewriter keyboards in five separate stages as opposed to each assembling the keyboards individually. Another method of job restructuring is to revise certain job tasks or to alter the sequence of job tasks. An example of the former would be where a sightless clerical worker would require brailled outlines for necessary business forms. The latter is illustrated by changing from a continuous to a batch operation when a mobility impaired worker is involved. The environment where the work is performed may also have to be modified, which may take the form of removing any of the architectural barriers to employment discussed in a previous section.

One caution about the use of occupational information—since a lag exists between writing, publishing, and distribution, by the time the information is available it is already out of date. Information published in 1978 was probably gathered in 1975 and 1976. Hands-on information of the local job market is therefore the most reliable type of information. This practical understanding provides the basis for good selective placement decisions and the knowledge necessary to initiate appropriate job modifications.

There will be times when even thorough knowledge of a labor market will not be enough to find appropriate placements for clients. New employment opportunities will have to be expanded or opened. The rehabilitation worker attempting to influence employer receptivity to hiring people with disabilities will find salesmanship a helpful process (Table 7-4). The modern notion of salesmanship is to identify customer needs and to match your product with those needs (Thompson, 1966). Labor market analysis, job analysis, and plant surveys all are tools used to discover employer needs. Presentations to employers should be based on a pragmatic assessment of how a specific client or group of clients can perform in specific capacities in the employer's organization. Because of the various negative employer perceptions previously presented, most employers will express some concern (objection) about employment of people experiencing certain handicaps. Rather than being negatively affected by such statements, the rehabilitation advocate must view these objections as salesmen do—a chance to provide more information about the product. Most of these employer objections deserve an answer and, if they cannot be answered, the employer is probably justified in not hiring your client. Some of the most common employer beliefs and corresponding rehabilitation rebuttals follow.

Table 7–4 Process of Salesmanship

Stage	Action
Preapproach	Knowledge of product Knowledge of employer's needs
Approach	Setting appointment Selling self Presentation of how product fits employer's needs
Answering Objections	Responding to employer's concerns Providing information
Closing	Getting a commitment or Leaving an opening for future contacts
Follow-up	Contacting on regular basis by phone, visit, or letter

My insurance rates will rise if I hire a disabled person.

Workmen's compensation rates are in fact based on the relative hazards in the work involved and on the company's accident experience and not on physical characteristics of employees (Williams, 1964; Sinnick, 1968). As far as group insurance is concerned, insurance companies do not dictate hiring practices to employers and insurance companies in general have very little actuarial data as to the effect of preexisting conditions on insurance rates (Loban, 1972).

I can't afford to hire disabled people.

This concern for cost is based on fear of lower productivity, more sick leave, and higher accident rates as a result of hiring disabled workers. These fears receive little objective support (Wecksler, 1960; Schlesinger, 1966; President's Committee on Employment of the Handicapped, 1968, 1970; Ware, 1958) as most studies show people with disabilities have equal or higher performance ratings in these areas compared to nondisabled people in the same company.

My other workers (or customers) wouldn't react well to the disabled worker.

This statement is based on a stereotype of a broad group labeled "disabled." Close contact between persons with and without disabling conditions is the best way to overcome this stereotype (Strauch, 1970; Anthony, 1972). Perhaps the employer would consider a trial placement. This employer needs education about specific clients and the varying effects of different disabilities.

Disabled people can't perform this type of work.

The obvious response is to provide information about how a specific client could perform a specific job in the employer's organization. Educating the employer about the effects of differing disabilities is again indicated. Examples of disabled people working successfully can create an interest and then, if possible, give the employer a chance to talk to another employer who is currently employing disabled people. A businessman is more likely to be more credible to a colleague than an advocate.

We don't believe in making special considerations for some workers and not others.

The concerns here are that special training or supervision will be required, that the "disabled" will not be as adaptable to job changes as their peers, and that other special considerations will have to be made. The concept of selective placement implies that the individual is competitive within a work environment in comparison to other workers. If this is the case then the best response to the above concern is that no special considerations are required.

To influence employers and answer such objections specific details are required both about the client and about the employer's job. This in-depth information can only be attained and maintained through a continuous systematic interaction with the world of work as well as the world of the client.

Preparing for Work

To help a client prepare for the world of work the counselor should develop an insight into the client; establish short- and long-range goals; and identify and implement a plan to remove the discrepancy between current client functional level and the levels necessary for goal achievement. The client is the focus of this process, since the client must ultimately make the decisions and perform the actions.

Essentially the desired outcome is selective placement with the client's abilities and interests matched to the best available job. To effectively facilitate good job-person matching a systematic approach is suggested (Daniels & Dollar, 1978). Each client must be assessed individually and the assessment must be geared to identifiable rehabilitation goals and not to simply labeling the disability. Assessment should consider the environment of the client in addition to within-client variables. Observations, counseling sessions, informal tests, psychological test batteries, medical examinations, and specialist examinations may all yield useful information, but the most essential information is pragmatic. What can the client do? What does the client want to do? How much assistance does the client need? Information from this assessment can then be used to identify client goals and the discrepancy between current functioning and these goals. Next an action plan to remove the discrepancy is identified and implemented. Client progress toward established goals is continuously monitored and the plan periodically evaluated. If the plan is not working, a period of reassessment is required and the process is repeated.

This general process can be used to attain any type of goal. For example for the goal of work, client John Doe walks into a counselor's office requesting assistance to return to work.

The first step would be to get to know John Doe:

What work has he done in the past?

What is his disability?

What are his financial responsibilities?

What is he doing currently?

When does he want to return to work?

How does he feel about work?

How successful has he been at past jobs?

These questions are only a sample of the ones that must be answered in order to establish where he currently is and where he wants to go. Through conversation it is discovered that John had been a heavy construction equipment operator for the past twenty-five years. He has a large family to support, has less than a high school education, and has just been terminated from his social security payments. He also has recently recovered from a stroke resulting in left hemiparesis (weakness of the left side of the body). He considers it important that he return to work, but has little idea of what job he could perform adequately.

At the next step more specific information about John may be needed:

What limitations does his disability impose?

What work skills does he currently possess?

What are his interest areas?

What are his feelings toward and abilities for further training?

Interest, aptitude, and values tests; work samples; work simulations; on-the-job tryouts; and work evaluations may be utilized to help answer these questions. As a result of this process and interpretation of the results to John, he may be able to more clearly see his current abilities and future alternatives.

The third step would then be to explore alternative plans of action. Perhaps John has high interests and aptitudes in the mechanical area, but his physical limitation precludes his returning to his previous line of work. In addition, John is able to utilize his left hand somewhat in light mechanical work, he performs better while seated, and with practice his performance could become competitive. The jobs vertically related to John's old job are laborer and supervisor; however, both require physical abilities similar to those required in John's old job. In exploring horizontally related jobs we find that there are many positions involving operating/controlling of machines that can be done with one hand. These are primarily indoor jobs involving bench work. When we explain to John that with a period of on-the-job training he could almost immediately move into one of these factory machinist jobs, he balks at the idea. It seems that he does not like sitting in one place performing the same task repeatedly. Since we are not able to completely transfer his skills to another job, we begin to explore other alternatives. One alternative in which John was highly interested was a small engine repair course offered at a local trade school.

The fourth step involves establishing a mutually agreeable plan. In this case John decides to attend the repair course and then attempt to find employment doing small engine repair. John completes the course but reports from his instructor indicate his speed is still very slow. Consequently, John is unable to secure employment.

A reevaluation of the plan is now required. John is to the point where he needs income very soon, but still maintains his interest in small engine repair. A sheltered workshop in town takes donated items, and repairs and sells them. The counselor discusses with John the possibility of working there repairing small engines they receive. This will allow him time to improve his working speed, begin to receive some income, and continue working toward competitive employment.

This example demonstrates the relevance of a systematic approach to job preparation. The alternatives and content were specific to John Doe's case, but the process was general. The information gathered and specific plans made will vary with each individual. With John Doe the counselor dealt with a vocationally mature individual with an adventitious disability. The counselor's intervention may have been different had the person been younger, had a poor work history, had a disability with varying effects, or had more severe impairments, but the counselor would still have followed the same general steps. The type of intervention must vary according to client characteristics, but the goal is always to improve the client's level of independent functioning. Toward this end rehabilitation workers must provide all assistance that is required but never more than is necessary.

SUMMARY

In this chapter, the world of work, disabling conditions, and the effects of disability on an individual's relationship with the world of work have been discussed. The employment goal for clients of vocational rehabilitation requires that professionals in the field develop competencies to facilitate entry of their clients into the world of work. Requisite knowledge includes employment market information and detailed understanding of disabling conditions and their effects on the individual. Skills are required to modify the employment market and to prepare the client to enter employment. A primary emphasis of this chapter has been on viewing clients and jobs individually. The rehabilitation worker is in the position of synthesizing the myriad of diverse facts about the local world of work and the specific client into a set of alternatives from which the client must choose. This is a heavy responsibility and a difficult challenge. The extent to which this challenge is met determines the success of a specific rehabilitation effort and cumulatively of vocational rehabilitation in general. This challenge is most likely to be met by those counselors who have the necessary information and skills.

REFERENCES

Anthony, W. Societal rehabilitation: Changing society's attitudes toward the physically and mentally disabled. *Rehabilitation Psychology,* 1972, *19,* 117–126.

Barsch, R. *Cerebral palsy work classification and evaluation project.* Milwaukee, Wis.: United Cerebral Palsy of Milwaukee, Inc., 1962.

Barshop, I. Policy and practice in hiring impaired workers. *Journal of Rehabilitation,* 1959, November-December, 23–25.

Baxt, R. *Survey of employers' practices and policies in the hiring of physically impaired workers.* New York: Federation Employment and Guidance Service, 1959.

Berkowitz, M., Johnson, W., & Murphy, E. *Public policy towards disability.* New York: Praeger, 1976.

Bolles, R. *What color is your parachute?* Berkeley, Calif.: Ten Speed Press, 1978.

Carlson, R., Dawis, R., England, G., & Lofquist, L. *The measurement of employment satisfactoriness.* Minnesota Studies in Vocational Rehabilitation, Minneapolis: University of Minnesota, 1963.

Daniels, J., & Dollar, S. Career planning model. Unpublished manuscript. Education Building 306, University of Texas, Austin, 1978.

Dembo, T., Diller, L., Gordon, W., Levitan, G., & Sherr, R. A view of rehabilitation psychology. *American Psychologist,* 1973, *28,* 719–722.

Felton, J. *Blocks to the employment of the paraplegic.* Los Angeles: University of California, School of Public Health, 1962.

Flanagan, J., Tiedeman, D., Willis, M., & McLaughlin, D. *The career data book.* Palo Alto, Calif.: American Institutes for Research, 1973.

Getzel, J., & Guba, E. Social behavior and the administrative process. *The School Review,* 1957, *65,* 423–441.

Ginzberg, E., Ginzberg, S., Axlerad, S., & Herma, J. *Occupational choice.* New York: Columbia University Press, 1951.

Haber, L. Disabling effects of chronic disease and impairment. *Journal of Chronic Diseases,* 1973, *26,* 135–142.

Hollander, J. Development of a realistic vocational choice. *Journal of Counseling Psychology,* 1967, *14,* 314–318.

Hopke, W. (Ed.). *Encyclopedia of careers and vocational guidance.* Garden City, N.Y.: Doubleday, 1967.

Jackson, D. More jobs for the deaf. *Social and Rehabilitation Record*, 1974, *1*, 7–10.

Jeffrey, D. A living environment for the physically disabled. *Rehabilitation Literature*, 1973, *34*, 98–103.

Landy, D., & Griffith, W. Placement of the emotionally handicapped ... Employer willingness and counselor practice. *Journal of Rehabilitation*, 1958, *24*, 17–18.

Levitan, S., & Taggert, R. *Jobs for the disabled*. Baltimore: John Hopkins Press, 1977.

Loban, L. *Group insurance and the handicapped*. Santa Barbara: Governor's Committee on Employment of the Handicapped, 1972.

McGregor, D. *The human side of enterprise*. New York: McGraw-Hill, 1962.

Neff, J. *The meaning of work*. New York: New York University Press, 1968.

Phelps, W. Attitudes related to the employment of the mentally retarded. *American Journal of Mental Deficiency*, 1965, *69*, 575–585.

Pirdell, H. Employer attitudes about psychiatric applicants. *Journal of Rehabilitation*, 1958, *24*, 5–7.

President's Committee on Employment of the Handicapped. *Guide to job placement of the mentally retarded*. Washington, D.C.: U.S. Government Printing Office, 1969.

President's Committee on Employment of the Handicapped. *Epileptics man the machines*. Washington, D.C.: U.S. Government Printing Office, 1970.

President's Committee on Mental Retardation and Employment of the Handicapped. *These, too, must be equal*. Washington, D.C.: U.S. Government Printing Office, 1969.

Rusk, A. *Specialized placement of quadriplegics and other severely disabled*. New York: New York University Medical Center, 1963.

Schlesinger, L. Epilepsy: Unemployment and rehabilitation. *Rehabilitation Literature*, 1966, *27*, 98–105.

Shartle, C. Occupational analysis, worker characteristics, and occupational classification systems. In H. Borow (Ed.), *Man in a world of work*. Boston: Houghton Mifflin, 1964.

Sinnick, D. Educating the community. *Journal of Rehabilitation*, 1968, *34*, 25–27.

Sterling, T. *Training of the blind for professional computer work*. Cincinnati: University of Cincinnati College of Medicine, 1967.

Strauch, J. Social contact as a variable in the expressed attitudes of normal adolescents towards EMR. *Exceptional Children,* 1970, *36,* 495–500.

Super, D. *The psychology of careers.* New York: Harper, 1957.

Texas Rehabilitation Commission. *Government supervisors training handbook on the handicapped.* Austin, Tex.: Texas Rehabilitation Commission, 1974.

Thompson, J. *Selling: A behavioral science approach.* New York: McGraw-Hill, 1966.

Torre, M., & Askenasy, A. *Attitudes toward mental illness: A cross-cultural study* (Part II). New York: World Federation for Mental Health, 1963.

U.S. Department of Labor. *Employment and earnings: United States 1909–72.* Bulletin 1312–9. Washington, D.C.: Bureau of Labor Statistics, 1974.

U.S. Department of Labor. *Occupational outlook handbook, 1976–1977 Edition.* Bulletin 1875, Washington, D.C.: U.S. Government Printing Office, 1976.

U.S. Department of Labor. *Dictionary of occupational titles* (4th ed.). Washington: U.S. Employment Service, 1977.

Vuris, M. Attitudes toward disabled persons as function of cognitive versus emotional appeals to hire the handicapped. Unpublished Master's Thesis, University of Texas, 1970.

Ware, E. *Some social factors in job placement and community life of the handicapped.* Garden City, N.Y.: Adelphi College, 1958.

Waters, G., Geham, J., & Barrette, R. *Job development project.* New York: HEW-SRS, 1970.

Wecksler, A. Handicapped employees—Real worker assets. *Mill and Factory,* 1960, *67,* 85–96.

Williams, J. Some of the most commonly held objections by management to employment of the handicapped. Unpublished speech before the Rehabilitation Counselor Training Program at Oklahoma State University. Stillwater, Okla.: Rehabilitation Clearing House, 1964.

Wright, B. *Physical disability—A psychological approach.* New York: Harper and Row, 1960.

Zawada, A. A report from the study group on rehabilitation of the severely disabled. Eleventh Institute on Rehabilitation Services, Research and Training Center, West Virginia, 1973.

Part III

Rehabilitation Counseling Practice—Delivering Services to People with Handicaps

The vocational rehabilitation process generally follows the same pattern regardless of the rehabilitation agency. Nevertheless, considerable variation in elements of the pattern occurs from rehabilitation client to client and from one agency setting to another. The first step usually involves casefinding and the initial interview. The counselor must actively seek potential clients from a variety of agencies and professional people, as well as accepting self-referrals. The initial interview provides the opportunity for the counselor to establish a counseling relationship; seek medical, psychological, vocational, and educational information from the client; and provide information to the client about agency policies and services.

The second step includes the evaluation of rehabilitation potential and eligibility determination. Evaluation discerns the extent of the disability as well as the degree of functional handicap. The disability is evaluated primarily through medical, and in some cases by psychological examinations. The degree of handicap may also be determined by these exams, but frequently further study is needed, for example, vocational evaluation. Vocational evaluation may involve job samples, job tryouts, on-the-job assessment, and job simulations. In-depth evaluation leads to the decision of whether the client can benefit from available services (eligibility determination) and also provides data upon which the client and counselor can base a plan of services to reach the rehabilitation goal. The Individually Written Rehabilitation Plan (IWRP) utilized in state rehabilitation agencies is a contract that indicates that the counselor and the rehabilitation agency agree to provide specified rehabilitation services to the rehabilitation client who in turn agrees in good faith to pursue a specified vocational goal or objective. The IWRP represents a culmination of evaluative efforts by specifying those rehabilitation services deemed beneficial and necessary for the client to achieve his or her rehabilitation goal. State rehabilitation agencies may provide one or more of the following services:

1. Counseling and guidance;
2. Medical, psychological, and evaluation;
3. Physical and mental restoration services;
4. Prevocational evaluation and training;
5. Vocational and other training services;
6. Maintenance expense allowances;
7. Transportation;
8. Interpreter services for the deaf;

9. Reader services and orientation and mobility services for the blind;
10. Prostheses and other technological aids and devices;
11. Work adjustment and placement counseling;
12. Job placement services;
13. Occupational licenses, tools, equipment, etc.;
14. Other goods and services that will benefit the client in achieving employability (McGowan & Porter, 1967).

Third, *counseling,* the core of rehabilitation, is provided throughout the process, but may intensify following the evaluation phase. Since handicapping conditions and resulting psychosocial pressures may lead to emotional difficulties, clients may need personal adjustment counseling. However, even with well-adjusted clients the degree of success of the rehabilitation enterprise frequently rests on the client-counselor relationship. Knowledge and experience with theories and approaches to counseling comprise the core professional competency required of rehabilitation counselors.

In addition to relationship skills, counselors must possess skills and knowledge to foster client career development, a fourth step. For too long rehabilitation agencies have emphasized job placement as the focused goal of rehabilitation. Ideally, though, effective job placement must occur within the broader context of long term client career and life skills development. Experienced counselors will attest to the problems encountered when short-sighted job placement is implemented without concern for a client's broader career and life goals.

A fifth aspect that spans the total process and will determine, to a large extent, the outcome of client-counselor efforts is the counselor's skills in caseload management and time utilization. Counselors ineffective in managing their work will be ineffective in helping clients regardless of the degree of other skills they may possess. Management of time, services, paperwork, and case processing as well as decision-making strategies are essentials of rehabilitation counseling that have been largely ignored by counselors and educators. This oversight has occurred in spite of the finding that rehabilitation counselors spend from 30 to 36 percent of their working hours in caseload management and related administrative tasks such as reporting, recording, and clerical duties, as well as coordinating clients' plans of service. In contrast counselors spend 25 to 34 percent of their time in counseling with clients; and they spend no more than 15 percent of their time in any other task (Fraser & Clowers,

1978; Miller, Muthard, & Barillas, 1965; Muthard & Salomone, 1969; Office of Vocational Rehabilitation, 1956). This aspect of the process certainly deserves much greater attention than it has received (Henke, Connolly, & Cox, 1975).

The final step is follow-up and case closure or termination. This step signifies that rehabilitation services have been rendered and that the client has obtained maximum benefit from them. A client's return to competitive employment has been the most highly prized culmination of rehabilitation, since it reflects the client's attainment of a high degree of economic, psychological, and physical independence. Other outcomes, however, are being recognized as equally desirable, for instance, the client's return to a productive, satisfying, and independent life in the sheltered workshop, home, or other noncompetitive settings. Counselors and their employing agencies are more and more coming to respect and highly regard the latter outcome. This attitude exemplifies the truly humanitarian foundation of the rehabilitation movement. In the remaining chapters, four aspects of the rehabilitation process of paramount importance are presented in detail. Chapter 8 considers the topic of evaluation of rehabilitation potential and includes discussions of state agency eligibility determination and IWRP development. Chapter 9 presents the theoretical bases for personal adjustment counseling. Major counseling theories are reviewed to provide a knowledge base upon which the counselor may later wish to develop practical skills. Chapter 10 discusses job placement within the context of career development, and Chapter 11 presents both theoretical and practical information for managing the delivery of rehabilitation services.

REFERENCES

Fraser, R., & Clowers, M. Rehabilitation counselor functions: Perceptions of time spent and complexity. *Journal of Applied Rehabilitation Counseling*, 1978, 9, 31–35.

Henke, R., Connolly, S., & Cox, J. Caseload management: The key to effectiveness. *Journal of Applied Rehabilitation Counseling*, 1975, 6, 217–227.

McGowan, J., & Porter, T. *An introduction to the vocational rehabilitation process*. Washington, D.C.: U.S. Government Printing Office, 1967.

Miller, R., Muthard, J., & Barillas, M. A time study of vocational rehabilitation counselors. *Rehabilitation Counseling Bulletin,* 1965, *9,* 53–60.

Muthard, J., & Salomone, P. The role and function of rehabilitation counselors. *Rehabilitation Counseling Bulletin,* 1969, *13,* 1–53.

Office of Vocational Rehabilitation, HEW. Utilization of counselor's services in state V.R. agencies. Washington, D.C.: Ninth Annual Workshop on Guidance, Training and Placement, Report of the Proceedings, 1956.

Chapter 8

Evaluation of Rehabilitation Potential

Jason W. Andrew

INTRODUCTION

Every day, in the United States, thousands of decisions are being made concerning the rehabilitation potential of people with disabilities for rehabilitation services. Based on sheer volume alone, one would assume that the techniques and procedures for evaluating rehabilitation potential must be well developed. This is not the case. For the most part, rehabilitation counselors are faced with a difficult and complex task for which they are poorly prepared in terms of both training and, even more importantly, resources.

Perhaps the best way to understand the complexities surrounding the process of evaluating rehabilitation potential is to consider the results of attempts to define this process for people with a specific disability. One such attempt is reported in the monograph, *Assessment of Vocational Potential of Sickle Cell Anemics* (Allesberry, 1977). This monograph reports an intensive effort to establish guidelines that would be of assistance to rehabilitation professionals in their attempts at rehabilitating people with sickle cell anemia. To understand the dimensions of the problem of establishing guidelines for serving this population, the size of this population must be compared with the size of other disability groups. In the state of Pennsylvania, where the research was conducted, there are more than one million black people. It is estimated that within the black population, 2,000 people with sickle cell anemia could be identified and of this number, 1,113 might be individuals with vocational rehabilitation potential. Comparing this number with the thousands of mentally ill or mentally retarded people in Pennsylvania, for example, clearly shows that the research population was extremely small. With such small numbers, it would seem reasonable to expect that the research would lead to a clearly defined process for assessing the vocational potential of people with sickle cell anemia. Such was not the case.

A brief quote from the project summary reflects the difficulty in establishing guidelines for assessing vocational potential within the confines of this single disability group (Allesberry, 1977, p. 59).

> The experiences of the project to assess the vocational potential of sickle cell anemics was not a simple task of a single dimension. Rather, the task was multi-dimensional involving educational, social, vocational, medical, physical and psychological factors. The range within variables which were obtained to reflect the dimensions listed above reveal that there was no single description of the sickle cell anemic; and thus, there was no one pattern of services nor needs profile for this disability group.

This study is a microcosm of the problem facing rehabilitation counselors as they attempt to evaluate rehabilitation potential. Our inability to lay out a roadmap for carrying out this process with a specific disability group suggests the scope of the problem when we further compound the situation by expanding the disability dimension.

The complexities involved in the evaluation of rehabilitation potential are beyond the ability of any single individual to comprehend. The combinations of interactions between the multiple variables that could influence rehabilitation potential are almost without number. It is not surprising that in many state agencies the "hit rate" for predicting rehabilitation success is little better than what could be achieved by chance. It is against this austere picture of the situation confronting the rehabilitation counselor that the description of the process of evaluating rehabilitation potential begins.

PURPOSES FOR CONDUCTING THE EVALUATION OF REHABILITATION POTENTIAL

From the standpoint of the disabled applicant for state rehabilitation agency services, the most critical reason for conducting an evaluation of rehabilitation potential is to determine eligibility. There are two basic criteria for establishing eligibility:

1. The presence of a physical or mental disability that for the individual constitutes or results in a substantial handicap to employment; and
2. A reasonable expectation that vocational rehabilitation services may benefit the individual in terms of employability. (National Archives, 1975, p. 54706)

The second criterion, having to do with a reasonable expectation, is dependent upon the outcome of the evaluation of rehabilitation potential for its resolution.

The evaluation of rehabilitation potential is generally considered to be made up of the preliminary diagnostic study and the thorough diagnostic study. In practice, for most applicants, this process is continuous and no clear separation exists or is perceived by the applicant.

Preliminary Diagnostic Study

In the preliminary diagnostic study, the counselor first determines the presence of a physical or mental disability that is resulting in a substantial handicap to employment. Establishing the presence of the disability is relatively straightforward. This generally involves only an examination, or series of examinations, by the appropriate specialists. A psychological examination, for example, may establish the presence of mental retardation; or a general medical examination may be the basis for confirming a diabetic condition or hearing loss.

Determining that the disability results in a substantial handicap to employment is, however, much more complicated. At this point counselors are going beyond the simple presence or absence of a malfunction in a body system, and must begin to deal with the interaction of these body systems with such factors as age, sex, education, prior vocational training, prior work experience, attitudes, and motivation.

The classic example of where a disability *may* not result in a vocational handicap is the bookkeeper who has a stable employment history with a firm where the requirements of the job call for little moving about, and who suffers the loss of a leg in an auto accident. In the majority of such situations, the bookkeeper could return to his or her previous job as soon as the medical condition was stable. Contrast the preceding example with exactly the same loss of a leg when the individual is a 50-year-old steelworker with a tenth grade education. Suddenly, the lost limb has a tremendous vocational implication. It is because of the complex interaction of sociological, vocational, and other factors that rehabilitation counselor training programs must cut across disciplinary lines in the coursework contained in their curricula.

When it has been determined that the applicant does have a disability that constitutes a substantial handicap to employment, the counselor is then faced with the task of determining whether or not there is a reasonable expectation that vocational rehabilitation services will benefit the individual in terms of employment. Remember that throughout the preliminary diagnostic study, the primary emphasis is placed upon the determination of the applicant's potential for achieving a vocational goal.

Extended Evaluation

In many instances, conditions may be present that make it virtually impossible for the state agency rehabilitation counselor to resolve the question of "reasonable expectation" at a given point in time. For example, the applicant may have only recently suffered traumatic injury that clearly resulted in a disability that constitutes a substantial handicap to employment. In instances of this type, it may be too early to determine the amount of functioning that will return or that can be induced through physical restoration procedures. Without a fairly accurate estimate of the applicant's ultimate functioning level, it might appear that there is no reasonable expectation that the individual will benefit from vocational rehabilitation services, in terms of employability.

Provision has been made in the rehabilitation program for situations such as those already cited. The counselor is allowed up to eighteen months in which to make an extended evaluation of a client's rehabilitation potential. Two fairly common situations where extended evaluations are employed involve severely retarded adolescents, and recently hospitalized mental patients. In the first situation, the counselor may be assessing the effect of increasing maturity on employment potential. With a recently hospitalized mental patient, extended evaluation may allow a period of time in which the effects of decreased medication and increased social interaction can be observed.

The two criteria necessary for making use of a period of extended evaluation are (1) the presence of a physical or mental disability that constitutes a substantial handicap to employment and,

(2) an inability on the part of the counselor to make a determination that vocational rehabilitation services might benefit the applicant in terms of employability, unless there is a period of extended evaluation to determine the presence of rehabilitation potential.

For all practical purposes, any vocational rehabilitation service that is considered to be necessary to aid in the determination of rehabilitation potential may be provided during the period of extended evaluation. The services of rehabilitation facilities, both medical and vocational, are frequently used during extended evaluations. Common among the services used in this process and purchased from rehabilitation facilities are physical restoration and adjustment services.

Periodic review is required when extended evaluation is used. The applicant's progress should be assessed as frequently as necessary, but must be assessed at least once in every ninety-day period during the extended evaluation. This assessment should include periodic reports from the providers of services so that the applicant's progress can be determined and so that the rehabilitation counselor can assess whether or not a determination of eligibility can be made at that time.

Only a single period of extended evaluation is allowed during the time that a case is open. If the case is reopened at a later date an additional period of extended evaluation may be used, provided that the applicant meets the previously stated criteria for the use of extended evaluation. Extended evaluations must terminate in an eligibility decision. This decision is based on the counselor's determination that there is, or is not, a reasonable expectation that the provision of rehabilitation services will lead to employability.

Thorough Diagnostic Study

The purpose of the thorough diagnostic study is to determine and delineate the nature and scope of services needed by the applicant in order for that individual to reach the vocational goal. This study will consist of a comprehensive evaluation of the relevant information, including medical, psychological, vocational, educational, and other information that has a bearing on the applicant's handicap to employment and rehabilitation needs. As stated in the rules and regulations of the Rehabilitation Act of 1975 (National Archives, 1975), the thorough diagnostic study will include

in all cases to the degree needed, an appraisal of the individual's personality, intelligence level, educational achievements, work experience, personal, vocational and social adjustment, employment opportunities, and other pertinent data helpful in determining the nature and scope of services needed. (p. 54707)

It is further stated that the thorough diagnostic study will include

as appropriate for each individual, an appraisal of the individual's pattern of work behavior, feasibility to acquire occupational skill and his capacity for successful job performance, including the utilization of work, simulated or real, to assess the individual's capabilities to perform adequately in a work environment. (p. 54707)

In addition to the areas mentioned in the 1975 Act, the need to evaluate life skills (often called survival skills) is reinforced by the independent living sections of the 1978 Act. Life skills include such areas as home maintenance (e.g., cooking, cleaning, shopping, child care), finances, housing, family, and activities of daily living.

Given the preceding, it is easy to see why there can be no clear separation among the processes involved in determining if the disability is a handicap to employment, determining if there is a reasonable expectation that rehabilitation services will lead to employability, and determining the service needs of the disabled applicant. As the state agency counselor thinks about the ways in which the disability constitutes a handicap to employment, it is only logical that the counselor will also be thinking about the services that could be provided that would ameliorate the effects of the disability. Entering into the thought process must also be a consideration of the effects that the provision of specific services will have upon the question of a reasonable expectation that employment will be achieved.

Impacting upon applicants for state rehabilitation agency services is a special provision contained in the rules and regulations associated with the Rehabilitation Act of 1975. This provision is contained in the section on evaluation of rehabilitation potential, and has to do with the provision of specified examinations when certain disabilities are present and the specifying of qualifications for people providing specific diagnostic services. For example, if the applicant is blind, a hearing evaluation is mandated. This is, of course, simply a preventative measure that reflects the fact that people who are blind are increasingly dependent upon their ability to hear. Consequently, the prevention and/or early detection and remediation of hearing loss constitute an extremely valuable service to the blind individual.

Before proceeding, a word of caution would seem to be in order. Rapid change is taking place on at least two fronts that have dramatic impact upon the provision of rehabilitation services to disabled people. Both the field of rehabilitation engineering, as reflected through devicing and instrumentation, and the field of medical science are advancing at rates that make it virtually impossible for the rehabilitation practitioner to stay current with the state of the art. This condition may impact upon the disabled applicant for services from the standpoint that the application may be denied on the basis of a lack of knowledge of the changing prognosis for a specific type of disability.

The dramatic change in life expectancy for people with certain types of cancers would be an excellent example of where an eligibility decision may be made on the basis of antiquated prognostic information. Equally devastating to the disabled person being provided rehabilitation services is the situation in which the counselor is not aware of devicing or instrumentation that would be of assistance in overcoming the handicapping effects of a particular disabling condition. The entire field of rehabilitation must share with the counselor the responsibility for seeing to it that new knowledge and innovation are disseminated to the farthest reaches of the service delivery system.

Although the eligibility determination represents the first critical use to which the evaluation of rehabilitation potential is put, its use in the planning process is equally critical. Both the likelihood of success and the degree of success in the rehabilitation process are heavily dependent upon how well the evaluation of rehabilitation potential is carried out. Mistakes made in the evaluation of rehabilitation potential will be reflected in service delays, frequent plan modifications, and high failure rates.

Individualized Written Rehabilitation Program and Placement Plan

Before services can be provided to an eligible handicapped individual, or an individual being provided extended evaluation services by a state rehabilitation agency, an Individualized Written Rehabilitation Program must be developed. This document is the plan that controls the provision of rehabilitation services throughout the entire rehabilitation process. Contained within the plan are such things as the vocational goal, services needed to achieve that goal, the terms and conditions under which these services will be provided, a procedure and schedule for assessing progress toward achieving the goal or intermediate objectives, and the disabled individual's views concerning the goal and services being provided. Decisions reflected in the original plan and any subsequent revisions of the plan must be made with the full participation of the handicapped individual.

Ideally, when the Individualized Written Rehabilitation Program is developed at the completion of the thorough diagnostic study, it would be a comprehensive program. It has been found, however, that the development of a separate placement plan increases the chance of a successful rehabilitation (Zadny & James, 1978). This finding implies that in addition to the normal sequence of activities that includes looking at the handicap to employment, providing services to overcome the handicap, and reducing the disabled person's marginality in the employment market through the provision of special skills, counselors must also examine placement-related dimensions. The dimensions include the individual's job seeking/job search skills, on-the-job behaviors, and other critical employment coupled behaviors (Krantz, 1971).

In each of these areas, services may be required to prepare the individual not only to meet the technical requirements of the job, but also to be able to search out potential job sites, carry out activities necessary for making application and being selected, and exhibit behaviors on the job that will contribute to job retention. The full purpose of the evaluation of rehabilitation potential must then include both the determination of eligibility and the development of comprehensive plans that will reduce the effects of the disability, prepare the disabled individual for employment, and assure that the individual will be able to find and retain employment.

RESOURCES AVAILABLE TO THE COUNSELOR FOR CONDUCTING THE EVALUATION OF REHABILITATION POTENTIAL

There are a number of resources available to the rehabilitation counselor that will be of assistance in the process of evaluating rehabilitation potential. For the most part, these resources fall in the category of other professional disciplines and rehabilitation speciality areas that may be called upon to carry out diagnostic procedures or to provide specific forms of treatment. Some of these resources for

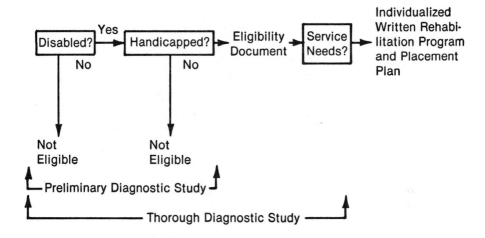

Figure 8–1 The Diagnostic Process

the evaluation of rehabilitation potential will only be touched upon while others will be given more intensive coverage.

Medical and Psychological Resources

Medical/psychological resources represent one category that will only be given limited coverage. Generally, medical and psychological resources are used for the purposes of establishing the presence of disabling conditions. A commonly occurring problem with medical/psychological resources is that they provide a label for the disabling condition, but do not provide the description of limitations of particular interest to the rehabilitation counselor. The best solution to this problem involves the development of an open channel of communication between the medical/psychological resource and the rehabilitation counselor, in view of the fact that the resource person carried out the examination and thereby possesses firsthand knowledge of the existence of limitations and the most likely prognosis.

Federal regulations and guidelines associated with the rehabilitation program, and state laws, which vary from state to state, influence the use of medical and psychological specialists. The federal regulations, for example, specify that in the case of mental or emotional disorder, the examination must be obtained from "a physician skilled in the diagnosis and treatment of such disorders, or a psychologist licensed or certified in accordance with state laws and regulations" (National Archives, 1975, p. 54706). Guidelines from the federal government further delineate the use of specialists by stipulating such things as the conditions under which, for example, a chiropractor may be used to provide services reimbursable with federal funds. Finally, the states get into the act through their licensing and certification procedures. New counselors would be well advised to spend some time reviewing this topic in the context of the state in which they are employed.

A backup system is available to the rehabilitation counselor for ferreting out from the various medical/psychological reports, the existence of specific limitations. This backup system is in the form of medical consultation purchased by the agency and made available to the counselor. Although the medical consultant will not have personally examined the client, all of the records contained in the casefile are available and are used by the consultant to aid in identifying limitations and establishing prognoses. The disadvantage of never having personally examined the disabled individual is probably offset by a greater knowledge of the relationship between disabilities and employment.

The greatest challenge facing the rehabilitation counselor who uses medical/psychological reports is in the area of translating limitations into their corresponding vocational implications. For example, the distorted speech pattern associated with cerebral palsy would tend to rule out jobs where clear, rapid, oral communication is an integral part of the job. In most cases, however, the translation of the limitation imposed by the disability into its corresponding vocational implication, will not be so obvious. In these cases other vocational resources will be required if the counselor is to obtain a true picture of the vocational implications resulting from the disability. Of equal importance to the identification of limiting vocational implications, is the need to identify positive vocational implications resulting from such factors as skills, abilities, and knowledge possessed by the disabled individual.

Vocational Resources—Vocational Evaluation

Before counselors examine the vocational resources available they must consider the potential for discrimination inherent in the techniques that historically have been used to assess such things as interest, skills, and work behaviors. The Equal Employment Opportunity Act of 1972 specifically declared it unlawful for an employment agency to

> fail or refuse to refer to employment . . . any individual because of his race, color, religion, sex, or national origin, or to classify or refer for employment an individual on the basis of his race, color, religion, sex, or national origin. (Equal Employment Opportunity Commission, 1975)

As defined in the Act, the term "employment agency" very probably includes vocational rehabilitation counselors in their traditional roles, and certainly includes vocational rehabilitation counselors who engage in placement activities on behalf of their clients.

The crux of the problem, as it relates to the question of evaluation of rehabilitation potential, is that "tests" are being used as a basis for employment decisions when no evidence indicates that the tests are valid predictors of performance on the job. At the same time, evidence exists that the same tests yield lower "scores" for the classes of people protected by the Equal Employment Opportunity Act. To fully appreciate the scope of this issue the definition of the term test must be reviewed. According to the regulations:

> The term "test" is defined as any paper and pencil or performance measure used as a basis for any employment decision. . . . This definition includes, but is not restricted to, measures of general intelligence, mental ability and learning ability; specific intellectual abilities; mechanical, clerical and other aptitudes; dexterity and coordination; knowledge and proficiency; occupational and other interests; and attitudes, personality or temperament. The term "test" includes all formal, scored, quantified or standardized techniques of assessing job suitability including, in addition to the above, specific qualifying or disqualifying personal history or background requirements, specific educational or work history requirements, scored interviews, biographical information blanks, interviewers rating scales, scored application forms, etc. (Equal Employment Opportunity Commission, 1975)

In the remainder of this discussion the term test shall be used with this definition as the reference point.

This issue is relevant to the rehabilitation counselor for two reasons. First, many of the people served by the rehabilitation program are members of groups protected by the Act. The second reason for examining this issue is the critical one, however. The real value of the Equal Employment Opportunity Act lies in the fact that it has made the testing industry and those who have come to rely on the products of that industry, extremely aware of the questionable practices that have been followed for many years. This piece of legislation has forced a reexamination of how various testing instruments and pieces of information are used in employment-related decisions. Simply stated, counselors now clearly carry a responsibility to determine for themselves that information used in employment-related decisions has a demonstrated relationship to a person's subsequent ability to perform on the job.

Validity. The process of determining whether or not a test measures what it purports to measure, or what one may be using it to measure, is known as establishing the validity of the test. Validity, which is frequently expressed as a correlation coefficient, refers to the degree of relationship between two measures. Some measures are quite valid predictors of others. For example, high school grade point average is usually a valid predictor of college grade point average. On the other side of the coin, however, is the fact that college grade point average is a poor predictor of success on the job. Tests, for the most part, are more in the category of the second example (poor predictors of job success). For a concise and easily understood discussion of the problems associated with predicting what jobs a person will be successful at in the future, see Dunn, Korn, and Andrew (1976).

Establishing the validity of a test may appear to be a simple process, but in reality, it is complex, particularly when the test is being used in employment decisions. Under such circumstances it may be necessary to attempt to establish a link between the test results and employment, an event that may take place a number of years later, and then only after specific vocational preparation has been provided. The number of intervening events (e.g., the quality of the vocational preparation provided, a change in the handicapping effects of the disability, or changes in the labor market) that could influence whether or not a person became employed in an occupation as predicted by one or more tests, is astronomical.

The message for rehabilitation counselors and vocational evaluators would seem to be to use these tests as "screen-in" devices, rather than "screen-out" devices, which would recognize the lack of predictive validity for most tests and would help avoid ruling out an occupation that holds potential for providing a rewarding and satisfying career. Counselors and evaluators must share with the client the knowledge that the instruments of the trade leave much to be desired. A selection of an occupation, far from being a scientific process, is still very much an art. Success in this endeavor is probably equally dependent upon the skills and knowledge of the rehabilitation professional and the degree to which the client is a fully informed and active participant. Although the discrimination that takes place as a result of the use of an invalid instrument is unintentional, the effect remains the same for the person who is discriminated against.

The following brief review outlines some of the more valuable vocationally oriented resources available to rehabilitation professionals as aids in determining rehabilitation potential. This review simply calls attention to these resources and provides limited information on their potential value. Knowledge in far greater depth than provided here would be required before people could consider themselves qualified to make use of these resources.

Psychological Tests. Certainly psychological tests have the longest history of the various vocationally oriented resources available to aid in the evaluation process. Based on the early work of Binet in the area of intellectual ability, and progressing through the extensive development associated with the world wars, psychological testing became a powerful force in the area of personnel selection. During the 1960s and well into the 1970s, psychological testing represented the most widely used method of selection in industry. Paralleling the industrial use of psychological tests has been the tremendous growth in their use within educational settings. Much of the growth was, of course, attributable to the fact that psychological tests were quick, inexpensive to administer, objective, and reliable.

The decline of psychological testing began when serious questions were raised about the validity of this approach. When it became apparent that the ability to predict performance based on most psychological tests was quite low and the tests were not necessarily measuring what they were reported to be measuring, a major change in the pattern of using psychological tests began. This change received further reinforcement from the Equal Employment Opportunity Act of 1972, as previously mentioned.

There are a number of reasons for the validity problems associated with testing. Chief among these has to be the poor quality of the outcome measures used during the development of the test. These measurements frequently included such things as foreman's ratings and subjective ratings of quality or production. Because of the lack of reliability of such ratings of performance, it is difficult to develop a psychological test that adequately predicts such performance.

Testing ethics, or the lack of ethics, has also contributed to the decline in use of psychological tests for employment-related decisions. At one point, business became heavily involved in personality testing as a part of their selection process, particularly for positions in the higher echelons. Education appears to have fallen into this practice, resulting in charges that current educational administrators are defining the personality characteristics of people who wish to enter the field.

There are other problems associated with psychological testing. Included among these problems would be the vast difference in attention and concentration required during testing as opposed to what would be required on the typical job. The most significant problem, however, has to do with the testing environment in contrast to the work environment. The importance of providing an accurate environment as a part of the evaluation process will be discussed in more detail later, but it should be readily apparent that the usual sanitary testing environment, where sound is controlled and interruptions are eliminated, is far different from the typical work setting.

Perhaps the following brief summary can serve as a starting point for the counselor in determining the role psychological tests should play in the evaluation of rehabilitation potential. Scholastic ability tests such as those that measure reading ability can contribute important information needed in the vocational planning process. Aptitude tests have almost no value for predicting the performance of an individual unless that individual's performance is at the extremes of the range. Interest tests have problems in the area of social desirability and faking, but they can serve as a starting point in the process of determining a vocational goal, as long as the test results are not used in isolation. Psychological tests can play a minor role in the evaluation of rehabilitation potential, but they must be used with extreme caution.

Situational Assessment. Situational assessment is defined by the Vocational Evaluation and Work Adjustment Association (VEWAA) as "a clinical assessment method utilizing observational techniques in established or created environments" (VEWAA, 1978,

p. 10). This is the latest, most inclusive definition in a long string of definitions that have been identified by Dunn (1973). As he documents, the term has meant many things to many people. Some would limit situational assessment to assessing work personality (Neff, 1966; Roberts, 1969), while others would also include work behaviors along with work personality as areas that can be assessed (Sankowsky, 1969).

Situational assessment has also been seen as an approach that was confined to use in a simulated work environment found in a workshop setting. At other times situational assessment included real work and the types of assessments that can be done in real work settings. The VEWAA definition is preferred over all of those that came before it because this definition is inclusive enough to cover both simulated and real work, as well as sheltered and competitive work settings. Situational assessment has the most to offer the rehabilitation professional when interests, skills, and work behaviors are to be assessed because the approach includes the most valid methods of assessment including on-the-job evaluations and job tryouts.

The range of methods included within situational assessment is quite broad (see Figure 8-2). On the lower end of a validity continuum would be work samples. Although work samples may quite

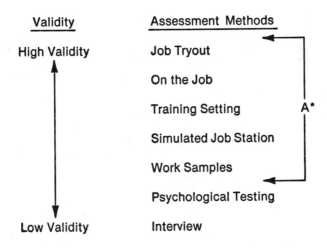

*These methods are included in the VEWAA definition of situational assessment (VEWAA, 1978).

Figure 8–2 Validity of Assessment Methods

accurately reflect the tasks involved in specific jobs, they are traditionally found in rehabilitation facilities where the environment is quite different from what an individual would encounter in an actual work setting. The atmosphere surrounding the work sample is more likely to be perceived as one of testing or learning/school, as opposed to the type of atmosphere that would normally be associated with the tasks being performed as a part of the work sample. This means that it is extremely difficult to assess an individual's reaction to such factors as the physical environment (e.g., temperature, noise levels, cleanliness of the work setting) and interactions with coworkers and supervisors, using work samples as they are generally found in rehabilitation settings.

However, work samples are an efficient method of providing an individual with exposure to a wide variety of jobs in a relatively brief period of time. In this way, work samples can be a major resource in an occupational exploration process. Work samples are also valuable as a first step in the assessment of skills and work behaviors.

Farther along on the validity continuum, a number of assessment methods that are more valid than work samples are encountered. These include the simulated job station, evaluation in a vocational training setting, on-the-job evaluation, and finally, the job tryout. Even without knowing the formal definitions for each of these methods of assessment, it should be readily apparent that factors in addition to the tasks required on the job can be assessed.

It is difficult to draw a clean line between the work sample approach to assessment and the simulated job station. Perhaps the easiest way to understand the simulated job station is to think of a work sample that is designed to replicate, as nearly as possible, all aspects of the job including the environmental factors. Like the work sample, the simulated job station is normally found in a rehabilitation facility. Because more dimensions of the job are included, the ability to predict a person's potential for being able to successfully perform a job is substantially greater using a simulated job station than it is when typical work samples are used in the assessment process.

The complexity and skill level requirements of many jobs make it extremely difficult to use the simulated job station as an assessment technique. In these situations, the technique that frequently is employed is assessment in a vocational training setting. This technique is particularly effective when the training resource employs an open enrollment policy. Open enrollment generally means that new students may begin a program on any Monday throughout the school year and the course of study is designed so the students may move at their own pace. Such settings are ideal for a training site assessment.

Using this approach clients, who may or may not be enrolled as students, are assessed by both the evaluation staff and the instructional staff. Particular attention is paid to a client's ability to learn the required skills and perform the job tasks after acquiring the necessary skills. With cooperative training institutions, it is possible for clients to try out and be assessed in several vocational training programs. This opportunity aids in the achievement of the goals of both occupational exploration and evaluation.

On-the-job evaluation is the logical next step in the assessment techniques being discussed. As the statement implies, the technique simply refers to the practice of arranging with an employer to allow a client the opportunity to be evaluated on an actual job. Typically, the evaluator will either remain on the job site with the client, or will make repeated visits to the job site for the purpose of assessing the client's performance. The major advantage of this assessment technique is that virtually all aspects of an actual job are present. Those factors that are missing include the relationship between the client and the employer as a result of the fact that both know the client is not an actual employee and will be leaving at the end of the assessment period.

Job tryouts are the ultimate valid assessment technique. In a job tryout the client becomes an employee with all the related responsibilities and benefits. Perhaps the best way to view the job tryout is as a conditional placement. Everyone, including the client, the employer, and the rehabilitation professional knows that if the client succeeds, he or she will continue on the job. However, should the client fail, the rehabilitation professional stands ready to provide additional services as required. In the event of failure, the elements leading to that failure are used for planning in the same way that information that has been obtained from other assessment techniques is used. When failure has occurred, the job tryout becomes an assessment technique, rather than a placement.

The value of natural work settings as assessment resources cannot be overstated. Although they have drawbacks, particularly regarding the time consumed by the rehabilitation professional in setting up and carrying out assessments in these settings, natural work settings represent the least used and potentially, the most valuable evaluation resource. Using the natural work setting in an evaluation has an added benefit. It requires that the rehabilitation professional get out into the world of work, resulting in increased exposure to, and knowledge of, jobs and their requirements.

Graduate rehabilitation training has traditionally short-changed the rehabilitation professional in the area of occupational information and knowledge of the world of work. What instruction is received has generally been provided through course work outside of the rehabilitation program, where the breadth and depth of knowledge needed by rehabilitation professionals may not be present. It is extremely difficult, if not impossible, to assess the rehabilitation potential of a person with a handicapping disability, if the person making the assessment has little or no knowledge of the world of work.

Independent Living

The final resource available to the counselor for the evaluation of rehabilitation potential that will be presented is in the area of independent living. Although at least one graduate level training program (University of Nebraska-Lincoln) has been training professional rehabilitation personnel to work in the area of independent living, the real significance of this area is only beginning to be perceived. With passage of the Rehabilitation, Comprehensive Services, and Development Disabilities Amendments of 1978, independent living rehabilitation, for the first time, is being recognized as an integral part of the rehabilitation process.

A number of concepts and techniques have been found to be common to both independent living and employment (Institute on Rehabilitation Issues, 1978). These include such things as adjustment to disability, medical aspects of disability, awareness of resources, basic nutrition, personal care, physical care, and psychological care. These examples represent only a partial listing of concerns common to both independent living and employment, but the list does indicate a few areas where an evaluation of independent living capability has direct carry-over to employment potential.

Under the amendments of 1978, independent living goes beyond being a support service for attaining the goal of employment. Increasing the ability of a disabled individual to live independently may now be the sole goal of rehabilitation, where employment potential does not exist. This means that new types of linkages and crossovers need to be developed between counselors and independent living specialists. Where, in the past, the state rehabilitation agency client's case would be closed when the applicant lacked rehabilitation potential as defined in employability terms, the case now may remain open and independent living services may be provided. Whether the counselor will continue to serve as the case manager in these situations remains to be seen. Perhaps a parallel path will be developed where the independent living specialist becomes both the case manager and primary service provider when employment potential does not appear to be present. If this parallel system comes about, there must be a built-in capacity for ongoing reevaluation of employment potential as the individual gains independent living skills. It has been the experience of the Nebraska Rehabilitation Agency, that as the ability to live independently is developed, the potential for employment also increases. In cases where the employment potential increases significantly, there must be the capacity to move the individual back into the employment-oriented track. Regardless of how the independent living service delivery system develops, the independent living specialist has much to offer during the process of evaluating the rehabilitation potential of individuals with disabilities.

EXPECTED OUTCOMES

As stated earlier, within the state rehabilitation agency setting there are three outcomes that should result from the evaluation of rehabilitation potential. In every instance, an eligibility decision should be forthcoming. A decision that the applicant is eligible for rehabilitation services indicates that a disability is present that constitutes a substantial handicap to employment, and that a reasonable expectation exists that vocational rehabilitation services may benefit the individual in terms of employment. The process to this point constitutes the preliminary diagnostic study.

The thorough diagnostic study encompasses the remaining two outcomes for those applicants found eligible as a result of the preliminary study. These outcomes are the Individualized Written Rehabilitation Plan (IWRP) and the placement plan. In the best of all worlds, the placement plan would constitute one element of the IWRP. The point, however, is not in what form the placement plan appears, but rather the fact that it occurs as an outcome of the evaluation of rehabilitation potential. A comprehensive plan for the rehabilitation program and associated placement activities completes the thorough diagnostic study and the evaluation of rehabilitation potential.

Before closing, there are four seemingly unrelated points that need to be touched upon. These points are related, however, to the extent that they should be included as key elements of a rehabilitation counselor's overall philosophy.

First, as emphasized by Brown and Koltueit (1977), the evaluation should suggest ideas for overcoming handicaps, not just put labels on people. Too often service providers become caught up in the need to diagnose and label, forgetting that the goal is to bring about change. The value of the diagnostic process is to point out the proper direction so that services may be provided to overcome the handicap, or at least diminish its effects on the employability of those being served.

The second point deals with Miller's (1970) concept of "coping level." Miller believes that the standard model employed by rehabilitation professionals in the process of evaluating rehabilitation potential is an "ideal man model." Using this model, clients are in effect compared with the professional's concept of what an ideal person in a given situation or occupation would be like. It is not surprising that clients frequently come up short when compared to this nonexistent ideal man.

As an alternative to this approach, Miller suggests that coping levels be substituted for ideals. Coping levels may be thought of as the lower limits of any dimension being considered that would still allow a person to be counted in the "accept" rather than the "reject" group. For example, using the ideal man model, a banker might be viewed as a person who has a master's degree in business administration, a bachelor's degree in finance, a strong minor in accounting, was an honor student, has distinguished looking silver-gray hair and an honest face. Using the coping level model, a banker would be a person with a bachelor's degree who got mostly Cs, has no hair and looks just a shade more honest than the latest sales person for Honest Jane's Used Cars.

Look around. How often do people fit the ideal man model for their occupation? Probably not often. Most are copers who have put together a package of knowledge, skills, and qualifications that allowed them to make it through the door before it slammed shut. People should not demand more of handicapped individuals than they demand of nonhandicapped people. It may even be necessary to go one step further and join the fight to eliminate the meaningless requirements that have been established for many jobs.

Wolfensburger (1978, pp. 99–100) in a presentation on the concept of normalization to a group of vocational rehabilitation professionals, made the point that "as deviancies and stigmata increase in number, severity, or variety they tend to have a multiplicative rather than additive impact." The implications of this statement for a counselor are many. In a situation where a given client may possess more than one handicapping disability, the "effect" of multiple disabilities is frequently greater than the simple total of the number of disabilities present.

The concept applies across people as well. For example, the effect of a group of people with disabilities is somehow more powerful than the simple total of the number in the group. What may take place in these situations is that the image of disability is perceived at a level substantially above the level at which it really exists. This phenomenon must be considered when determining rehabilitation potential, assessing individuals in the presence of other people with disabilities, housing people with disabilities together in the community, and seeking to employ clients with that handful of willing employers who have hired in the past.

The concept of normalization should be carefully studied by anyone serving people with disabilities. It can help professionals step outside their roles and examine the image of the people they serve that is projected to society.

The final point to be made cuts across everything that has been previously presented with regard to evaluating rehabilitation potential. It is a simple statement, but once again, one that is much more difficult to put into practice than into words. The rehabilitation potential of an individual *cannot* be separated from the environmental factors associated with that person's past, present, and future. Or, stated positively, to assess the rehabilitation potential of an individual a counselor must consider the environment surrounding that individual before he or she sought services, the environment during the provision of services, and the environment in which the individual will find himself or herself upon the completion of the program of services. This is quite an assignment, but the possibly devastating effects of an inaccurate assessment and resulting decision on the lives of clients should be enough to cause rehabilitation professionals to both remove the barriers of ignorance that currently exist and develop the knowledge and resources necessary to successfully rehabilitate handicapped people.

REFERENCES

Allesberry, D. *Assessment of vocational potential of sickle cell anemics.* Harrisburg, Penn.: Pennsylvania Bureau of Vocational Rehabilitation, 1977.

Brown, J., & Koltueit, T. Individual assessment: A systematic approach: *Personnel and Guidance Journal,* 1977, 55, 271–276.

Dunn, D. J. *Situational assessment: Models for the future.* Menomonie, Wis.: University of Wisconsin-Stout, Research and Training Center, January, 1973.

Dunn, D. J., Korn, T. A., & Andrew, J. D. *Critical issues in vocational evaluation.* Menomonie, Wis.: University of Wisconsin-Stout, Research and Training Center, October, 1976.

Equal Employment Opportunity Commission. *Laws and rules you should know.* Washington, D.C.: Equal Employment Opportunity Commission, 1975.

Institute on Rehabilitation Issues. *The role of vocational rehabilitation in independent living.* Fayetteville, Ark.: Arkansas Rehabilitation Research and Training Center, University of Arkansas, 1978.

Krantz, G. Critical vocational behaviors. *Journal of Rehabilitation.* July-August, 1971, 37(4), 14–16.

Miller, L. A. Everyman's system for interpreting client information like a vocational counselor. *Rehabilitation Research and Practice Review,* Summer, 1970, 1(3), 19–23.

National Archives of the United States. Vocational rehabilitation programs. *Federal Register.* Tuesday, November 25, 1975, 40(228), 54695–54733.

Neff, W. Problems of work evaluation. *Personnel and Guidance Journal,* 1966, 44, 682–688.

Pruitt, W. *Vocational (work) evaluation.* Menomonie, Wis.: Walt Pruitt Associates, 1978.

Roberts, C. Definitions, objectives, and goals in work evaluation. In W. Pruitt, & R. Pacinelli (Eds.), *Work evaluation in rehabilitation.* Washington, D.C.: Associates of Rehabilitation Center, 1969.

Sankowsky, R., State of the art in vocational evaluation: Report of a national survey. Pittsburgh, Penn.: University of Pittsburgh, Research and Training Center, 1969.

Vocational Evaluation and Work Adjustment Association. *Vocational evaluation and work adjustment standards with interpretive guidelines and VEWAA glossary.* Menomonie, Wis.: University of Wisconsin-Stout, Materials Development Center, 1978.

Wolfensburger, W. A brief overview of the principle of normalization. In S. A. Grand (Ed.), *Severe disability and rehabilitation counseling training.* Albany, N.Y.: National Council on Rehabilitation Education, 1978.

Zadny, J. J., & James, L. F. *Job placement in state vocational rehabilitation agencies: A survey of techniques.* Portland, Ore.: Regional Rehabilitation Research Institute, Portland State University, 1978.

Chapter 9

Counseling for Personal Adjustment

Kenneth R. Thomas   Alfred J. Butler

INTRODUCTION

Problems associated with disability are rarely limited to the finding and retention of appropriate employment. In recognition of this fact, the goals of rehabilitation as a field, objectives of the state-federal vocational rehabilitation program, and roles of the rehabilitation counselor include the resolution of client adjustment problems that may or may not impinge directly on the client's ability to work.

Among some of the more common problems that people with disabilities must frequently confront are personal acceptance of the disability, the reactions of others to the disability, lack of accessibility of the environment, reintegration of their self-concepts, and possible changes in their relationships with family members and other significant people in their lives. People with long-term disabilities, especially those who have been sheltered by their families or other social institutions, may require even more extensive personal adjustment counseling and training to learn how to function effectively.

The role of the rehabilitation counselor in helping clients resolve problems of personal adjustment varies somewhat depending on the objectives of the employing agency and intensity of the client's difficulties. Counselors working for agencies and facilities emphasizing work adjustment and job placement may decide to deal only with those clients' problems that directly affect their ability to maintain employment. However, counselors employed by agencies with a more general focus may consider almost any client problem (short of severe psychopathology in poor remission) deserving of their professional attention.

Speculations on the relationship between personal and vocational adjustment range from the often cited psychoanalytic point of view that all problems of work adjustment are basically problems of general adjustment to the more recent idea (Neff, 1968) that work and other areas of personality are only semiautonomously related. In support of his position, Neff points out that some frank psychotics are able to meet the demands of work with reasonable adequacy. The weight of research evidence over the years generally supports the idea that personal and vocational adjustment are related; however, it is also apparent that this relationship is not high enough to conclude that the two are identical (Crites, 1969). In any case, since problems of personal adjustment often affect clients' employability and almost always their sense of well-being, the ability to help clients resolve such problems is clearly a skill the rehabilitation counselor must possess.

A related issue concerns whether the methods of personal adjustment counseling differ from the methods of vocational counseling. Most of the counseling strategies applied to the solving of personal adjustment problems can also be used by the counselor when confronted with clients who primarily demonstrate problems of vocational choice, development, or adjustment. Although this chapter discusses the major counseling approaches used to facilitate personal adjustment, a creative application of the theories and ideas presented can assist in the resolution of problems and can facilitate positive development in a variety of life areas.

BACKGROUND—REVIEW OF RELEVANT LITERATURE

Scope of the Literature

In the space of a few pages one cannot truly "review" the relevant literature in any comprehensive way. The intent here is to present a reasonable picture of the extent of the literature, to recommend some representative readings, to summarize major themes, and to provide some specific examples of the literature of particular interest to rehabilitation counseling.

Few professionals in the field can retain command of the extensive literature in counseling and psychotherapy. There are several hundred books, including general overview texts, research reviews, and presentations of specific viewpoints. In 1977 alone, approximately 1400 new books, journal articles, and monographs devoted to the field were identified in *Psychological Abstracts*. In Bergin and Garfield's (1971) *Handbook of Psychotherapy and Behavior Change*, probably the most ambitious review to date, approximately 3000 authors were cited.

To keep reasonably up to date, it would be necessary to read at least a score of the several dozen relevant journals available. Two, specifically directed to rehabilitation counselors, are the *Rehabilitation Counseling Bulletin* and the *Journal of Applied Rehabilitation Counseling*. Of more general interest are the *Journal of Counseling Psychology* (as well as several other journals published by the American Psychological Association), the *Journal of Clinical Psychology, Psychiatry, American Journal of Psychiatry, American Journal of Orthopsychiatry,* and *Psychotherapy: Theory, Research and Practice* to name but a few.

In addition to this chapter, consider one or more of the following texts that summarize major theories or approaches: Barclay (1971), Corsini (1973), Downing (1975), and Patterson (1973). A majority of the expositions of specific viewpoints cited in this chapter are referred to in these summaries. For overviews of research in the field, see Bergin and Garfield (1971), a comprehensive summary of all major research aspects; Kiesler (1973), on counseling process; Luborsky, Chandler, Auerbach, and Cohen (1971), on outcome research; and Meltzoff and Kornreich (1970), on principles and methods, as well as outcome research. There are also periodic reviews of counseling, psychotherapy and behavior therapy in the *Annual Reviews of Psychology*. For a compendium of techniques, albeit from a medical and psychoanalytic slant, see Wolberg (1977).

From the literature, the following themes have been selected for brief attention: the general effectiveness of counseling; relative effectiveness of various counseling strategies; relationship of client, counselor, and process characteristics to counseling outcome; and special issues in rehabilitation counseling.

Outcome Studies

Eysenck's (1952, 1961) highly critical papers are a landmark in the research on counseling and psychotherapy. In essence, he challenged whether traditional therapies had any demonstrable positive effects. He argued that those positive results that had been reported could readily be accounted for in terms of spontaneous remission that approximates the success rates claimed in the literature. He acquired a substantial following of critics, most of whom argued for behavior modification techniques in favor of formal psychotherapy. Many of his detractors replied in highly emotional and defensive style but several have rebutted with comprehensive and well-documented counterarguments in favor of psychotherapy (e.g., Bergin, 1971; Luborsky et al., 1971; and Meltzoff & Kornreich, 1970). In these rebuttals, Eysenck's interpretation of data has been challenged, spontaneous remission as a universal phenomenon has been questioned, and reasonable evidence has been accumulated to demonstrate that positive results exceed chance expectations. From such reviews, the focus of concern has been shifted from *whether* psychotherapy is effective to *under what* conditions and *for whom* it is effective.

A significant confounding issue has been setting criteria for, and measurement of, successful outcome. After an in depth review and critique of the outcome literature, Bergin (1971, p. 256) made this comment,

> ... the process of therapeutic change in patients is multifactorial. As simple and obvious as this sounds, it has profound implications for both research and practice. It means that divergent processes are occurring in therapeutic change ... and that divergent methods of criteria measurement must be used. ...

Criteria for successful outcome for counseling in general range through affective, cognitive, and behavioral change. In rehabilitation counseling, criteria for successful outcome must be considered within the context of the broader goals of the rehabilitation process. In addition to the psychological indices noted, a number of others have been employed primarily on economic and/or vocational status. These include the "closed-rehabilitated" criterion, income, occupational status, occupational adjustment, and vocational adequacy. Others reflect client satisfaction with services and/or income, adjustment to disability, and physical functioning skills. For a comprehensive review and critique of rehabilitation outcome criteria see Bolton (1974b) and Walls and Tseng (1976).

Client, Counselor, and Process Variables Related to Outcome

This section will attempt to identify only the major themes in recent research and to recommend some useful relevant readings. Complexity and extent of this literature tend to dismay newcomers and seasoned researchers and practitioners alike.

For overviews on the relationship of client characteristics to outcome, see Garfield (1971) and Meltzoff and Kornreich (1970). Although a number of client variables, e.g., age, sex, marital status, socioeconomic status, problem type and severity, maturation, and attitudes, in isolated studies, have shown some promise as predictors of outcome, no generalizations can be made.

Greater attention has been paid to the importance of counselor characteristics, particularly those of professional qualifications and personal attributes (see Truax & Mitchell, 1971; Meltzoff & Kornreich, 1970; and Luborsky et al., 1971). Intense controversy has been generated from the fact that trained therapists have not been shown to be consistently superior to untrained or paraprofessional therapists. Although this research has been severely criticized on methodological grounds and on narrowness of criteria used in assessing impact of professional training, the type and extent of professional training, e.g., psychiatry, social work, or psychology, also have not been shown to be related to outcome in any systematic manner.

Substantial research has been directed to what occurs within the counseling process (see Howard & Orlinsky, 1972; Kiesler, 1973; Marsden, 1971; and Truax & Mitchell, 1971). Under this rubric, studies attempting to relate types of techniques, particularly those associated with specific theories, have been generally inconclusive. Research associated with correlates of the Rogerian counselor conditions has been most ardently reported and appears to have been more productive in positive findings.

For the student or practitioner searching for definitive answers and sure-fire techniques, the literature related to outcome and its correlates will be a disappointment. To date, it has mainly served to destroy myths and preconceptions, but also can provide for the careful and persistent readers guidelines for training and practice.

Topics Relevant to the Rehabilitation Counselor

Research on counseling process and outcome in rehabilitation parallels conceptually that of generic counseling, but has been modest in productivity. Overview works such as those of Bolton and Jacques (1978) and Moses and Patterson (1971) tap many of the relevant issues. Major issues include the application of counseling to specific rehabilitation populations, special orientation and/or adaptation of counseling within rehabilitation, and measurement of client outcomes.

The client as a variable was reviewed from the perspective of the counselor in their study of counselor professional concerns by Thoreson, Smits, Butler and Wright (1968). Client motivation and counselor responsibilities in coping with the "unmotivated client" emerged as primary concerns. Most studies, however, have focused on requirements and procedures with specific disability groups, for example, with adolescents who are chronically disabled (Beyrakal, 1975), sexual adjustment of physically disabled people (Boyle, 1976), individual versus group counseling with physically disabled people (Bryan, 1974), group therapy with spinal cord injured people (Cimperman & Dunn, 1974), counseling with the renal dialysis patient (Ebra, 1975; Fisher, 1976), and working with loss and grief in traumatically disabled people (Krieger, 1976). These examples, representative of the rehabilitation-oriented literature on counseling of people who are physically handicapped, are paralleled in studies focusing on people who are mentally retarded, emotionally disturbed, or abusing drugs.

The counselor as a variable has received attention primarily in terms of his or her professional orientation, counseling style, and type of training. Work by Sather, Wright, and Butler (1968) provided instrumentation for measuring orientation on two dimensions, relationship oriented and situation oriented. Recent work by Bolton (1974b) has distinguished three verbal interaction styles of rehabilitation counselors, namely, therapeutic, information giving, and information exchanging styles.

Evidence that two approaches are related to counselor case performance have been given by Ayer, Wright, and Butler (1968) and by Bolton (1976). Studies on correlates of training within the counseling process for rehabilitation counselors have been as inconclusive as they have in the generic field of counseling and psychotherapy. Finally, for a recent assessment of methodological issues in the assessment of rehabilitation counselor performance see Bolton (1978).

CURRENT STATUS—DIVERGING POINTS OF VIEW

Criteria for Comparison of Counseling Approaches

In the search for a personal vantage point in counseling with the rehabilitation client, the student and practitioner have the option of selecting from at least a dozen major approaches. These approaches include psychoanalysis and its recent offshoots, client-centered therapy, Gestalt therapy, rational-emotive therapy, reality therapy, and a number of behaviorally oriented therapies.

Models for comparison vary considerably in scope with that of Ford and Urban (1963) being the most extensive. The average "shopper" for a suitable counseling approach in rehabilitation practice may wish to consider the following points.

First, what are the basic philosophical notions underlying the approach? To what extent are such basic assumptions as the basic goodness of man congruent with the searcher's own beliefs? In a related vein, how well developed and verified are the theoretical bases? Regardless of the verifiability of the theoretical underpinnings, for example, those related to the development of normal and abnormal behavior, or the principles of change, these tenets usually must be congruent with views of the counselor or the approach will not be seriously accepted, except by the most blatant hypocrite.

Another consideration is the range and type of clients who can feasibly be served by the approach. Are limits imposed by such factors as the client's presenting problems, intellectual functioning, verbal expressivity, or expectations? In most rehabilitation settings, the counselor is expected to work with clients with a wide range of characteristics and the counselor's approach must be commensurate with this range.

What demands does a selected approach place upon the counselor with respect to training, experience, personality attributes, verbal ability, and values? Although there are some nominal expectations concerning the counselor's input in most systems, there are demands made by some that make them impractical for use by many practitioners.

Another major concern is the goal, explicit or implicit, for the counselor. In many employment contexts counselors are expected to limit their function to a narrower role than is commensurate with the use of a given approach. When the agency's goal for its clients is rigidly defined, for example, as vocational placement, counseling approaches that stress the goal of a more comprehensive personality integration become difficult to justify. Not only is the goal itself important but also the question of who assumes the responsibility for setting the goal. Approaches vary considerably in the relative role of counselor and client in goal formulation.

Techniques used to achieve the goal(s) must also be considered regarding the demands placed on the counselor and the client, their appropriateness for the agency context, their cost and other practical constraints. For example, a behavioral approach that requires cooperation of outsiders to implement reinforcement schedules may be inappropriate to the client who is a "loner." Some techniques place heavy demands on the counselor for specialized training, others place unrealistic requirements for client cooperation.

Criteria for measurement of change are a concern for many counselors. These practitioners require more than blind faith that their approach is effective. Not all approaches make these criteria explicit or are geared to reliable, empirical measurement of change. Often the criteria for change are not theoretically congruent with the approach itself.

A final and global consideration is the relevance and appropriateness of a counseling approach for rehabilitation. This judgment stems from both the sum and the cross-products of the factors cited. The approach selected ideally should be congruent with the basic philosophy and theoretical orientation of the counselor; be congruent with his or her training and personality; be applicable to the clients within the agency context; be directed to goals acceptable to the client, counselor, and the agency; be accountable in terms of benefits accrued; and in general mesh well with the specific rehabilitation context. No single approach has yet been blessed with a consensus of endorsements. The onus is upon the student and practitioner to apply their training, experience, and professional judgment to select an approach that best suits their unique responsibilities.

In the summaries that follow, these major considerations will be highlighted. References will be made to additional readings that will aid the reader in making comprehensive evaluations of these divergent points of view. With the exception of psychoanalysis, which is presented primarily for its historical role as a precursor to most modern counseling viewpoints, all the approaches cited have their advocates in the broad field of rehabilitation. Each approach should be assessed from two perspectives, its applicability for direct use by the rehabilitation counselor and its applicability for referred or purchased service for the rehabilitation client. The second perspective has been grossly ignored in rehabilitation practice. In referring clients for training, or purchasing training services, the counselor traditionally assesses closely the resources, capabilities, and relevance of the training facility. Generally, selection of psychotherapeutic services has been made less critically.

Other than the psychoanalytic viewpoint, the approaches reviewed here were chosen for their predominance in the general field of counseling and psychotherapy and potential relevance to rehabilitation. The grouping, although it represents a somewhat arbitrary classification, is based on similarity of major theoretical viewpoints, as well as different methods of classification and criteria for selection. See Barclay (1971), Corsini (1973), Downing (1975), Morse and Watson (1977), and Patterson (1973).

Psychoanalytic Approaches

Strategies for facilitating personal adjustment based on psychoanalytic theory date back to the earliest writings of Sigmund Freud (Freud & Breuer, 1895). Classical psychoanalysis is a long-term therapy process used primarily in the treatment of neurosis; it relies on the techniques of free association, interpretation, and analysis of transference and resistance. In its original form, psychoanalysis stressed the role of the unconscious, infantile sexuality, and anxiety on psychic functioning. However, later theorists such as Alfred Adler (1963), Carl Jung (1959), Otto Rank (1945), Karen Horney (1945), Harry Stack Sullivan (1947), and Erich Fromm (1947) have considerably modified or elaborated on Freud's original concepts, especially in terms of deemphasizing the role of infantile sexuality and stressing the role of social variables in anxiety and personality development. Other theorists, particularly Franz Alexander (1963) and Edward Bordin (1955), have incorporated psychoanalytically derived concepts and techniques into shorter term therapy and counseling systems.

Basic to the use of classical psychoanalysis as a treatment method is an understanding of the role of the unconscious in psychic functioning. Briefly, Freud believed that the motivational forces in human behavior are both conscious and unconscious. He further believed that the individual retains in the unconscious primitive biological and sexual impulses which, if expressed, would cause retribution from society at large. To prevent this punishment the individual relies primarily on the defense mechanism of repression. That is, the individual represses these unacceptable impulses from conscious expression.

When the material repressed in the unconscious constantly threatens to escape into consciousness, the individual experiences anxiety. To alleviate this anxiety, the individual develops a variety of defense mechanisms such as compensation, sublimation, reaction formation, rationalization, displacement, and projection. Although both adjusted and distressed individuals use these defense mechanisms, their use is considered indicative of neurosis when it becomes excessive.

The therapist's role in helping neurotic individuals is to facilitate the bringing of the repressed material into consciousness where it can be dealt with in a rational and socially acceptable manner. To accomplish these goals the therapist relies primarily on the techniques of free association, transference, and interpretation. Although psychoanalytic theorists differ considerably on their speculations regarding the cause of anxiety (e.g., Freud attributes it to repressed biological and sexual impulses; Adler and Horney, to feelings of discouragement and helplessness; Rank, to primal anxiety evoked at birth; and Sullivan, to inner impulses that threaten relations with others) psychoanalysis is almost always a long and intensive modality of treatment.

With the exception of Bordin (1955) psychoanalytic theorists offer little to the counselor who is primarily involved in the resolution of vocational or educational problems. However, Adler's (1963) conceptualization of striving for superiority as an innate drive may be useful for understanding the motivational aspects in these areas. In addition, concepts such as compensation for organic defect or organ inferiority may be viewed as potentially useful for better understanding psychological adjustment to disability. A further contribution of psychoanalytic theory to rehabilitation practice is the recognition that early life experiences and child-rearing practices may have a considerable impact on later development and behavior.

While psychoanalysis is an inappropriate method for use by rehabilitation counselors due both to the length of time and level of training required, a knowledge of psychoanalytic theory can contribute significantly to the counselor's understanding of human behavior and practice of counseling. In addition to those contributions already cited, psychoanalytic theory provides a framework for better understanding the structure of personality, the role of the unconscious, and the mechanisms of defense. It has also served as the basis for many of the other approaches to counseling and associated techniques.

Humanistic Approaches

The approaches reviewed under this classification, client-centered therapy and Gestalt therapy, represent only two of several that have a common fundamental belief in the client as the active agent of change in the context of an interpersonal relationship that stresses the uniqueness of the individual's own experience. Emphasis is placed on the client's feelings and emotions rather than behavior or on rationality of beliefs. The counselor's role is deemphasized in favor of an optimistic view that clients can, with a modicum of guidance and interaction, redirect their own lives.

Client-Centered Therapy. This approach owes its origin to Carl Rogers (1942, 1951, 1961). It has been extended by the writings and research of a substantial group of active associates and followers as documented by Bergin and Garfield (1971), Carkhuff and Berenson (1977), and Kiesler (1973). In large part a reaction to psychoanalytic therapy, the basic philosophical and theoretical foundations differ significantly.

Man is viewed as innately good, basically rational, socialized, forward moving, and realistic. The theory of therapy is based upon an extensively developed theory of personality and development. Rogers recognized a number of innate components that include the actualizing tendency as an inherent proclivity of the organism to develop all of its capabilities in ways that serve to maintain the organism; the tendency toward self-actualization that is symbolized in the self; awareness and symbolization, representing the capacity to perceive situational events and internal stimuli and to represent the awareness in symbolic form; and the organizing principle that integrates new experiences with past behavior and experience.

A fully functioning individual is one who symbolizes his experiences accurately in awareness. Needs for positive regard from others and positive self-regard are met. Self-structure is consistent with perceived experience. Experience will not be distorted or denied to awareness. Under conditions of less than optimal functioning the individual senses a lack of congruence between self and experience; is defensive, anxious, and lacks positive self-regard; and tends to deny, to ignore, or to distort the perception of discrepant responses.

The goal of counseling under this approach has been variously stated, but essentially it permits clients to become self-actualized through the development of all capacities that serve to maintain or enhance the self. Specific goals of counseling are determined primarily by clients who are assumed capable of developing a greater congruence between their behaviors and perception of self. Potential positive outcomes from the process of therapy include greater congruence, openness to experience, reduction of defensiveness, and more realistic, objective, and comprehensive perceptions. As a further result of successful client-centered counseling, clients become more effective in problem solving, less threatened, acquire a more positive self-regard, and perceive the real self as more congruent with the ideal self. Frequently other people are perceived more accurately, and as more accepting. Finally, clients perceive their own behavior as being under their self-control.

Appropriate and effective techniques are not clearly specified, but conditions of the therapeutic process are. The necessary and sufficient conditions of therapeutic change identified by Rogers (1957) may be summarized as follows:

1. Two persons are in contact.
2. One, the client, is in a state of incongruence, being vulnerable or anxious.
3. The other, the counselor, is congruent in the relationship.
4. The counselor experiences unconditional positive regard toward the client.
5. The counselor experiences an empathic, understanding, positive regard of the client's internal frame of reference.
6. The client perceives, to some extent, the positive regard and empathic understanding of the counselor.

Process of therapy, then, is described not in terms of specific dos and don'ts, but is seen as a logical outcome of the conditions just listed and the basic assumptions concerning personality change. During the process, the client becomes more open to experiencing feelings, more aware of incongruence between experience and self, and more aware of feelings that were previously denied to awareness or distorted. The counselor is expected to express and communicate acceptance, congruence, and understanding. How this is done is not spelled out, but counselor reflection of feeling tends to be the major counselor response. Giving advice or directive provisions of alternative solutions, interpretation, probing, role playing or information giving, admonishment, or other intrusions of the counselor's values are regarded as detrimental to client growth. Counselor introduction of psychometric test data or case history material is similarly excluded.

Criteria for change are implied by the expected outcomes of this therapy. In operationalizing these for purposes of research, client self-report techniques are most consistent with the underlying philosophy. The most commonly used techniques of evaluation are measures of self-concept and indices of congruence between real and ideal self.

Application of client-centered therapy to rehabilitation settings has received mixed reviews. Serious questions have been raised about the appropriateness for clients with limited intelligence and/or limited verbal expressivity, particularly those who are mentally retarded or severely psychotic. Rogers himself has reversed his original dictum against using his approaches with retarded people and has conducted extensive research with a schizophrenic population (Rogers, Gendlin, Kiesler, & Traux, 1967). Because this approach emphasizes personal attributes (which may or may not be modified by training rather than formal training in psychotherapy), the approach is within bounds for the majority of rehabilitation counselors. Goals of therapy may conflict with those set by the agencies in many settings. Perhaps most important is the potential role of conflict for counselors, particularly those in state rehabilitation agencies who are required to make substantive decisions such as those concerning eligibility for rehabilitation services. Another commonly expressed criticism is that extensive counseling time is required. Other than cost, however, there have been no serious objections raised to referral of clients to client-centered therapists for purchased services during the rehabilitation process.

Gestalt Therapy. Gestalt therapy may be attributed primarily to Fritz Perls with the books by Perls, Hefferline and Goodman (1951) and Perls (1969) being landmark publications. It is based upon Gestalt psychology in that both emphasize dealing with humans from a holistic rather than analytic framework. Perls also drew upon psychoanalysis and existential philosophy. A major concept from Gestalt psychology is the perceptual field that represents the context and extent of what an individual perceives. The individual is viewed as striving to organize stimuli into wholes. This is done in the context of figure-ground relationships, the figure constituting the immediate need and the activities associated with meeting these needs, the ground with the physical and psychological surrounds. As shifts in stimuli occur, a Gestalt or unified understanding is formed. Somewhat simplistically, people's abilities to shift, meet needs, and form complete Gestalts are related to their complete and accurate awareness of both figure and ground. Anything that detracts from comprehensive and accurate awareness interferes with people's capacities to act effectively as fully functioning people.

According to Passons (1975, p. 14), Gestalt therapy is based on several assumptions that include:

1. Man is a whole who is (rather than has) a body, emotions, thoughts, sensations, and perceptions, all of which function interrelatedly.

2. Man is a part of his environment and cannot be understood outside of it.

3. Man is proactive rather than reactive. He determines his own responses to external and proprioceptive stimuli.

4. Man is capable of being aware of his sensations, thoughts, emotions, and perceptions.

5. Man, through self-awareness, is capable of choice and is thus responsible for covert and overt behavior.

6. Man possesses the wherewithal and resources to live effectively and to restore himself through his own assets.

7. Man can experience himself only in the present. The past and the future can be experienced only in the now through remembering and anticipating.

8. Man is neither intrinsically good or bad.

An important concept in understanding personality development is what Perls referred to as the "ego boundary." Children soon learn to differentiate what is within themselves and what is outside. During development the self and self-image are formed, the self being what the individual really is, the self-image reflecting the expectations of others.

Growth is characterized by contact, sensing, excitement, and Gestalt formations. Frustration facilitates growth in that it encourages people to mobilize resources and act on their own. Fully functioning people are those who are comprehensively aware of their senses, can fully express themselves, have no major "incomplete" life experiences, are self-supporting, and are not maintaining self-images incongruent with the self.

In Gestalt therapy, the goal is the integration of the individual, of bringing together all the parts that have been disowned to the point that the client is self-directive. The major intermediate goal is increased awareness; only with increased awareness can the "unfinished business" of life be recognized and confronted.

Perls (1969), Kempler (1973), and Polster and Polster (1973) have proposed a wide range of techniques, although there are significant differences of opinion as to the appropriateness of some. Throughout all techniques, emphasis is on experiencing and awareness in the "here and now." Counselors are active, confrontative, probing, and authoritative. Role playing, the "hot seat," dream review, and client fantasizing are a number of acceptable techniques, but all are designed to facilitate clients' experiencing fully concerns, feelings, attitudes, or disowned aspects of themselves. Nonverbal behavior is considered significant, the bowed head or clenched fist is challenged to encourage clients to share the associated feeling. Frustration is used to discourage dependency, mobilize resources, and encourage expression of feeling. Intensive group workshops are often used for the emotional impact and elicitation of awareness. For a comprehensive listing of "rules" and "games" of Gestalt therapy, see Levitsky and Perls (1970).

Criteria for change and evaluation of success are elusive in Gestalt therapy. Level of goal attainment is assessed primarily through clinical judgment. Appropriate objective measures of change have not been developed. The approach has not been verified by significant research.

Implications for rehabilitation do not differ significantly from those cited for client-centered therapy. It has been used with children, adolescents, adults, alcoholics, the mentally ill people, and mentally retarded people. Presenting problems may include generalized anxiety, discomfort, psychosomatic disorders and anomie. It is appropriate for clients who have difficulty in interpersonal relationships, as well as those with distorted or limiting self-images. Counselor requirements are not as precisely specified as in the client-centered approach, but the counselor should be capable of a dynamic and active role in the counseling relationship. In view of the typical level of risk-taking with clients, extensive training and personal therapy are required for recognition as a Gestalt therapist. The latter requirement makes the approach impractical for the majority of rehabilitation counselors. The techniques are sufficiently unconventional to rule out the approach in many agencies. However, counselors may wish to refer clients who require this form of confrontative and unconventional therapy to Gestalt therapists.

Rational Approaches

Contrasted to the humanistic approach, which focuses on client feelings, experiencing and awareness, rational approaches emphasize a logical and intellectual solution of the client's problems. The two approaches extensively discussed, trait-factor counseling and rational-emotive therapy, have considerably less similarity than the two humanistic approaches. They have different historical precedents and have generally focused on quite different clientele. They are grouped together somewhat arbitrarily on the basis of their "rational" emphasis. Reality therapy is also briefly discussed under the same rubric.

Trait-Factor Counseling. The major spokesman for this approach was Edmund Williamson (1950, 1965) although it represented a point of view shared by a number of his colleagues at the University of Minnesota. It was a logical precursor of the Minnesota Studies in Vocational Rehabilitation (see Dawis, 1967, for a summary description). Unlike Rogers and Perls whose views stemmed from reaction against the clinical application of psychoanalysis, Williamson's viewpoint appeared to develop from a long career in university testing and counseling services. Unlike all others cited in this chapter, it is the only approach that emerged from vocational counseling and emphasizes educational and vocational adjustment. It stresses the use of psychological testing in the counseling process.

A basic assumption of his approach is that each individual is born with the potential for both good and evil. The individual strives to develop his or her full potential, which may be viewed as excellence in all aspects of human development. But, quite important in this approach, the individual needs others to realize the fullest of this potential. Development is more likely to be fostered by rational processes than an affective or intuitive capacity. Assumptions more directly related to counseling itself include the following:

1. Major traits of the individual are measurable and can be used as guides to matching that person to a vocation or job.
2. Information derived from the individual in testing and diagnostic interviewing can be used in decision making relative to vocational and general life adjustment.
3. Information derived from the individual must be considered in the light of demands made in the environment.
4. A major task in counseling is the systematic synthesis of information so that reasonable predictions can be made about the individual's "fit" with the job and other important dimensions of the environment.

The goal of counseling is a broad one; to assist clients toward the optimal development in all aspects of their personalities. Considerable stress is placed on "social enlightenment, self-understanding and self-direction" rather than an autonomous individuation. The client is expected to be a responsible member of society and conform to its mores and values.

Techniques of counseling are not fully explicated, but the steps in the counseling process have been rather clearly delineated as follows:

1. Analysis, the initial step, involves the systematic collection of data and information about the client to acquire an understanding of the client's problem and the demands of current and future adjustment. Specific tools will vary with the setting, but include the initial interview, case history, medical history, and psychological tests. From these are derived family history, health history, educational and work history, and an overview of social, avocational and vocational interests and objectives.

2. Synthesis is the summarizing and organizing of data to determine the client's assets, liabilities, adjustments, and maladjustments.

3. Diagnosis pertains to the summary of problems, their causes, and implications for future adjustment (prognosis). Unlike medical diagnosis, which is almost solely the practitioner's responsibility, diagnosis involves the client's participation to the extent of his or her intellectual and emotional capabilities.

4. Counseling is viewed as that phase in which the counselor assists the client in utilizing internal and external resources to achieve optimum adjustment. It involves a process of guided reeducation. Five categories of techniques have been identified, including forcing conformity, changing the environment, selecting the appropriate environment, learning needed skills, and changing attitudes. These are general headings; specific techniques vary with the individual client and the presenting problem. Some common threads throughout include establishing rapport, cultivating self-understanding, and advising or planning a program of action. The counselor is active in the process, avoids being dogmatic, but may offer advice and information freely, while encouraging the client to express and bring out ideas. Direct assistance in implementing the plan is proffered when necessary and the counselor will involve others as deemed appropriate.

5. Follow-up is not fully explicated, but implies availability of the counselor to deal with recurring problems and to determine if the counseling has been effective.

No systematic procedures have been developed as criteria for change under this approach. Since the approach has been used extensively in the university setting, educational and vocational success have been cited as appropriate indicators. Client satisfaction and satisfactoriness on the job, measurement concepts developed in the Minnesota Studies on Vocational Rehabilitation, could be logically used under this approach as indices of effectiveness.

Of all the approaches reviewed in this chapter, trait-factor counseling most closely parallels the practice of the majority of rehabilitation counselors, particularly within state agencies. If a client is eligible for service under the state-federal system, there are no serious restrictions to the use of the trait-factor approach. Clients served in other settings who have serious thought disorders, or quite limited intelligence, may not be appropriate. A major counselor requirement is the ability to interpret psychological test results and to understand the merits and liabilities of psychological measurement. Goals of counseling are generally congruent with the broader goals of rehabilitation. Techniques are usually well within the repertoire of skills of most rehabilitation counselors and deemed appropriate in most settings. Some counselors, however, will have difficulty in accepting the philosophical underpinnings of this approach.

Rational-Emotive Therapy. Rational-Emotive Therapy (RET) is the product of Albert Ellis, who like Rogers and Perls made a significant departure from psychoanalysis. His approach emerged from his clinical practice which was primarily in marital counseling.

A key to understanding RET is the so-called A-B-C paradigm. "When a highly charged emotional consequence (C) follows a significant Activating Event (A), A may be seen to, but does not actually, cause C. Instead, emotional consequences are largely created by B, the individuals' Belief System" (Ellis, 1973, p. 167). In other words, it is not what happens that causes difficulty and stress, but the person's irrational beliefs. If these beliefs can be rationally challenged and disputed, the undesirable emotional consequences will cease. Major assumptions underlying this approach to therapy include:

1. Humans have an innate potential for rational thinking.
2. Irrational thinking is acquired by learning, usually at an early age.
3. Perception, thinking, and emoting are interdependent and occur simultaneously.
4. Irrational beliefs, when they cause emotional disturbance, are primarily faulty and/or negative self-verbalizations.

5. These irrational beliefs may be supplanted and thus overcome by inducing the individual to verbalize positive self-verbalizations.

A focal point in the theory is that eleven illogical ideas form the basis of self-defeating attitudes and neuroses (Ellis, 1960). In outline, these illogical beliefs are:

1. It is imperative to be loved or approved by everybody.
2. People must be perfectly competent, adequate, and achieving to consider themselves worthwhile.
3. Some people are bad, wicked, or villainous and therefore should be blamed and punished.
4. It is catastrophic when conditions are not as people want them to be.
5. Unhappiness is caused by outside circumstances over which people have no control.
6. Dangerous or fearsome things are causes for great concern and continuing preoccupation.
7. It is easier to avoid certain difficulties and self-responsibilities than to face them.
8. People need to be dependent on others.
9. Past experiences and events determine present behavior, and their influence cannot be eradicated.
10. People should be quite upset over other people's problems and disturbances.
11. There is always a right or perfect solution to every problem and unless found, results will be catastrophic.

A succinct statement of the goals of therapy must be implied; essentially, it is to eliminate emotional disturbance by substituting rational beliefs and thinking for the irrationality. As a result of successful RET, clients become more independent of the evaluations of others and rely more on positive self-reinforcement for their behavior.

Conventional techniques used in psychoanalytic and client-centered therapy are avoided. The client is discouraged from relating past history, abreacting, or free associating. Ellis views such techniques as free association, dream analysis, dynamically oriented interpretation and reassurance as inefficient and sidetracking. Generally, the therapist uses an active directive approach to identify the core of irrational ideas that are basic to disturbed behavior, challenges the client to validate those ideas, demonstrates to the client the illogical nature of the ideas, and directively shows how they do not work. Rational substitutes are introduced and the client is taught how to sequence them. Homework assignments are often made in which the client may listen to cassette recordings of the previous session or record situations between sessions in which irrational beliefs have been assailed.

Criteria for success of the approach are couched in general terms, as in the following quote from Ellis (1973, p. 200),

> Rational-emotive therapy is a method of personality change that quickly and efficiently helps the individual to foster and implement his human tendencies to gain more individuality, freedom of choice and enjoyment and also helps him to discipline himself so that he minimizes his natural human tendencies to be conforming, suggestible and unenjoying.

These criteria have been operationally defined primarily by therapist report. However, researchers are developing "irrational" belief scales that show promise for assessing the effectiveness of the approach.

Applicability of RET to rehabilitation settings may be assessed on a number of points. It does not appear to be feasible for individuals of low intelligence or thought disorders associated with brain damage. It does not appear to be routinely called for in educational and vocational decision making, but is more appropriate when lack of acceptance of disability interferes with this process, or when the client is overwhelmed by the transition from the hospital or institution to the community. Counselors may have philosophical reservations about the approach, and those who do not should receive specific training in the techniques beyond that usually incorporated in most formal counselor education programs. The didactic and directive aspects would blend reasonably well with the training programs in most settings. Referral of selected clients for formal RET would be feasible and appropriate.

Reality Therapy. One other rational approach should be briefly noted. Reality therapy, a relative newcomer to the field of psychological treatment, was introduced by Glasser (1965, 1969). Glasser and Zunin (1973, p. 287) describe reality therapy as being applicable to individuals with behavioral and emotional problems—focusing on the present and on behavior, the therapist guides the individual to enable him to fulfill his own needs without harming himself or others. The crux of the theory is personal responsibility for one's own behavior, which is equated with mental health.

In the counseling process, the counselor is verbally active, sets limits, is guided by a precise behavior contract with the client, and may engage in a wide variety of interactional techniques (e.g., confrontation and constructive arguing) that directs the client to the realities of the present and immediate future. The focus is on behaviors, not on feelings, and particularly on how clients will act in a responsible manner on their own behalf.

Reality therapy has not yet been widely used in rehabilitation settings, but it does appear to have potential value for those with "responsibility" problems, for example, the public offender and the overly dependent client. Although the basic tenets have been thoroughly documented, little research has been conducted to verify their utility.

Behavioral Approaches

The term behavioral approaches may be extended to include those counseling strategies that involve learning theory principles and focus on change of behavior rather than feelings, attitudes, or beliefs, but do involve a therapist-client relationship rather than a behavior management paradigm. Two approaches have been selected for more detailed review, Krumboltz's behavioral counseling and Wolpe's psychotherapy by reciprocal inhibition. Two others, Rotter's Social Learning approach and Dollard and Miller's marriage of reinforcement and psychoanalytic theories will be briefly noted.

Krumboltz's Behavioral Counseling. Expounded by John Krumboltz and a number of associates and students at Stanford University, this approach was developed initially for counseling services in the public school setting. Basic references include Krumboltz and Thoresen (1969; 1976) and Hosford and de Visser (1974). Highly eclectic in the use of techniques, its theoretical principles stem primarily from learning theory. Basic concepts include the following:

1. People have equal potentialities for good and evil.
2. People are capable of change.

3. Each person has unique problems that must be appreciated on an individual basis.
4. Behavior is guided by external conditions that are interpreted by the individual's cognitive processes.

There is little preoccupation with the causality and classification of maladaptive behavior. No assumptions are made about psychopathological processes. Current problems may stem from either learned maladaptive behavior or failure to have learned specific adaptive behaviors. The focus is on identifying the client's current problem, establishing specific behavioral goals to alleviate the problem, and selecting the most appropriate techniques to achieve the goal.

In their introduction, Krumboltz and Thoreson (1969) identify four general types of problems:

1. Deficient decision-making skills;
2. Ineffective academic (vocationally related) skills;
3. Inappropriate social skills;
4. Self-defeating fears and anxieties.

Essential features include four interrelated characteristics that enable behavioral counselors to respond flexibly and adapt new continuously improving procedures to help their clients.

The first concerns the process of formulating counseling goals. Of all the major approaches, behavioral counseling places the greatest emphasis on the process of goal formulation. A goal should meet three essential criteria:

1. It must be desired by the client.
2. The counselor must be willing to help the client achieve the goal.
3. It must be possible to assess the extent to which the client achieves the goal (Krumboltz, 1966).

A second feature is that the same technique not be universally applied. A procedure or combination of procedures is selected to help clients accomplish their unique goals. Third, there are no restrictions on the possible techniques to be used, except those imposed by ethical considerations. There is no recommended approved list; counselors are encouraged to experiment and systematically explore new techniques, provided, of course, these are within their repertoire of skills. Finally, procedures need to be modified and changed on the basis of empirical evidence.

Three classifications of goals are recognized: altering or diminishing maladaptive behavior, learning the decision-making process, and preventing problems. The latter includes the acquisition of new behaviors, for example, job seeking skills, which will be needed to prevent difficulties in the future.

With the wide range of continually evolving techniques permissible under this approach, no single listing is feasible. See Krumboltz and Thoresen (1969; 1976) for a comprehensive overview that includes reinforcement techniques, role playing, social modeling, counterconditioning, and cognitive techniques such as simulation and planning. Certain traditional procedures that focus primarily on feelings, experiencing, and insight, while not expressly "forbidden," do not logically fit the system. One procedural element common to most techniques is the written behavioral contract in which the commitments of the client and counselor toward achievement of the goal are clearly identified.

Criteria for success under this approach tend to be unique to each client. Generally, these can be defined as the acquisition of adaptive behavior or extinction of problem behavior as reported by the counselor, the client, or significant others.

The approach appears to be applicable to a wide range of rehabilitation settings and clientele. No categories of clients are arbitrarily excluded. Presenting problems of substantial numbers of rehabilitation clientele, for example, absence of job seeking and maintaining skills, inappropriate social behaviors, and fears related to changing vocations, are amenable to behavioral counseling. Counselors would require special training in the application of techniques based on the learning theory model as well as training in the skills of problem identification and goal formulation. Techniques that require cooperation of others, for example, maintaining reinforcement contingencies, may set some limits on application.

Wolpe's Psychotherapy by Reciprocal Inhibition. Joseph Wolpe (1958; 1969) developed his approach from a background in psychiatry and as a reaction to psychoanalysis. His approach evolved mainly from his studies of experimental neuroses in animals. In the course of his investigations, he induced in cats, neurotic reactions that he found could be reduced by conditioned inhibition. The basic concept, reciprocal inhibition, refers to the inhibition, elimination, or weakening of old responses, such as anxiety or fear, by new responses through the process of conditioning. Wolpe is not explicit regarding his philosophy concerning the nature of humans. Inherent in his approach, however, is the belief that the same laws of behavior apply to humans as they do to lower animals. Although humans are recognized as rational beings, the higher aesthetic or spiritual qualities have been largely ignored. The focus is on conditioning, the laws of which apply to humans as they do to other animals. His focus in therapy is primarily on removing neurotic behavior—learned, persistent, and maladaptive habits.

The goal of therapy is to overcome and assuage the suffering associated with neurotic systems. Once clients have identified their difficulties, it becomes incumbent upon the therapist to apply experimentally established principles of learning to change maladaptive behavior. Responsibility for change rests primarily with the therapist. Emphasis is on the techniques rather than on the therapist-client relationship, although the importance of the latter is recognized in facilitating conditioning.

In therapy three categories of conditioning are recognized:

1. Counterconditioning is the elimination of such maladaptive responses as anxiety, usually by a competing relaxation response developed through reciprocal inhibition.
2. Positive reconditioning is the establishment of new behaviors usually through operant conditioning precepts.
3. Experimental extinction occurs when maladaptive behavior is systematically not reinforced and consequently weakens.

The process of therapy begins with an exploration of the client's presenting problems. Life history is reviewed including family and social relationships, education, vocational history, and sexual development. Selected psychological testing is done; the Willoughby Questionnaire and a Fear Survey Schedule are often used. A medical evaluation is conducted primarily to rule out organic causes or other confounding conditions. As the therapist reviews the treatment plan with the client, an objective nonjudgmental stance is maintained. Care is taken not to place blame on clients and to assure them that behavior is learned and can be unlearned. Treatment is preceded by a didactic introduction to the principles and procedures of behavior therapy.

Specific techniques are selected to match the unique problem of the client. The major ones include assertiveness training, systematic desensitization (which includes a number of variants), aversion therapy, therapeutic sexual arousal, and operant conditioning methods. Of these, the first two are the best known and probably are most relevant to rehabilitation clientele.

Assertiveness training is used when clients recognize they need to be more assertive but are unable to change; simple instructions, urging to act, or behavioral rehearsal are used to elicit assertive behavior. Clients are encouraged to practice outside the therapy period, report their progress, and are commended for assertive action.

Systematic desensitization is used to reduce phobic reactions and involves the breaking down of neurotic anxiety responses step by step. The treatment may be conceptualized in three phases. The first is the induction of a state that is physiologically inhibiting to anxiety. Relaxation, used in most cases, is acquired by training. A second and overlapping phase is the development of an anxiety hierarchy related to the focal fear identified from the history and psychological testing. To illustrate, an anxiety hierarchy related to fear of snakes may range from imagining a picture of a snake to imagining touching one. The treatment phase entails the sequential presentation of stimuli contiguously with relaxation. Successful systematic desensitization requires the client to use both relaxation and imagery. Criteria for change require evaluation of improvement in the unique problem behaviors of the individual clients. Measurement is contingent upon observations by the client, therapist, or significant others.

There is no evidence that Wolpe's approach has been applied extensively in rehabilitation settings. Assertiveness training has been used selectively, although usually not in the context of Wolpe's reciprocal inhibition. Desensitization procedures appear appropriate not only for clients with nondisability related anxiety and specific fears, but also for clients with concerns directly related to traumatic disabilities, for example, return to work, maintaining family and social relationships, and sexual readjustment. Certainly many unadaptive behaviors that directly interfere with vocational adjustment may be treated under this approach. The training required would rule out direct use by most rehabilitation counselors. Consideration may be given, however, for referral of selected cases to practitioners specializing in Wolpe's behavior therapy.

Other Behavioral or Learning Theory Approaches. Among the other behavior therapy approaches, two warrant brief mention. Dollard and Miller (1950) are of particular interest because of their attempt to integrate learning theory and psychoanalysis. Their techniques are reminiscent of psychoanalysis, but their explanation of behavior change is couched primarily in learning theory concepts. For a recent summary of their approach see Patterson (1973).

Rotter's (1954) social learning theory, also summarized by Patterson (1973), is of interest more for its potential than for its direct impact on the field of counseling and psychotherapy. Its potential lies in the extension of learning theory to include concepts such as the locus of control in which there is a resurgence of interest in rehabilitation counseling research. Locus of control refers to clients' perceptions of whether behavior is controlled by outside forces or by themselves. For populations such as those in rehabilitation settings who find themselves in highly dependent situations, this concept is relevant. The potential of this approach appears to be not so much in the techniques proposed but in the use of constructs for explanation and measurement in the counseling process generally.

FUTURE TRENDS

Eclectic and Problem-Solving Approaches

Although it was once considered questionable for counselors to utilize techniques based on differing views of counseling and human development, the eclectic approach to counseling (best exemplified by Frederick Thorne, 1968) has recently gained a considerable measure of respectability. The eclectic approach represents attempts by counselors to develop their own systems of counseling based on all available scientific data on human behavior and the practice of counseling. Essentially, it allows the counselor to use techniques derived from a variety of theoretical systems as long as these techniques and related theoretical underpinnings can be logically integrated and are contextually appropriate.

Arguments against utilization of an eclectic approach have been primarily based on the idea that counselors risk considerable confusion and inconsistency when they select techniques derived from differing perspectives on human development and behavior. In other words, since different counseling theories suggest vastly different reasons for the ways people behave and develop, counselors should select one of these theories as a primary frame of reference. Otherwise, counselors might be using techniques that are inconsistent with their view of human behavior and development.

While this line of reasoning has merit in pointing out to counselors that they should attempt to avoid conflicts of purpose and strategy in their practice, it ignores the fact that no one counseling theory explains or provides for the remediation of all types of behavior problems. Also ignored is the fact that clients with similar behavior problems do not always respond well to the same types of treatment. Therefore, by limiting their practice to one "school of counseling," counselors are forced to assume a universality that simply does not exist.

The number of ways different counseling theories and techniques can be used to facilitate the attainment of positive personal adjustment is extensive. For example, counselors could combine the use of the client-centered theorist's facilitative relationship with the behaviorist's operant reinforcement techniques to facilitate the adjustment of a rebellious and hostile disabled client who finds it difficult to maintain old or establish new friendships due to a poor self-concept. Principles of facilitative confrontation could be combined with behavioral techniques to assist a client facing a difficult choice situation where rigorous self-assessment and environmental assessment are required. The possibilities are almost endless, as long as counselors carefully explore and resolve the philosophical and value conflicts that exist among the different theories.

A closely related, yet distinctive approach to counseling in which various theories and techniques are used is the problem-solving approach. In using this approach, the emphasis is on the systematic resolution, using all of the client, counselor, and environmental resources available, of whatever problems the client is presenting. For a recent review of problem solving to the counseling process, see Heppner (1978). Although one rather automatically associates the problem-solving approach with the behavioral approach because of their common emphasis on problem solving, it really transcends any particular school of counseling and is basically eclectic. However, it remains somewhat distinctive from what is traditionally thought of as an eclectic approach due to the amount of emphasis placed on systematic problem solving.

The influence of both the eclectic and problem-solving approaches to personal adjustment counseling in rehabilitation settings may be expected to increase because of the advantages they offer the counselor for flexibility and goal-orientedness.

Group, Milieu, and Environmental Strategies

In addition to recognizing the efficacy of using techniques derived from a variety of counseling theories, counselors are becoming more aware of the impact the environment can have on their clients' personal adjustment. This appreciation has resulted not only in changes in the counselor's role perception, but also in the use of a broader range of counseling techniques.

For rehabilitation counselors in particular, the days when counselors could limit their practice to "cubicle counseling" are over. In fact, it is really rather remarkable that counselors ever assumed that their one-hour-per-week contact with a client would be sufficient to signicantly impact on the client's behavior or development. After all, that left only about 111 of the client's waking hours per week for other influences.

Rehabilitation counselors working in either agency or facility settings can, and indeed should, use the environment in a variety of ways to facilitate their client's personal adjustment. For example, counselors in both settings can assign "homework" to their clients that involves practicing new and more effective ways of interacting with others. Or, counselors can work closely with the family, school, or other social institutions in arranging cooperative reinforcement schedules, or in providing more appropriate role models and greater opportunities for social interaction. Self-help groups such as Alcoholics Anonymous or Parents Without Partners can also be effectively used to complement individual counseling programs.

Because of its malleability, the rehabilitation workshop offers a particularly favorable setting for the application of an environmental or milieu approach to personal adjustment counseling. Although one normally associates the rehabilitation workshop with work adjustment and vocational training, it also offers considerable potential for helping clients attain improved levels of personal adjustment. Specifically, the same workshop staff and environment used to simulate real work conditions and facilitate positive work adjustment can also function as an adjunct to individual personal adjustment counseling.

An obvious reason why the workshop milieu offers potential as a personal adjustment counseling technique is that many of the same client learnings and behaviors contributing to positive work adjustment also contribute to effective interpersonal functioning. For example, the well-adjusted worker will possess good habits of personal hygiene, favorable interactions with other significant people, and characteristics of conscientiousness, dependability, and independence. Since the workshop milieu is almost always designed to foster these client characteristics as they relate to participation in the world of work, the counselor can work cooperatively with the client and workshop staff to promote the generalization of these learnings to other life areas.

Another strategy that rehabilitation counselors may use to

complement one-to-one methods is the group approach. Groups can be used for the specific purpose of providing clients with information, or as a personal adjustment counseling tool. Moreover, most of the major counseling theories presented earlier in this chapter allow for the application of their techniques on both a group and individual basis.

Utilization of the group approach in conjunction with one-to-one counseling may have many advantages over the use of individual methods alone. Not only do groups offer counselors a potentially more efficient use of their time, groups also facilitate the exchange of feelings and problems leading toward a social reality testing. Groups also offer the potential of providing clients with feedback on their interpersonal behavior, as well as the opportunity to discuss with others sharing similar problems the pros and cons of various solutions. Group members can also serve as positive role models and can provide a strong sense of support for clients learning to take risks in social situations. The group also provides clients with the opportunity to practice social skills learned, as well as the opportunity to share feelings with others. Since clients are often convinced that they are the only ones with particular concerns or feelings, the sharing of feelings can be an especially beneficial aspect of the group process.

While it is unlikely that the environmental, milieu, and group approaches will ever totally replace the one-to-one counseling relationship, utilization of these approaches as part of the counselor's overall strategy for facilitating personal adjustment provide the counselor with several treatment modalities to be selectively employed depending on the client's problem and social context.

CONCLUSIONS AND IMPLICATIONS FOR PRACTICE

An overview of the major counseling theories and related techniques rehabilitation counselors may use to facilitate positive personal adjustment has been presented in this chapter. The counselor's success in applying these theories and techniques will necessarily depend on the interaction of a number of counselor, client, process, outcome, and contextual variables. However, counselors are most likely to succeed when they genuinely care for the client's welfare and sincerely respect the client as a person. It is also important that counselors seek to develop in their clients and in themselves a sense of planfulness, and that they help their clients identify and capitalize on their abilities rather than dwelling on their disabilities.

Finally, it is important that counselors remain flexible enough in their practice to capitalize on the assets of different counseling theories and techniques in attempting to ameliorate the problems of different types of clients. Each and every approach to counseling presented in this chapter has something of value to offer the rehabilitation counselor—even to the counselor who almost exclusively practices vocational counseling, vocational evaluation, or job placement. The professional challenge and obligation is to develop a sense of when a particular theory or technique is appropriate and then to apply it creatively and effectively.

REFERENCES

Adler, A. *The practice and theory of individual psychology.* Paterson, N.J.: Littlefield, Adams, 1963.

Alexander, F. M. *Fundamentals of psychoanalysis.* New York: Norton, 1963.

Ayer, M. J., Wright, G. N., & Butler, A. J. Counselor orientation: Relationship with responsibilities and performance. In G. N. Wright (Ed.), *Wisconsin studies in vocational rehabilitation.* Madison, Wis.: University of Wisconsin Regional Rehabilitation Research Institute, 1968, *10*, 1–34.

Barclay, J. R. *Foundations of counseling strategies.* New York: Wiley, 1971.

Bergin, A. F., & Garfield, S. L. *Handbook of psychotherapy and behavior change.* New York: Wiley, 1971.

Beyrakal, S. A group experience with chronically disabled adolescents. *American Journal of Psychiatry,* 1975, *132,* 1291–1294.

Bolton, B. *Introduction to rehabilitation research.* Springfield, Ill.: Charles C Thomas, 1974a.

———. Three verbal interaction styles of rehabilitation counselors. *Rehabilitation Counseling Bulletin,* 1974b, *18,* 34–40.

———. Case performance characteristics associated with three counseling styles. *Rehabilitation Counseling Bulletin,* 1976, *19,* 464–468.

———. Methodological issues in the assessment of rehabilitation counselor performance. *Rehabilitation Counseling Bulletin,* 1978, *21,* 190–193.

————, & Jacques, M. E. (Eds.). *Rehabilitation counseling: Theory and practice.* Baltimore: University Park Press, 1978.

Bordin, E. S. *Psychological counseling.* New York: Appleton-Century-Crofts, 1955.

Boyle, P. S. Totally rehabilitating the physically disabled client: Recognizing the sexuality of the physically disabled individual. *Journal of Applied Rehabilitation Counseling,* 1976, *7,* 176–181.

Bryan, W. V. The effects of short-term individual and group counseling on the self-concept of physically handicapped workers in a sheltered workshop setting. *Dissertation Abstracts International,* 1974, *34* (8A, Pt. 1), 4729–4730.

Carkhuff, R. R., & Berenson, B. G. *Beyond counseling and therapy* (2nd ed.). New York: Holt, Rinehart and Winston, 1977.

Cimperman, A., & Dunn, M. Group therapy with spinal cord injured patients: A case study. *Rehabilitation Psychology,* 1974, *21,* 44–48.

Corsini, R. (Ed.). *Current psychotherapies.* Itasca, Ill.: F. E. Peacock, 1973.

Crites, J. O. *Vocational psychology.* New York: McGraw-Hill, 1969.

Dawis, R. V. The Minnesota studies in vocational rehabilitation. *Rehabilitation Counseling Bulletin,* 1967, *11,* 1–10.

Dollard, J., & Miller, N. E. *Personality and psychotherapy.* New York: McGraw-Hill, 1950.

Downing, L. R. *Counseling theories and techniques: Summarized and criticized.* Chicago: Nelson-Hall, 1975.

Ebra, G. Rehabilitation in end-stage renal disease. *Journal of Applied Rehabilitation Counseling,* 1975, *6,* 96–105.

Ellis, A. *Reason and emotion in psychotherapy.* New York: Lyle Stewart, 1960.

————. Rational-emotive therapy. In R. Corsini (Ed.), *Current Psychotherapies.* Itasca, Ill.: F. E. Peacock, 1973, pp. 167–206.

Eysenck, H. J. The effects of psychotherapy: An evaluation. *Journal of Consulting Psychology,* 1952, *16,* 319–324.

————. The effects of psychotherapy. In H. J. Eysenck (Ed.), *Handbook of abnormal psychology.* New York: Basic Books, 1961, pp. 697–725.

Fisher, S. The renal dialysis patient: A rational counseling approach. *Rehabilitation Counseling Bulletin,* 1976, *19,* 556–562.

Ford, D. H., & Urban, H. B. *Systems of psychotherapy: A comparative study.* New York: Wiley, 1963.

Freud, S., & Breuer, J. *Studies in hysteria* (1895). New York: Basic Books, 1957.

Fromm, E. *Man for himself*. New York: Holt, Rinehart and Winston, 1947.

Garfield, S. L. Research on client variables in psychotherapy. In A. E. Bergin & S. L. Garfield (Eds.), *Handbook of psychotherapy and behavior changes*. New York: Wiley, 1971, pp. 271–298.

Glasser, W. *Reality therapy*. New York: Harper & Row, 1965.

———. *Schools without failure*. New York: Harper & Row, 1969.

———, & Zunin, L. M. Reality therapy. In R. Corsini (Ed.), *Current psychotherapies*. Itasca, Ill.: F. E. Peacock, 1973, pp. 287–316.

Heppner, P. P. A review of the problem-solving literature and its relationship to the counseling process. *Journal of Counseling Psychology*, 1978, *25*, 366–375.

Horney, K. *Our inner conflicts*. New York: Norton, 1945.

Hosford, R. E., & deVisser, L. A. *Behavioral approaches to counseling: An introduction*. Washington, D.C.: American Personnel and Guidance Association Press, 1974.

Howard, K. I., & Orlinsky, D. E. Psychotherapeutic processes. In P. H. Mussen & M. R. Rosensweig (Eds.), *Annual Review of Psychology* (Vol. 23). Palo Alto, Calif.: Annual Reviews, Inc., 1972, pp. 615–668.

Jung, C. G. *Basic writings*. New York: Random House, 1959.

Kempler, W. Gestalt therapy. In R. Corsini (Ed.), *Current psychotherapies*. Itasca, Ill.: F. E. Peacock, 1973, pp. 251–286.

Kiesler, D. J. *The process of psychotherapy*. Chicago: Aldine, 1973.

Krieger, G. Loss and grief in rehabilitation of the severely traumatically disabled. *Journal of Applied Rehabilitation Counseling*, 1976, *7*, 223–227.

Krumboltz, J. O. Behavioral goals of counseling. *Journal of Counseling Psychology*, 1966, *13*, 153–159.

Krumboltz, J. O., & Thoresen, C. E. (Eds.). *Behavioral counseling: Cases and techniques*. New York: Holt, Rinehart and Winston, 1969.

———. *Counseling methods*. New York: Holt, Rinehart and Winston, 1976.

Levitsky, A., & Perls, F. S. The rules and games of Gestalt therapy. In J. Fagan & I. Shepherd (Eds.), *Gestalt therapy now*. Palo Alto, Calif.: Science and Behavior Books, 1970, pp. 140–149.

Luborsky, L., Chandler, M., Auerbach, A. H., & Cohen, J. Factors influencing the outcome of psychotherapy: A review of quantitative research. *Psychological Bulletin*, 1971, *75*, 145–185.

Marsden, G. Content analysis studies of psychotherapy: 1954–1968.

In A. E. Bergin & S. L. Garfield (Eds.), *Handbook of psychotherapy and behavior change.* New York: Wiley, 1971, pp. 345–407.

Meltzoff, J., & Kornreich, M. *Research in psychotherapy.* New York: Atherton, 1970.

Morse, S. J., & Watson, R. I. (Eds.). *Psychotherapies, A comparative casebook.* New York: Holt, Rinehart and Winston, 1977.

Moses, H. A., & Patterson, C. H. (Eds.). *Readings in rehabilitation counseling* (2nd ed.). Champaign, Ill.: Stipies, 1971.

Neff, W. S. *Work and human behavior.* New York: Atherton, 1968.

Passons, W. R. *Gestalt approaches in counseling.* New York: Holt, Rinehart and Winston, 1975.

Patterson, C. H. *Theories of counseling and psychotherapy* (2nd ed.). New York: Harper & Row, 1973.

Perls, F. *Gestalt therapy verbatim.* Lafayette, Calif.: Real People Press, 1969.

Perls, F., Hefferline, R. F., & Goodman, P. *Gestalt therapy.* New York: Julian Press, 1951.

Polster, E., & Polster, M. *Gestalt therapy integrated.* New York: Brunner/Mazel, 1973.

Rank, O. *Will therapy and truth and reality.* New York: Alfred A. Knopf, 1945.

Rogers, C. R. *Counseling and psychotherapy.* Boston: Houghton Mifflin, 1942.

————. *Client-centered therapy.* Boston: Houghton Mifflin, 1951.

————. The necessary and sufficient conditions of therapeutic personality change. *Journal of Consulting Psychology,* 1957, *21,* 95–103.

————. *On becoming a person: A therapist's view of psychotherapy.* Boston: Houghton Mifflin, 1961.

————, Gendlin, E. T., Kiesler, D. J., & Truax, C. B. (Eds.). *The therapeutic relationship and its impact: A study of psychotherapy with schizophrenics.* Madison, Wis.: The University of Wisconsin Press, 1967.

Rotter, J. B. *Social learning and clinical psychology.* Englewood Cliffs, N.J.: Prentice-Hall, 1954.

Sather, W. S., Wright, G. N., & Butler, A. J. An instrument for the measurement of counselor orientation. In G. N. Wright (Ed.), *Wisconsin studies in vocational rehabilitation.* Madison, Wis.: University of Wisconsin Regional Rehabilitation Research Institute, 1968, 9, 1–37.

Sullivan, H. S. *Conceptions of modern psychiatry.* Washington, D.C.: William Alanson White Psychiatric Foundation, 1947.

Thoreson, R. W., Smits, S. J., Butler, A. J., & Wright, G. N. Counselor problems associated with client characteristics. In G. N. Wright (Ed.), *Wisconsin studies in vocational rehabilitation.* Madison, Wis.: University of Wisconsin Regional Rehabilitation Research Institute, 1968, 3, 1–32.

Thorne, F. C. *Psychological case handling. Vol. 1: Establishing the conditions necessary for counseling and psychotherapy.* Brandon, Vt.: Clinical Psychology, 1968.

Truax, C. B., & Mitchell, K. M. Research on certain interpersonal skills in relation to process and outcome. In A. E. Bergin & S. L. Garfield (Eds.), *Handbook of psychotherapy and behavior change.* New York: Wiley, 1971, pp. 299–344.

Walls, R. T., & Tseng, M. S. Measurement of client outcomes in rehabilitation. In B. Bolton (Ed.), *Handbook of measurement and evaluation in rehabilitation.* Baltimore: University Park Press, 1976, pp. 207–226.

Williamson, E. G. *Counseling adolescents.* New York: McGraw-Hill, 1950.

———. *Vocational counseling.* New York: McGraw-Hill, 1965.

Wolberg, L. R. *The technique of psychotherapy* (3rd ed.). New York: Grune & Stratton, 1977.

Wolpe, J. *Psychotherapy by reciprocal inhibition.* Stanford, Calif.: Stanford University Press, 1958.

———. *The practice of behavior therapy.* New York: Pergamon, 1969.

Chapter 10

Placement and Career Development Counseling in Rehabilitation

David Vandergoot

INTRODUCTION: IMPORTANCE AND SCOPE OF CHAPTER

Since the 1920s, the state-federal system of vocational rehabilitation (VR) has maintained a goal of achieving employment for people with disabilities. Since employment was, and is, the focus of VR services, it is obvious that job placement would become an important target. Other rehabilitation service sectors, such as rehabilitation workshops and centers, have followed this lead.

Over the years, the focus on placement has become more intense as program funding and counselor evaluation in state rehabilitation agencies were often contingent on the number of placements achieved. A brief review of the literature, presented in the next sec-

The assistance of Dr. John D. Worrall and Mr. Richard J. Jacobsen is gratefully acknowledged.

tion, indicates that even with an intense focus for almost sixty years, there is little consensus in the field regarding what placement is or how to achieve it.

The Rehabilitation Act of 1973 did not include the word "vocational" in the title. This change was seen as a harbinger of a broadening expectation of what rehabilitation is to achieve. There have long been advocates of a more global approach to rehabilitation that would target psychosocial, family, leisure, and other important human accomplishments besides the vocational. The rehabilitation legislation enacted in 1978 continues and broadens this emphasis with the concept of independent living. How this will affect rehabilitation services is expected to gradually emerge over the next few years.

A parallel movement however, has also been taking place since 1973 that has actually increased the attention given to placement. As stated, there has long been debate over the status of placement as a central point in the rehabilitation process. Studies continually show that rehabilitation counselors, although acknowledging the centrality of placement, spend little time on actually providing placement services. A possible explanation may be that many graduate programs in rehabilitation counseling teach little about placement. Little attention has been given to developing placement theory; concentrated research efforts have been few; and placements may be more dependent on external factors such as labor market conditions. It is therefore reasoned that counselors cannot be held entirely responsible for not attending to placement. They may lack placement skills, have few guidelines to use in making service delivery decisions relevant to placement, and have little control over the factors that affect placement success.

The Rehabilitation Services Administration (RSA) of the federal government has responded by increasing the extent of funding for training and research in placement. Master's degree programs at Michigan State, Southern Illinois, and Drake Universities graduating placement specialists have been supported and others are being developed. A Regional Rehabilitation Research Institute with a placement emphasis has been funded at Portland State University and several other placement research and training projects have received substantial support. This approach is based on the assumption that more knowledge and better trained personnel will result in more effort directed at placement with a resulting increase in the effectiveness of vocational rehabilitation.

A second factor contributing to the attention given to placement can also be linked to the Act of 1973. A major emphasis of the Act was to redirect services to those who had *severe disabilities.* The types of disabilities now to be given priority were, in the past, usually relegated to the unfeasible category. People with these severe disabilities were thought to have little chance to be competitive in the labor market. Now that vocational services were to be directed toward people with severe disabilities, it would be reasonable to emphasize the development of new and more extensive placement techniques. The assumption appeared to be that people with severe disabilities would require different and more extensive placement services than people with less severe disabilities.

Whether or not this assumption and the one concerning training was valid is less important than the fact that rehabilitation professionals do not yet have a conceptual framework from which to draw guidelines for developing services and research. This fact reveals that the vocational rehabilitation profession is basically in its infancy. A central concern of this chapter is to suggest a conceptual framework that will contribute to the overall development of a comprehensive rehabilitation services model that views placement as an event within a person's overall career development. As important as placement is, it is a stepping stone. The real outcome that needs to be considered is the career that a person will pursue *over a working lifetime.*

Rehabilitation services are typically applied over a relatively brief period of a person's life. For that reason, these services cannot be expected to account for all potential career outcomes. However, while services are provided, a comprehensive career orientation may reduce the uncertainties involved and provide rehabilitants with more control over the direction of their careers.

A compelling reason for highlighting placement and other career development services is the discrepancies between the employment experiences of people with disabilities compared to people without disabilities. For the past ten years, studies have been directed at establishing how many people have work disabilities in the United States; for example, Haber (1968) reported an estimate of 17.8 million, and Fechter and Thorpe (1977), one of 12 million. The differences in estimates can be attributed to varying definitions used for work disability and differing age ranges covered.

One of the purposes of the landmark Comprehensive Service Needs Study (Urban Institute, 1975) was to establish the extent of work disability in the United States. The 1966 Survey of Disabled Adults was used as the basis for obtaining estimates. A figure of

23.3 million was derived that accounted for 18.7 percent of the population within the 18 to 64 year old age range.

A more important aspect of this study described how well people with disabilities fared in the labor market and labor force. Chapter 13 of the Comprehensive Service Needs Study reported findings summarized as follows:

1. People with disabilities tend to have labor force participation rates that are less than rates for nondisabled people (p. 292).
2. People with disabilities tend to do more part-time work and have lower annual and weekly earnings than nondisabled people (p. 294).
3. People with disabilities are generally members of the secondary labor market (pp. 295–297).
4. The demand for workers who have disabilities is less than the demand for workers in general (p. 299).
5. Employers tend to expect that hiring workers with disabilities will increase costs (p. 312).
6. Employer attitudes are generally unfavorable toward hiring people with disabilities (p. 324).
7. Certain groups of people with disabilities have a poorer record in the labor market than others. These include people who are mentally ill, mentally restored, mentally retarded, congenitally disabled, and older people with disabilities (p. 329).

Participation rates in the labor market can be affected by many factors. Among these, discrimination on the part of the employers to exclude certain groups, is likely. However, some individuals may decide not to pursue employment. This may occur, for example, when a person with a disability might lose disability benefits if employment is accepted, although the extent to which such factors actually operate is unclear. Again, a concentration on theory may suggest how influential these variables may be in certain circumstances. In any case, people with disabilities seem to be a hard-to-employ group.

The next section will briefly summarize literature relevant to placement and career development. Subsequent sections will include a reconceptualization of the rehabilitation process and include implications for practice. A concluding section will discuss the implications of this reconceptualization on the professional status of rehabilitation practitioners.

Background: Review of Rehabilitation Placement Literature

Two extensive placement literature reviews recently completed (Dunn, 1974; Zadny & James, 1976) both indicate that there has been a lack of synthesis regarding the placement process. Research and development projects concerning the placement process have proliferated without a clear-cut view of how innovations or even traditional practices can be integrated for application purposes. Without a conceptual framework, this situation cannot be expected to improve.

The field of counseling has had a similar problem of diversity without synthesis. One remedy suggested by a counseling researcher is a system of analysis guided by the following question: "What treatment, by whom, is most effective for this individual with that specific problem, and under which set of circumstances"? (Bergin & Garfield, 1971). This question can be transposed into a question relevant for the placement process: "What kind of *placement intervention,* by whom, is most effective with which individuals, and under which set of circumstances?" The following sections will review important placement literature that corresponds to the various segments of the question.

Placement Intervention: Treatment Approaches

Many strategies have been devised for facilitating placement. Only a few of the more recent ones will be reported here. Placement approaches can vary along several dimensions. They can be oriented either to groups or individuals. They can also be categorized according to the degree of responsibility residing with the client or counselor for various placement functions. Some strategies require more of counselors and others more of clients.

Selective placement has been described by McDonald (1974) as an approach that stresses direct intervention by the counselor within the labor market on behalf of the rehabilitation client. Direct intervention and job development techniques have been devised to aid the counselor in selective placement (Multi-Resource Centers, 1971). Salomone (1971) proposes a different method that stresses a "client-centered" approach requiring that the client assume most of the responsibility for job procurement. The counselor is required to serve as teacher and resource person to the job seeker.

Job-seeking skills packages have been developed to aid clients in finding their own jobs. Most of these emphasize a group-process approach for instructional purposes. Jones and Azrin (1973) apply behavioral analysis techniques to the study of the job-seeking process and formulate a group approach called the Job Finding Club. This process teaches job seekers to create their own informal networks of labor market information that will produce job leads. Members remain a part of the group until a job is found. Job leads and information are shared throughout the group. A description of how the approach works and a research study of a successful group is presented in Azrin, Flores, and Kaplan (1975). Keith, Engelkes, and Winborn (1977), in contrast, develop an individualized, programmed-learning format for teaching job-seeking skills. Molinaro (1977), on the other hand, recommends an approach that stresses that the rehabilitation professional should serve as a resource person to employers. As employers' needs are met, they will become more willing to hire qualified people who have been rehabilitated. Among the employer services that Molinaro (1977, p. 125) recommends are:

1. Worker compensation assistance;
2. Affirmative action consultation and implementation;
3. Awareness training;
4. Selective placement;
5. Follow-up;
6. Troubled employee assistance.

It is interesting to speculate about the potential effectiveness of various combinations of these approaches.

Ugland (1977) points out that the intensity with which an approach is used is also important. The implication is that job seeking requires a planful strategy, and concentrated, enthusiastic effort and time expenditures. In any case, traditional and formal approaches to job seeking, such as answering want ads and using the employment service, seem grossly inefficient as they account for only 10 to 15 percent of placements made by rehabilitation agencies (Zadny & James, 1976, pp. 27–28).

Placement Personnel: Who Is to Do Placement?

Placement has been a traditional part of the array of tasks required of rehabilitation counselors. In spite of this fact, there seems to be a long-term reluctance on the part of counselors to engage extensively in this task (Muthard & Salomone, 1969; Hagan, Haug, & Sussman, 1975). Recent literature has emphasized ways counselors can assume a more active placement role (Echols, 1972; Flannagan, 1974). An alternative approach is to use placement specialists in cooperation with counselors (Hutchinson & Cogan, 1974; Usdane, 1974). Placement specialists in this model would assume responsibility for job development after the counselor had helped the client attain job readiness. Empirical evidence remains to be developed on the efficacy of either of these strategies, and further research could explore different ways of integrating counseling and placement functions and personnel.

The role of the client in the placement process and, specifically, how much responsibility the client has for self-placement are intriguing issues raised by Salomone (1971). The degree to which a client can participate in placement depends on identifying relevant tasks and determining how clients can best work mutually with placement professionals. Clarifying this issue is an important research task.

Placement Techniques with Specific Disability Groups: Are Different Approaches Needed for Different Disability Groups?

The literature that describes placement practices in rehabilitation is extensive and is highlighted by the recent reviews by Dunn (1974) and Zadny and James (1976). Many efforts have been made to describe various kinds of placement programs and techniques for different disability groups. Rubin (1976) describes procedures for the placement of psychiatric patients. Mallik and Sablowsky (1975) describe a program that considers the placement needs of those with severe disabilities. The Second Institute on Rehabilitation Issues (1975) has developed a counselor's guide to placement of those with severe disabilities. People with hearing impairments (Vescovi, 1973), learning disabilities (Brolin & Kokaska, 1974), and various other disabling conditions have also received special attention in the placement literature. Whether the placement process can be assumed to be generally the same regardless of disability, or whether unique processes will need to be developed for people with different disabilities requires further investigation. Of interest in this regard is the development of techniques to measure the severity of disability by functional limitation rather than by disability classification. Granger and Sherwood (1975) report experimental work with the Barthel Index (Mahoney & Barthel, 1965) to measure severity. This kind of approach may improve the ability of placement professionals to individualize placement services.

Education, age, work experience, and socioeconomic status are variables that can be expected to relate to occupational achievement. However, Westerheide and Lenhart (1974) review the literature pertaining to the relationship of client characteristics to eventual rehabilitation success. They conclude that little can be consistently relied upon regarding predicting outcome from demographic characteristics. This conclusion may indicate that it is too early to specify placement approaches on the basis of disability type.

Situational Considerations: Are Different Placement Approaches Needed for Different Circumstances?

The context in which placement services are provided can also be expected to impact upon the success of those services. Several questions have already been raised in this review that are relevant. The group interaction format versus individual instruction is one such issue. Another issue relates to the type of instructional package, such as paper-and-pencil programmed instruction versus audiovisual instruction. The amount of client-counselor interaction in various placement-related activities is an important concern that also needs further study.

The situational context is being explored by research that considers job restructuring and modification (Mallik & Sablowsky, 1975). Affirmative action requires that entire working environments become accessible. The proper techniques for helping employers deal with affirmative action requirements must be developed (Molinaro, 1977). These are just a few of the concerns that relate to the situational context in which placement service delivery occurs.

Career Development Theories

Even a brief review of the literature exposes many uncertainties within the placement domain. Priorities for research and development need to be established, but even before this can occur, a clear understanding of the placement process must be developed. The effort to devise a conceptual framework for the placement process is an essential next step. Toward this end, brief overviews of several major career development theories will be presented.

The Career Development Theory of
Donald Super

Super has devoted approximately forty years to the study of career development (Super, 1942). His work is widely known and respected. A basic premise underlying Super's theory is that the self-concept of an individual will be reflected in the behavior exhibited by that person (Super, 1953; 1957). Thus, behaviors directed toward the pursuit of a career will be greatly determined by the self-concept. A job goal, level of education sought, and training attained by a person will all be dependent to an extent on how that person views himself or herself.

Implementation of the self-concept occurs throughout a person's life. Super hypothesized, however, that this process will take different forms according to the developmental stage a person is in. Each of the stages requires different tasks in order for the self-concept to be consistently implemented (Super, 1964, 1972; Super, Starishevsky, Matlin, & Jordan, 1963). Super's stages are as follows:

1. The growth stage—to about age 14;
2. The exploratory stage—to about age 25:
   a. Tentative;
   b. Transition;
   c. Uncommitted trial;
3. The establishment stage—to about age 45:
   a. Committed trial;
   b. Advancement;
4. The maintenance stage—to about age 65;
5. The decline stage—after age 65.

For rehabilitation purposes the second through the fourth stages are of primary concern in terms of career planning. Some of the particularly relevant tasks that Super hypothesized are:

1. Crystallizing ideas of a career orientation congruent with the self-concept—age 14 to 18;
2. Specifying a particular career direction—age 18 to 21;
3. Implementing a vocational preference by accepting a relevant placement—age 21 to 24;
4. Stabilizing in an occupation without major directional change—age 25 to 35;
5. Consolidating status and advancing vocationally—age 35 plus.

Super further suggests that other factors that affect career development need to be considered for planning purposes. A career is influenced by parental socioeconomic level, a person's mental ability and personality characteristics, as well as environmental factors such as labor market conditions. Adding these factors to those of the self-concept, developmental stages, and life tasks reveals the complexity that must be dealt with when attempting to control the direction of a career. To operationalize his theory, Super has researched the viability of a vocational maturity index. His efforts culminated in the development of the Career Development Inventory (Super, Zelkowitz, & Thompson, 1975). This index is comprised of several elements, including a measure of task accomplishment to indicate a person's developmental stage. It also provides an appraisal of a person's self-concept to indicate the degree of congruence between career direction and self-concept. Research with the Inventory has supported Super's ideas, although there appears to be a great deal that still needs to be incorporated into both the theory and the instrument to help account for more of the variability observed in making and implementing career decisions.

Super's theory provides a broad map with some of the signposts for planning career direction. More of the specifics need to be filled in before precise directions can be charted. One important task, particularly for rehabilitation professionals, is an elaboration of the impact disability may have on career development, especially in the cases where a disability is acquired in adult developmental stages. Literature discussing the impact of disability on the self-concept and other personality characteristics may be helpful in this regard. Wright (1960), McDaniel (1976), and Shontz (1975) have presented various viewpoints on this subject.

The Career Development Theory of John Holland

John Holland has been exploring career development for over two decades (Holland, 1959). He too has had a major impact on how the field of counseling conceptualizes the career development process. Whereas Super formulated his theory around the implementation of the self-concept, Holland used other personality variables to explain the course of a career. Career direction is viewed as an expression of personality. The quality of a career will depend on the extent to which the work environment is congruent with the personality (Holland, 1966; 1973).

Holland's research has led him to conclude that there are six basic personality types. These are labeled realistic, investigative, social, conventional, enterprising, and artistic. Similarly, he postulates that there are six environmental types that correspond in name and structure to the six personality types. In a work context, it is anticipated that the most suitable career outcomes will result when a match occurs between a personality and an environmental type. (See Table 10-1).

In practice personality types may consist of more than just one dominant characteristic. Personalities are frequently comprised of combinations of types. The interaction between environmental types occurs in much the same way. Therefore, arriving at a measure of congruence is more difficult than it might seem at first. Table 10-2 provides a sketch of the dominant personality types and the kinds of occupations that provide congruent work environments.

The thrust of Holland's theory deals with occupational choice. He presents two types of choice. The first, of course, is the overall decision itself, linking the personality with an appropriate work environment. The second type of choice involves the specific level within an occupation to which a person aspires. Occupational level is frequently dependent on a person's ability and intelligence,

Table 10–1 Elements of Holland's Theory

1. Organizing axioms
   a. In our culture, all persons can be assessed by their resemblance to each of the following personality types—Realistic, Investigative, Social, Conventional, Enterprising, and Artistic.
   b. The environments in which people live and work can be assessed by their resemblance to each of the following model environments —Realistic, Investigative, Social, Conventional, Enterprising, and Artistic.
   c. A person's behavior is determined by his or her interaction with his environment.
2. Personality types and patterns
3. Environmental models and patterns
4. Interrelationships between personalities and environments
5. Outcomes—Vocational behavior, social behavior, etc.

Source: Taken from Holland (1972; p. 56). Copyright 1972 by the American Personnel & Guidance Association. Reprinted with permission.

Table 10–2 Holland Personality Types and
Congruent Environments

Personality Type	Occupational Environment
Realistic	skilled trades, technical and some service occupations
Investigative	scientific and some technical occupations
Artistic	artistic, musical, and literary occupations
Social	educational and social welfare occupations
Enterprising	managerial and sales occupations
Conventional	office and clerical occupations

Source: Adapted from Holland (1974) with permission of the author and publisher.

whereas the initial choice is more dependent on personality variables.

Holland's theory outlines the types of choices a person is confronted with in the pursuit of a career. The variables upon which these choices depend are more explicit than those of Super. Holland has developed several widely used instruments, the Vocational Preference Inventory (Holland, 1965) and the Self-Directed Search (Holland, 1970), which permit the appraisal of the personality according to types. The Self-Directed Search also contains a system where the personality types can be related to the jobs classified in the Dictionary of Occupational Titles (DOT) (Holland, 1974). Similarly, ability and intelligence factors can be drawn from DOT job descriptions to see what levels of potentially congruent occupations are appropriate for these characteristics of an individual.

Holland's system has evolved practical applications useful in the counseling context. His integration of specific occupational information from the DOT is a practical aid to the counselor. His theory focuses on the individual's problem of deciding on a career direction. However, the theory does not explore longer range career direction, since there is no provision for predicting how the personality might evolve as a person becomes older, as Super's theory attempts to do. The theory also does not anticipate the effects a disability may have on career development.

The Minnesota Theory of Work Adjustment

The Theory of Work Adjustment (Dawis, England, & Lofquist, 1964; Dawis, Lofquist, & Weiss, 1968; Lofquist & Dawis, 1969) grew out of RSA-sponsored research at the University of Minnesota's Industrial Relations Center. Although much of the empirical work was done with various disability groups, the theory does not specifically address the impact disability may have on work adjustment or career development.

The theory was not actually directed at career development. Rather, it was intended to provide a system in which employment-related counseling services could be developed and subsequently evaluated. It evolved in a similar way to Holland's in that personality variables and congruent environmental matches became the focus of study. Ability factors and job characteristics were also considered relevant. Although the overall process and classes of factors seem much like Holland's, the individual elements are different. Table 10-3 provides a brief sketch of the theory's components.

Although as in Holland's theory, it might be assumed that a suitable outcome would be a close match between a worker's personality and ability with an appropriate work environment, the Theory of Work Adjustment extends the concept of successful outcome beyond this concept. Work adjustment is a continuous process that precedes and follows the initial placement. A successful work adjustment is earmarked by a worker's tenure in a job. Tenure is predicted by worker job satisfaction and job performance. A person will be more likely to stay on a job if satisfaction is present. If not, and if other factors permit, a dissatisfied worker can be expected to quit. An unsatisfactorily performing worker will probably be fired. Successful employment-related services result in a satisfied and capable worker who remains on the job and advances over time (See Figure 10-1).

Needs are the personality factors of most concern within the Theory of Work Adjustment. Twenty-one needs have been identified, for example, the need for advancement, using abilities, compensation, creativity, recognition, security, social service, social status, and autonomy. These needs vary in importance from person to person and reflect an individual's requirements in a work environment. Work environments, in turn, provide a variety of rewards. As rewards become available to satisfy needs, one degree of correspon-

Table 10–3 Propositions in the Theory of Work Adjustment

Proposition I. An individual's work adjustment at any point in time is indicated by his concurrent levels of satisfactoriness and satisfaction.

Proposition II. Satisfactoriness is a function of the correspondence between an individual's abilities and the ability requirements of the work environment, provided that the individual's needs correspond with the reinforcer system of the work environment.

> *Corollary IIa.* Knowledge of an individual's abilities and of his satisfactoriness permits the determination of the effective ability requirements of the work environment.

> *Corollary IIb.* Knowledge of the ability requirements of the work environment and of an individual's satisfactoriness permits the inference of an individual's abilities.

Proposition III. Satisfaction is a function of the correspondence between the reinforcer system of the work environment and the individual's needs, provided that the individual's abilities correspond with the ability requirements of the work environment.

> *Corollary IIIa.* Knowledge of an individual's needs and of his satisfaction permits the determination of the effective reinforcer system of the work environment for the individual.

> *Corollary IIIb.* Knowledge of the reinforcer system of the work environment and of an individual's satisfaction permits the inference of an individual's needs.

Proposition IV. Satisfaction moderates the functional relationship between satisfactoriness and ability-requirement correspondence.

Proposition V. Satisfactoriness moderates the functional relationship between satisfaction and need-reinforcer correspondence.

Proposition VI. The probability of an individual being forced out of the work environment is inversely related to his satisfactoriness.

Proposition VII. The probability of an individual voluntarily leaving the work environment is inversely related to his satisfaction.

Combining Propositions VI and VII, we have:

Proposition VIII. Tenure is a joint function of satisfactoriness and satisfaction.

Given Propositions II, III, and VIII, this corollary follows:

> *Corollary VIIIa.* Tenure is a function of ability-requirement and need-reinforcer correspondence.

Proposition IX. Work personality-work environment correspondence increases as a function of tenure.

Source: Quoted from Dawis, et al. (1968, p. 11) with permission.

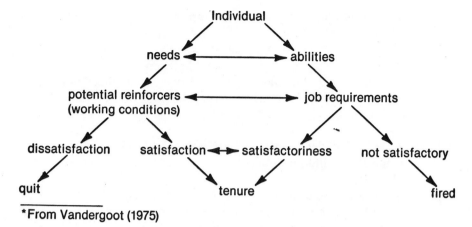

*From Vandergoot (1975)

Figure 10–1 Schematic of the Minnesota Theory of Work Adjustment

dence will be achieved. This correspondence is evident in the satisfied worker. The Minnesota Importance Questionnaire (Gay, Weiss,
Hendel, Dawis, & Lofquist, 1971) was developed to identify the
important needs of a person, and research has been done to specify
the types of rewards many occupations offer (Borgen, Weiss, Tinsley, Dawis, & Lofquist, 1968). The fact that the same terminology
is used to define needs and job rewards results in conceptual par-
simony. A disadvantage lies in the rather small pool of occupations
that have been analyzed for their reward systems.

Worker ability characteristics and job demands form the factors that determine the second necessary correspondence, if work
adjustment is to be achieved. An appropriate degree of congruence
between these factors will yield a satisfactory worker. The Theory
of Work Adjustment employs the General Aptitude Test Battery
(GATB) to operationalize the measure of abilities (United States
Training and Employment Service, 1966). The Dictionary of Occupational Titles presents the ability demands of jobs using the
same system as the GATB, thereby facilitating the matching of
worker abilities and viable job alternatives.

Additional research has been completed that illustrates the degree to which satisfaction and satisfactoriness are interdependent.
Many additional variables mediate this interaction, and a clear understanding for counseling purposes is difficult to achieve. However, this research attempts to explore the critical area of career
enhancement following placement. If rehabilitation services are to
become meaningful for long-range career development, this type

of research must be pursued and practical counseling applications developed. The Theory of Work Adjustment has offered rehabilitation professionals a capability to ascertain some of the prerequisites of choosing an initial career direction or placement. It has potential to aid in the development of practical approaches for helping people with disabilities prepare for their longer range career enhancement.

A Model for Placement and Career Development in the Rehabilitation Process

It is evident from the review of the literature that rehabilitation has a number of resources on which to draw for placement and career-oriented services. However, many of the placement techniques have not been researched, making their adequacy uncertain. This is not to say they are inadequate, only that the outcome of these services may not be predictable. And although current theories of career development have explored some of the important variables that affect careers, much remain to be explained. As a result, completely developed theories or concepts are not yet available for organizing placement and career development in rehabilitation.

Other information from the fields of economics and sociology highlights additional factors that affect labor market and labor force participation. The field of rehabilitation has not drawn extensively from these resources. One effort has been made to analyze labor markets and career development from available research in economics, sociology, and other fields such as industrial and organizational psychology (Vandergoot, Jacobsen, & Worrall, 1978). These authors demonstrate that rehabilitation research can be integrated with information from other disciplines, illustrating the unique interdisciplinary potential rehabilitation has. When viewed from this perspective, the rehabilitation professional possesses a unique and exciting challenge. The role of the rehabilitation professional will gain in status, since no other professional will be as uniquely prepared to offer employment services to people with handicaps.

Labor market analysis is an important facet of career development. One of the most important factors in labor market participation and maintenance in the labor force is productivity. People are hired and advanced on the basis of their perceived and observed level of productivity. An employer must ascertain a worker's productive potential in terms of that employer's specific needs. This, of course, has implications for the job searcher. Information must be sought regarding a specific employer's needs, and any information a job searcher uses should be tailored to address these needs.

Labor market participation is costly. Time and transportation requirements typically are demanding. A minimum of six weeks may be necessary for developing a job offer (Rosenfeld, 1975). It is important to plan a job search carefully to attain efficiency and thus increase the incentive for finding work. Such efficiency requires relevant up-to-date local labor market information about jobs that are in demand. Other desirable information would be data regarding advancement possibilities for the future.

To enhance placement and career development, rehabilitation services must attend to identifying and enriching a person's productivity by developing the necessary information base to plan and implement an effective job search. It is, therefore, proposed that the rehabilitation process consists of three phases. The first phase is *productivity enrichment* during which previously achieved levels of productivity are confirmed, and additional vocational preparation and training is pursued. The direction of this preparation should be determined on the basis of local labor market demand as well as personal preference. The second phase of rehabilitation is labeled *productivity realization* to denote the specific attempt to achieve placement that permits a full expression of a person's productivity. The third phase is concerned with a person's utilization of productivity and is therefore referred to as *career enhancement*. Each rehabilitation service can be identified as relevant to one or more of these phases.

The rest of this section will explore these phases in more depth and provide specific directions for service delivery. Prior to this, however, one caution must be offered in relation to the decision people make to participate in the labor market. This decision process is merely an alternative way for expressing the concept of motivation. Motivation is usually described in emotionally laden terms, which tends to cloud the fact that many individuals may make a rational decision to not participate in the labor force based on their assessment of the costs and benefits of working. Their assessment may be inaccurate, but the decision based on the perception may be logical. For people with disabilities, costs may exceed the benefits, which highlights the need to carefully consider costs and benefits, psychologically and financially, when helping a person make a decision regarding whether to pursue work.

The remainder of this section will review each of the three phases of the rehabilitation process. Stages within each phase will be described along with specific services that facilitate the process at each stage (see Figure 10-2).

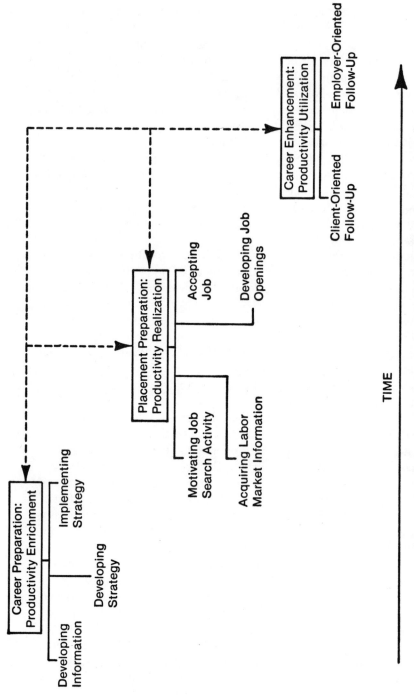

Figure 10–2 A Career Development Model of the Rehabilitation Process

The first phase is *productivity enrichment* in which vocational preparation is emphasized. The three stages of this phase include (1) information development, (2) strategy development, and (3) strategy implementation.

Information Development refers to that process whereby the data gathered by and for an individual client is put into the world-of-work context. Without grounding the extensive amount of information available about a person into a vocational context, a proper integration of a person's rehabilitation services with the desired vocational outcome is less likely to occur.

The information gathered regarding the individual should focus on needs and skills. The professional, as a vocational expert, must help the client understand these personal characteristics in vocational terms. Personal needs can usually be expressed by an individual. Identifying problems from which needs can be inferred is a traditional counseling practice. Skills can also be identified in this way, but documentation, such as school records, training reports, and interviews with previous supervisors might be helpful. At the outset skills should be defined rather broadly and include anything that might be advantageous in the labor market.

Skills can be broken down into general and specific categories. General skills are applicable across a wide range of occupations; specific skills may be appropriate to only one specific job. Both are valuable and an appropriate balance is important in the labor market.

A person's educational level and previous work experiences may give a view of general skills. Specific skills, if thought to be present, should be documented by achievement tests or on-the-job evaluations. Hidden aptitudes might be uncovered through standard work evaluations. Specific vocational concerns, such as work tolerance and coworker relationships, can also be discovered by work evaluation. However, these specific concerns should be phrased in question form prior to the evaluation, so that the evaluator may weigh a variety of hypotheses regarding specific vocational concerns.

Medical and psychological evaluation may be important, depending on the stability of any disability. However, here too, the rehabilitation professional should make special efforts to direct these evaluations to specific questions. Too often, physicians and psychologists report their findings in general terms and do not translate results into vocational implications.

Other skill areas also are important, particularly as they might influence work readiness. These include community living skills, personal care skills, leisure and recreational pursuits, problem-solving skills, and self-placement skills.

Finally, information must also be obtained regarding a client's current and future income and costs and the potential impact of rehabilitation on this financial picture. As previously indicated, a comparison of costs and benefits of working and not working may indicate a person's desire, or motivation to pursue rehabilitation. This assessment might also suggest what strategies are necessary to reduce costs and increase benefits. A rehabilitation professional's knowledge of community resources might be particularly relevant for this purpose. This initial financial assessment might be done in a general way. As rehabilitation proceeds, the precision of estimates should increase, and prior to planning the job search, this financial review should be repeated.

Financial costs and benefits are difficult enough to predict; psychological costs and benefits are even more difficult. However, they may be more important to the individual than financial concerns. The value of work for its own sake and for potential secondary benefits and costs should also be considered. These factors are often very personal and quite idiosyncratic. A highly individualized process is needed to effectively assess the full range of costs and benefits.

Strategy development is the second stage of productivity enrichment. The essential task is to construct a plan of rehabilitation services that will enable a person with a disability to obtain the desired placement and career goals. It is essentially a problem-solving and decision-making activity.

Goal setting initiates strategy development. Goals might be set rather broadly depending on how much information was obtained and integrated during information development. It is not necessary to concentrate specifically on vocational goals. Other life pursuits, such as recreation, might also be targeted. It is presumed that other activities are affected by a person's vocational experiences and vice versa. For example, recreational pursuits may be contingent on having employment that yields a certain excess amount of income. These recreational activities might then serve as delayed reinforcers to help motivate a person to become rehabilitated. The relationships among a person's personal goals, vocational or otherwise, should be explored for possible vocational implications.

Goals are valuable only as they become translated into concrete objectives that are further divided into steps or activities. These activities should be discrete tasks. The responsibility for completing each task should be clearly assigned to the client or rehabilitation professional. Other resources should also be considered.

This stage of the process requires precise counseling, communication, and coordination skills on the part of the rehabilitation professional. A great deal of information must be condensed into useful categories depending on its vocational significance, which must be done with the cooperation of the person with a disability. It, therefore, can become an instructional procedure during which a client can learn how to identify relevant information and use it for planning how to overcome problems or achieve desired goals. A crucial concern for the rehabilitation professional is to help the client perceive the interdependence of all of life's spheres. An appreciation of the impact of the family, for example, on vocational activities and vice versa is an intended outcome of strategy development.

Community resources should be a part of any plan. The rehabilitation professional should have a personal network that permits quick access to services. Although time is required to form close working relationships with other professionals, it can be expected that the flow of information will be greatly expedited and services offered with a greater amount of personal concern. Granovetter (1974) has indicated how such networks can improve job searching results. The same principle is likely to apply to other community resources as well. Allowing a client to have access to a diverse network also provides a learning opportunity that, in the future, should contribute to the independence of the client.

Although rehabilitation services can attend to a variety of needs, it is important to maintain emphasis on vocational preparation and productivity enrichment. Vocational services must be related to the demands of the local labor market unless a person has the capability of relocating to an area with a better demand.

Excellent resources are available on helping the rehabilitation professional develop expertise in strategy development. The field of counseling is particularly relevant. D'Zurilla and Goldfried (1971) outline a problem-solving and decision-making model that seems suitable. Mager (1962) details a procedure for generating objectives that are explicit and measureable. A comprehensive approach to strategy development can be found in Stewart, Winborn, Johnson, Burks, and Engelkes (1978).

The final stage of productivity enrichment is *strategy implementation*. When planning is completed, strategies should be developed and implemented without delay. This stage requires that strategies be clearly defined by task and person responsible for the task. Also, completion dates should be charted.

The rehabilitation professional is responsible for monitoring the progress of strategies. Documentation should be obtained from the client and professionals involved, such as training or classroom instructors. Contacts with the family may also be appropriate. Face-to-face meetings with the client may or may not be necessary. Maintaining an exchange of information is necessary, however. In addition, the rehabilitation professional must be prepared to play a supportive role and provide encouragement, counseling, and other resources as necessary.

Monitoring is important because even the best laid plans are usually deficient in some way. Flexibility should be maintained and plans should be revised regularly. However, revisions should be based on pertinent information just as during the initial planning stage.

It is important to recognize that not all plans, even when revised, will be successful. Again, motivation could be a factor. As recommended earlier, costs and benefits of participating in rehabilitation should be reviewed. This process might indicate the value a rehabilitation client attaches to successfully completing a rehabilitation plan.

After an adequate degree of productivity enrichment has been obtained, the rehabilitation process flows into the *productivity realization* phase. The ultimate outcome of productivity realization is expected to be placement. Placement is viewed as an event that marks a person's acceptance of a job offer. The rehabilitation process during this phase focuses on activities that will increase the likelihood of obtaining job offers. Productivity realization consists of four stages: (1) acquiring motivation for the job search, (2) acquiring labor market information, (3) developing job openings, and (4) accepting appropriate placement.

Acquiring motivation for the job search is crucial to rehabilitation. A careful analysis of financial and psychological costs and benefits may indicate how well a client will participate. As the rehabilitation process approaches placement, cost benefit analyses should become specific in two ways. First, the expected costs and benefits of actual employment should be estimated. At this point, it may be desirable to specify an intended range of occupations that are suitable placement goals in terms of their potential rewards. Second, costs of the job search should also be clarified. The time and financial investment in job searching is often overlooked. These items should be clarified in advance so that a job searcher does not have unrealistic expectations. Time involvement should be specified on a weekly basis and most likely, a minimum of six weeks of search might be expected. Such search costs as transportation should be estimated. If these costs appear excessive, additional funds or services should be secured.

A person with no previous, or negative, work experience, may have failed to understand the full meaning, benefits, and costs of work. The meaning of work for a client should be reviewed. If perceptions seem unrealistic, job site visitations and interviews with workers in the desired occupations might clarify matters.

Another factor in motivation might be a lack of job search skills. These skills should be carefully assessed by accurate simulations such as making practice telephone contacts, developing a resume, completing an application, and participating in an interview. If skills are deficient, job search skills training should be arranged. Special attention should be given to training that includes the identification and development of informal networks that produce job leads (Keith et al., 1977; Azrin et al., 1975). These networks typically include relatives, friends, and acquaintances. An increase in job search skills seems likely to be related to greater confidence in the performance of job search behaviors.

Careful job search planning that specifies goals and tasks will tend to increase motivation. Plans should seek to minimize costs. Appropriate labor markets should be identified that are accessible to the searcher. Search strategies should accommodate disabilities of clients, for example, transportation might be needed for a person with a mobility impairment or interpreters might be necessary for a person with a hearing impairment. Existing community resources, such as public and private employment services, should be integrated into the search plan. Such preparation would effectively instruct a client how to look for work.

Rehabilitation professionals must also be concerned with their own motivation to pursue placement. Studies continually show that little perceived time is spent in placement, even though it is acknowledged to be an important function (Muthard & Salomone, 1969; Fraser & Clowers, 1978). Possibly, caseloads are too large, paperwork too burdensome, business people too uncooperative, or required specialized skills are not acquired by typical rehabilitation professionals. Also, certain people with disabilities may appear to be unemployable. If rewards for the professional are dependent on placements, frustration may ensue. This negative relationship may result in avoidance of the placement function or a search for alternative means that require little personal involvement. The administrators of rehabilitation programs must seek to provide the structure and reward system to enable rehabilitation professionals to skillfully and energetically fulfill their placement function.

Once motivation is apparent and job search plans are formalized, productivity realization proceeds to *acquiring labor market information.* The job search is dependent on a flow of information from the labor market to the searcher (Granovetter, 1974), and, then, from the searcher to the market of choice (Lippman & McCall, 1976).

Appropriate labor markets must be identified in terms of geographical area, types of industries, and occupational classifications in which a job or job families can be found (Heneman & Yoder, 1965). *The Dictionary of Occupational Titles* and the *Occupational Outlook Handbook* are useful in this regard. Also, information previously obtained during information development can be applied again.

Once appropriate local labor markets have been identified, relevant information networks should be uncovered. Information networks can be formal, such as the want ads or an employment agency, or informal such as friends and relatives. Prime network contacts should be sought in the labor markets of choice and if specific firms can be identified, personnel of those firms should be tapped. Informal networks usually rely on word of mouth rather than written information that makes them more up to date. Also, since personal communication is involved, the credibility of the information may be less suspect.

These networks should be used not only to uncover job openings, but also to learn about employer recruitment practices. When these are known, particularly employer needs, the job searcher can tailor application information to maximize its attractiveness to the employer. Also, if one of these information resource people employed in a firm is willing to vouch for an applicant, the employer is likely to exercise greater care in making the hiring decision.

It must be recognized that employers use application blanks to screen out unlikely applicants. Resumes can counter this and should be constructed to express the capabilities of the job searcher. Resumes and applications serve to acquire interviews. Interview proficiency should be emphasized since job offers are dependent to an extent on successful interviews (Clowers & Fraser, 1977).

Again, acquiring information can be costly. Although information reduces uncertainty, diminishing returns may be expected. At some point, before information costs become excessive, the information should be put to use to develop job openings, the next stage of productivity realization.

Developing job openings is a difficult task because rehabilitation professionals and job searchers do not control demand in the labor market. The real job developers are employers. Employers incur costs, however, when they conduct transactions in the labor market. Job development practices within rehabilitation should concentrate on reducing employer hiring costs in instances where qualified rehabilitated people are available. Qualified applicants are, of course, necessary, and the proper information should be supplied to employers to certify an applicant's capabilities. Prior research should uncover exactly what type of qualities an employer desires.

Rehabilitation helps employers to reduce hiring costs by gaining their confidence in the client labor supply. Other employer cost-reducing services are helping employers develop hiring and performance rating criteria that are based on job requirements; providing postplacement adjustment services; consulting on job and work site modifications; job task restructuring; and helping employers develop career enhancement opportunities. The counselor's development of a consultative relationship with employers provides many mutual benefits, even though a specific placement may not be a particular focus.

One seemingly successful means of developing productive employer relationships is to use an employer and, possibly, a union advisory council. Such a formal relationship can provide benefits for all and can lead to successful job development. Advisory councils are most effective when they are actively used. Members can provide labor market data regarding current and future demands to plan training programs. Councils have developed training curricula and secured necessary equipment for rehabilitation facilities. This involvement insures them of gaining a qualified labor supply since training was geared to their specifications. Employers and unions might even supply training through on-the-job or apprenticeship programs. Council members have also been used to provide simulated job search practice for clients. Mock interviews with actual hiring gatekeepers are valuable experiences for clients. Council members, even when they are unable to provide placement, are usually willing to vouch for candidates among their peers, thus increasing the informal rehabilitation placement network among highly credible contacts. Informal networks evolved from councils and other employer-union contacts can become steady sources of job leads.

Active employer contact by rehabilitation professionals can bring the affirmative action requirements of the Rehabilitation Act of 1973 to bear in a positive way. Helping employers satisfy these legislative demands will become an increasingly valuable rehabilitation employer service. In this context, job development is an ongoing process of meeting employers' needs so that individual client placement needs can be accommodated in a timely way.

The final stage of productivity realization, if reached, is *accepting appropriate placement*. Ideally, if job development has been successful, several job offers will be obtained by a job searcher. Realistically, any job offer is usually welcome and often readily accepted without much thought. However, even if only one offer is available, more consideration should be given to the acceptance decision. The first placement can be expected to have important long-range career implications.

Unfortunately, there are few guidelines for this important decision. One broad guideline is to view the labor market as consisting of primary and secondary jobs. Primary jobs are reasonably permanent, offer good wages and benefits, and have an identified career ladder for long-term security. Secondary jobs are often seasonal, deadend, and offer poor wages and working conditions. The primary labor market should be the target of those clients who can qualify. Clients capable only of the secondary sector might require additional means of ongoing support. Continued training for people in the secondary market might also be considered until they advance.

The Seventh Institute on Rehabilitation Issues (1969) has described criteria for suitable placement. These include among others:

1. Occupation is consistent with the client's capacities and abilities.
2. Client possesses acceptable skills to perform or continue the work satisfactorily.
3. Employment and working conditions will not aggravate the client's disability in the job setting and will not jeopardize the safety of himself or herself or others.
4. Wage and working conditions conform to state and federal statutory requirements.
5. Employment is reasonably permanent.
6. Client receives a wage commensurate with that paid other workers for similar work (p. 22).

To this list, Dunn (1974) adds two others:

1. The job provides for up-grading and advancement within a reasonable period of time.

2. The wage received is sufficient to enable the client and his or her family to obtain a minimally sufficient standard of living, as defined by the poverty level (p. 18).

In order to effectively apply these criteria, information will be needed, which again highlights the need for labor market data and regular employer-union contact.

Work has many rewards. In addition to financial returns are satisfaction, status, recognition, interpersonal relationships, and leisure opportunities. All of these factors suggest that placement is an event that has serious long-range implications and must be carefully weighed before any job offer is accepted.

The final phase of the rehabilitation process is *career enhancement*. As a process, rehabilitation services can typically apply only to a brief span of a person's life. Rehabilitation cannot be held directly responsible for long-range outcomes. However, it seems plausible that more preparation for long-range career development will permit rehabilitated people to exercise more control over the future direction of their careers. Hence, it is valuable to study those factors that current career development theories suggest are operable. Unfortunately, practical applications for service delivery are not readily at hand.

If the prior two phases of rehabilitation have been successful, the client has probably been exposed to learning opportunities for developing adequate productive potential and suitable job offers. If learned well, the client can repeat these, perhaps independently over the course of a lifetime for career up-grading. The rehabilitation professional can assess a client's capability for this accomplishment, and, if needed, provide additional instruction and practice.

Following placement, adjustment services might be required. No matter how well a job was researched, actual working conditions may differ from what was expected. To help a rehabilitated person deal with this discrepancy, counseling may be necessary much as when the rehabilitation process first began. Problem identification and resolution can proceed as before. In some cases, adjustment will occur; however, the first placement may turn out to be inappropriate and a new one might need to be considered. Although the client may feel like a failure, job change should be viewed as a learning opportunity to better prepare for the next placement.

Usually, work adjustment is geared to client concerns. However, career enhancement can be facilitated by maintaining employer follow-up as well. If employer job development activities had been implemented, follow-up will occur as part of the ongoing relationship. If the placement resulted from a new contact, development activities should begin as follow-up. The employer's primary need will be to insure that the new employee is successful. Adjustment services, therefore, serve employer needs as well. Other employer needs can be accommodated, such as job site and task restructuring. A new placement is a starting point, upon which an ongoing consultative relationship can be set up. This will help the employer gain confidence in the rehabilitation professional and the rehabilitation system. This regular contact will enable the rehabilitation professional to have an impact on the career development of the employed client. Although career enhancement is a major concern of rehabilitation, little is known about implementing such services. Rehabilitation researchers and practitioners need to attend creatively to this important facet.

CONCLUSION: IMPLICATIONS FOR REHABILITATION PROFESSIONALS

To some rehabilitation professionals, the terms used in the previous section may seem strange, but the examples of services may appear quite traditional. Why, then, the need for new descriptors? It is more than for just appearance's sake. Since vocational rehabilitation must interact with labor markets, what rehabilitation does must have an impact on these markets. Rehabilitation has not evolved a strong theoretical or research base of its own. If the conceptual view of rehabilitation presented here as emerging primarily from economics and sociology, is valid, then it makes sense to structure services accordingly. It is to the credit of rehabilitation that much of what it does seems consistent with this conceptual view.

The rehabilitation process presented here is directed at placement and long-term career development for people with disabilities. It is evident that career outcomes depend on professionals expert in labor market economics, information development and utilization, communication skills, community organization, and development. All of this environmental input requires translation into a personally meaningful vocational context for clients. When viewed this way, the value of a rehabilitation professional, for people with disabilities and for society in general, becomes clear.

The career development perspective of the rehabilitation process presented here indicates the information that is needed from a variety of sources, and suggests when and how it can be used best. This information is intended to be used for explicit economic reasons, namely, the reduction of costs to the client and employer, and an increase in benefits. These costs and benefits refer to psychological as well as economic factors.

Rehabilitation professionals, when using this framework, will have a clear idea of the functions to be performed in order to deliver appropriate services that will lead to suitable placement and career outcomes. They will be able to give clients a strong rationale for each service they recommend. Clients should be able to understand why things happen the way they do and how their chances for labor market and labor force participation will be increased. Using the conceptual view offered here, rehabilitation professionals can structure and communicate rehabilitation services to clients, employers, and others interested in productive rehabilitation services.

REFERENCES

Azrin, N. H., Flores, T., & Kaplan, S. J. Job-finding club: A group assisted program for obtaining employment. *Behavior Research and Therapy,* 1975, *13,* 17–27.

Bergin, A. E., & Garfield, S. L. The evaluation of therapeutic outcomes. *Handbook of psychotherapy and behavior change.* New York: Wiley, 1971.

Borgen, F. H., Weiss, D. J., Tinsley, H. E., Dawis, R. V., & Lofquist, L. H., Occupational reinforcer patterns (first volume). *Minnesota studies in vocational rehabilitation,* No. XXIV, 1968.

Brolin, D., & Kokaska, C. Critical issues in job placement of the educable mentally retarded. *Rehabilitation Literature,* 1974, 35(6), 174–177.

Clowers, M. R., & Fraser, R. T. Employment interview literature: A perspective for the counselor. *Vocational Guidance Quarterly,* 1977, 26(1), 13–26.

Dawis, R. V., England, G. W., & Lofquist, L. H. A theory of work adjustment, *Minnesota studies in vocational rehabilitation,* No. XV, 1964.

Dawis, R. V., Lofquist, L. H., & Weiss, D. J. A theory of work adjustment—A revision. *Minnesota studies in vocational rehabilitation,* No. XXIII, 1968.

Dunn, D. *Placement services in the vocational rehabilitation program* (Tech. Rep.). Menominee: University of Wisconsin-Stout, Research and Training Center, 1974.

D'Zurilla, T. J., & Goldfried, M. R. Problem solving and behavior modification. *Journal of Abnormal Psychology*, 1971, 78, 107–126.

Echols, F. H. Rehabilitation counselor's responsibility for placement. *Journal of Applied Rehabilitation Counseling*, 1972, 3(2), 72–75.

Fechter, A. E., & Thorpe, C. O. *Labor market discrimination against the handicapped: An initial inquiry*. Washington, D.C.: The Urban Institute, 1977.

Flannagan, T. Whatever happened to job placement? *Vocational Guidance Quarterly*, 1974, 22(3), 209–213.

Fraser, R. T., & Clowers, M. R. Rehabilitation counselor functions: Perceptions of time spent and complexity. *Journal of Applied Rehabilitation Counseling*, 1978, 9(2), 31–35.

Gay, E. G., Weiss, D. J., Hendel, D. D., Dawis, R. V., & Lofquist, L. H. Manual for the Minnesota Importance Questionnaire. *Minnesota studies in vocational rehabilitation*, No. XXVIII, 1971.

Granger, C., & Sherwood, L. *Preliminary analysis of the Barthel Index and Granger Modifications*. Unpublished manuscript, 1975.

Granovetter, M. S. *Getting a job: A study of contracts and careers*. Cambridge: Harvard University Press, 1974.

Haber, L. D. Disability, work, and income maintenance: *Prevalence of disability, 1966* (Report No. 2). Social Security Survey of the Disabled, 1966, U.S. Department of HEW, SSA, Office of Research and Statistics, May 1968.

Hagen, F. E., Haug, M. R., & Sussman, M. B. *Comparative profiles of the rehabilitation counseling graduate: 1965 and 1972*. Cleveland: Case Western Reserve University, 1975.

Heneman, H. G., & Yoder, D. *Labor economics*. Cincinnati: South-Western, 1965.

Holland, J. L. A theory of vocational choice. *Journal of Counseling Psychology*, 1959, 6, 35–44.

———. *Manual for the Vocational Preference Inventory* (6th rev.). Palo Alto: Consulting Psychologists Press, 1965.

———. *The psychology of vocational choice*. Waltham, Mass.: Blaisdell, 1966.

———. *The self-directed search*. Palo Alto: Consulting Psychologists Press, 1970.

———. The present status of a theory of occupational choice. In J. Whiteley & A. Resinkoff (Eds.), *Perspectives on vocational development*. Washington, D.C.: American Personnel and Guidance Association, 1972.

————. *Making vocational choices: A theory of careers.* Englewood Cliffs, N.J.: Prentice-Hall, 1973.

————. *The Occupations Finder.* Palo Alto: Consulting Psychologists Press, 1974.

Hutchinson, J., & Cogan, F. Rehabilitation manpower specialist: A job description of placement personnel. *Journal of Rehabilitation,* 1974, *40*(2), 31–33.

Jones, R. J., & Azrin, N. H. An experimental application of a social reinforcement approach to the problem of job-finding. *Journal of Applied Behavior Analysis,* 1973, *6*(3), 345–353.

Keith, R. D., Engelkes, J. R., & Winborn, B. B. Employment-seeking preparation and activity: An experimental job-placement training model for rehabilitation clients. *Rehabilitation Counseling Bulletin,* 1977, *21*(2), 159–165.

Lippman, S. A., & McCall, J. J. The economics of job search: A survey. *Economic Inquiry,* 1976, *14,* 155–189.

Lofquist, L. H., & Dawis, R. V. *Adjustment to work.* New York: Appleton-Century-Crofts, 1969.

Mager, R. F. *Preparing instructional objectives.* Palo Alto: Fearon, 1962.

Mahoney, F. S., & Barthel, D. W. Functional evaluations: Barthel Index. *Maryland State Medical Journal,* 1965, *2* (February), 61–65.

Mallik, K., & Sablowsky, R. Model for placement: Job laboratory approach. *Journal of Rehabilitation,* 1975, *41*(6), 14–20.

McDaniel, J. W. *Physical disability and human behavior* (2nd ed.). New York: Pergamon, 1976.

McDonald, D. J. The rehabilitation counselor: A resource person to industry: A revitalized approach to selective placement. *The Journal of Applied Rehabilitation Counseling,* 1974, *5*(1), 3–7.

Molinaro, D. A placement system develops and settles: The Michigan model. *Rehabilitation Counseling Bulletin,* 1977, *21*(2), 121–129.

Multi-Resource Centers. *Job development reference manual.* Minneapolis: Minneapolis Rehabilitation Center, 1971.

Muthard, J. E., & Salomone, P. R. The roles and functions of the rehabilitation counselor. *Rehabilitation Counseling Bulletin,* 1969, *13*(1-SP), 1–168.

Rosenfeld, C. Job seeking methods used by American workers. *Monthly Labor Review,* 1975, *98,* 39–43.

Rubin, S. E. *Service intervention factors related to successful vocational placement of the hospitalized psychiatric patient.* Paper presented at the Region VII Rehabilitation Continuing Education Program on Rehabilitation of the Mentally Ill, Omaha, June, 1976.

Salomone, P. A Client-centered approach to job placement. *Vocational Guidance Quarterly*, 1971, *19*(4), 266–270.

Second Institute of Rehabilitation Issues. *Placement of the severely handicapped: A Counselor's Guide.* Institute, W. Va.: Research and Training Center, 1975.

Seventh Institute on Rehabilitation Issues. *Recommended standards for closure of cases.* Washington, D.C.: Rehabilitation Services Administration, 1969.

Shontz, F. C. *The psychological aspects of physical illness and disability.* New York: Macmillan, 1975.

Stewart, N. R., Winborn, B. B., Johnson, R. G., Burks, H. M., Jr., & Engelkes, G. R. *Systematic counseling.* Englewood Cliffs, N.J.: Prentice-Hall, 1978.

Super, D. E. *Dynamics of vocational adjustment.* New York: Harper, 1942.

――――. A theory of vocational development. *American Psychologist*, 1953, *8*, 185–190.

――――. *The psychology of careers.* New York: Harper, 1957.

――――. A developmental approach to vocational guidance: Recent theory and results. *Vocational Guidance Quarterly*, 1964, *13*, 1–10.

――――. Vocational development theory: Persons, positions, and processes. In J. M. Whiteley and A. Resinkoff, *Perspectives on vocational development.* Washington, D.C.: American Personnel and Guidance Association, 1972.

Super, D. E., Starishevsky, R., Matlin, N., & Jordan, J. P. *Career development: Self-concept theory.* New York: College Entrance Examination Board, 1963.

Super, D. E., Zelkowitz, R. S., & Thompson, A. S. *Career development inventory* (Tech. Rep.). New York: Columbia University, Teachers College, 1975.

Ugland, R. P. Job's seeker's aids: A systematic approach for organizing employer contacts. *Rehabilitation Counseling Bulletin*, 1977, *21*(2), 107–115.

United States Training and Employment Service. The General Aptitude Test Battery, Washington, D.C.: United States Training and Employment Service, 1966.

Urban Institute. *Report of the comprehensive service needs study.* Washington, D.C.: Urban Institute, 1975.

Usdane, W. M. Placement personnel: A graduate program concept. *Journal of Rehabilitation*, 1974, *40*, 12–13.

Vandergoot, D. An application of the Minnesota theory of work adjustment in a vocational rehabilitation agency. Unpublished dissertation, Michigan State University, 1975.

Vandergoot, D., Jacobsen, R. J., & Worral, J. D. *New directions for placement related research.* Albertson, N.Y.: Human Resources Center, 1978.

Vescovi, G. M. Factors related to successful employment of adult deaf workers. *Journal of Rehabilitation of the Deaf,* 1973 6(3), 1–11.

Westerheide, W. J., & Lenhart, L. *Case difficulty and client change: Monograph I.* Oklahoma City: Department of Institutions, Social and Rehabilitative Services, 1974.

Wright, B. A. *Physical disability: Psychological approach.* New York: Harper & Row, 1960.

Zadny, J. J., & James, L. F. *Another view on placement: State of the Art, 1976.* Portland, Ore.: Regional Rehabilitation Research Institute, School of Social Work, Portland State University, 1976.

Chapter 11

Managing the Delivery
of Rehabilitation Services

Jennings G. Cox   Sean G. Connolly   William J. Flynn

INTRODUCTION

The effective delivery of services to clients with disabling conditions is the great challenge for rehabilitation practitioners. This delivery is managed and administered at various levels, but the key professional in its accomplishment is the rehabilitation counselor. It is the individual rehabilitation counselor in this role, whether in a private or public agency, who usually has the responsibility of delivering the services needed by clients in the rehabilitation process. The functions involved in this position are diverse, and the counselor's management and coordination skills must be developed for most effective functioning. These skills include the management of individual clients (on a timely schedule) through the rehabilitation process and the management of a large number of clients on a caseload at any one time. These separate challenges of *case* and *caseload* management are considered the core functions of the effective delivery of client services (Henke, Connolly, & Cox, 1975). This chapter addresses itself to those functions, and two skills that permeate both areas—decision making and time utilization. While other skills are significant, for example, the ability to communicate,

record and document case services, and utilize community resources, the core competencies in caseload management are making
decisions and utilizing time effectively.

The growing movement over the last few years in all rehabilitation organizations is to enhance the quality of services provided
to people with disabling conditions. This movement has been a
function of both the influence of disabled consumers and the development of the rehabilitation profession. The contributions of both
groups have been directed toward the improvement of the quality
of services. The increased number of options and opportunities for
disabled clients, although as yet not comprehensive, reflects the
growth of the rehabilitation profession. The experienced voice of
disabled clients has already molded the rehabilitation profession for
years to come. The management of "quality services" to large numbers of disabled clients is the challenge of the rehabilitation counselor. *Quality* and *quantity* are key words in all human service agencies, and professionals must face the reality and challenge of
accountability.

The education of rehabilitation counselors devotes considerable time to developing skills associated with specific services such
as counseling, placement, and evaluation techniques as well as specific knowledge in the medical, psychological, and vocational areas.
It is only in recent times that consideration has been given to the
function of caseload management. However, while this training deficiency is often identified by agency and facility administrators,
other factors impact on case and caseload management. Such factors might include size of caseload and type of disability, rural versus urban location, changing emphases on different aspects of the
rehabilitation process by administrators, inadequate supervision,
lack of established criteria of performance, conflicts about quantity
and quality objectives, and changing legislation and regulations.
Any of these factors can markedly change the pattern of client services, but the rehabilitation counselor will need to assess and develop the skills required to effectively manage the delivery of client
services regardless of these factors.

One of the major sources of conflict for the rehabilitation practitioner in the delivery of client services is the discrepancy between
the counselor's own professional goals and organizational goals. For
several years quantity was the primary organizational goal, but it
was perceived as an obstacle to the professional goal of quality. The
distance between these apparently divergent goals has lessened in
recent years, and counselors and administrators are searching for a
"happy medium" that will be realistic and feasible. One of the

greatest problems in accomplishing this objective is the lack of clear and meaningful performance criteria for the rehabilitation practitioner. The traditional criterion of the "26 closure" (case closed as rehabilitated) is now generally accepted as inadequate in evaluating the rehabilitation process.

How individual counselors perceive their roles in the delivery of services is a key issue when the management of client services is discussed. For many years rehabilitation counselors have considered their primary function counseling, rather than managing or coordinating. The issue of counselor versus coordinator has been discussed in several sources (Patterson, 1957; 1968), and the recognition of managing and coordinating skills has expanded the professional's role rather than taken away from the counseling function. The reality of the situation in all rehabilitation organizations is that the professional who delivers service to disabled clients must be knowledgeable about the skills involved in case and caseload management.

CASE MANAGEMENT

Case management refers to the movement of an individual client through the rehabilitation process, and includes the management and coordination of all services needed to successfully achieve the rehabilitation goal. In terms of managing individual cases, the counselor must utilize decision-making skills. These skills allow the counselor to determine client readiness and ability to benefit from services, to manage the individual's step-by-step process, and to obtain feedback on the completion of a step in order to continue progress toward the rehabilitation goal or to decide what reassessment may be needed. To conceptualize the counselor's role in case management it becomes important to address the rehabilitation helping model. This model offers certain criteria for the case management process that are not considered significant in the more traditional medical model.

Rehabilitation and Medical Models

In the past, rehabilitation services to people with disabling conditions were provided through the medical model approach that is best exemplified by the physician-patient relationship. As the field of rehabilitation has developed, changes in the professional-patient relationship have evolved. Neither model is necessarily a better approach, but the rehabilitation movement has molded a more holistic, helping model. Similarities between the models are numerous, but the differences are emphasized in order to show the effects and implications in the case management process.

In the medical model the professional takes the active role. The client tends to be more passive and follows prescribed recommendations (Anderson, 1977). Problems are solved through the professional's direct questioning of the client to identify problems and symptoms, and the subsequent determination of a diagnosis and solutions. Responsibility for success of the problem solving is usually placed on the professional, and when a new or recurring problem arises the client must return to the professional for assistance. This model has been successful in many health fields, and is necessary with some particular problems or clients. This approach makes case management a relatively easy process of prescribing solutions for problems. While in the past this model has served well in the provision of rehabilitation services, recent years have witnessed a development in conceptualizing the delivery of rehabilitation services to reflect a more holistic approach. This approach accentuates the cooperative process of professional and client in delivering rehabilitation services. This broader concept of rehabilitation has resulted in a model in which the counselor and client mutually define problems and issues, and the counselor listens and assists in determining the appropriate rehabilitation service. This rehabilitation model emphasizes that action is taken by the client with the counselor acting as a facilitator. The goal of the model is the client's learning specific coping and developmental behaviors and skills, which will be available when new problems arise. The acquisition of these skills leads toward the accomplishment of the rehabilitation goal, and the counselor's reward consists of observing this self-development and growth on the client's part. This model avoids the development of client dependency by not solving all the client's problems and depriving the individual of self-help. This significant factor in the helping field is often overlooked (Resnick, no date). Client involvement in his or her own rehabilitation process is the key to the rehabilitation model as well as to effective case management skills for the counselor.

Planning for the Provision of Services

Working on one case at a time is a prerequisite for overall effective caseload management. As will be discussed in a later section, decision making provides the basis of the delivery of services to the individual client. Counselors must monitor their own work behaviors and determine the point in case movement where the process is most frequently interrupted in order to improve their case management skills. Systems have been established for the delivery of services and the counselor can benefit from using parts of the whole of a service delivery system (Grantham, 1976). The integration of a model of casework or rehabilitation services in case management will greatly facilitate the delivery of services. This model can be broad, such as *diagnostics-remediation-evaluation,* or can incorporate specific statuses reflecting client movement in the rehabilitation process. The planning component will facilitate control of crises, interruptions, indecision, or procrastination. The major benefit of a conceptual approach is in the assessment and determination of the client's need for services at any point in the process. Services are planned and provided on the basis of where the client is in the rehabilitation process, and what service would alleviate the need in an efficient manner.

Rehabilitation Process

The objective in rehabilitation case management is usually specific: vocational rehabilitation, or the process of assisting an individual with a disabling condition to return to gainful employment. While many factors are involved in attaining this objective such as the severity of the disability, employability, motivation, physical and psychological demands of the job, and the labor market, the individual case management involves many of the traditional casework principles of assisting a client achieve a mutually desirable objective. What makes rehabilitation unique is the consideration of abilities and disabilities of the person as they relate to appropriate vocational placement. Accomplishing this objective must involve attention to emotional, interpersonal, intellectual, medical, motivational, and family factors. Throughout the rehabilitation process there are times when accomplishing the objectives may be hindered.

One point at which the process may slow down for the counselor is in the diagnostic stage. Determining the diagnostic needs and coordinating the assessment data are usually completed with ease, but the determination of eligibility and the identification of functional limitations of the disabling condition are often more difficult tasks. From the medical, social, psychological, and vocational evaluations, the counselor must assess the functional limitations of an individual's disability. It is the determination of these limitations that dictates the specific needs of the client and helps insure timely movement through the rehabilitation process. The documented limitations assist in anticipating problems and selecting a priority system of case management.

Synthesizing diagnostic information collected on a client is essential, and a system must be established for translating the diagnostic data into functional limitations for employment. Dudek and his associates (1977) have developed a system that focuses on life function needs. Limitations are categorized in five broad areas, and each area is subcategorized providing comprehensive data on potential restrictions. The counselor may specify the life function restricted by a specific disabling condition. Utilizing this framework, a skeletal plan of the entire rehabilitation process and the priority items or stages within a specific case can be determined. This procedure allows for less complicated case management. The categorization of life factors as established by Dudek and his associates (1977) includes:

1. Health—being able to maintain physical well-being associated with proper physiological functioning;
2. Mobility—being able to operate in and negotiate the physical environment;
3. Communication—being able to send and receive communications with other human beings and the environment;
4. Cognitive-intellectual processes—being able to interpret events, to learn, and to apply learning;
5. Social-attitudinal processes—being able to regard oneself positively and to interact successfully with others (pp. 2–4).

The use of a comprehensive model such as Dudek's can assist the rehabilitation counselor in making decisions during the casework process. Assessing and clarifying the limitations to vocational success also allows the case management concept of potential problem analysis to be implemented. Counselors must make professional judgments as to the proper movement of an individual case, by assessing clients' readiness to move on to the next stage in the process. The ability to assess clients comes from knowledge of the rehabilitation process and counseling skills, as well as the ability to make decisions and to carry through with an anticipatory planning program. After the counselors determine the functional limitations, they may enhance case management by studying the potential problems that might arise, and thereby eliminate them or at least prepare for a possible breakdown in the case flow.

The analysis of potential problems in the rehabilitation process can be achieved from an assessment of the individual case history and current status (Region III RCEP, no date). This analysis requires planning, but it can prevent or minimize potential problems that might interfere with the movement or process of the case. As a technique to control the unpredictable outcome of the client's behaviors, it can improve the effectiveness of case management. Of the four steps suggested in this analysis, the first step demands the greatest attention as it speaks to a technique already established in the rehabilitation process.

1. State the purpose of the plan. Through the determination of the functional limitations the counselor and client can begin to establish the rehabilitation goal and the steps to achieve that goal. In many agencies and facilities this statement is already a formal part of the process through the formulation of the Individualized Written Rehabilitation Plan (IWRP). The counselor can use the IWRP to anticipate problems if the plan is clear and specific in the implementation steps and delineation of intermediate objectives.

2. Anticipate potential problems. This suggests a brainstorming activity to determine what could go wrong, considering past history and current state of emotional, motivational, and behavioral assets and deficits in an individual case. Generally, if a plan is well developed the potential problems are few. If many problems are anticipated, perhaps the original plan is not reasonable and should be reconsidered.

3. Determine the likely cause of problems. When potential problems have been identified, attempts should be made to explore the likely causes. If these causes can be avoided, case service interruption is less likely. Professional judgment is an important part of the process that allows counselors to ignore problems that have little likelihood of occurring.

4. Plan and initiate preventative action. If the anticipated problem appears likely, the final step is to initiate preventative action or a contingency plan. The counselor who can avert the problem by planning an action, for example, transportation for a client missing appointments with the physician, has a case that requires less continuous monitoring, and thus enhances

case management. The counselor can also enhance case management by establishing a contingency plan when it is difficult to plan preventative actions. The contingency plan increases the likelihood that case progression will not be interrupted.

These steps can be applied to many decisions and services in the rehabilitation process, and will enhance case management of services provided the individual client. Many counselors and other rehabilitation professionals use this technique in a less systematic way, and have, from experience, developed an intuitive sense for contingency plans. For example, with a client who has borderline reading skills, the opportunity for on-the-job training as an alternative to formal vocational training is such a contingency plan.

Client-Counselor Responsibilities

Much of what has been discussed relates to the counselor's management of a client's case. When this case management is based upon the rehabilitation helping model, the coordination of services becomes a joint responsibility of the counselor and client. The introduction of the IWRP and similar programs reflects this philosophy, and it must state specifically what the client and counselor will do cooperatively. If this type of behavioral contract is agreed to, the client can help maintain the case flow. The counselor's explanation of the process in a manner that emphasizes this shared responsibility will increase the ease with which client involvement takes place. The client, for example, can remind the counselor of important transitional stages such as the movement from training to ready-for-employment status. Making arrangements for their own appointments and following up on getting reports are both examples of clients' involvement in case management. Planning and coordinating systems take time, but it can prevent breakdowns in the provision of case services.

Counselor Values

Case management can be easily affected by counselors' values, but an awareness of their values can be enough to prevent them from creating problems. Denial of values, however, can impede the case flow. The values that appear most important in the effective management of rehabilitation services include: (1) like/dislike of casework, (2) like/dislike of clients, and (3) like/dislike of job duties.

The professional who denies disliking casework but avoids casework tasks preventing timely completion of a case, is creating additional case management problems. Whether counselors like or dislike casework, commitment to the task is essential for the client's achievement of goals. A counselor's willingness to commit to a task of perceived dislike is frequently a significant ingredient in successful client rehabilitation.

Awareness of attitudes toward clients must also be considered. Most counselors prefer some clients to others on an individual or group basis, that is, physically disabled persons as opposed to mentally retarded individuals. As with other values there may be no problem necessarily associated with this dislike if services are provided as needed. Disliking a client may result in unconsciously avoiding the case management process with that particular client, unless the counselor is aware of these personal feelings. Dislike of specific job tasks, such as job placement or training clients in job-seeking skills, can also restrict opportunities and services. Systems may be developed to avoid case process sabotage because of personal dislikes. Delegation of certain duties, use of outside resources, or whatever is needed to complete the disliked task, becomes the responsibility of the counselor.

In summary, the counselor evaluates the steps to be taken to assist the disabled client complete the rehabilitation process from application to closure. Decisions about what services to provide and the appropriate timing of these services constitute the essence of case management. These tasks must be applied to the unique circumstances of each case so that the delivery of services for each client will be managed effectively. Unless case management is effective, services to the person with the disabling condition are limited or delayed, and caseload management systems are impeded.

CASELOAD MANAGEMENT

Whereas case management reflects the counselor's efforts to meet the challenges presented by the individual client, caseload management concerns itself with the overall flow of all clients comprising the caseload. There is a direct relationship between the two functions, and many skills apply to both, but the perspective offered by caseload management is more global, since it affects all cases to some degree. An individual client, for example, may need a specific action to insure the development of a program of services, and an overdue diagnostic report may be the key factor. However, a breakdown in one of the overall process steps, such as the lack of fully developed referral or placement resources, will cause stagnation in the flow of cases, and may make efforts with specific clients fruitless until the breakdown has been resolved. The source of the problem, individual or global, must be identified and action taken to correct it.

It may be useful to consider how organizational administrators or supervisors frequently distinguish between case and caseload management. Cases are reviewed primarily to determine their consistency with regard to established policies and procedures. Caseloads are evaluated to assess continuity of services and to perhaps provide a quick indicator of the counselor's accomplishments with the total number of clients. Process problems that are causing logjams can be identified, and supervision may center around ways to eliminate them. As mentioned earlier, numerous factors influencing this flow include the type of disability being serviced, counselor experience, rural or urban setting, knowledge about and diversity of community resources, and cyclical variations in referrals and local job markets. These and other factors must be considered when counselors attempt to analyze the goals and the action they require.

The specific skills, distinct from case management, needed by professionals for effective caseload management include: (1) selecting certain cases to work on each day, (2) reviewing the total caseload in order to monitor how cases are spread throughout the rehabilitation process, (3) assessing the time a particular client or a specific action for a client is warranted, (4) recognizing and allotting more time to "difficult cases," (5) balancing the time and effort devoted to clients within any one day, (6) avoiding spending too much time providing a specific rehabilitation service to the detriment of another, for example, counseling versus placement activities, (7) monitoring input and output of the caseload, (8) determining what event is an emergency and needs immediate attention, (9) managing emergency case problems, and (10) keeping the caseload at a manageable level. The focus is on a global perspective rather than on the needs of the individual client. A number of these functions deserve special consideration.

Selecting the Case File

The size of caseloads in the field of rehabilitation varies greatly in agencies, facilities, or rehabilitation centers. Many counselors have reported caseload sizes of 300 or more. Some caseloads, especially in rehabilitation centers or facilities, may be as low as 25. Numbers alone do not give a complete picture of the caseload. Disabilities and job functions must be included if caseload size is to be compared. Regardless of the size of the caseload, one of the most significant skills for caseload management is the process of selecting which client to work with on a particular day, or how to move from one case to another. The decision to select a particular client file is one that can be based on thoughtful consideration, convenience, guilt about procrastination, whim, or a reminder telephone call. One of the problems for professionals working in rehabilitation is to develop alternatives to the fire bell syndrome where they are controlled by the events and fire bells of the day. The decision to select a case for work or to move from one case to another requires systematic and thoughtful consideration.

Management System

To facilitate the provision of appropriate and timely services, professionals must establish and utilize a system of reviewing the total caseload. Such a system is indispensable for effective caseload management. The choice of a system must be consistent with their professional needs and personal skills. The approach ought to be individual and pragmatic. A particular approach may work well for some, but unless it increases the effectiveness of the counselor's management skills, it will lead only to frustration. The relationships between the methods selected and the evaluation of counselor performance must be acknowledged. A basic compatibility between personal and organizational goals is important; otherwise, the experience of the burn out syndrome will be inevitable. In establishing a system of caseload management counselors must first consider organizational priorities. Since it is unlikely that these priorities will lend themselves to significant change, and because performance is frequently measured in relation to them, the management system selected must be designed to meet those priorities.

One of the first steps is the selection of a system. A number of such systems may be utilized, and counselors should remain flexible in choosing among them. Such methods include the use of monthly computer printouts of caseload statuses, an index card system of clients in various statuses, color-coded filing, a schedule of action steps recorded on calendar dates, and specific days scheduled for special units of the caseload, for example, selected statuses. Any of these or similar systems offer an orderly process through which counselors may obtain a global perspective of clients. Selection of a particular method depends as much on counselor preference as administrative effectiveness.

Management Guidelines

Once a system has been selected, goals for the caseload can be established and a reasonable way to evaluate the accomplishments of these goals introduced. Realistic variables may be considered, and with supervisory assistance accountability standards can be determined for the year. The goals can be broken down into monthly or weekly targets, and used as indicators to show areas needing attention. Based on the percentage of people who are accepted for services, who complete services, and who are placed in employment (or whatever may be the final objective), the counselor may determine how many referrals will be needed to compensate for cases that are unsuccessfully closed. Progress can be reviewed periodically, and adjustments to activities made accordingly.

A method of monitoring the caseload from a global perspective is important. A decision must be made or a guideline established as to how many clients are acceptable at each stage in the process. The flow can be analyzed by following one of the systems suggested, and action points, that is, referral, diagnostics, services, and placement, will require special attention to remove logjams and establish balance. Resources needed to facilitate movement at these points can be selected, and a plan outlined that will have the desired effect.

The system selected for caseload management can be used to keep track of the wide variety of deadlines that must be met in a rehabilitation agency or facility. It can also be used to schedule the timely movement of a client in the rehabilitation process. The deadlines may be categorized in the following way: *urgent, one-time,* or *routine*. *Urgent* actions imply a sense of immediacy and significance in order to maintain stability in the process and might include such things as rescheduling appointments to accommodate an unanticipated occurrence. *One-time* actions are significant in that they have a deadline by which the task must be completed. Such an action may be completing activities or reports in order to close a case on schedule. *Routine* actions involve tasks that are generally predictable, recurring, and have established due dates. Through a daily review, counselors can keep actions from moving from routine to urgent. As emergencies occur, counselors must develop skills to deal with them efficiently. Procrastination of deadline actions can compound the problem considerably by removing breathing space that the counselors have built into their schedules.

It is imperative that counselors have easy access to information in order to meet a wide variety of needs. The system selected for managing a caseload should ideally lend itself to accurate and rapid input and retrieval. The availability of computer assistance in accomplishing this task is particularly helpful, but may not be available in some agencies or facilities. The types of data that may be included in such an information system are:

1. Information on individual clients to refresh the counselor's memory prior to an appointment or during a telephone conversation;
2. The current financial status of the caseload and how it might be budgeted effectively;
3. A listing of community resources typically utilized, services provided, costs involved, and a specific contact person;
4. The names of key people in the community, and their spheres of influence—employers, judges, county and city officials, leaders in the consumer/parent groups and related professional organizations, facility operators, emergency service providers, and other resource people. (It will be beneficial to keep this list current.)

Personal and Organizational Goals

A basic reason for the skillful management of a caseload is the attainment of personal and organizational goals. Rehabilitation professionals have reasons for their chosen careers, and they must select the professional environment through which the majority of their needs can be met. If organizational and personal goals differ significantly, the counselor's energy and motivation to manage the caseload will be seriously restricted. In human service agencies, organizational goals must be compatible with the professional's basic philosophy and values (see Chapter 3). Simply stated, caseload management begins with a consideration of the organizational goals. How individual counselors integrate their own values, philosophy, preferred functions, and interests into the organizational goals becomes a significant task in the development of effective management skills.

When viewing the caseload as a whole, the counselor should consider a number of variables in developing overall management strategies. Of primary importance are time, people, material resources, and the individual counselor. The management of time will be discussed later. The involvement with individual people is probably the greatest challenge of rehabilitation counseling. Clients are not served in a vacuum. By the very nature of the job, rehabilitation counselors must enlist the skills and services of a wide variety of other people; positive working relationships must be developed. This task begins in the counselor's office and extends to each person who may influence the services provided. Whether this challenge is labeled salespersonship or public relations it is an essential ingredient of modern day rehabilitation. Without this involvement, the rehabilitation team is nonexistent and the most gifted counselor will be less effective. Counselors must clearly understand what their organization is capable of providing, what is expected and needed from others, and how these expectations and needs can be integrated for the benefit of the client. These factors permeate every stage of the process from referral through diagnostics, evaluation, service delivery, and placement to closure and follow-up services. Until the counselors are knowledgeable about the policies, procedures, and guidelines of their rehabilitation organization, it will be difficult for them to properly negotiate the best alternatives for the client.

Perspectives on Caseload Management

In addition to organizational support, it is important that the broad spectrum of available community resources be explored, and those most applicable to clients' needs be identified. There may be a temptation to relegate this function to a lower priority than it deserves. This task is time consuming, and its results may not be as readily apparent or as immediately rewarding as those gained in the one-to-one atmosphere of direct client contact. However, until counselors become aware of the full range of services available locally, or perhaps statewide or nationally, the options from which they may choose are limited. This stage in development of professional capabilities is not unique to new counselors, but is faced by experienced counselors moving to a new position where location or organizational goals differ significantly from previous ones.

Knowledge of counseling techniques, decision-making models, problem-solving methods, effective time utilization, and familiarity with policies and procedures can withstand a change of caseload or location. External factors that are initially foreign to new counselors are intimately associated with caseload management, and considerable time and effort are required to "learn the territory." The anxiety caused by this transitional condition can be lessened through input from other rehabilitation professionals and supervisors. Time is also needed to become acclimated to the new environmental factors, and counselors should not permit frustration to lessen efforts in this area.

Finally, a major task involves the management of the counselors' own resources and behaviors. As in case management, counselors each bring a unique personality to the professional role undertaken. Professionals must be willing to honestly evaluate personal deficits and take appropriate action so that these will have minimal effect on the services provided. Knowing when to seek aid, develop untested skills, or perhaps transfer a client to a more experienced counselor are all part of the process of professional growth, which is linked to an awareness of personal limitations. Such an appraisal is as much a part of the foundation of counseling as is the selection of a basic philosophical approach to clients.

The basic reason for caseload management is a natural outgrowth of case management. It allows counselors, on a larger scale, to control or manipulate resources, prioritize actions, and move toward a greater economy of effort. No matter what the setting—sheltered workshop, half-way house, state agency or private practice—the rehabilitation goal is to move clients through a process that insures the timely and appropriate provision of services. This objective relates to case management to the degree that the system permits smooth progression from one stage to another as the client is ready. It allows counselors to anticipate future requirements, and insures that resources will be available.

MAKING DECISIONS

In case and caseload management, making decisions is a perennial task if delivery of rehabilitation services is to occur. Many types of decisions are being made as the client progresses through the rehabilitation process. Some decisions are made independently of the client, but most decisions in providing services are made with client involvement. The level of involvement may vary with client, disability, and the decision to be made. Case management includes decisions about eligibility, diagnostic specialities needed, evaluation resources, vocational objective, training facility to be used, client readiness for job placement, and the selection of a placement position. All such steps in the rehabilitation process involve decision-making skills, and the development of these skills will enhance rehabilitation counselors' endeavors. Caseload management decisions include such functions as selecting the next client with whom to work, adequacy of referral sources, diagnostic resources, adequacy of training facilities, time and effort allotted to clients, and quality of services. The literature offers little in the area of decision making for rehabilitation counselors. When these skills are discussed in rehabilitation, they are usually explored in the context of a supervisor's management skills (RAMP, 1977). However, making decisions is a significant skill for counselors and is an essential ingredient for success in their job.

Decisions about client evaluation and services are often made rapidly without thoughtful consideration, and many of the actions resulting from such decisions are appropriate and effective. They are based on experience, intuition, knowledge, educated guesses, and sound professional judgments. As counselors develop experience in the field, they make decisions with less hesitancy and caution. That wealth of experience brings a competency that is unique to human service professionals. But people are creatures of habit and, despite informed experience, decisions are sometimes made on whims or "gut feelings" rather than thoughtful judgment. Some factors and systems to minimize the guesswork will be discussed next.

In the field of rehabilitation counseling, as well as other human service fields, many decisions are relative. They cannot easily be classified as correct or incorrect, right or wrong. It is client progress that can determine the rightness or wrongness, but that evaluation can only be made with hindsight, and probably many months or years later. It is the effectiveness of decisions, then, that is the key test. Does the decision facilitate the client's progress through the rehabilitation process, even if the decision is to delay a particular service? Does the decision help achieve the goal of vocational rehabilitation? In evaluating a decision about a client, counselors might consider such criteria as follows:

1. Consistency with the client's abilities and disabling conditions—does the decision take into account important client variables?

2. Responsiveness to an identified client need—does it achieve the desired objective?

3. Contribution toward the goal of rehabilitation—are there any undesirable side effects?

4. Cost-effectiveness—is the most effective use made of case service monies?

Seldom do counselors evaluate each decision made in terms of these criteria; such activity would be time consuming and laborious for each decision. But counselors' awareness of their decision-making process can be a helpful professional experience. An over-concern with the rightness or wrongness of a decision can interrupt the rehabilitation process, but the awareness of reasons why some decisions are made can help improve skills.

Reasons for Making Decisions

Rehabilitation counselors, like other professionals, make decisions for a variety of reasons: because the decision fits the facts, because they like the decision, because it is the first alternative that came to mind, because it will please a supervisor, because it is an easy solution, because the client will support it, because changing a decision may make them lose face, because they like the person who suggested the decision, because they want to avoid administrative criticism, because they fear the client's possible reaction to alternatives, because they don't want to copy someone else's decision, or for a variety of other reasons (Maier, 1970). Making decisions with client involvement can significantly influence how counselors make decisions. Fears about saying "no," about client reaction, about not following regulations, as well as concerns about the unpredictability of the client's behavior, can all influence counselors' approaches to the decision-making process. Developing an awareness of why even routine decisions are made can help counselors to assess the effectiveness of the decisions and offer an opportunity for professional development. The literature on personal and organizational decision making is extensive (Dyckman, Smidt, & McAdams, 1969; Elbing, 1970; Kuhn, 1974; Maier, 1963, 1970). Theories and systems have been developed in an effort to make better decisions. A selection of ideas from the literature can be made; their application to rehabilitation counseling is useful.

Decision-Making Steps

Most approaches recommend various steps for effective decision making, and while there may be slight differences in terminology or specificity, all approaches tend to have the same steps (Gordon, 1977; Kite, 1977; RAMP, 1977). A problem can be defined as any situation that requires a decision (Kuhn, 1974). A decision is the selection of a solution to a problem from two or more alternatives. This process of selecting the best option constitutes the decision-making process. It can be analyzed through various steps that may be helpful in arriving at a decision or assessing its effectiveness. Some of the major steps are as follows:

1. *Problem identification.* A well-known saying states that "a problem well stated is a problem half solved." The need to identify the *real* problem as opposed to the *obvious* problem is important. Every problem has many factors involved, and a clear definition of the problem must be made before an effective solution can be found.

2. *Goal determination.* Once the problem has been identified, a goal needs to be clarified. The goal can be developed directly from the identified problem, and will give direction to activities involved. This goal needs to be defined by involved parties so that it is clearly understood and accepted as realistic and feasible.

3. *Information gathering.* In order to make an informed decision, as much relevant information as is practically attainable should be accumulated. The type of information may vary, and may come from various sources. Key factors include the relevance of information, its utility in problem solving, and the ability to determine when sufficient information has been obtained to proceed with the decision. This information may include listing all possible options and their consequences.

4. *Evaluation of information.* This step includes an assessment and integration of all pieces of information in order to select the best alternative or combination of options. It is in this step that the decision maker attends to the objective data in order to arrive at a high quality decision. It is important to examine the sources of information and the consistencies and discrepancies in the information as patterns are identified and alternatives eliminated.

5. *Making the decision.* This step advances the process by making a determination of some activity or inactivity about a certain situation. In some cases it will be the selection of the best possible option or combination of options to resolve the problem.

6. *Execution of the decision.* Once the solution is selected the decision plan needs to be converted into action and this is best done by identifying *who* will do *what* and *by when.* Implementation within certain

time limits is an important aspect of the effectiveness of a decision.

7. *Evaluation of the decision.* Once the decision is made and implemented, it is often assumed that the situation or problem is resolved. However, a useful step in the decision-making process is an evaluation of the decision at some later date to assure that the decision is resolving the identified problem. This assessment may lead to the identification of a new problem, and the process begins over again.

Some authorities include more detailed and separate steps. Kite (1977) emphasizes the need to set time limits to avoid the postponement of the decision due to a variety of factors. Some decisions are delayed because sufficient information is not available, the outcome is too unpredictable, counselors tend to procrastinate on difficult decisions, or they hope the problem will go away. Consequently, the setting of time limits is considered a useful step within the process, but is suggested here as a factor that pervades each individual step as counselors work toward a final solution to a problem. Another important aspect of making decisions is the awareness of people's own needs and values, and how these influence the decision. It is important for professional counselors to monitor their biases and preferences to avoid restricting clients because of their influence.

Decision Making and Predictability

One of the greatest problems with all decision making is the uncertainty of the outcome. Many decisions in rehabilitation counseling consist of judgments about the future behavior of other people. Clients with disabling conditions seeking rehabilitation services have a number of complex factors influencing their behavior, and the skill in predicting their behavior influences most decisions the rehabilitation counselors and clients will jointly make about the client's rehabilitation. The reasons for uncertainty might include such factors as the nature of the information, the inability to verify certain critical information, the complex interplay of motivational factors, the array of subtle family influences, or the nature of the disabling condition. The uncertainty of human behavior and the difficulties in predicting behavior make decision making an immense challenge. Some writers suggest ways of decreasing the unpredictability of the outcome by formulating hypotheses (Elbing,

1970) or by utilizing the method of Potential Problem Analysis as discussed under case management (Region III RCEP, no date). Such exploration of potential consequences of various alternatives may facilitate the decision-making process and limit the sources of uncertainty about the outcome. Through weighing potential consequences counselors can begin to anticipate problematic situations that might occur.

In evaluating the data for making a decision, the professionals' degree of certainty in making the decision involves differentiating facts, inferences, speculations, and assumptions (Elbing, 1970). An awareness of this categorization may be helpful for the rehabilitation professional. These categories distinguish fact and opinion, and emphasize the verification potential of data. Some decisions require more verifiable information than others, for example, terminating client services. Some professionals may require more verifiable data than others before they reach a decision.

As counselors make decisions based on questionable data, the greater is the "leap in judgment" (Roskin, 1975). The development of decision-making skills in rehabilitation counseling, no matter how advanced, must maintain a flexibility and patience with human change. In the helping field, professionals must always remain open to the human factor and the challenges it presents.

Kinds of Decisions

Rehabilitation counselors face five kinds of decisions in case and caseload management. (1) *Technical decisions* are ones that involve the consistency of a chosen action with the organization's policy and procedures. (2) *Economic decisions* involve the consideration of cost effectiveness of certain actions and budgetary restrictions or planning. (3) *Clinical decisions* involve judgments about the client's motivation, vocational potential, or psychological adjustment. (4) *Selective decisions* usually involve the client in selecting a course of action, or choice (e.g., vocational objective, or training facility) from a number of alternatives. (5) *Allocative decisions* involve the distribution of resources, including time, effort, and people, for optimal effectiveness. These situations underscore the different types of decisions rehabilitation counselors face. While applying the decision-making steps to these decisions may be helpful, certain kinds of decisions may require special attention. Additionally, an awareness of a particular difficulty with any of these kinds of decisions in rehabilitation can aid in assessing case and caseload management deficits.

Evaluation of Decisions

Maier (1963; 1970) has extensively researched two dimensions of making decisions: quality and acceptance. These dimensions are helpful in appraising a decision's potential effectiveness. The *quality* of a decision refers to the objective validity of a decision based on facts and professional opinions, and refers to the overall evaluation of a decision in terms of whether it is valid, based on the information available at the time. Examples might include a decision of ineligibility of a client eager for services based on the evidence of no disabling condition, or a mild disabling condition that does not constitute a handicap to employment; or, a decision not to send a client to college based on the data from the psychological evaluation, despite the fact that the client has expressed a strong desire to pursue a college education. The *acceptance* of a decision refers to the subjective attractiveness or desirability of the decision to the client or the person who must execute the actions required by the decision. This dimension does not refer to the facts relevant to the decision, but to the feelings associated with the decision. Examples of this dimension in rehabilitation counseling might include the reaction of the client who was determined ineligible, or who was informed that providing the service of college training was not a feasible alternative.

Both dimensions, quality and acceptance, are important for rehabilitation counselors. In some decisions quality or acceptance alone will be more important. If the decision or its execution does not involve people, the need for acceptance may not be significant. Factors that can influence these dimensions are the client, the counselor, the decision, and such outside factors as regulations, supervisors, and administrators. In the human service field, both dimensions must be considered. Problems differ in the degree to which quality and acceptance are vital to success. Making decisions based on available information and pertinent regulations without consideration of the client's reaction or involvement can be as restrictive as making decisions that please clients regardless of the objective data or regulations in the case. The selection of a vocational objective when there is some discrepancy between the counselor's judgment and the client's wishes is a situation where attention to both quality and acceptance is necessary.

In order to avoid the evaluation of a decision in terms of goodness or correctness, Maier (1963) suggests a system of assessing the effectiveness of a decision using quality and acceptance as criteria. Applying these principles to the rehabilitation process, *quality* refers to factual information and objective data on clients, organizational guidelines and regulations, the recommendations of administrators or supervisors, and such factors as consistency between disabling condition and vocational objective. *Acceptance* refers to the client's cooperation, motivation, and achievement needs. Each decision requires some attention to both dimensions, and the more major the decision, the greater attention it requires. These dimensions may assist in the development of insight into individual approaches for the decision-making process. Counselors sometimes attribute greater significance to quality and others to acceptance. Through several exercises professionals can develop an awareness of their tendency to focus on quality or acceptance in making decisions (Roskin, 1975; Connolly & Cox, 1977).

Maier (1963) points out that the traditional but ineffective decision-making model is one in which the counselor makes the decisions and solicits the acceptance of the client. The primary factor according to the traditional model is achieving quality; acceptance is only a secondary objective. For effective decision making, however, Maier believes that acceptance must be an initial objective and that quality is achieved later through a cooperative approach. This model corresponds to the current philosophy of rehabilitation of involving clients in all decisions. Acceptance can be developed through counseling and the development of rapport from the time of the initial interview. As the relationship develops, high-quality decisions can be integrated well into the process.

UTILIZATION OF TIME

A final skill that is easy to understand but difficult to practice is that of effective time utilization. Since the mid-1960s, business and industry have been teaching employees methods to effectively use work time. Lakein (1973) summed up the objective of effective time utilization with the phrase "work smarter, not harder." Others in the field also emphasize the concept that organization and personal commitment are the keys to utilizing time effectively (Lakein, 1973; Bliss, 1976). The term *time management* suggests that time can be controlled. The authors' preferred term, *time utilization*, reflects the uncontrollability of time itself and the fact that it is a resource equally distributed to all people. This term also emphasizes the individual's responsibility to utilize the time available in the most effective way.

For rehabilitation counselors effective utilization of time is a necessity if organizational and client goals are to be accomplished. A fundamental tenet of time utilization is that counselors develop an attitude that promotes change and development of new personal systems. Time utilization can be discussed in helpful generalities, but it becomes a professional responsibility to develop methods of utilizing time that are appropriate and acceptable to the individual.

Counselors are faced with large amounts of paperwork necessary to render services to the client. At the same time the responsibilities of counseling and other person-to-person contact exist. Counselors making a commitment to improving their time utilization can benefit from the work established in industry.

Issues of Time Utilization

Time is one of the few universal commodities that is equally distributed. People each have the same amount of time to use as they deem important. People have many misconceptions regarding the effective use of time, and it is important to be aware that several time-honored traditions will not be beneficial to counselors. The myths that appear most important for counselors to discard include:

1. Counselors who are most active get the most done. Activity does not mean results; effective time management may eliminate some activity.

2. Delaying decisions improves quality. Typically the longer people wait, the more difficult it is to make the decision. Waiting until all pieces of the puzzle fit together can hinder effective service delivery.

3. Efficient counselors are effective. Efficiency has been acclaimed in business and human service fields as a significant goal for many years. However, efficiency without consideration of effectiveness is shortsighted. Effectiveness cannot take second place to efficiency. Effectiveness means optimizing results with the least expenditure of resources, not just being efficient.

4. Counselors often feel they get work done faster and better by doing it themselves. Refusing to delegate responsibility and teach others how to do certain tasks will only increase personal time demands.

5. Being available to clients at all times will improve effectiveness. This may actually limit effectiveness. The goal is to be optimally available. This means that both counselor and client needs must be jointly con-

sidered within the context of time constraints imposed by other professional activities.

6. Identifying the problem is the easy step in problem solving. Superficial problem identification frequently leads clients and counselors on wild goose chases. Using more time to properly identify the problem will typically provide for a time savings by the completion of the rehabilitation process.

These points emphasize that getting control of time in a manner that is personally effective will enhance work quality for rehabilitation counselors. How do people gain better control of time? Lakein (1973) has delineated six points that appear appropriate for counselors:

1. *Set goals and priorities.* Before getting involved in any activity, it is important that counselors set up the goals of the job as well as the personal priorities. This global and initial stage of planning allows for a general scheme that can then be broken down into parts that are easily managed.

2. *Make a daily "to do" list.* Of all time utilization techniques the "to do" list appears most frequently as *the* important step. It is recommended that either at the beginning or end of the day the counselor make a list of things that need to be accomplished during the subsequent work period.

3. *Prioritize the "to do" list into three categories.* This rule prevents wasting time. Frequently a list includes many items that can be accomplished easily and quickly. It is typical for people to start with these tasks, and end the day without accomplishing the major, more difficult goals. Categories should include those items that are very important, important but not so urgent, and busy work. After prioritizing, it is important to start with the very important category, and not waste time on the busy work. Typically the busy work will take care of itself.

4. *Self-monitoring should periodically be done by asking, "what is the best use of my time right now?"* If this question is asked frequently during the day, it can serve as a reminder when time is being wasted.

5. *Handle a piece of paperwork only once if possible.* Counselors' paperwork often requires multiple action. Generally time will be saved if counselors complete

all activities regarding a particular piece of paper-work at one time.

6. *Do it now.* It is easy to put aside a task and plan to get to it later. This procrastination is particularly true of tasks with which a person is uncomfortable. Putting aside the task only increases its aversiveness and frequently causes counselors to waste time on other tasks because of the anticipatory dread associated with the delayed task.

These six rules offer general guidelines for using time effec-tively. Problems frequently expressed by counselors show that certain situations consume inordinate amounts of time. Use of the six rules does not necessarily allow the counselor to avoid or handle the time wasters. The major time wasters identified by counselors include procrastination, meetings, telephone interruptions, drop-in visitors, disorganization, and the inability to say "no." To study options available for handling these time wasters, it is important to look at (1) personal changes and planning, and (2) controlling the environment.

Personal Changing and Planning

Making the commitment to attempt new methods of time utiliza-tion remains the biggest, and probably most difficult, personal change that is required. Following the commitment counselors may avail themselves of the numerous suggested approaches to utilize time. Planning includes the prioritizing that has been discussed, but it also includes the ability to say "no." As helpers, counselors have a tendency to feel that saying "no" to a client is unprofessional. In reality, saying "yes" may be a disservice to the client, particularly if it infringes upon the counselor's professional time and results in resentment for the time spent on the task.

Another aspect of personal change falls in the area of perfec-tionism. Workers, especially those that are new to the field, tend to want all details of their work to be error free. While this is a worthy goal, it can also be a time waster. Again, it becomes important for the counselor to realize which tasks must be executed "perfectly" and which ones can be less than perfect and still achieve their objective. For example, it is important that forms be correct or more time will be wasted in their return and correction, but minor grammatical errors in a contact report may be inconse-quential.

Taking time for planning is vital. The Pareto Principle (Bliss, 1976) indicates that 20 percent of the effort brings about 80 percent of the accomplishment. It is also referred to as the concept of the "vital few" and the "trivial many," or the 80/20 rule (Bliss, 1976). In other words, if there are ten items to get done, the rule implies that completion of two of these items will result in 80 percent of the value of the items. Taking time to determine which of the items will provide this desired result can keep the counselor concentrating on the important issues of work. The principle can be helpful in coping with a long list of tasks to be accomplished.

Some specific techniques that counselors can employ include the use of a "quiet hour," which entails scheduling one hour each day when they are not to be disturbed to allow time to get tasks accomplished. This technique frequently can prevent the feeling of being behind schedule. Committing themselves to doing jobs that are difficult or unpleasant first thing in the morning may also help counselors' efficiency. They accomplish the task and thus eliminate worrying about this task that would interfere with their work.

Counselors can save time by setting clear time limits on themselves and others. Personal limits can include making deadlines for each task and sticking to them. Also, if the counselor is responsible for arranging meetings of any type, having a specific meeting termination time will expedite the accomplishment of tasks. Time limits can also help the counselor through control of telephone calls and interruptions, and office visits. Limiting the receiving of calls to certain hours of the day and then returning all other calls during that time is one way of eliminating continuous telephone interruptions. Central to the success of time limiting is the effective training of a secretary to screen calls and determine which calls are important enough to require an exception to the plan. Care must be taken, however, that callers do not feel "put off;" they should be assured that their message will be delivered. Unscheduled office visits by clients and fellow workers may also be time wasters subject to the same rules of the telephone. Establishing "visiting hours" makes the counselor available to clients and also allows time for completion of all the other tasks that are essential to providing services to people with handicaps.

Controlling the Environment

Ordering their work environment is paramount in counselors' achievement of effective time utilization. Of particular importance are arranging the office for effective functioning and making use of appropriate time-saving devices. The office should be arranged in a manner that allows as few distractions as possible. Eliminating distractions involves arranging things so that while working it is difficult to hear noises or observe people through a door or window. It also means having necessary tools and equipment (dictaphone, stapler, files, address book) readily available.

A cluttered desk may signify a cluttered mind; time efficiency studies show that the cluttered desk results in lost time looking for material and adds to the likelihood of jumping from task to task without evaluating its priority. A cleared desk that holds no work materials other than the task at hand is a most helpful time saver. Dealing with mail when it arrives by responding, filing, or discarding assists in keeping the desk clear and saves handling business more than once. Sorting the mail into that needing immediate attention versus that which can be dealt with only once a day or week is another way of keeping the desk clear. Delegation of this duty to the secretary can be easily accomplished as long as he or she is aware of priorities.

Using a pocket calendar is one helpful way for counselors to control their environment. The calendar provides them ready access to their personal schedule. In this way scheduling a new appointment can be done readily and put aside, allowing counselors to continue the current task with little interruption. Dictating is also a time saver when compared to the use of shorthand or longhand. Dictating allows counselors to perform the task when it is convenient, and permits secretaries to complete the task when it is convenient for them. It is a time saver for two people.

Counselor-Secretary Team

A final aspect of time utilization that is important to the rehabilitation process is the relationship between counselor and secretary. Effective delegation of duties and the development of a mutually supportive work system constitutes one of the most potent methods of time utilization. The team approach can become a reality. The counselor and the secretary should discuss and agree upon the secretary's job description. They may allow ten minutes in the morning to preview the day's priorities with each other. The secretary can be taught preferred approaches to time utilization by screening phone calls, scheduling appointments, etc. Methods to avoid interruptions and determine which questions or problems can be postponed may also be discussed.

Communication and respect are the basic elements in the

counselor-secretary relationship that allow team work and time management techniques to work. Supporting and listening to the secretary are important basic techniques of developing this relationship. Appropriate involvement in the rehabilitation process is as important for the secretary as any other member of the team.

SUMMARY

Rehabilitation counselors are responsible for developing methods of case and caseload management that will insure that appropriate services are provided on a timely basis. Case management skills include the ability to determine individual functional limitations, negotiate services, set goals for the rehabilitation program, analyze factors that may be potential problems, and decide on actions that will minimize those factors. Caseload management requires a workable system that provides a global perspective, and is designed to meet client, organizational, and counselor needs. Administrative skills in decision making and time utilization are basic prerequisites in this area. While the coordination and decision-making skills are often assumed to be developed prior to employment, academic training normally focuses attention on case management functions. It is only in recent years that attention has been devoted to the skills required for caseload managment, and methods developed in business and industrial management are now being applied to rehabilitation counseling. The helping model requires that the efforts of many individuals, including the client, be incorporated into an administrative approach that fosters optimum service delivery to people with disabilities. Skills in this area, if not previously developed, must be acquired and practiced for the successful movement of people through the rehabilitation process.

REFERENCES

Anderson, T. P. An alternative frame of reference for rehabilitation: The helping process versus the medical model. In R. P. Marinelli & A. E. Dell Orto (Eds.), *The psychological and social impact of physical disability.* New York: Springer, 1977.

Bliss, E. C. Getting things done: The ABCs of time management. New York: Scribner, 1976.

Connolly, S. G., & Cox, J. G. Rehabilitation counselor decision-making style inventory. In *Basic decisions in the vocational rehabilitation process: A training manual*. Dallas: Region VI RCEP, University of Texas Health Science Center, 1977.

Dudek, R. A. (Project Director). *Human rehabilitation techniques: A technology assessment, Vol. 1, Part A. Final Report*. Lubbock, Tex.: Texas Technological University, 1977.

Dyckman, T. R., Smidt, S., & McAdams, A. K. *Management decision making under uncertainty*. New York: Macmillan, 1969.

Elbing, A. O. *Behavioral decisions in organizations*. Glenview, Ill.: Scott/Foresman, 1970.

Gordon, T. *Leader effectiveness training*. New York: Wyden, 1977.

Grantham, R. J. A comprehensive service delivery system for rehabilitation. *Rehabilitation Counseling Bulletin*, 1976, *20*(1), 5–14.

Henke, R. O., Connolly, S. G., & Cox, J. G. Caseload management: The key to effectiveness. *The Journal of Applied Rehabilitation Counseling*, 1975, *6*(4), 217–227.

Kirkpatrick, D. L. *How to plan and conduct productive business meetings*. Chicago: Dartnell Corp., 1976.

Kite, J. Decision making. In J. Thompson, J. Kite, & S. M. Bruyere, *Caseload management: Training package*. Seattle: Region X RCEP, Seattle University, 1977.

Kuhn, A. *The logic of social systems*. San Francisco: Jossey-Bass, 1974.

Lakein, A. *How to get control of your time and your life*. New York: Wyden, 1973.

Maier, N. R. F. *Problem-solving, discussions, and conferences: Leadership method and skills*. New York: McGraw-Hill, 1963.

———. *Problem-solving and creativity in individuals and groups*. Belmont, Calif.: Brooks/Cole, 1970.

Patterson, C. H. Counselor or coordinator? *Journal of Rehabilitation*, 1957, *23*(3), 13–15.

Patterson, C. H. Rehabilitation counseling: A profession or a trade? *Personnel and Guidance Journal*, 1968, *46*, 567–571.

RAMP (Rehabilitation Administration Management Program), *Decision making in the rehabilitation environment: A training manual*. Norman, Okla.: University of Oklahoma, 1977.

Resnick, R. Chicken soup is poison. Los Angeles: Gestalt Institute of Los Angeles, no date.

Region III RCEP (Rehabilitation Continuing Education Program).
    Effective caseload management: An instructor's manual. Fish-
    erville, Va.: Department of Vocational Rehabilitation, no date.
Roskin, R. Decision style inventory. In J. E. Jones & J. W. Pfeiffer
    (Eds.), *The 1975 annual handbook for group facilitators*. La
    Jolla, Calif.: University Associates, 1975.

Appendix A

Selected Professional Organizations in Rehabilitation and Related Areas

INTRODUCTION

Just as a characteristic common to professions in general is the formation of professional associations, a trait of a professional rehabilitation counselor is membership and participation in professional rehabilitation organizations. Some professionals choose not to belong to any organizations even though the efforts and fees contributed by members are typically devoted to a number of humanitarian and professional endeavors. Associations in and related to rehabilitation counseling usually state as their purposes the betterment of people with handicaps. This betterment is accomplished directly through lobbying for legislation addressed to meeting the needs of these people, and indirectly through setting professional standards for training and practice of professionals, through providing continuing education for professionals, and through encouraging the conduct and publication of relevant research.

The reader may wish to consider the following associations for membership and/or subscription to their publications. They represent only a selected listing of organizations commonly identified with rehabilitation counseling or related professions. Specific information regarding the size, nature, membership fees, and membership requirements is not included because they are subject to frequent change. Up-to-date information may be obtained from the organizations' main office at the address listed here. For information regarding other organizations or other publications consult the *Encyclopedia of Associations* (13th Ed.), Detroit: Gale Research Co., 1979, and *Ullrich's International Periodicals Directory* (17th Ed.), New York: R. R. Bowker, 1977.

The following is a listing of rehabilitation and related associations. The first two, the National Rehabilitation Association and the American Personnel and Guidance Association, are of primary import; the remainder are of related interest.

Association Name and Address

National Rehabilitation Association
1522 K Street, N.W.
Washington, D.C. 20005

Journal Publication

Journal of Rehabilitation

**Divisions of Parent Organization and
Journal Publication**

Administrative and Supervisory Practices Division
Journal of Rehabilitation Administration

Job Placement Division
Job Placement Digest

National Association of Rehabilitation Instructors

National Association of Rehabilitation Secretaries

National Congress on the Rehabilitation of Homebound
and Institutionalized Persons

National Rehabilitation Counseling Association
The Journal of Applied Rehabilitation Counseling

Vocational Evaluation and Work Adjustment Association
Vocational Evaluation and Work Adjustment Bulletin

Association Name and Address

American Personnel and Guidance Association
Two Skyline Place, Suite 400
5203 Leesburg Pike
Falls Church, Virginia 22041

Journal Publication

Personnel and Guidance Journal

Divisions of Parent Organization and Journal Publications

Division 1: American College Personnel Association
Journal of College Student Personnel

Division 2: Association for Counselor Education and
   Supervision
Counselor Education and Supervision

Division 3: National Vocational Guidance Association
Vocational Guidance Quarterly

Division 4: Association for Humanistic Education and
   Development
The Humanist Educator

Division 5: American School Counselor Association
*The School Counselor; Elementary School Guidance and
   Counseling; ASCA Newsletter*

Division 6: American Rehabilitation Counseling Association
Rehabilitation Counseling Bulletin

Division 7: Association for Measurement and Evaluation
   in Guidance
*Measurement and Evaluation in Guidance; AMEG
   Newsnotes*

Division 8: National Employment Counselors Association
Journal of Employment Counseling

Division 9: Association for Non-White Concerns in Personnel and Guidance
*Journal of Non-White Concerns in Personnel and Guid-
   ance; ANWC Newsletter*

Division 10: Association for Religious and Value Issues in Counseling
Counseling and Values

Division 11: Association for Specialists in Group Work
Journal for Specialists in Group Work

Division 12: Public Offender Counselor Association

Division 13: American Mental Health Counselors Association
AMHCA News (Bimonthly Newsletter), AMHCA Journal

REHABILITATION-RELATED ORGANIZATIONS

Association Name and Address and Publication

American Association on Mental Deficiency
5101 Washington Ave., N.W.
Washington, D.C. 20016
American Journal of Mental Deficiency
Mental Retardation

American Association of Workers for the Blind
1511 K St., N.W., Suite 637
Washington, D.C. 20005
News and Views
Blindness

American Psychological Association
1200 Seventeenth Street, N.W.
Washington, D.C. 20036
American Psychologist

Divisions of Special Interest

Division 17: Counseling Psychology
The Counseling Psychologist

Division 22: Rehabilitation Psychology
Rehabilitation Psychology

American Speech and Hearing Association
10801 Rockville Pike
Rockville, Maryland 20852
ASHA

Journal of Speech & Hearing Disorders
Journal of Speech & Hearing Research
Language, Speech & Hearing Services in Schools

Council for Exceptional Children
1920 Association Drive
Reston, Virginia 22091
Exceptional Children
Exceptional Child Evaluation Resources
Teaching Exceptional Children

National Association of the Deaf
814 Thayer Ave.
Silver Spring, Maryland 20910
Deaf America

Appendix B

Commission on Rehabilitation Counselor Certification (CRCC)

SOME COMMONLY ASKED QUESTIONS
ABOUT REHABILITATION COUNSELOR
CERTIFICATION

How Did the Certification Program Develop and How Is It Organized?

The certification program is an outgrowth of the professional concerns of two associations: the National Rehabilitation Counseling Association and the American Rehabilitation Counseling Association. These organizations deemed it desirable to establish a national professional scale of minimum standards for the practice of rehabilitation counseling and to provide a baseline for professional growth. These two Associations appointed a joint Committee on Certification which became the Commission on Rehabilitation Counselor Certification (CRCC), an independent, incorporated non-profit organization.

Prepared 1/1/79 by Commission on Rehabilitation Counselor Certification and reprinted with their permission.

CRCC consists of five appointees from NRCA, five appointees from ARCA, three appointees from the American Coalition of Citizens with Disabilities, and one appointee each from the Council on Rehabilitation Education, Council of State Administrators of Vocational Rehabilitation, Association of Rehabilitation Facilities, National Association of Non-White Rehabilitation Workers, and the National Council on Rehabilitation Education.

What Is the Purpose of Certification and What Will Be Its Effect on Rehabilitation Counseling as a Profession?

The primary purpose of certification is to provide assurance that professionals engaged in rehabilitation counseling will meet acceptable standards of quality in practice. Such standards are considered to be in the best interests of clients, rehabilitation counselors and related professionals. It is evident that rehabilitation counselors are encouraging, through their participation in the certification program, a higher level of performance and qualification that will benefit both the public and the profession.

It is not CRCC's intent to certify that any individual is suitable for employment or to impose personnel requirements on any agency; rather, the intent is to establish a national professional scale that any interested group, agency or individual may use as a measure. However, even though certification standards have existed for only a short time, they have already been incorporated into the Federal Regulations for Intermediate Health Care Facilities; accreditation standards for private rehabilitation facilities; education standards for rehabilitation education programs; licensing standards for rehabilitation counselors; and employment and/or promotion standards for some agencies and facilities.

How Do I Become a Certified Rehabilitation Counselor?

Initial certification, valid for five years, is achieved by satisfying specific criteria in the areas of education, employment experience, peer assessment and supervisor assessment; acceptance of a Code of Ethics; and passing a Certification Examination composed of problem-solving type questions designed to be relevant to the day-by-day decision-making processes of rehabilitation counselors. Questions about these criteria and about the Certification Examination are answered in following paragraphs.

How Do I Maintain My Certification?

Because rehabilitation counseling is a dynamic profession in which knowledge, skills and techniques are continually evolving, CRCC in 1974 endorsed the principle of certification maintenance for rehabilitation counselors. Consequently, CRCC formally set in motion in January 1978 a Certification Maintenance Plan under which Certified Rehabilitation Counselors are required to demonstrate continuing competence at five year intervals.

The stated objectives of the Certification Maintenance Plan are to encourage Certified Rehabilitation Counselors to participate in continuing education activities in which they will be provided with new information, explore new knowledge in a specific content area, master new skills and techniques, expand approaches toward the management of clients, and develop critical inquiry and balanced professional judgment. The maintenance plan also includes options for those unable to participate in continuing education activities.

Certification maintenance represents an essential step in the development of a comprehensive certification process for the profession and should significantly enhance the acceptance of rehabilitation counselor certification standards by consumers, administrators, peer-professionals and legislators.

Who Is Eligible to Take the Certification Examination?

To be eligible for the Certification Examination, a candidate must meet *one* of the following requirements of education combined with acceptable professional employment experience. Education and employment experience requirements must have been *fully satisfied* at the time the candidate's application is submitted.

How Do I Become Eligible If I Do Not Have Experience under the Supervision of a Certified Rehabilitation Counselor?

If the candidate cannot at the time of application meet the requirement of employment experience under the supervision of a CRC, CRCC offers these two alternatives:

1. Only until July 1, 1979, a rehabilitation counselor who has at least a bachelor's degree and at least five years

Education	RCE Program Accreditation	Internship	Acceptable Employment Experience[1]
1. Master's—Rehabilitation Counseling	Accredited by CORE[2] when candidate's degree was granted	Must be supervised by a CRC[3]	None required
2. Master's—Rehabilitation Counseling	Not accredited by CORE when candidate's degree was granted	Must be supervised by a CRC	One year under the supervision of a CRC
3. Master's—Rehabilitation Counseling	Not accredited by CORE when candidate's degree was granted	None	Two years, one of which must have been under the supervision of a CRC
4. Master's related to a Master's in Rehabilitation Counseling	N/A	N/A	Three years, one of which must have been under the supervision of a CRC
5. Master's unrelated to a Master's in Rehabilitation Counseling[4]	N/A	N/A	Five years, at least one of which must have been under the supervision of a CRC
6. Bachelor's—Rehabilitation	N/A	N/A	Four years, at least one of which must have been under the supervision of a CRC
7. Bachelor's in any other area	N/A	N/A	Five years, at least one of which must have been under the supervision of a CRC

[1] See the following question for a definition of "acceptable employment experience."
[2] Council on Rehabilitation Education, Inc.
[3] Certified Rehabilitation Counselor.
[4] Such relatedness or unrelatedness to be determined by the Credentials Committee on the basis of the candidate's transcript.

experience in the field of rehabilitation, with at least one year as a practicing, case-carrying rehabilitation counselor, will be allowed to sit for the examination without meeting the requirement of one year's supervision by a CRC *upon submission of two reference letters from Certified Rehabilitation Counselors* (in addition to the reference discussed in following paragraphs).

2. *Provisional Certification.* A candidate may submit a Supervision Plan to CRCC outlining a method for acquiring one year of supervision under a CRC in his/her geographical area. "Supervision" is defined as a systematic and periodic evaluation of the quality of delivery services. If one meets all educational and employment experience requirements, and the Supervision Plan is approved by CRCC's Credentials Committee, he/she will be allowed to sit for the Certification Examination. If a passing score is achieved, Provisional Certification will be issued pending documented completion of the candidate's Supervision Plan.

Provisional Certification is granted for a specified period of time and expires on one of two dates:

a. The date on which completion of the Supervision Plan is documented and full certification is granted; *or*

b. Twenty-four (24) months from the date on which the candidate sat for the Certification Examination. A candidate may begin implementing the Supervision Plan as soon as he/she has been notified of the Credentials Committee approval of the plan. If Provisional Certification expires without documented completion of the Supervision Plan, full certification will not be granted.

How Does CRCC Define "Acceptable Employment Experience in Rehabilitation Counseling"?

In order for employment experience to be considered acceptable by CRCC, it must be full-time paid employment or its equivalent. Internship time is not acceptable as employment experience. The candidate's job description must contain the first experience component listed below and at least two of the other experience components listed. Experience gained prior to the granting of the master's or bachelor's degree will be considered only if it has been under the supervision of a CRC.

1. Techniques of counseling special populations and groups;
2. Vocational exploration;
3. Psychological and vocational assessment;
4. Use of social, medical, vocational, psychiatric information;
5. Job placement and/or job development;
6. Rehabilitation methods in an agency, public or private, business or industry, hospital or clinic, in which the applicant is under professional supervision and has employed such methods and measures.

What Is the Certification Examination Like and How Was It Developed?

An intensive field testing process, which spanned a two-year period and involved over 8,000 rehabilitation counselors, educators and administrators, has resulted in a pool of examination items statistically validated across levels of education, experience, geography and professional function. The Commission maintains a Task Force of rehabilitation counseling professionals who continually add to and upgrade the examination item pool.

Each Certification Examination consists of approximately 300 multiple choice questions drawn from the item pool. Questions are practice-based and put a higher premium on application of knowledge in serving clients than on isolated bits of factual information. In scoring the examination, credit is given for the "best response" as determined by the item authors and verified by the field testing process.

What Are the Content Areas Tested by the Certification Examination?

To qualify for certification the candidate is required to demonstrate competence in the following content areas by achieving a minimum passing score on the Certification Examination as a whole:

Rehabilitation philosophy, history, structure, ethics and laws;

Medical aspects of disability;

Psychological aspects of the handicapping condition;

Job placement and job development of job opportunities for the handicapped;

Occupational information, the world of work, job modification and re-engineering;

Counseling theory and techniques of counseling;

Community organization and resources;

Psychology of personal and vocational adjustment;

Evaluation and assessment (work evaluation);

Ability to utilize research findings;

The delivery of rehabilitation services.

How Will My Application Be Processed?

1. When your application is received by CRCC, you will be sent an acknowledgment indicating your Candidate Identification Number and enclosing appropriate reference forms. Should there be any question about your eligibility, you will be advised of this fact and the date when the Credentials Committee will convene to consider your application.

2. *If your application was not sent to the Credentials Committee,* a status letter from CRCC will be sent to you about eight weeks after the application deadline date, indicating what materials may still be missing from your file. With this status letter for approved candidates will be enclosed a Site Questionnaire, a Guide to Candidate Orientation to aid you in preparing for the examination, and a request to remit your Examination and Certificate Fee.

3. *If your application was considered by the Credentials Committee:*

   a. *And you have been approved* to sit for the examination, you will receive notification of this decision along with the materials mentioned in Step #2 above about eight weeks after the application deadline date.

   b. *And your application has been rejected,* you will be so notified and informed of the right to appeal the Credentials Committee decision. Such notification is also sent about eight weeks after the application deadline date.

A Credentials Committee rejection is an absolute rejection for the upcoming examination. The Appeals Committee will meet to consider the files of those candidates who wish to appeal their rejection by the Credentials Committee *during the next examination cycle.* Those candidates whose appeals are accepted will be so notified and scheduled for the next examination. Candidates whose appeals are denied will be so notified and their certification files will be closed.

4. About one month before the Certification Examination, approved candidates will be sent an Admissions Pass with detailed site information. The Examination and Certificate Fee will be refunded to an applicant who is unable to sit for the scheduled examination *only* if the applicant notifies CRCC ten calendar days prior to the scheduled examination date.

5. *Examination Results and Certificate.* About six weeks after the examination, each candidate will be sent a computer-generated profile of examination results. Somewhat later, each passing candidate will be sent a Certificate attesting to his/her Certified Rehabilitation Counselor status. The designation "CRC" may be used by each *passing* candidate as soon as the candidate has received the profile indicating that a passing score has been achieved.

Some Details About Examination Administration

The Certification Examination is given twice each year in the spring and in the fall. Barrier-free examination sites are arranged for each administration according to the geographical mix of approved candidates to minimize travel expenses for counselors insofar as possible. An additional city will be considered by CRCC as an examination site on scheduled examination dates upon petition to CRCC by 20 or more approved candidates.

If a candidate cannot take the examination under usual testing conditions because of physical limitations, special arrangements may be made. The examination can also be administered in Braille or in Spanish on scheduled examination dates if CRCC is so notified at the time of application. Accommodations will be made for candidates who cannot sit for the examination on scheduled examination dates for religious reasons.

After a candidate's application has been approved, he/she will be notified of the sites at which the examination will be administered. If for any reason the candidate is unable to sit on the scheduled date, *one deferral to the next scheduled examination date is allowed.* A deferral fee of $10.00 is required at the time a deferral is requested to cover processing costs. Applicants who defer participation to the next scheduled examination date and subsequently are unable to sit for that examination will be required to submit a new Application for Certification with another non-refundable fee.

A candidate who fails to achieve a minimum passing score on his/her first examination is allowed to retake the examination *once* within the following 15 months, upon notice to CRCC and payment of another Examination and Certificate Fee. If the candidate fails to pass on the second attempt, or for any reason is unable to sit again during the 15-month period, a new Application for Certification with another non-refundable processing fee will be required if he/she wishes to pursue certification.

What Does Certification Cost?

Until January 1, 1980	$35.00	*Non-refundable* Application Processing Fee which must be submitted with the Application; and
	$40.00	Examination and Certificate Fee, due when the applicant is approved for the Certification Examination.
	$75.00	*Total Certification Fee to January 1, 1980*
After January 1, 1980	$35.00	*Non-refundable* Application Processing Fee which must be submitted with the Application; and
	$50.00	Examination and Certificate Fee, due when the applicant is approved for the Certification Examination.
	$85.00	*Total Certification Fee After January 1, 1980*

How Do I Apply for Certification?

All inquiries regarding certification and requests for application forms should be directed to the Commission on Rehabilitation Counselor Certification, 162 North State Street, Suite 602, Chicago, Illinois 60601.

Appendix C

Council on Rehabilitation Education (CORE)

COUNCIL ON REHABILITATION
EDUCATION, INC.

The Council on Rehabilitation Education (CORE) is a not-for-profit organization incorporated in the District of Columbia. It is recognized by the Council on Postsecondary Accreditation as the accrediting body for master's degree programs in rehabilitation counselor education in the United States.

History

CORE grew out of a 1969 meeting of rehabilitation professionals who met to discuss the need for an accreditation procedure for rehabilitation counselor education (RCE) programs. The organization was formed in June 1971 and incorporated in June 1972. It is composed of two representatives from each of the following professional rehabilitation organizations: American Rehabilitation Coun-

Adapted from a pamphlet entitled, "1978–79 Fact Sheet," prepared by the Council on Rehabilitation Education, November, 1978.

341

seling Association (ARCA), National Council on Rehabilitation Education (NCRE), Council of State Administrators of Vocational Rehabilitation (CSAVR), Association of Rehabilitation Facilities (ARF), and National Rehabilitation Counseling Association (NRCA).

With support of the Rehabilitation Services Administration (RSA) of HEW during its first three years, CORE conducted a developmental phase to establish a unique research-based evaluation procedure that relies heavily on assessing the performance of graduates. The research aspects of the project were subcontracted to the Regional Rehabilitation Research Institute at the University of Wisconsin-Madison. The procedures were implemented with the accreditation of RCE programs for the first time in 1975. Developments currently underway through a two-year RSA grant are for the purposes of revising and revalidating the standards, increasing the efficiency of data collection, building ongoing validation into the accreditation process, and promoting the applicability of the procedures to other areas of rehabilitation education.

Accreditation of Rehabilitation Counselor Education Programs

The basic purpose of RCE accreditation is to promote the effective delivery of rehabilitation services to handicapped people by stimulating and fostering continuing review and improvement of master's degree level RCE programs. The accreditation process promotes program self-improvement rather than outside censure. A concomitant purpose is to meet the manpower needs of both public and private rehabilitation agencies by providing graduates who have been equipped with the skills and knowledge necessary to help decrease dependence among disabled and disadvantaged persons.

"Accreditation" should not be confused with "certification," although both are assessment procedures. "Certification" is concerned with the competency of individual members of a profession and their performance on the job. "Accreditation" is concerned with the quality of education programs that offer training in a profession.

Forty-eight Rehabilitation Counselor Education programs are currently accredited by CORE. The evaluation of these programs, as well as the continual review of the standards and procedures themselves, is the responsibility of the Commission on Standards and Accreditation for Rehabilitation Counselor Education. The Commission is responsible to CORE and is composed of one CORE member from each of the five sponsoring organizations, one non-CORE member appointed directly by each of the five sponsoring organizations, and five representatives from professional and consumer groups in rehabilitation and the general public.

Once a program has applied for recognition, it is the responsibility of the Commission to assess its compliance with the standards and to provide recommendations for program improvement. At the point a program is deemed to be in essential compliance with the standards, the Commission recommends to CORE that it be recognized as a Candidate for Accreditation, be granted Preliminary Accreditation or be granted Accreditation—based on how long the program has been in existence. This recommendation may be made at the time of the first review or may be made after the completion of specified program improvements.

While CORE's initial focus was rehabilitation counselor education, it is actively exploring the development of standards and accreditation procedures with professional groups in other areas of rehabilitation education. CORE's Council and Commission structure allows for expansion into other areas where the need and interest are evident through the creation of appropriate Commissions.

Inquiries should be directed to Council on Rehabilitation Education, Inc., Suite 3301, 8 South Michigan Ave., Chicago, Illinois 60603.

Appendix D

National Rehabilitation Counseling Association Ethical Standards for Rehabilitation Counselors

ETHICAL STANDARDS FOR REHABILITATION COUNSELORS

Prepared by the NRCA Ethics Sub-Committee, and accepted at San Juan, Puerto Rico, September, 1972

A rehabilitation counselor has a commitment to the effective functioning of all human beings; his[1] emphasis is on facilitating the functioning or refunctioning of those persons who are at some disadvantage in the struggle to achieve viable goals. While fulfilling this commitment he interacts with many people, programs, institutions, demands and concepts, and in many different types of relationships. In his endeavors he seeks to enhance the welfare of his

Reprinted from the *Journal of Applied Rehabilitation Counseling*, 1972, 3(4), 218–228, with permission of the coeditors.

[1] The masculine noun and pronoun is used throughout the standards. Although such "sexist" language may be objectionable and does not conform to present stylistic standards of writing, the Ethical Standards are reproduced in their original form.

clients and of all others whose welfare his professional roles and activities will affect. He recognizes that both action and inaction can be facilitating or debilitating and he accepts the responsibility for his action and inaction.

The acceptable rules of behavior which the rehabilitation counselor himself observes and which he urges his colleagues to observe are in relationships with (1) his client, (2) his client's family, (3) his client's employer or prospective employer, (4) his fellow counselors, (5) his colleagues in other professions, (6) his own employer or supervisor, (7) the community, (8) other programs, agencies and institutions, (9) maintenance of his technical competency, and (10) research. The ethical rules presented here are organized to group specific rules or principles as they cluster about these various relationships.

Counselor—Client

I. The primary obligation of the rehabilitation counselor is to his client. In all his relationships he will protect the client's welfare and will diligently seek to assist the client towards his goals.

A. The rehabilitation counselor will keep confidential any information he acquires concerning the client, the divulgence of which might be inimical to the best interests of the client.

1. The rehabilitation counselor will persist in claiming the "privileged" status of confidential information concerning his clients in court proceedings.

2. Where there are conflicts between the client's interests and the interests and welfare of the community, the rehabilitation counselor will protect the client, unless by his doing so there is created a real and imminent danger to others.

a. The counselor will try to persuade the client to report knowledge of crimes or planned crimes to the appropriate law enforcement authorities.

b. The client will be warned that information acquired in the counseling relationship might have to be reported in court proceedings; that it might not be possible to withhold the information as "privileged."

3. Where illegal behavior of the client is destructive to himself as well as to the community, the rehabilitation counselor will report such behavior to the appropriate authorities, after advising the client that this must be done.
4. In situations where it is necessary to share information with others in order to advance the rehabilitation goals of the client, consent of the client or his guardian or parent will be secured before release of such information.
   a. Only information essential to advancing the goals of the client will be given to others.
   b. Only those persons for whom it is essential to have information about the client in order to advance his rehabilitation will be given information.
5. Only such information as the client requires to advance his rehabilitation will be given to him. The counselor will personally give and interpret information to the client that is within the scope of the rehabilitation counseling specialty to develop and establish.
6. Only information essential to advancing the goals of the client will be included in the records kept on the client.
7. Client records will be safeguarded to insure that unauthorized persons shall not have access to them.
   a. All nonprofessional persons who must have access to the client's records will be thoroughly briefed concerning the confidentiality standards to be observed. Compliance with these standards will be continuously monitored by the counselor and will be his responsibility.
   b. The counselor will insist on an administrative plan for retirement and destruction of client records that will afford satisfactory protection of the client's future interests and welfare.
B. The rehabilitation counselor will maintain objective and professional standards in his personal relationships with the client.
1. He will refrain from urging the client's ac-

ceptance of values, life styles, plans, decisions and beliefs that represent only the counselor's personal judgments or values.

2. If he learns of criminal and destructive activities of the client, either current or planned, he will advise the client that this must be reported to law enforcement authorities.

3. He will refer to others for service those to whom he is not able to relate objectively, *e.g.*, relatives, close friends, persons against whom he is prejudiced.

4. He will, in serving the client, function within the limits of his defined role, training, and technical competency. In discussing probable or hoped-for outcomes of services to be offered, he will refrain from promising greater results than can reasonably be expected. He will not misrepresent his role or his competency to the client or to others. He will refer the client to other specialists as the client's needs dictate. He will not discuss with the client any professional incompetency he might feel is characteristic of his colleagues or other professional persons or agencies involved in the client's rehabilitation plan.

5. He will know thoroughly the legal or regulatory limits or the extent of the services that he may offer. He will operate within these limits. He will brief his clients on these limits, as appropriate.

6. He will not exploit the client or the counselor-client relationship for agency or personal advantage.

7. He will assist the client in devising an integrated, individualized rehabilitation plan that he believes offers reasonable promise of success in reaching the stated goals.
   a. He will approve only those services that the client needs for his rehabilitation and which the client is capable of accepting in an effective way.
   b. He will persistently follow up on the client's rehabilitation plan to insure its continued viability and effectiveness.

8. He will act responsibly in the client's behalf in emergency situations.

9. A counselor not in private practice will accept no fee or gratuity from clients for services given.

10. He will not become involved with clients in any fiscal or business arrangements or commitments beyond those required for delivery of services.

11. He will recommend the client's employment in only such jobs and circumstances as fit the capabilities of the client, his welfare, and his needs.

Counselor—Client's Family

II. The rehabilitation counselor recognizes that the client's family is typically a very important factor in the client's rehabilitation. He will strive to enlist the understanding and involvement of the family as a positive resource in promoting the client's rehabilitation plan and in enhancing his continued effective functioning.

A. The rehabilitation counselor will promote the interest, involvement, and cooperation of the client's family in his rehabilitation plan if the family is of sufficient significance to the client to exert an impact on the plan.

B. The counselor will communicate to the family such information as will facilitate the client's welfare and rehabilitation, but will refrain from including information that would represent a violation of essential confidentiality.

C. The counselor will refrain from becoming a partisan in any intra-family conflict; he will try to resolve such conflicts where they are interfering with the welfare and rehabilitation of the client.

Counselor—Client's Employer or Prospective Employer

III. The rehabilitation counselor is obligated to protect the client-employer relationship by adequately apprising the latter of the client's capabilities and limitations. He will not participate in placing a client in a position that will result in damaging the interests and welfare of either or both the employer and the client.

A. The rehabilitation counselor will refrain from recommending a client to an employer for employment in work for which the client is not properly qualified in terms of the job's requirements and the standards set by the employer.

B. The counselor will give a prospective employer only such information about the client as is necessary to identify the client's fitness for the job under consideration. The counselor will secure the consent of the client, or his parent or guardian, for the release to employers of any information that might be considered confidential.

C. The counselor will not collaborate in placing a client for employment in a situation where the client is likely to be unfairly exploited or where he is likely to experience management prejudice or discrimination.

D. If the client finds a job without the intervention of the counselor or his agency, the counselor will supply information about the client to the employer only if requested by the client.

E. The counselor will not collaborate in placing a client in a job where his functioning would be illegal or detrimental to his health and welfare or a threat to the safety of his fellow workers.

F. The counselor will recommend the client for only those jobs that appear to be compatible with the client's rehabilitation plan and long-term welfare.

Counselor—Counselor

IV. The rehabilitation counselor will relate to his colleagues in the profession so as to facilitate their ongoing technical effectiveness as professional persons.

A. The counselor will encourage his colleagues to observe ethical rules and professional standards such as will protect clients and the rehabilitation counseling profession.

1. If defections from acceptable standards are observed, the counselor will discuss the be-

havior directly with the defector, reporting the problem to the local ethics committee only when direct discussion brings no corrective results.

B. The counselor will not knowingly withhold information from his colleagues that would enhance their effectiveness.

C. The counselor will not disseminate information about his colleagues that would tend to erode their professional status or effectiveness.

D. Clients will be accepted readily in transfer or will be transferred to a colleague whenever it is deemed to be in the best interest of the client.

1. The counselor will not transfer a client to a colleague without the latter's consent.

2. In transferring a client the counselor will refrain from committing the receiving counselor to any prescribed course of action in relation to the client and his problems. The receiving counselor will continue with the rehabilitation plan formulated by the transferring counselor unless the best interests of the client dictate a change in the plan.

3. The transferring counselor will not disparagingly discuss with the client the receiving counselor's capabilities, deficiencies or methods.

4. The receiving counselor will not discuss in a disparaging way with the client transferred to him the competencies of the transferring counselor or agency, the judgments made, the methods used, or the quality of the client's rehabilitation plan.

5. The transferring counselor will withdraw from involvement in the case when a client has been transferred, except to act as a resource for the receiving counselor.

a. If the client is received on a temporary basis for continuation of services when the regular counselor cannot continue his relations to the client for a time, the receiving counselor will refrain from making basic changes in the client's rehabilitation plan without the prior approval of his colleague.

E. The counselor will refrain from public display or behavior and from expression of opinions, complaints or frustrations that might bring discredit to rehabilitation, to his profession, or his colleagues.

F. The counselor will give active support to his colleagues who experience administrative or other pressures because of observance of ethical and professional principles.

Counselor—Other Professionals

V. Typically, the implementation of a rehabilitation plan for a client is a multidisciplinary effort. The rehabilitation counselor will conduct himself in his interdisciplinary relationships in such a way as to facilitate the contribution of all the specialists involved for maximum benefit of the client and to bring credit to his own profession.

A. The rehabilitation counselor will not abdicate his role in relation to the client by delegating his responsibilities to other specialists; he will accept and discharge his responsibilities to the client. If necessary, he will request involved others to refrain from altering the client's rehabilitation plan for which he is responsible or committing him or his agency to giving services not prescribed by him. He will insist on proper controls on confidential information made available to other professionals by himself or his agency. If there is noncompliance with his requests, he will ask that the offending persons or agencies be withdrawn from participation in implementing the client's rehabilitation plan.

B. If "team" decisions are involved in formulating procedures, he will abide by and help to implement those decisions even though he might not personally agree with them.

C. The rehabilitation counselor will not waste the resources of his agency and of the client by requiring more other-professional services than are indicated for adequately serving the client.

D. The rehabilitation counselor will request such other-professional examinations, data and advice as are indicated for adequately evaluating, counseling and otherwise serving the client.

E. As far as possible, the rehabilitation counselor will defer to other specialists the responsibility of interpreting their findings to the client; he will ask for reports from these specialists for his own guidance in counseling the client.

F. The counselor will defer to the other specialists involved in releasing information confidential to the client that is wholly within the scope of such specialists to develop and establish.

G. The rehabilitation counselor will report his findings and conclusions to other involved specialists to the extent necessary for them to cooperate effectively in implementing the client's rehabilitation plan.

1. Reports will be made and requested promptly so that the client's progress will not be impeded.

2. Procedures and reports ("red tape") will not be permitted to inhibit the progress of the client in his rehabilitation plan.

3. Reports of findings, decisions and results will be made to referring agencies and individuals within proper limits of confidentiality.

H. The rehabilitation counselor will avoid any economic advantage to himself resulting from referrals for evaluations, training, or opinions to other persons or agencies.

Counselor—His Employer, Agency, Supervisor

VI. The rehabilitation counselor will be loyal to the agency that employs him and to the administrators and supervisors who supervise him. He will refrain from speaking, writing, or acting in such a way as to bring discredit on his agency.

A. The rehabilitation counselor will persistently try to have amended those regulatory and administrative conditions of his employment that require him to act in an unethical or unprofessional manner or that erode the effectiveness of his professional functioning.

B. The counselor will act at a professional and responsible level by carrying his administrative and professional duties efficiently, devoting the hours to his work as required by the conditions of his employment. When he decides upon resignation or separation from his position, he will give his employer timely and adequate advance notice and will leave his work in such condition that his successor can continue effective services to clients.

C. When there are differences in opinions and values between the counselor and his agency, he will attempt to resolve these differences through discussion and other communication with the appropriate persons in the agency. He will not carry his dissent to persons and agencies outside his own agency.

D. The rehabilitation counselor will promptly inform his supervisors of any situations in his work that might develop into problems that would become difficult or embarrassing for the agency.

Counselor—Community

VII. The rehabilitation counselor will regard his professional status as imposing on him the obligation to relate to the community (the public) at levels of responsibility and morality that are higher than are required for persons not classified as "professional." He will use his specialized knowledge, his special abilities, and his leadership position to promote understanding and the general welfare of handicapped persons in the community, and to promote acceptance of the viable concepts of rehabilitation and of rehabilitation counseling.

A. The rehabilitation counselor will not compromise the professional and ethical correctness and quality of his functioning in response to political or economic pressures.

B. The counselor will resist any arrangements or operations that will result in exploitation of his clients by business or other interests.

C. The counselor will resist situations where his relationships with business or other activities might be interpreted in the community as a "conflict of interest."

D. The counselor will refuse to participate in or apply any policies that involve discrimination of any type.

Counselor—Other Programs, Agencies, and Institutions

VIII. In his relationships with other programs, agencies and institutions that will participate in the rehabilitation plan of the client, the rehabilitation counselor will follow procedures and insist on arrangements that will foster maximum mutual facilitation and effectiveness of services for the benefit of the client.

A. The counselor will insure that there is full mutual understanding of the client's rehabilitation needs and plan on the part of all agencies cooperating in the rehabilitation of the client.

B. If the counselor cannot concur in the rehabilitation plan for a client referred to him, he will resolve the differences between the plan and what he believes should be done.

C. The counselor will keep himself aware of the actions being taken by cooperating agencies on behalf of his client and act as an advocate of the client to insure services delivery and effectiveness. He will insist on discontinuance of any procedures that exploit the client or threaten his welfare.

D. The counselor will take action to correct a situation where the client is improperly exploiting the agencies involved in the client's rehabilitation.

E. The counselor will insure that there are defined policies and practices in the other agencies cooperating in serving his client that effectively protect information confidentiality and the general welfare of the client.

1. All information necessary for the cooperating agencies to be effective in serving the client will be promptly supplied by the referring counselor.

2. Information supplied to a cooperating agency will be limited to that which is necessary for effective delivery of service.

Counselor—Maintenance of Technical Competency

IX. The rehabilitation counselor is obligated to keep his technical competency at such a level that his clients receive the benefit of the highest quality of services the profession is capable of offering.

A. The counselor will continuously strive, through reading, attending professional meetings, and taking courses of instruction, to keep abreast of new developments in concepts and practices and will apply those that appear to be viable and effective for his practice.

B. The counselor will take the initiative to arrange for in-service instruction adequate for him to perform his assigned duties competently and efficiently. He will not permit himself to be placed in a situation where he must carry out his duties without understanding what he is to to do, how he is to do it, and what effects his doing it will have on his clients.

C. If the agency provides "time off" training to enhance the professional status of the counselor, he will arrive at an understanding of his obligation to remain with the agency for a period of time following such training and he will honor any such obligation.

Counselor—Research

X. The rehabilitation counselor is obligated to assist in the efforts to expand the knowledge needed to serve handicapped persons with increasing effectiveness.

A. The counselor will cooperate in research efforts whenever it is feasible for him to do so without jeopardizing his primary obligations and responsibilities to his clients and his agency.

B. In supplying data for research, the counselor will insure that it meets rigid standards of validity, honesty and protection of confidentiality.

C. In cooperating with research projects, the counselor will supply the data or action to which he commits himself, timely and in a form usable in the projects.

Index

Adler, Alfred, 235, 236
Affirmative action, 23–24, 29, 268, 285
Alcoholism, 129, 158
American Association on Mental Deficiencies, 124
American Coalition of Citizens with Disabilities, 107
American Heart Association, 127
American Personnel and Guidance Association (APGA), 49, 71
code of ethics, 71, 72, 74, 76
American Psychological Association (APA)
code of ethics, 71, 72, 74–76
publications, 229
Amputations, 120, 128–29
Andrew, Jason W., 205–26
Antipoverty program, 17
Anxiety, 235–36
Architectural and Transportation Barriers Compliance Board, 28–30
Architectural barriers, 183
Architectural Barriers Bill, 20
Aristotle, 61
Arthritis, 113, 124
Assertiveness training, 251
Asset values, 152–53
Attitudes to disability, 106, 107, 144, 153–59, 184–85
of employers, 189–91
methods for changing, 159–61, 185
of professionals, 157–59, 161, 303
of public, 154–57, 161
research on, 155–57

Barriers in environment (see also Architectural barriers), 22–23, 161
Behavior modification techniques, 69
Behavioral counseling, 247–49
Behaviorist approach, 4, 65, 66, 70, 76, 79
Bergin, A. F., 230
Blind, 62
attitudes to, 156, 183
in industry, 17
information gathering, 181–82
population, 126
Blindness and visual impairments, 113, 120, 125–26, 184
Bolton, Brian, 83–102

Bozarth, Jerold D., 59–81
Brubaker, David, 37–58
Bureau for the Education of the Handicapped (BEH), 24
Butler, Alfred J., 227–60

Cancer, 129, 157
Cardiovascular disorders, 113, 127–28
Career Data Book, 170
Career development theories, 268–76
Holland's, 270–73
Minnesota, 273–76
Super's, 269–70
Carter, Jimmy, 11
Case management, 297–303
client-counselor responsibilities, 302
contingency plan, 301–2
counselor values, 302–3
planning, 298–99
rehabilitation process, 299–302
Caseload
future outlook, 137–38
in 1976, 133–36
size, 304–5
Caseload management, 202, 295–97, 303–9
access to information, 307
factors impacting on, 296, 308
guidelines, 306–7
involvement with people, 308
personal vs. organizational goals, 307, 308
perspectives on, 308–9
selecting the case file, 304–5
skills needed, 304, 322
system, 305–6
time utilization, 307, 316–22
Cases vs. caseloads, 304
Cerebral palsy, 130
Certified Rehabilitation Counselor (CRC), 38–39
Chicago Jewish Vocational Service, 92, 99
Chicago Mental Health Center, 92
Chicago State Hospital work-therapy program, 85, 92–94
Children
with arthritis, 124
Freudian theory and, 144, 146, 236
mentally ill, 123
Chronic conditions, 117–18
Client-centered therapy, 237–39, 245, 265

Client characteristics, 231
Client participation, 68, 298, 302, 309, 311, 315, 316
Closure, 203
  criteria, 135–36
Collingwood, T. R., 87–92
Commission on Chronic Illness, 122
Commission on Rehabilitation Counselor Certification (CRCC), 38, 47–49, 54
Committee on Developmental Disabilities, 30–31
Communication problems, 183–84
Community facilitator, 78
Community resources, 280, 281, 308
Community service employment programs, 28
Comparative values, 153
Compensation defenses, 145, 147, 236
Comprehensive Service Needs Study, 263–64
Connolly, Sean G., 295–324
Control group, 90, 91, 100
Cook, Daniel W., 143–67
Counselor Client Interaction Project, 95–97
Counselor-client relationship, 64, 72–73, 131, 202
Council of State Administrators of Vocational Rehabilitation, 13
Council on Rehabilitation Education (CORE), 47, 51
Cox, Jennings G., 295–324
Credentialing Health Manpower, 53, 54

Daniels, Jim L., 169–97
Deaf, 62, 126
Deafness and hearing impairments, 113, 120, 126–27
Decision making, 297, 299, 300, 303, 309–16
  criteria for, 310
  evaluation of, 315–16
  kinds of decisions, 314
  literature, 311
  predictability, 313–14
  problem identification, 304, 312, 318
  steps in, 311–13
Defense mechanism, 145, 146, 235, 236
Defensive behavior, 149
Delivery of services, 19, 29, 200–204, 295–324
  changes in field, 211
  services of state agencies, 201–2
Denial, 149, 150, 162
Department of Education, 11

Department of Health, Education, and Welfare, 11, 14, 20, 25, 52
Department of Housing and Urban Development, 29, 30
Department of Transportation (DOT), 29–30
Desensitization, 251
Determining eligibility, 201, 207, 211, 223, 299
Diagnostic studies, 207–11, 223
Dictionary of Occupational Titles, 170, 187, 272, 275, 284
Disability
  impact on individual, 143–67
    attitudes of professionals, 157–59, 161
    attitudes of public, 154–57, 161 (*see also* Attitudes to disability)
    personality theories, 144–53
    phases of adjustment, 162
    psychosocial adjustment, 143
    research, 162
    vs. handicap, 177–78
  work and, 177–87 (*see also* Employment; Job placement; Work)
    factors influencing, 179–82
    handicapping aspects, 182–86
Disability and Rehabilitation Handbook, 119–20
Disabled person
  age and, 110–12, 118
  common problems, 227
  defined, 9, 14, 16, 114–16, 179
  employment, 112–13 (*see also* Employment; Job placement; Work)
  number, 30
  participation in labor force, 264
  social rights, 30 (*see also* Human rights)
Disabling conditions, 109–38, 179–80
  amputations, 128–29
  blindness and visual impairments, 113, 125–26, 184
  cardiovascular, 113, 127–28
  chronic, 117–18
  deafness and hearing impairments, 113, 126–27
  mental illness, 113, 120–23, 184–85
  mental retardation, 120, 124–25, 185
  orthopedic, 123–24
  other, 129–30
  population characteristics, 110–13
  severely disabled, 118–19 (*see also* Severely physically disabled)
Discrimination, 24, 29, 75, 183–85, 214–15, 217, 264

Discrimination *(continued)*
 law against, 28, 30, 107, 215
Dix, Dorothea, 62
Dollard, J., 251
Dudek, R. A., 300

Education for All Handicapped
  Children Act (1975), 24–25, 29
Education for the Handicapped Act
  (1970), 24
Elementary and Secondary Education
  Act (1965), 24
Ellis, Albert, 244–46
Employees by industry, 171
Employer, 73
 attitudes, 189–91
 costs to, 285
 services to disabled, 266
Employment (*see also* Job placement;
   Work)
 barriers to, 107, 183–86
 independent living and, 222–23
 right to, 67–68
Employment agency, 215
Employment opportunities, 23, 30, 160,
  189
Employment Opportunities for
   Handicapped Individuals Act,
   28
*Encyclopedia of Careers and
   Vocational Guidance,* 170
Environment
 counseling approach, 253–55
Epilepsy, 129
Equal Employment Opportunity Act
  (1972), 215–17
Equal opportunity, 68
Ethics, 69–76
 codes, 70–76
 current status, 76–78
 violations, 75–76
Ethnocentrism, 155–56
Evaluation, 76, 201, 205–26
 continuing, 18, 19
 expected outcomes, 223–25
 extended, 208–9, 223
 purposes, 206–12
 resources of counselor, 212–23
 vocational, 201
Existential-humanistic approach, 66
Eysenck, H. J., 229–30

Facts About Handicapped People,
  109–13
Family
 focus on, 18, 19
 role of, 73
 stress and, 106

Federal Board for Vocational
   Education, 8
Federal funding, 3, 8, 17, 24–26
Federal guidelines, 213–14
Federal legislation, 7–28
Flynn, William J., 295–324
Fort Logan Mental Health Center,
  84–85
Freud, Sigmund, 144–45, 150, 235,
  236

Galen, 61
Gallaudet, 62
Gestalt therapy, 239–41
Glasser, W., 246–47
Goal setting, 280–81
Group approach to counseling, 255

Halo effect, 179
*Handbook of Measurement and
   Evaluation in Rehabilitation,* 97
Handicap (*see also* Disability;
   Disabled person; Disabling
   conditions)
 causes of, 178
 definitions, 114–16
 environment and, 225
 vs. disability, 177–78
Handicapped, 105–7
 adjustment process, 106
 age at onset, 105, 181
 characteristics of, 105
 economic impact, 106
 historical view, 61–62
 noninstitutionalized, 105, 116–17
 number served, 19
 population of, 105
 progress in service to, 29
 public attitudes to, 106–7, 144, 183
   (*see also* Attitudes to
   disability)
 rights of, 23, 24
Hauy, Valentin, 62
Health care expenditures, 119
Health Training Improvement Act of
  1970, 52
Holland, John, 270–73
Human rights, 13, 31
Human service occupations, 47, 52–53,
  131
Humanistic approach, 4, 66, 70, 76, 79

Independent living, 222–23
Independent Living Program (ILR),
  27–29
Individualized Written Rehabilitation
   Plan (IWRP), 68, 76, 201,
   211–12, 223, 301, 302

Information regarding injury, 160–61
Institute for the Crippled and
    Disabled, 99
Instrumentalism, 64
Interaction strain, 107, 155, 159–61,
    185
International Committee Against
    Mental Illness, 122–23

Jenkins, William M., 7–35
Job analysis, 187, 189
Job placement, 64, 76, 185, 192, 202,
    211–12, 261–63, 282–84 (see
    also Employment; Work)
Job satisfaction, 176
Job search, 277, 282–83
Job-seeking skills, 265–66, 283
Job station, 219–20
Job titles, 175–76
Job tryouts, 221

Kidney disease, 130
Krumboltz, John, 247–49

Labeling, 157, 179, 184
Labor market analysis, 186–91, 276
Lakein, A., 318–19
Leadership style, 176
Learning theory, 247, 249, 251–52
Lewin, Kurt, 150–53
Life expectancy, 137–38, 211
Life factors framework (Dudek), 300
Life skills, 210
Locus of control, 252

McGregor's Theory X and Theory Y,
    176
Maier, N.R.F., 315–16
Management philosophy, 176
Medical consultation, 214
Medical specialists, 131, 214
Mental illness, 113, 120–23, 184–85
Mental retardation, 120, 124–25, 185
Mental Retardation Amendments, 20
Mentally handicapped, 14, 15, 17, 19
Miller, L. A., 224
Miller, N. E., 251
Minnesota Importance Questionnaire,
    275
Minnesota Studies in Vocational Re-
    habilitation, 242, 244
Minnesota Theory of Work Adjust-
    ment, 86, 273–76
Minorities, 111, 154–56, 161, 178
Multiple sclerosis (MS), 113
Muscular dystrophy, 130

National Association for Mental Health,
    122
National Census of the Deaf Pop-
    ulation, 126–27
National Center for Health Statistics,
    117, 118, 122
National Civilian Vocational Act, 8–9
National Commission for Health
    Certifying Agencies
    (NCHCA), 53
National Council on Rehabilitation
    Education, 13
National Council on the Handicapped,
    28
National Defense Act of 1916, 8
National Health Education Committee,
    138
National Institute of Handicapped
    Research, 28
National Rehabilitation Association
    (NRA), 11–13, 29, 32
National Rehabilitation Counseling
    Association (NRCA), 49, 50–
    51, 53, 71–76
National Society for the Prevention of
    Blindness, 125
Nebraska Rehabilitation Agency, 223
Normalization, 224–25

Obermann, C. E., 70
Occupational Outlook Handbook, 284
Occupations, 170, 176, 284
Office of Human Development Ser-
    vices, 11
Office of Special Education and Re-
    habilitation Services, 11
Office of Vocational Rehabilitation, 14,
    16
On-the-job evaluation, 220–21
Organizations for handicapped, 107
Orthopedic disabilities, 120, 123–24

Pareto Principle, 320
Passons, W. R., 239–40
Perls, Fritz, 239–41
Personality theories, 144–53
Personologists, 150–51
Philosophy, 59–67, 79 (see also
    Ethics)
    current status, 76–78
    development of, 61–62
    framework for rehabilitation coun-
        seling, 67–69
    views of human beings, 65–67
Physical examinations, 186
Physically disabled, 9–10, 123, 137,
    185 (See also Amputations, or

Physically disabled *(continued)*
    name of specific illness; Se-
    verely physically disabled)
Physiological-medical approach, 65–66
Placement and career development,
    261–93 (*see also* Employment;
    Job placement; Work)
    acquiring labor market information,
        284
    career development theories, 268–76
    career enhancement, 287–88
    implications for counselors, 288–89
    intervention, 265–66
    personnel, 266–67
    placement literature, 265–76
    techniques for specific disability
        groups, 267–68
    work adjustment, 287
Placement plan, 211–12, 223, 283
Porter, Thomas L., 109–42
Prejudice, 155, 158 (*see also* Dis-
    crimination)
President's Committee on Employment
    of the Handicapped, 109, 110,
    117
Private counseling, 54, 75
Profession, 39–46
    advertising, 42–43
    autonomy, 44, 50
    community sanction, 43–44, 51
    ethical codes, 44–46, 50, 51, 55, 70–
        76 (*see also* Ethics)
    key elements, 40, 46
    professional authority, 42–43, 48, 50
    social values, 44, 50
    systematic body of knowledge, 40–
        42, 47, 55
Professional organizations, 12–13, 21,
    22, 38, 43, 45
    competing, 50, 51, 55
    ethics, 70–75
    membership, 55
Psychiatric rehabilitation, 84–85
Psychoanalysis, 234, 239, 245, 251–52
Psychoanalytic approach, 4, 65–66, 70,
    234–36
Psychoanalytic theory, 144–47, 234
Psychological environment, 151
Psychological tests, 97, 217–18, 242,
    244, 250
Psychoneurotic disorders, 121–22 (*see
    also* Mental illness)
Psychotherapy, 66, 229–30
Psychotic disorders, 120–21 (*see also*
    Mental illness)
Public Law 565, 15–17
Public Law 113, 14–15

Random assignment, 91–92, 94, 100
Rational-emotive therapy, 244–46
Reaction formation, 145
Reactive effect, 90–91
Reality therapy, 246–47
Reciprocal inhibition therapy, 249–51
Rehabilitation Act of 1975, 209–10
Rehabilitation Act of 1973, 24–25, 27,
    28, 49, 114, 262, 263
Rehabilitation, Comprehensive Ser-
    vices and Developmental Dis-
    abilities Amendments of 1978,
    28, 222
Rehabilitation counseling, 202, 227–
    60
    approaches
        behavioral, 247–52
        criteria, 232–35
        eclectic, 69, 252–53
        group and environmental, 253–55
        humanistic, 236–41
        problem-solving, 253
        psychoanalytic, 235–36
        rational, 241–47
    cornerstones, 3
    credentialing, 53–54
    goal, 233, 263
    legislation on, 3, 7–28, 49–51, 77
    literature on, 228–32
    personal adjustment vs. vocational,
        228
    profession, 3–4, 22, 37–58, 60, 65, 79
        (*see also* Ethics; Philosophy;
        Rehabilitation counselor,
        values)
Rehabilitation Counseling Bulletin, 100
*Rehabilitation Counseling: Theory and
    Practice*, 97
Rehabilitation counselor (*see also*
        Rehabilitation counseling)
    characteristics of, 231
    colleague relationships, 73, 281
    coordinator role, 17, 295, 297
    decision making, 297–99, 300, 303,
        309–16, 322
    education, 296
    federal regulations and, 77
    influencing employers, 189–91, 194
    number of, 3, 131
    performance of, 77–78
    philosophy, 223–25
    professional vs. organizational goals,
        296–97
    relations with community, 74, 78,
        280–81
    relevant skills, 202, 228, 279–80,
        295, 296, 304

role of, 131, 227–28, 298
values, 302–3
Rehabilitation engineering, 211
Rehabilitation outcome criteria, 230,
    263
Rehabilitation process, 277–88
    career enhancement, 277, 287–88
    productivity enrichment, 277, 279–
        82
    productivity realization, 277, 282–
        87
    relevant skills, 279–80
Rehabilitation services, 131, 169 (see
        also Delivery of services)
    questions, 115–16
    rationale for, 67–69
Rehabilitation Services Administration
        (RSA), 11, 29, 98, 117, 130,
        262
Rehabilitation workshop, 254
Rehabilitations
    estimate of, 130
    outlook, 137–38
    severe and nonsevere cases, 136–37
Report on Licensure and Related
        Health Personnel Creden-
        tialing (HEW), 53
Repression, 145, 146, 235
Research, 4–5, 16, 19–20, 74, 83–102
    on attitudes toward disability, 155–
        57, 161
    on counseling and outcome, 231–32
    literature, 229–30
    measurement methodology, 97
    need for, 83–84
    one-group pretest-posttest design,
        87–92
    scientific method, 85–87
    strategies, 87–89
    utilization of, 97–101
Research and training centers, 28, 99
Research BRIEFs, 99
Research design, 87, 89
    ex post facto design, 94–95, 100–
        101
    external validity, 89, 95
    internal validity, 89
    one-group pretest-posttest design,
        87–92, 100
    posttest only control group design,
        92, 100
    sources of error, 90–91
Richmond, Frederick, 49
Right to education laws, 24–25
Rogers, Carl, 64, 237–39
    self-concept theory, 147–50
Rorschach responses, 147

Rotter, J. B., 252

Scientific method, 41, 85–87, 100
Second Institute on Rehabilitation
        Issues (1975), 267
Self-actualization, 147, 237
Self-concept theory, 147–50
    adjustment and, 148–49
    physical disability and, 148
    research evidence, 150
Self-help groups, 254
Service industries, 171
Seventh Institute on Rehabilitation
        Issues, 286
Severely handicapped, 114–15, 263
Severely physically disabled, 15, 23,
        27–28, 118–19, 134–38, 178
Severely retarded, 208
Sheltered workships, 18, 194
Sickle cell anemia, 205–6
Situational assessment, 218–22
Smith-Hughes Vocational Act of 1917,
        8
Smith-Sears Rehabilitation Act, 8
Social learning theory, 252
Social psychologists, 151
Social Rehabilitation Service, 20
Social Security Acts, 12, 13, 17, 18
Socially handicapped, 16, 18
Somatopsychology, 150–53
Specialized work stations, 184
Spinal cord injuries, 124
State Administration of Vocational
        Rehabilitation, 26–29
State boards of vocational education, 9
State-federal vocational rehabilitation
        program, 10, 12, 13, 18–19, 26,
        32, 106, 132–36
State laws, 25, 213–14
State licensing, 44, 49, 53
State rehabilitation agencies, 3, 9, 14,
        16, 18, 19, 26–28
    economic factors, 21, 26
    employment guidelines, 38, 49, 50
    services, 201–2
Statistical significance, 87, 93, 100
Super, Donald, 269–70
Superego, 144
Survey of Disabled Adults (1966),
        263–64
Survival camping, 87–89
Switzer, Mary E., 20, 137

Test, 215 (see also Psychological tests)
Testing, 216–18
Therapeutic responder, 78
Thomas, Kenneth R., 227–60

Thoresen, R. W., 247–49
Time utilization, 202, 307, 316–22
Trait-factor counseling, 242–44

Ugland, D., 77
Union advisory council, 285
Union membership, 186
United States Public Health Service,
      53–54
University of Nebraska-Lincoln, 222
Urban Institute, 105, 106, 114, 115,
      118, 122

Vandergoot, David, 261–93
Veterans, 8
Visibly disabled, 153, 160
Visually impaired (see Blindness and
      visual impairments)
Vocational Act (1920), 8–10, 12
Vocational diagnostician, 78
Vocational Evaluation and Work
      Adjustment Association
      (VEWAA), 218
Vocational Rehabilitation Act, 9, 12
      (see also State-federal voca-
      tional rehabilitation program)
   Amendments, 15–17, 20, 25
Vocational rehabilitation movement,
      20, 21, 32
Vocational rehabilitation services (see
      also Employment; Job place-
ment; State-federal vocational
      rehabilitation program; Work)
   defined, 16–17, 299
   need for, 117
   professional competencies, 169
   specialists, 25
Vocational stereotyping, 180, 184

White collar workers, 171
White House Conference on Handi-
      capped Individuals, 29, 30
Wilensky, H., 46, 49
Williamson, Edmund, 242
Wolpe, Joseph, 249–51
Work, 169–97, 283, 287
   competitive, 170–71, 177, 178, 203
   environment, 176–77
   interventions, 186–94
   modifications, 189
   noncompetitive, 171, 175, 177
   skills, 182
   work stations, 184, 219, 220
   worker's perspective, 175–76
Work behavior, 210, 212, 219
Work ethic, 175
Work samples, 219, 220
Work therapy, 84–85, 100
   research center, 92–94
Workmen's Compensation Law, 54
Workmen's compensation rates, 190
World War II, 14
Wright, B. A., 151–53, 161, 162